AA

Explorer
Cyprus

George McDonald

AA Publishing

Front cover
Top: *Pissouri Bay* (Steve Day); Centre (left to right): (a) *Statue of Archbishop Makarios* (Steve Day); (b) *Mosaic at Kampanopetra Basilica, Salamis* (Alex Kouprianoff); (c) *Famagusta Beach* (Alex Kouprianoff); (d) *Agios Rafaelis at Pachyammos* (Steve Day); (e) *Lacemaker* (Alex Kouprianoff)
Spine *Kourion* (Malc Birkitt)
Back cover
Left: *Monastery, Omodos* (Steve Day); Right: *Nissi Bay* (Roy Rainford)

Page 3: *Nun working in the garden at Agios Irakleidos monastery*
Page 4: *Enjoying a day's cruise off the coast of Agia Napa*
Page 5 (top): *Sunset over the Troodos Mountains*
Pages 6–7: *Moutoullas, Marathasa Valley, Troodos*
Page 8: *Episkopi*
Page 9: *Lefkara village, southwest Cyprus*
Page 25: *Votive statue from Golgoi (ca 600 BC)*
Page 251: *Road sign*
Page 269: *Hilton Park Hotel, South Nicosia*

Written and revised by George McDonald

Published by AA Publishing, a trading name of Automobile Association Developments Limited, whose registered office is Fanum House, Basing View, Basingstoke, Hampshire RG21 4EA. Registered number 1878835.

ISBN-10: 0-7495-4826-6
ISBN-13: 978-0-7495-4826-6

The contents of this publication are believed correct at the time of printing. Nevertheless, AA Publishing accepts no responsibility for errors, omissions or changes in the details given, or for the consequences of readers' reliance on this information. This does not affect your statutory rights. Assessments of the attractions, hotels and restaurants are based upon the author's own experience, and contain subjective opinions that may not reflect the publisher's opinion or a reader's experience. We have tried to ensure accuracy, but things do change, so please let us know if you have any comments or corrections.

A CIP catalogue record for this book is available from the British Library.

Colour separation by M.R.M. Graphics Ltd, Bucks, UK
Printed and bound in Italy by Printer Trento Srl

Find out more about AA Publishing and the wide range of travel publications and services the AA provides by visiting our website at www.theAA.com/bookshop.

Revised fifth edition 2006
First published 1995

Titles in the Explorer series:
Australia • Boston & New England • Britain • Brittany California • Canada • Caribbean • China • Costa Rica • Crete Cuba • Cyprus • Egypt • Florence & Tuscany • Florida France • Germany • Greek Islands • Hawaii • India • Ireland Italy • Japan • London • Mallorca • Mexico • New York New Zealand • Paris • Portugal • Provence • Rome San Francisco • Scotland • South Africa • Spain • Thailand Tunisia • Turkey • Venice • Vietnam

A02698

How to use this book

ORGANIZATION

Cyprus Is, Cyprus Was
Discusses aspects of life and culture in contemporary Cyprus and places the island in its historical context, exploring those past events whose influences are felt to this day.

A-Z
Breaks down the island into regional chapters, and covers places to visit, including walks and drives. Within this section fall the Focus On articles, which consider a variety of subjects in greater detail.

Travel Facts
Contains the strictly practical information vital for a successful trip.

Hotels & Restaurants
Lists recommended establishments throughout Cyprus, giving a brief summary of what each has to offer.

ABOUT THE RATINGS
Most places described in this book have been given a separate rating. These are as follows:

▶▶▶   **Do not miss**
▶▶   **Highly recommended**
▶   **Worth seeing**

KEY TO ADMISSION CHARGES
An indication of an establishment's admission charge is given by categorizing the standard, adult rate (for South Cyprus in Cyprus pounds; for North Cyprus in Turkish lira and approximate equivalent in British pounds) as:
Inexpensive: under CY£2 and
     YTL3 / £1.25
Moderate: CY£4.50–6 and
     YTL4–12 / £1.90–2.50
Expensive: over CY£6 and
     YTL9 / £3.75

MAP REFERENCES
To make each location easier to find, every main entry in this book has a map reference to the right of its name. This comprises a number, followed by a letter, followed by another number, such as 176B3. The first number (176) refers to the page on which the map can be found, the letter (B) and the second number (3) pinpoint the square in which the main entry is located. The maps on the inside front cover and inside back cover are referred to as IFC and IBC respectively. A red square indicates a place of interest.

Contents

Feeding the pelicans, Limassol

Agios Nikolaos

The coastline of Akamas

George McDonald dates his love of travel writing from a career move that saw him switch from editing local newspaper stories to, a few weeks later, being paddled down the River Ganges in Bangladesh. He has rarely taken a backward glance since then. He has written articles for magazines in Europe, North Americ, and Asia and written or contributed to more than 20 guidebooks, among them AA guides to the Aegean Islands, Amsterdam, Belgium, Germany and China.

My Cyprus

From my house in a village near Pafos I look downhill past citrus orchards, olive groves and banana plantations —and, alas, an ever-increasing clutter of villas and holiday apartments—to the sparkling blue of the Mediterranean. The sea is generally empty but every now and then a black dot appears on the horizon. It usually resolves itself into a cruise liner or a rustbucket freighter heading for Limassol, though not before I have indulged my pastime of imagining a bronze-tipped trireme cutting through the water, bringing the latest news—and, of course, ideas—from ancient Greece.

It is easy to get carried away in Cyprus. This is Aphrodite's Island, after all, where the goddess of love drifted ashore on a sea shell. I have scented her perfume all over the island in the white anemones that are said to be her tears over the death of her lover, Adonis. At the Baths of Aphrodite, a freshwater pool where she bathed, I have dipped my hands in crystal-clear water, hoping a little of the eternal youth it promises might seep in.

Cyprus has romance in abundance, and I experienced much of that quality while researching this guidebook. It is mixed, however, with rather too much concrete in resorts where 'development' has overwhelmed the natural beauty. But even this fades to insignificance compared with the still unresolved 'problem' between the island's Greek and Turkish Cypriots that led to the 1974 Turkish invasion and division of the island.

I once stood beside the sea at the Apostolos Andreas Monastery in the North, gazing across the water towards Turkey. The elderly Greek Cypriot caretaker wept as he told me that 'not many pilgrims' came any longer to the shrine where St. Andrew called forth a sacred spring. Now the pilgrims are coming again. Since the opening of the border in 2003, there are grounds for being optimistic that the days of division are numbered.

Cyprus specializes in idyllic days. Minoans, Phoenicians, Mycenaeans, Egyptians, Persians, Romans, Arabs, Byzantines, Crusaders, Venetians, Turks and British all crossed Cyprus' shores, only to be seduced by her soft Levantine ways and absorbed by the landscape. You have every reason to expect that the same experience lies in store for you.

George McDonald

Cyprus Is

Cyprus's landscape, people, climate and history offer visitors unsurpassed interest and charm, but it must guard against the overdevelopment that threatens some of its most scenic places. It must also work out a just and permanent solution to the division between its Greek and Turkish communities.

Gazing back through the mists of time, all nations like to think their birth was attended by some portent of greatness, by heroes who left future generations an indelible legacy of virtue, or by a mystic sign of heaven's special favour. But only Cyprus can claim to be the birthplace of the goddess of love, for this is indeed Aphrodite's island.

❏ Cyprus is the third largest island in the Mediterranean, after Sicily and Sardinia. It lies in the eastern Mediterranean, 65km (40 miles) from Turkey, 105km (65 miles) from Syria, 340km (210 miles) from Egypt and 385km (240 miles) from the Greek island of Rhodes. ❏

The beach is the big attraction

Here the favoured child of Zeus, gold-crowned and beautiful, made her abode after being wafted ashore from the wine-dark sea, and here she loved and bathed and rested. Cyprus is Aphrodite's garden, a mosaic of mountains, woodland and plains charmed by the spell of an enchantress.

That enchantment is evident in many ways. The peaks of two mountain ranges, the Troodos in the west and the Pentadaktylos (Beşparmak) in the north, grasp at the sky, and between them stretches the Mesaoria (Mesarya) Plain, fraying into rugged foothills along the edge of the mountains. Broad bays sweep the coastline, sharpening to points on peninsulas whose layout led ancient writers to compare the shape of Cyprus to a spread-out sheepskin. Nowadays, a frying-pan is a more popular—and, in view of the long, hot summers,

perhaps more appropriate—image, with the Karpasia (Karpaz) Peninsula forming its handle.

THE OTHER FACE Veterans of past tourist campaigns will not be surprised to find that this Mediterranean holiday destination has attributes less amenable to legendary treatment: rush-hour traffic jams, for example, and cheek-by-jowl holiday hotels that no amount of tourist-board doctoring can re-create as traditional dwellings set in groves of lemon trees. Similarly, beaches

> ❑ The permanent population of Cyprus is estimated at 985,000, of whom 640,000 are Greek Cypriots, 180,000 are Turkish Cypriots or Turkish immigrants, and about 6,000 are Maronites or Armenians. The remainder are foreign residents and temporary workers. ❑

exist on which it may scarcely be possible to find a few grains of sand to call your own, and not all the local cuisine has been approved by rhapsodic gourmets before appearing on your plate. There are even Cypriots who look upon visitors as cash-dispensers on the hoof—herds to be shepherded, milked and fleeced.

In most aspects, however, the downside is the exception rather than the rule. The island's ethnic Greek and Turkish populations, who have caused each other so much grief, extend a welcome to their foreign visitors that is all the more refreshing for being genuine. 'Friendly natives' is such a patronizing cliché that the phrase is best avoided, but Cypriots come close

enough to the ideal. Their island (Kypros in Greek; Kıbrıs in Turkish) boasts a wild beauty that does not submit easily to the dictates of 'development', and even if large tracts along the coast have by now submitted, there remains much that is fresh and untamed.

A NEW HOPE Yet a serpent has been loose in Aphrodite's garden. The island of love is divided by more than 40 years of conflict between its Greek and Turkish communities, split across the middle by a United Nations buffer zone separating the two parties. Since the border was opened in 2003 peaceful contact between the communities has indoubtedly improved the atmosphere and created an opening for change. Tough issues still have to be addressed and resolved if the vision of the Cypriots living together in harmony once more is to be realized.

A place of escape in the Troodos

The reward for turning your back on the beach is a glimpse of another Cyprus, one far removed in spirit from the heavily developed resorts that crowd sections of the coast. With scarcely a backward glance at the turquoise shimmer of the warm Mediterranean, the adventurous spirit heads for the hills.

When the English writer Lawrence Durrell first set eyes on Cyprus in the 1950s, his ship berthed in 'a gloomy and featureless roadstead, before a town whose desolate silhouette suggested that of a tin-mining village in the Andes' (*Bitter Lemons*, 1957). Resort hotels and real-estate developments have replaced this bedraggled scene and, although the coastal strip can still beguile, the real Cyprus lies elsewhere. You could do worse than leave the toasting bodies behind occasionally to follow the road into the Troodos or Pentadaktylos (Beşparmak) Mountains.

Dusty trails lead into the wild interior and to the few remaining sections of coast (in the South) where the development bandwagon has never rolled. There is nature aplenty, although this is not to say the natural world remains intact. Prehistoric flora and fauna have been drastically modified by agriculture, logging, mining and other human activity. In the mountains, terraces provide a level platform for orchards.

SCENIC HIGHS There are few good roads into the Troodos Mountains in the west, and once you're there the going can get tough. The Troodos draw their attraction from cool mountain air, pretty villages, Byzantine churches and the chance to get close to nature. On the western slopes is the Pafos Forest, where the wild mountain sheep of Cyprus, the moufflon, roams. If the Pentadaktylos peaks are less dominant, they are no less scenic, nor are their crusader castles less noteworthy than the

Lara Bay (top). The Akamas Peninsula wilderness area (below)

12

❏ Nature has been a victim of the Cyprus conflict. The Greek Cypriot economy was virtually ruined by the 1974 war and subsequent refugee influx. Development, particularly tourism development, on a massive and uncontrolled scale revived it, but only at the expense of the natural world. ❏

Foxes breed all over the island

13

Troodos churches. The Pentadaktylos Mountains run parallel to the north coast before petering out in the Karpasia (Karpaz) Peninsula. This mountain chain is less frequented by tourists than the Troodos, improving the chances of a peaceful escape.

COASTAL DELIGHTS The coast also has its wild places, with more open coastline than developed; in this respect the Turkish Cypriot zone is better off. Peninsulas are favoured areas for wilderness and wildlife protection, both the Akamas Peninsula (see page 159) and the Karpasia Peninsula (see page 241) are potential locations for national parks dedicated to preserving their unique character—or at least some of it. The Akrotiri Peninsula (see page 102) is a semi-wilderness, partially protected by the presence of a British military base.

LIVING WORLD The moufflon, which is now thriving after only just avoiding extinction, is the star of Cyprus' wildlife show, but it is far from being a solo performer. Foxes, hedgehogs and shrews can be found all over the island, and wild donkeys roam the Karpasia Peninsula. Birdwatching is a popular activity, thanks to the many species that stop over in Cyprus during their migration—and despite the fact that thousands of birds continue to be slaughtered on the island in the name of sport. The Salt Lakes at Akrotiri and Larnaka (see pages 116 and 96) are prime observation sites in winter and spring, when pink flamingos and a host of ducks, waders and other water-orientated species fly in. Indigenous birds like the Cyprus warbler can also be seen.

Flowers and butterflies, many unique to Cyprus, are abundant, and this is also true of trees, plants and shrubs. Add freshwater fish species in reservoirs, marinelife seen on scuba-diving trips and the rare green and loggerhead turtles that lay their eggs on Cyprus's beaches, and you'll see that the natural world still has much to offer here.

❏ Extinction of indigenous species began at about the same time as the first evidence of human occupation is noted on the island, some 11,000 years ago. Fossils of pygmy hippopotamuses and elephants have been found at various locations (see pages 102 and 203). ❏

No country as strategically positioned as Cyprus, at the historic crossroads of the world's great civilizations, could avoid attracting so many different ethnic communities. The irony today is that community spirit has proved to be both a blessing and a curse.

Cypriot veins course with the blood of Phoenicians, Persians, Greeks, Romans, Arabs, French, Italians, Turks and Britons, to name just the more prominent sources. Heritage is not necessarily community, however, and at its worst the Cypriot concept of community has come down to armed individuals glaring at each other across a gulf of fear and hatred. At its best, on the other hand, community spirit is one of the island's greatest delights.

The two main communities are of Greek and Turkish origin. Whether or not Cyprus is Greek is a question that has taxed both experts in international law and historians peering back through the dimly lit corridors of time. All that can be said with confidence is that most Cypriots feel themselves to be either Greek or Turkish—with the historical bonds that this implies—and yet, as Cypriots, not exactly identical to either, so that the visitor must speak of Greek Cypriots and Turkish Cypriots and never confuse the two.

An elderly Greek Cypriot

14

NEW THINKING Cypriots are cosmopolitan, belonging to a well travelled community of emigrants, and there are large Cypriot communities—both Greek and Turkish—in Britain, the US, Australia and western Europe. Many young Cypriots go to university in Athens or Istanbul, although locally established universities have reduced this traffic. That said, a lack of career opportunities, even allowing for virtually full employment (in the South), still persuades young people to leave.

The Cypriot concept of community shows most strongly at village level, and one of the saddest results of economic growth is the death of villages as young people leave for a more prosperous life in towns and resorts. The Greek Cypriot government is almost obsessive about the health of its villages, supporting projects to keep them going concerns. However, such plans often lead to an artificial state which is arguably worse than extinction; wealthy newcomers buying quaint village houses are no substitute for the living communities that have left them.

COMMUNITY CHEST Beyond its two main ethnic groups, Cyprus is a melting-pot of minorities. Maronites (Syrian or Lebanese Christians), Armenians and Latins (Roman Catholics, mainly Italian in origin) are the main minorities, with the Maronite component reinforced by Lebanon's descent into chaos. Lebanese Muslims also came over, and Cyprus took on the mantle as the main entrepôt of the Middle East.

The British have long considered Cyprus to be the Mediterranean jewel of their lost empire, and today British communities are found all over the island, particularly around Limassol and Pafos, and at Keryneia (Girne) in the Turkish Cypriot sector. They are being joined by other expatriates, most notably Germans.

In Turkish Cyprus, the new arrivals have mostly been Turkish. Immigrants from Anatolia, and more recently from Bulgaria's Turkish minority, have boosted the Turkish Cypriot population. Greek Cypriots complain that these people are part of a demographic offensive, and that they are occupying land and houses that belong to Greek Cypriots. Many Turkish Cypriots, too, resent the influx from Turkey, feeling it has changed, for the worse, the character of their community. In Cyprus, sadly, community can be a source of conflict as well as a badge of distinction.

❏ After Nicosia and Limassol, the largest Greek Cypriot city is London, with some 100,000 residents, out of more than 200,000 people of Cypriot origin living in Britain. About 40,000 Cypriots live in the United States. ❏

In old Nicosia two Turkish Cypriot boys find fun in a tyre

15

Such is the mystical lure of Cypriot religious foundations, that people who at home rarely or never set foot inside places of worship can be seen marvelling at murals, following in the footsteps of monks or standing barefoot before a mosque mihrab *(prayer niche). Religious tourism, it seems, is sanctioned on high.*

Cypriot Christians happily venerate their icons and seek assistance from the saints in time of need, yet low attendance at religious services (except on festival days) can hardly be encouraging to the priests. Cypriot Muslims, in the main, have a laid-back approach to the mosque which would be anathema to a fundamentalist. Very few attend mosque or wear religious attire, but they do celebrate religious festivals—perhaps because these afford time off work and spent with the family.

Two millennia of Christian tradition have filled Cyprus with churches and monasteries, the finest of which have won the United Nations' badge of approval as key elements in the cultural patrimony of humankind. Some of the best mosques are churches with a minaret or two tacked on.

> ❑ The schism between Roman Catholicism and the Orthodox tradition has lasted a long time, encapsulated in the capture and sacking of Constantinople in 1204 by the Fourth Crusade. As recently as 1965, the Pope and the Orthodox Patriarch lifted recipricol excommunication orders that dated from 1054. ❑

PAST GLORIES The ruins of colossal early Christian basilicas are to be found at archaeological sites around the island—most notably at Kourion, Pafos and Salamis (see pages 172, 109 and 246). They symbolize the new religion's power and wealth soon after it had replaced paganism as the state religion of the Roman, and later Byzantine, Empire. Yet with their classical colonnades and multicoloured marble floors, the remains sometimes look little different from the ruined gymnasia, palaces and villas that surround them.

More evocative of the Christian empire of Byzantium is the constellation of little frescoed churches that glitters in the Troodos Mountains and a few other places. Externally, none of them is worth much more than a passing glance, being based, it would appear, on the same architectural principles as the barn. Inside, however, the Byzantine tradition's true impact can be seen in wonderful paintings that cover the walls and vaulted roofs with scenes from the Bible, the lives of the Holy Family and saints, and the primary images

A Greek Orthodox monk at the Royal Chapel of Agia Ekaterina

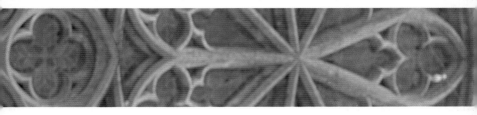

of Christ crucified, risen from the dead, and as 'Ruler of the World'.

LIVING LEGENDS The proudest institutions in Cyprus are the great hilltop monasteries of Panagia tou Kykkou, Stavrovouni and Machairas (see pages 142, 96 and 190), stout vessels which have borne the ideals of Orthodox Christendom and Hellenism safely down the stream of time. These monasteries have been the source of a determination that Byzantium should not die in spirit, although it is no longer counted among the powers of the earth. This timeless quality is impressive, with perspectives spanning a thousand years and more, yet ultimately such rigour passes the casual visitor by, leaving only a vague impression of bearded monks and glowing icons. More easily absorbed are the convents where nuns maintain a simpler spirituality, softened by flowers and spiced with sales of honey and souvenirs.

In recent years with the relaxation of border restrictions, saint's day worship has again become regular for Greek Cypriots at the monasteries of Apostolos Andreas in the Karpasia (Karpaz) Peninsula and Agios Mamas at Morfou (Güzelyurt) in the north, while Turkish Cypriots head south to worship at the Hala Sultan Tekke outside Larnaka.

Detail, Lala Mustafa Paşa Mosque, Famagusta (top). Modern frescoes, Panagia tou Kykkou (below)

17

Religious, folkloric and modern festivals are scattered conveniently through the calendar, ensuring that there is nearly always a colourful celebration taking place somewhere in Cyprus. Not all are major events, as the tradition of local village festivals remains strong.

Considering the island's religious legacy, it is no surprise that most Cypriot festivals are based on some holy day or event, while feast days, or 'name days', of the saints provide an eternal excuse for a party. Villages are the traditional venues for festivals, and the venues for traditional festivals. Nowadays, however, more people live in towns and cities, so either the celebrations have been adapted or celebrants return to their home village for the occasion.

Easter, culminating in the celebration of Christ's resurrection from the dead, is the principal festival. Palm Sunday, the Sunday before Easter, is the start of Holy Week. On Easter Thursday icons are shrouded in black, and on the next day, Good Friday, processions carry Christ's flower-bedecked image through the streets. On Easter Saturday the black shrouds are removed from the icons and in the evening bonfires are lit, onto which are thrown effigies of Judas. Easter Sunday itself is marked by feasting.

❏ The Curium Drama Festival takes place on various days during July and August, using the 2,000-year-old theatre at Kourion (see page 109) for performances of ancient Greek plays, as well as works by Shakespeare and other dramatists ❏

CARNIVAL CAPERS Easter begins, in a sense, with the pre-Lenten Carnival —ten days of fun, games, masquerades and feasting, ending on Green Monday, seven weeks before Easter Sunday. Limassol is the centre of Carnival, and the Carnival king's entry into the city by float kicks off the proceedings, which culminate in a massive float parade through Limassol on the final Sunday. Vegetarian picnics on Green Monday 'cleanse' the body in preparation for the coming fast.

Fun and games at Limassol's pre-Lenten Carnival

Christmas is the other important Christian festival. Olive twigs and branches, symbols of purity, are placed over doorways and inside houses as decoration, with a Christmas tree symbolizing life and prosperity. In the villages, fattened pigs are slaughtered for a feast, although turkey is also popular. Gifts are often exchanged on New Year's Day rather than at Christmas. Those not going to a village festival or special restaurant party stay at home and play simple games before cutting the *vasilopitta*, or New Year cake.

HIGH TIMES Other important events include the Anthestiria flower festivals at Limassol, Pafos and

18

several other towns in May, recalling the floral festivals of pagan times. The International State Fair, held in May at the State Fair Ground outside Nicosia, showcases Cypriot products and services.

At Kataklysmos (the Festival of the Flood) in June, three days of seafront fairs and mutual-soaking contests celebrate Noah's sojourn on the Ark during the 40 days and nights of the Great Flood. In the same month, the Carlsberg Beer Festival concentrates on liquid refreshment based on hops and water.

Another important religious event takes place on 15 August—the Assumption of Our Lady. Perhaps most eagerly awaited of all, however, is the Limassol Wine Festival in September, when the city's Municipal Gardens become an open-air venue for contemporary Dionysiac revelry.

In the Turkish zone most festivals are related to Islam or to political events associated with the Turkish Cypriots' struggle against Enosis (union with Greece) and finally for independence. Islamic festivals include Kurban Bayramı, which commemorates Abraham's willingness to sacrifice his son Isaac at God's command, and the three-day Şeker Bayramı festival at the end of Ramadan's 40 days of fasting.

For a calendar of public holidays and festivals, see pages 254–255.

19

❏ A ten-day International Arts Festival takes place in Limassol during June and July. The city's Municipal Gardens are the open-air venue for music, song and dance by both local and international artists. ❏

In the Republic of Cyprus, religion is the source of a strong festival tradition

As in other countries where mass production has overwhelmed demand for traditional products, Cyprus has struggled to retain a foothold on the artisanal ladder. Government support, assisted by burgeoning demand from visitors and collectors, has helped to bring about a renaissance in the old skills.

A case could be argued that Cypriot arts and crafts began with young women's need for a dowry. The men crafted objects from copper, gourds and wood, but the finest products emerged—and still do—from the fingers of home-working embroiderers. A self-respecting bride had to have a hundred sheets and pillowcases and towels, as well as heaps of table linen and other furniture- and floor-coverings. As families were large and girls many, both mother and daughters had to start laying in the linen early.

Hand-embroidered lace from Lefkara (*lefkaritika*) represents the stellar end of the spectrum, but products from other areas, including different forms of embroidery, have merit. Pafos, for example, is noted for *pafitika*, white material woven with bright, geometric designs. The cloth is made up into table-mats, cloths, runners, cushion-covers, bedspreads and curtains. Handloom weaving has all but disappeared, particularly as its finest exponents, from Lefkonikon (Geçitkale), abandoned their village ahead of the Turkish army in 1974. Re-established around Pafos, brightly coloured and striped Lefkonikon work is making a comeback.

The unique pattern of Lefkara lace

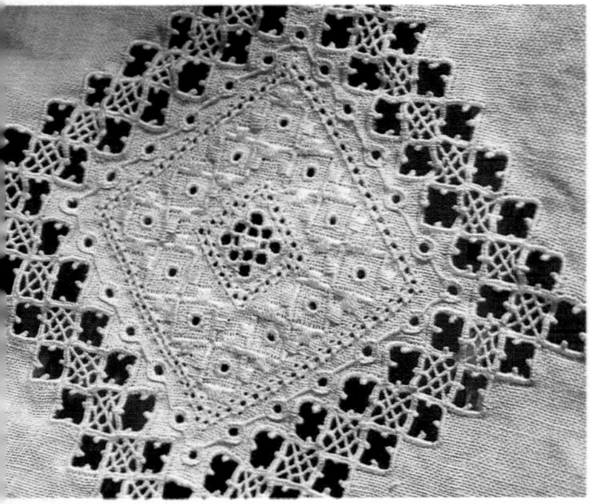

Selling lace in the village of Lefkara

MANLY VIRTUES In ancient times, the copper mines of Cyprus were famous and their metal formed a primary component of the Bronze Age. Even in the Iron Age the armies

❑ Lefkara's superb hand-made lace is generally thought to have originated when local women observed the lace-work of visiting Venetian noblewomen and adapted it to their own embroidery forms. Turkish Cypriots trace *lefkaritika* to the traditional patterns of Turkey's Antep region, and equally fine work of this kind is on sale in Northern Cyprus. In both cases the products are sold locally for one-third or less of the price in Europe and America. ❑

of Alexander the Great were said to have worn armour of Cypriot copper. Copper cauldrons coated with tin have lost their place in the kitchen to aluminium pots, but can still be found, along with copper ornaments, in handicraft shops.

Other metalworking crafts have retained their popularity, especially gold- and silverware, with demand existing for ecclesiastical vessels as well as elaborate jewellery worked in these materials.

Demand was once insatiable for hand-thrown *pitharia*, pots of a size and shape that allowed them to be used as a kind of individual 'sauna'—something you can still find today—although they were more usually used for storing olive oil and wine. The curvaceous forms of these pots can still be seen in gardens, monasteries and along roadsides, although they are now more likely to be filled with flowers than wine. Their production has been revived at Kornos (see page 109). Pottery cats were a speciality of Lapithos (Lapta—see panel on page 216).

❏ Turkish Cypriot crafts such as basketry, lace-making and kilim (rug) weaving, are maintained despite fears that they are dying out. Some attractive pottery, based on traditional designs, is hand-crafted at the Dizayn 74 workshop on the western edge of Keryneia (Girne). ❏

21

SKILLS SHORTAGE Nicosia's Cyprus Handicraft Centre workshop (see page 48) is a vital element in the drive to retain the island's heritage of traditional arts and crafts. Fewer people learn these skills now, as the practice of handing them down from parent to child gets broken. The ultramodern institute at the city's edge provides teaching and practical experience in the old ways. It is questionable whether such an organized place can also preserve the spirit of the original crafts, but it at least offers the possibility of doing so.

Handicrafts are popular souvenirs

Economic growth differs on either side of the demarcation line, for while a similar base sustains each part, the Greek Cypriot sector generates three times its neighbour's wealth. Both utilize their geographical situation to provide offshore centres for banking.

The location of Cyprus, which has brought unwelcome visitors in the past, has had compensations in its economy. Tourism is the most obvious of these, with the Greek Cypriot south welcoming around 2 million and Turkish Cypriot north 550,000 visitors each year, and the number is growing. Tourism forms the principal source of foreign exchange, and, in addition, is a major provider of jobs, both directly and indirectly.

HARVEST THE PROFIT Agriculture remains the biggest economic sector, comprising several subsectors, of which citrus fruit (including products such as processed juices) is the most important in terms of exports, followed by potatoes, grapes and wine. The light-industrial sector is large and growing, with exports of clothing and footwear combined outweighing the revenue generated by the island's agricultural exports. Greek Cyprus's principal trading partner is the European Union, which supplies just over half the island's imports and takes just under half its exports.

> ❏ Despite Cyprus's ancient reputation for mining, this is now a declining industry. Iron pyrites is the principal product at around 50,000 tonnes, with copper reaching barely one-twentieth of this amount. ❏

The Turkish Cypriot sector's main partner is Turkey, followed by the European Union.

BANKER'S DRAFT Banking is an important growth area, as Greek Cyprus develops as an offshore centre, but is one which has credibility problems to overcome before achieving widespread acceptance. The government has been cautious in granting licences, preferring to build slowly on a base of reputable banks. Recent years saw an influx of dollars from Russia and Yugoslavia—the origins of some of this money can really only be described as 'suspect'.

Women picking shallots in a field near Polis

Cyprus's misfortune is to be so located that no power of any consequence in the eastern Mediterranean could accept a competing power controlling it. The military forces swarming over the island are proof that little has changed in this respect.

PRIME LOCATION Geography is often the main determinant of history, and Cypriots could be forgiven for wishing they could attach sails to their island and slip away to a less desirable but more tranquil location. With its mines, forests and ports there have always been reasons enough for wanting the island, but even more important was to deny its use to a potential or actual enemy.

A vital consideration in Turkey's 1974 invasion of the island, in addition to protecting Turkish Cypriots, was to prevent the coup against President Makarios leading to Greek possession of a base off Turkey's southern shore. Ironically, Greece and Turkey were, and are, NATO allies, but the Atlantic Alliance often had better grounds for fearing a shooting match breaking out between them than a Soviet offensive into the Mediterranean.

AREA DEFENCE Britain's sovereign military bases at Akrotiri and Dhekelia undoubtedly have different *raisons d'être* than those highlighted in public relations briefings. The provision of good-weather exercise areas for air force and army units, and logistics support to United Nations peacekeeping forces, scarcely justifies such a commitment by the British government. Rather, it seems the bases are being retained for such events as Gulf War I and II, and for possible 'out of area' operations by NATO in the Middle East.

Tides of strategic thinking have ebbed and flowed over Cyprus for 3,000 years. Swords have been beaten into missile-armed jets, but the troops and the hardware are still there—and will probably remain so for quite some time yet.

This view of Europe dates from 1360 AD. and shows the borders of the Holy Roman Empire. Cyprus has remained important right up to the present day, a consequence of its strategic location at the crossroads between East and West

23

❑ 'A race advancing on the East must start with Cyprus. Alexander, Augustus, Richard and St. Louis took that line. A race advancing on the West must start with Cyprus. Sargon, Ptolemy, Cyrus, Haroun al-Rashid took this line.'
– W. Hepworth Dixon, *British Cyprus*, 1887 ❑

The island's state of division had seemed set in concrete, but the opening of the border and European Union membership have created a new dynamic. While the international community tries to help, only Greek and Turkish Cypriots can choose to live in harmony.

The generally peaceful character of divided Cyprus since the 1974 Turkish invasion spiralled into violence during the 1990s. Relations between Turkey and Greece deteriorated to the point of a narrowly averted war over territorial disputes in the Aegean. Turkey was incensed by a defence agreement between Greece and Cyprus and the establishment of Greek bases on the island.

Turkish occupation forces reacted harshly to challenges to the 'territorial integrity' of North Cyprus. Greek Cypriots who deliberately broke through demarcation line barriers, or even wandered apparently unwittingly into the UN buffer zone were at best arrested and at worst killed.

HOPE FOR THE FUTURE In 2000 a ray of light came along with a UN-sponsored project for restoration of a

...confronting Turkish and Turkish Cypriot flags across the way

monastery in the North and a mosque in the South. But the mood soured again in 2001, when the European Court of Human Rights found Turkey guilty of widespread human rights violations arising from its 1974 invasion.

By then, however, relations between Greece and Turkey were improving, thanks in part to each country having assisted the other after severe earthquakes, and both Cyprus and Turkey were on the list of candidates for European Union membership.

The surprise opening of the Green Line in Nicosia in 2003 for freer movement between the two sectors, began a process that has continued to deepen. In April 2004, however, Greek Cypriots voted in a referendum 3 to 1 against the Annan Plan to reunify the island in time for its accession to the EU. Although Turkish Cypriots voted 2 to 1 in favour, the plan was thereby rejected. A month later Cyprus joined the EU, with only the South gaining membership, for the time being at least.

But the outlook has clearly improved. In 2005 the UN began to consult once again with the various interested parties before deciding whether to launch a new initiative.

War of the flags: Greek and Republic of Cyprus flags...

24

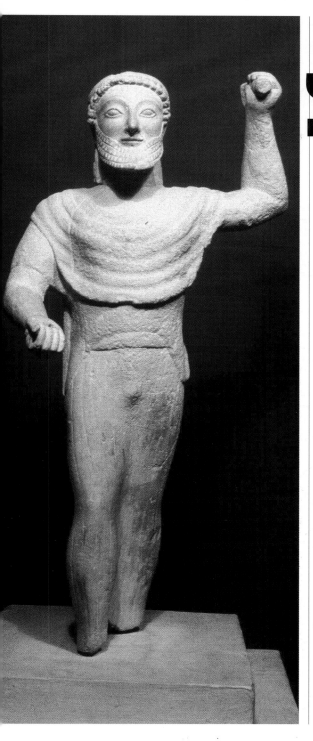

Cyprus was

Civilization in Cyprus developed slowly as the result of colonization from the Asian and European land masses, and trade with the more developed cultures of ancient Mesopotamia, Egypt and Greece. Already, at this early stage in its history, Cyprus had become a crossroads between east and west.

26

Ninety million years ago Cyprus lay under an ocean called Tethys that stretched from northern Europe to Asia. The majestic rhythms of geological time witnessed the formation of limestone and sandstone layers which were forced upwards by the slow collision of Africa with Eurasia. Mountains and volcanoes formed two chains of islands, today's Troodos and Pentadaktylos (Beşparmak) ranges, while erosion gradually laid down the Mesaoria (Mesarya) Plain and the coastal flatlands. Water from melting Ice Age glaciers poured into the Mediterranean basin and isolated Cyprus from Asia. The scene was set for the arrival of humankind.

Palaeolithic people must have stood on the shores of present-day Turkey and Syria, gazing thoughtfully at the green haze of Cyprus, 65km (40 miles) distant over the water. Primitive boats were prepared and Stone Age migrants set out across the sea. The first traces of human habitation date from the mesolithic period, in the 10th millennium BC, at the exciting but scientifically controversial site of Aetokremnos on the Akrotiri

Iconostasis in Panagia Angelostisti (top) and sculpture of a warrior (above) from the Cyprus Museum, Nicosia

Peninsula. Then there are neolithic settlements dating from the 7th and 6th millennia BC, at Kastros in the Karpasia (Karpaz) Peninsula, and at Khirokitia (Choirokoitia) between Limassol and Larnaka.

RISING CIVILIZATION By the Bronze Age, from 3000BC, Cyprus was at the forefront of the new metal technology, thanks to its copper mines. Contacts and trade with the ancient Middle East brought Babylonians, Assyrians and Egyptians, thereby opening the island to their influence. Tablets from the 18th century BC onwards found at Tel el-Amarna in Egypt refer to the copper-making centre of 'Alasia', which may refer to the city of Enkomi (Egkomi) alone, or possibly to the whole of Cyprus.

❏   The origins of the name 'Cyprus' are uncertain. In the *Iliad*, Homer calls it 'Kypros', which may come from the Greek word for the henna plant that flourished on the island. Its association with copper offers a more likely explanation—the Latin name for copper is *aes cyprium*. However, the question remains: Did Cyprus take its name from copper, or copper take its name from Cyprus? ❏

❑ Aphrodite, the goddess of love, like the first Cypriots and many since, was an immigrant. Despite Homer's colourful tale of her birth in the sea, Aphrodite originated with the Assyro-Babylonian earth goddess Ishtar and the Phoenician Astarte. ❑

The Phoenicians, seafarers from Lebanon and Palestine, set up trading cities around Cyprus at Kition, Amathous and Lapithos (Lapta). The Minoans of Crete also came to trade and settle, and they introduced the Cypro-Minoan script (based on Cretan Linear A) which remains undeciphered. The cities were prosperous, a sign of progress that brought its own problems, as may be inferred by the walls raised to ward off pirates and invaders.

Earthquakes, an ever-present threat in an area of colliding land masses, periodically struck and demolished the newly established centres of civilized life.

ENTER THE GREEKS From about 1400BC, Mycenaean Greeks traded with Cyprus, as seen in the many examples of their pottery and other implements found by archaeologists. Later, they came to colonize as their homeland was invaded by Dorian tribes from the north, who were equipped with superior iron weapons. The Greeks founded new cities and took over existing ones, although Cyprus remained under intermittent Egyptian, Assyrian and possibly Hittite control. The city-states, which included Egkomi, Salamis, Soloi, Marion, Kition, Palaia Pafos and Kourion, were kingdoms ruled by absolute monarchs.

Cyprus was on the periphery of the great civilizations of the period, never at the centre of trade or culture, but one of the first places that any expanding imperialistic power reached as it moved across the Mediterranean from east to west, or west to east. Colonized, courted, conquered: The pattern of Cyprus' history was set.

Detail of a bronze cauldron dating from the eighth century BC, on display in the Cyprus Museum, Nicosia

The tug-of-war between Persia and Greece over Cyprus had profound implications for the island. It was too vital to Persia's security to be relinquished except in the face of overwhelming force, but too far from Greece for that force to be applied, and so Cyprus remained under Persian control throughout the great age of classical Greece.

Egyptian hegemony over Cyprus ended in 540BC, when the Cypriot kings threw in their lot with the Persian Empire under Darius I, who was on the rampage throughout the Middle East, swallowing up rivals before breakfast and taking Egypt in his stride. Little Cyprus would have been unwise to do anything other than bow the knee, as it was later to discover in brave but foolhardy bouts of rebellion. In the meantime, it became part of the Persian Empire's Fifth Satrapy, which included

28

❑ The first known biography of a living person was the eulogy written by the Athenian teacher Isocrates on the Cypriot hero, King Evagoras I of Salamis, who expelled the Persians and united the island between 411 and 374BC. ❑

Palaia Pafos and Soloi, were taken under siege and eventually succumbed to the Persians.

WRONG SIDE Persia went on to invade mainland Greece twice, in 490BC and 480BC. So thoroughly cowed was Cyprus that when Greece was fighting for its life in the great battles at Marathon, Thermopylae, Salamis and Plataea, Cypriot naval forces served under the banner of the invader. At Salamis no fewer than 150 Cypriot galleys fought in Xerxes' fleet, but they performed so badly that perhaps their real allegiance was clear.

The golden age of classical Greece passed Cyprus by, running its course far beyond a horizon circumscribed by the island's role as a Persian naval base. One man, King Evagoras I of Salamis, a brilliant political and military leader, succeeded in uniting Cyprus by force and kicking out the Persians—not without resistance, however, from Cypriots of Phoenician origin and others who supported Persia. With Evagoras' assassination in 374BC, the old forces reasserted themselves.

CULTURAL QUESTION Cyprus had absorbed much of Greek culture, even if such developments as

The Kyrenia Ship (c300BC), in the Shipwreck Museum, Keryneia Castle

territory covering present-day Israel, Lebanon and Syria.

The quality of Persian rule can be judged by the fact that all the Cypriot cities, save Phoenician Amathous, raised the standard of revolt in support of the Ionian Greeks of Asia Minor, when they launched their great rebellion against Persia in 499BC. The Persians reacted swiftly, landing an army at Salamis. The city was soon recaptured after Stasenor, king of Kourion, deserted the rebel cause, and then Salamis itself deserted. Other cities, including

democracy never reached it, but it was never truly Greek, nor had it ever been allowed to become truly Greek. Its population make-up and geographical location inevitably determined that it looked east as well as west. The question of whether or not Cyprus has been Greek since the dawn of history is now an intensely political question. The historical record does not support those Hellenist partisans who say that no other indigenous cultural tradition ever flourished in Cyprus.

Ironically, by the time the island came under the undisputed control of Hellenism, Greece itself had been defeated by Macedon. The young Macedonian king, Alexander the Great, was off on the trail of conquest that would swamp Persia and extend the Hellenistic world to the borders

❑ The last independent king of Cyprus was Nicocreon, who ruled over Salamis. In 311BC he committed suicide, and he and his family are thought to have been commemorated by, but not buried in, the so-called Cenotaph of Nicocreon, a tumulus at the village of Egkomi (Tuzla) near Famagusta (Gazimağusa). ❑

29

of India. In such a vast scheme, Cyprus was a mere morsel. By 325BC the island was swallowed up into Alexander's empire. One of its great ages was about to begin.

Hellenistic rock-cut tombs, Makronisos (top). The Battle of Salamis, 480BC (below)

The might of Rome tore Cyprus away from the enfeebled grasp of Ptolemaic Egypt and incorporated it into the Roman province of Cilicia. Centuries of peace and prosperity followed, disturbed only by the occasional disastrous earthquake. During this time, Christianity took a firm hold on Cypriot hearts and minds.

Alexander the Great's approach to his succession was simple: Let the strongest rule. The island was finally won by Ptolemy, whose power-base was Egypt. In the Hellenistic Age that followed, Greek art, literature, language and philosophy were diffused throughout the three Hellenistic kingdoms. As a province of Ptolemaic Egypt, Cyprus was administered by a governor based at Salamis, and later at Pafos. The strongly eastern-influenced culture of the island became indelibly tinged with that of Greece.

For 250 years Cyprus developed in peace, with fine market-places and temples being constructed in the cities. Outstanding monuments, such as the Tombs of the Kings at Pafos, date from this period. In the 4th century BC Cyprus produced one of the brilliant minds of antiquity: Zeno of Kition, a Cypriot who founded the Stoic philosophy. A modified version of Zeno's ideas became the guiding philosophy of the Roman nobility.

ROMAN RULE The

Roman Emperor Septimius Severus in bronze at the Cyprus Museum in Nicosia (right). Mosaic at Soloi (top)

❏ In AD116, the Jewish inhabitants of Cyprus joined the revolt of their compatriots in Judaea. Some 200,000 non-Jews were said to have been massacred—a figure that is probably greatly exaggerated. The Roman general Lucius Quietus savagely suppressed the rebellion in AD117, and all Jews were expelled from the island. ❏

island's ruler, Ptolemy Auletes, refused to pay a ransom demanded by pirates for the release of a Roman aristocrat called Publius Claudius (or Clodius). Unfortunately, Publius was a friend of Julius Caesar and after his eventual release he was elected Tribune at Rome. It wasn't long before the invasion of Cyprus was underway. In 58BC the Roman general Marcus Portius Cato annexed Cyprus to Rome, which had brought the entire area of the Mediterranean under its rule.

Although Cyprus was at one time governed by the renowned orator Cicero, it gained a better indication of its position in the new order when Mark Antony, temporarily triumphant, gave the island to Queen Cleopatra of Egypt as a lover's gift.

From Emperor Augustus onwards, Cyprus was a tranquil backwater of the Roman Empire. For more than two centuries the island was a major beneficiary of the *Pax*

Greco-Roman theatre overlooking the sea at Kourion, west of Limassol

Romana. The Mediterranean was freed of pirates and hostile fleets, and trade flourished.

Pafos became the seat of Roman government, a city of villas, theatres and gymnasia. Archaeologists have uncovered some of the magnificent mosaic floors that graced the governor's palace and adjacent villas (see page 170). The coastline of Cyprus was dotted with other wealthy cities, a string of pearls connected by a Roman road that encircled the island.

CHRISTIAN VIRTUES Cyprus can, and does, claim to be the first Christian country. St. Paul converted the Roman governor, Sergius Paulus, in AD45, a remarkable 'catch' for a religion just off the theological drawing-board. Periods of persecution followed, but by AD313, when Emperor Constantine issued the Edict of Milan permitting religious freedom throughout the empire, Christianity was the dominant force in Cyprus. The ancient sanctuaries of Aphrodite and Apollo Ylatis (see pages 165 and 116 respectively) remained in business until AD392, when Emperor Theodosius abolished the pagan cults.

By then, Salamis had replaced Pafos as the island's capital. Demolished by an earthquake in AD342, Salamis was rebuilt by Emperor Constantius and renamed Constantia. Rome's empire subsequently split into a Greek east and a Latin west; when the western empire collapsed in the 5th century, Cyprus remained a province of the eastern empire, ruled from Constantinople.

31

❏ Roman tastes in performance art were less refined than those of the Greeks. Theatres like the one at Kourion (see page 109), more familiar with plays by Sophocles and Aristophanes, were converted to arenas for bloody spectacles between gladiators and wild animals. ❏

Column capital from the archaeological site at Kourion

No period of Cyprus's history left such an indelible legacy as the Byzantine. The era began as the swansong of classical civilization, was swept away when Islam's armies scorched the land, and then returned stronger than ever as the majestic empire whose twin fountainheads were Orthodox Christianity and Hellenism.

32

No citizen of 'Byzantium' would have recognised this modern term. Byzantium was an insignificant town occupying a strategically vital position on the Bosphorus. When the Roman Emperor Constantine transferred the imperial capital from Rome to Byzantium, he built a magnificent new city which was named Constantinople in his honour. From the start, it was a Christian city. When the Roman Empire in the west collapsed, Constantinople continued for another thousand years as capital of the east. In their own eyes, the Byzantines were Romans.

❑ The 6th-century Emperor Justinian, who is often considered to be the first important Byzantine emperor, was well aware of his own august Roman heritage. He had a commemorative medallion struck at Constantinople, preening himself as 'the Glory of the Romans'. ❑

While the empire's land frontiers were threatened on all sides, Cyprus continued to live the same peaceful existence it had known for centuries under Roman rule. Christian basilicas adorned its cities in place of pagan temples, and these new foundations lacked nothing of the wealth and elegance of their religious predecessors.

It was, in a sense, a golden age, but just as gold is the colour of a late afternoon in summer, so the drowsy centuries of the imperial peace were coming to an end for Cyprus. From the depths of Arabia, a storm was rising that would shake the Byzantine world to its foundations.

SWORD VERSUS SCIMITAR In AD622 Islam bloomed in the desert like a rain-blessed flower and the armies of the Prophet erupted from the sands, tearing across Syria, Palestine and Egypt to stand within a few years on

Brilliant Byzantine frescoes adorn the church of Panagia tou Asinou

the Mediterranean shore opposite Cyprus. The hard-pressed Byzantine armies could not defend the island. In AD632 an initial raid destroyed Kition, and a more determined attack in AD647 did the same to Constantia (Salamis). Pafos fell the following year. The Cypriots began scrambling inland, away from the coastal cities which were little more than sitting ducks to the new religion's rampaging warriors.

The island returned to its former role as a frontier outpost, fought over and ravished by the forces of two great, irreconcilable powers. By AD650 it was split between the Byzantines and Arabs, and gradually depopulated as its inhabitants fled to safer parts of the empire. In AD688 those who remained were forced to pay tribute to both the Byzantine emperor and the Muslim caliph.

The disasters of the 7th century were fatal to civilized life, and the roster of cities whose millennia-old histories reached an end at this time makes for a grim chapter in the archaeological record.

THE EMPIRE STRIKES BACK In 965, Byzantium, which at one stage had been on its knees with hostile armies at the gates of Constantinople itself, made a dramatic comeback in Cyprus under Emperor Nicephoros Phocas, who expelled the Arabs. For the next two centuries Christian arts and architecture flourished once more in what had again become a relatively peaceful backwater. Nicosia (Lefkosia) grew on the foundations of ancient Ledra, the castles in the Pentadaktylos (Beşparmak) Mountains were established, and monasteries and frescoed churches sprang up in the Troodos Mountains.

❑ In 1959, when Archbishop Makarios signed the London Accord in red ink, he was exercising a right to use that imperial colour granted in AD478 by the Byzantine Emperor Zeno to the head of the Cypriot Church and his successors. Zeno also allowed him to wear a purple cloak and to carry an imperial sceptre. ❑

33

Panagia Angeloktisti church, Kiti (top and below)

Cyprus remained unaffected by the blood and violence of the First and Second Crusades, but its luck ran out by the Third. The Cypriots had been invaded, repressed and auctioned like so many goods and chattels in the past. Now they were to see their island handed over to a dynasty of failed crusaders who would rule it for 300 years.

The fires of religious fundamentalism swept once more across the Levant. This time Islam was the victim. In 1095, Pope Urban II launched the First Crusade to recover the Holy Land from the infidels. The flower of European chivalry carried the crusader banner to the walls of Jerusalem and, in 1099, took the city by storm. A massacre of its Muslim population ensued. The Holy Land had been delivered, but the new Christian kingdom immediately came under intense pressure from Saracen armies bent on its destruction. Cyprus, dangerously close to the flames, had so far escaped unscorched...but not for long. In 1184 Isaac Komnenos, a member of Byzantium's imperial family, seized Cyprus and declared it independent. He ruled tyrannically for seven years until fate caught up with him in a drama worthy of Hollywood. Komnenos had promised the Saracen ruler Saladin, who had recaptured Jerusalem, that he would not help the Third Crusade to re-recapture the city. When the fleet of England's King Richard the Lionheart was scattered by a storm, the king's fiancée, Princess Berengaria, landed on Cyprus where Komnenos treated her badly. Richard promptly invaded, routed Komnenos's army, and had the usurper hauled before him.

England's King Richard (below), who first bought, then sold Cyprus Isaac Komnenos (top) pleads with him for his daughter's return

MUSICAL CHAIRS King Richard soon alienated the Cypriots by scooping up their wealth and forcing the Latin (Roman Catholic) Church on them. They revolted. As his mission was to fight for the Holy Land, not for Cyprus, Richard sold the island to the Knights Templar, an élite order of crusader monks. No strangers to repressing subject peoples, the Templars went to work on the rebels with a will, but even they could make no headway and they unloaded the island back on Richard. He then handed the Cyprus hot potato to his ally, Guy de Lusignan, the then out-of-work French King of Jerusalem. He proved an able ruler who began

❏ King Richard the Lionheart of England married Princess Berengaria of Navarre at Limassol in 1191. It was 800 years before another reigning British monarch dropped in— Queen Elizabeth II in 1993. ❏

34

Famagusta's 14th-century Citadel

the process of restoring Cyprus's wealth and stability. The island's Byzantine character was pushed into second place, however, and the Orthodox Church was likewise relegated as the Lusignans introduced a feudal system and granted Catholicism the privileges it enjoyed in France. Short of blue-bloods for the upper crust of his new realm, Guy issued an invitation to the French nobility of the Holy Land to join him. Comparing their current lot—hot, dusty and beset on all sides by Saracens—with an offer of land, servants and peace, many packed their bags and sailed for Cyprus.

BALANCE SHEET From 1192 until 1489, the Lusignans guided their ship of state through the treacherous currents of the Levant, although at times the hand on the tiller was a shaky one. Famagusta (Gazimağusa) became a source of awe to visitors from backward Europe as its merchants grew rich on profits from the crusaders and, after the Holy Land was finally lost, from trade with the Saracens.

Monuments of Lusignan rule remain throughout Cyprus, among them the Cathedral of St. Nicholas in

Famagusta (now the Lala Mustafa Paşa Mosque, see page 237), the Cathedral of St. Sophia in Nicosia (now the Selimiye Mosque, see page 64), and the Abbey of Bellapais at Bellapais (Beylerbeyi, see page 207).

> ❏ Thomas Aquinas dedicated his *De Regimine Principium* to the 13th-century Lusignan King Hugh III, a mild ruler who was both soldier and scholar. ❏

Geoffroy de Lusignan, of the French dynasty that ruled Cyprus for three centuries (1192–1489)

> ❏ In 1260 Pope Alexander IV issued a papal decree, the Bulla Cypria, establishing the Latin Church's sovereignty over the Orthodox. However, most Cypriots retained their allegiance to the Orthodox Church. ❏

The Ottoman Turks were the nemesis of the thousand-year-old Byzantine Empire. With Constantinople captured and the entire Levant in their hands, Cyprus was clearly next on the menu. Venice had replaced the Lusignans and taken over the island just in time to find the Turks heading their way.

The decline and fall of the Lusignans had a touch of comic opera, yet was preceded by the reign of a dashing soldier-king, Peter I, who thrashed the Turks and Egyptian Mamelukes before being assassinated by his own barons. Meanwhile, Genoa and Venice had been muscling in on the eastern Mediterranean trade routes and seizing bases to protect their investments. In 1372 the coronation of Peter's successor at Famagusta (Gazimağusa) was disrupted by clashes between the Genoese and Venetian representatives. To avenge their slighted honour, the Genoese invaded Cyprus and captured Famagusta. In 1426 the Mamelukes invaded and devastated the island, and were bought off only with a huge indemnity.

Anyone knowing Cyprus's history would have recognized the signs: Things were heading downhill. Venice, the Most Serene Republic, serenely bided its time. It helped

> ❑ The Venetians cared little for Lusignan art and architecture. Faced with an imminent Ottoman invasion, they drastically reduced the circuit of Nicosia's walls and demolished everything outside them to provide clear fields of fire for artillery. The Lusignan royal palace, as well as many Gothic churches and mansions, were destroyed in the process. ❑

King James II kick the Genoese out, then generously provided him with a Venetian wife, Caterina Cornaro. Such selfless benevolence was uncharacteristic, to put it mildly, and King James no doubt spent a lot of time watching his back—though not well enough, apparently. He died in

Map of Cyprus (1601) by the Flemish cartographer, Ortelius

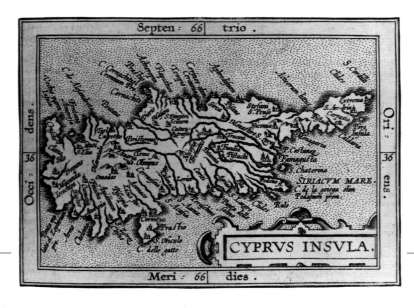

36

suspicious circumstances in 1473, as did his son James III, the last of the Lusignans, in the following year. Caterina Cornaro was 'persuaded' to turn Cyprus over to Venice, an act made official in 1489.

VICTOR'S SPOILS In one of Cypriot history's many ironies, Venice, which had schemed assiduously to annex Cyprus, now found that its new possession lay squarely in the sights of the Ottoman Turks. The Turks had captured Constantinople in 1453, an event that shook the Mediterranean world as no other had since the fall of Rome a thousand years earlier. While the Ottomans pushed ahead with their conquest of the adjacent mainland, Venice fortified the island, and in 1546 they suppressed a revolt of Cypriots embittered by brutal military rule and punitive taxation.

The long-awaited invasion, ordered by Sultan Selim II and commanded by Lala Mustafa Paşa, was launched in 1570. Venice concentrated its defence at Famagusta, Nicosia and Keryneia (Girne), whose walls had been strengthened to withstand artillery. Lala Mustafa drew up his vastly superior army before Nicosia and, after a six-week siege, stormed the defences and slaughtered 20,000 inhabitants. Keryneia quickly surrendered. Famagusta's commander, Marcantonio Bragadino, and his 8,000-man garrison kept Lala Mustafa's supposed 200,000-strong force at bay for 10 months before the

Nicosia's Venetian walls, raised in vain against the Ottoman threat

survivors finally surrendered in August 1571.

TURKISH TAKE-OVER Despite their harsh measures in wartime, the Turks were welcomed by most Cypriots. They eliminated the oppressive Latin (Roman Catholic) Church and restored Orthodoxy, not as a sign of goodwill but because the Orthodox Church was less threatening to their interests than Western-orientated Catholicism. Feudalism was abolished and freed serfs were given the right to own land, although Turkish immigrants tended to take the best of it and taxation remained heavy.

Apart from these measures, and converting a few Latin churches to mosques, the Turks allowed Cyprus to slide into that state of bureaucracy-infested indolence which is arguably among the Ottomans' principal bequests.

❑ Heavy taxation and greedy officials, along with poor harvests, led to famine, high mortality rates and emigration during Ottoman rule. In 1641 this deadly combination reduced the island's population to 25,000, down from 150,000 two years earlier. ❑

Britain first became involved in Cyprus as a by-product of shoring up Turkey against the might of Russia. When the island was ceded to Britain in 1878, however, its attractions became more appealing to the empire, and the British settled down for an indefinite stay.

One of the charges laid by Cyprus's Hellenist partisans against the Ottomans is that they left little of worth behind them. Maybe the Turks' cultural bent lay in other directions, and their state of graceful indolence may have been preferable to one where poor peasants footed the bill for palaces, cathedrals and villas that would one day be gawped at by visitors in air-conditioned coaches. Unfortunately, the poor peasants still paid, but their money went to venal officials in Cyprus and to the Sublime Porte in Istanbul, who no doubt made good use of it.

Seen from history's vantage-point, every empire's glorious trail of conquest fades ultimately to weakness and oblivion. So it was with the Ottomans, as it had been with the Persians, Greeks, Romans, Byzantines and Venetians.

By the 19th century, the 'terrible Turk', whose name once struck fear across Europe, had become 'poor little Turkey', a toothless tiger beset on all sides. Greece rebelled in 1821 and won its independence 11 years later, aided, if not achieved single-handedly as romantics imagine, by the British poet Lord Byron.

WAVING THE RULES Britannia had arrived. As the century progressed and the Suez Canal opened, Britain sought to protect its lifeline to India by bolstering Turkey. British naval power was deployed to keep Russia out of the Mediterranean. At first, Cyprus's only role in this drama was as a victim of Turkish paranoia, when several hundred leading Greeks—among them Archbishop Kyprianos and all of the island's bishops—were executed in 1821 to prevent the island joining Greece in rebellion. Turkey then only just managed to hang on to Cyprus, as Egypt broke free of Ottoman rule.

By 1878, Britain was in the driving-seat. The Union Jack fluttered aloft after the Ottoman Empire ceded Cyprus to Britain by a treaty that sanctioned British subsidies to Istanbul and other assistance against Russia, while retaining Ottoman sovereignty and allowing for the island's possible return to Ottoman rule. Britain's legal and administrative

British troops take over Cyprus in July 1878, under an agreement with the Ottoman government

38

❏ Luigi di Cesnola, the American consul-general, began excavating ancient monuments in Cyprus in 1873. He was thought to be a scientific investigator, but was in fact a con-man who plundered the sites and looted thousands of objects of great historical and monetary value. ❏

systems were introduced, as well as other political reforms. A road- and bridge-building schedule was begun, and reafforestation started in the Troodos and Pentadaktylos (Beşparmak) Mountains.

GREEK GIFT Greek Cypriots had high hopes that Britain would support their desire for Enosis (union with Greece), but strategic considerations ensured that the time for this was somehow never appropriate. In 1914 Turkey sided with Germany in World War I and Britain annexed the island. During the course of the war, the British offered Cyprus to Greece on condition that Greece declare war on Germany and Turkey. Greece declined, a decision that would later be the cause of some embarrassment in its claim to be the Cypriots' motherland.

In 1925 Cyprus became a British Crown Colony and a governor replaced the previous high commissioner, a development the average Cypriot probably did not even notice. As far as the British were concerned, Cyprus could look forward to no other future than as part of the empire on which the sun never set. Within a few years they would learn that not all Cypriots held the same views as His Britannic Majesty's government.

❏ Cyprus's historical record is well represented in Claude Delaval Cobham's *Excerpta Cypria*, published in 1908 (republished 1969) and incorporating material from some 80 writers, ranging from AD23 to 1849. ❏

British troops on patrol in the neutral zone of Nicosia in January 1964

The road to independence was hard and rocky, and the outcome was only accepted by Greek Cypriots as a second-best to their goal of union with Greece (Enosis). The machinations of international power politics had sown the seeds of future conflict in Cyprus.

By 1920 Greek Cypriots outnumbered Turkish Cypriots by five to one, so that in any vote on the island's future the Greek Cypriot viewpoint would prevail—and that viewpoint was in favour of Enosis. Britain permitted no such vote, and in 1931 serious rioting broke out in Nicosia, which resulted in Government House being burned down. British troops were brought in from Egypt to put down the rebellion, whose leaders were captured, tried and exiled.

40

Little more was heard of Enosis until after World War II. Some 36,000 Cypriots, both Greek and Turkish, served in the British Commonwealth armed forces during the war. The consciousness of having earned their right to self-determination revitalized the demand for Enosis among Greek Cypriots, and the slogan 'Enosis and only Enosis' began to appear on buildings. A referendum organized by the Orthodox Church, which had always seen itself as the guardian of Hellenism, resulted in a 96 percent vote in favour of Enosis. Greece took the Greek Cypriot case to the UN.

BLIND RESPONSE The writing was, literally, on the wall, but Britain ignored it. Rioting broke out. Britain invited Greece and Turkey to a conference on the island's future,

> ❏ The 1960 constitution allowed for a Greek Cypriot president and a Turkish Cypriot vice-president, each of whom had veto powers over government decisions. The House of Representatives had 35 Greek Cypriot members and 15 Turkish Cypriot members. ❏

which ended without positive result yet confirmed these three countries as arbiters of Cyprus's destiny. However, the Greek Cypriots determined to take a hand in that destiny. A Cyprus-born Greek army colonel, Georgios Grivas, landed secretly in 1955 on the coast near Pafos and formed EOKA (Ethniki Organosis Kyprion Agoniston, or the National Organization of Cypriot Fighters) to wage a guerrilla war against the British in order to achieve Enosis.

Bombs in crowded streets; bullets in the back of the head: EOKA's war lacked glamour, but it made its way. The British declared a state of emergency and drafted in troops to combat the guerrillas. Turkey and the Turkish Cypriots watched these

Greek Cypriot girls welcome EOKA fighters to Nicosia in 1959

developments with alarm and a determination that Cyprus must not be handed to Greece. In 1957 the United Nations adopted a resolution to establish an independent Cyprus. Two years later the Greek Cypriot political leader, Archbishop Makarios, signed treaties at Zürich and London, and in 1960 the Republic of Cyprus took its place among the nations.

CASE HARDENED Greek Cypriots believe that the problem began with Turkey's 1974 invasion and that the 180,000 refugees who fled from their homes in northern Cyprus had little choice, faced with a 'Peace Operation' whose instruments were tanks, rockets and napalm.

To many Turkish Cypriots, on the other hand, Turkey's intervention

41

UNCERTAIN FUTURE Under the treaties establishing the state, Britain, Greece and Turkey were 'guarantor powers', able to intervene militarily if Cyprus's independence was threatened. Britain retained two military bases which were (and still are) British sovereign territory. The real difficulty shifted to relations between the two communities, with the Greek Cypriots eager to move, albeit stealthily, towards Enosis, and the minority Turkish Cypriots unwilling to accept this. Calls within the Turkish population for Taksim (partition) grew as the power-sharing constitution broke down and Turkish communities came under attack, provoking the threat of Turkish intervention.

Bad as the situation became through the 1960s, with a UN peacekeeping force being deployed to keep the communities apart, the real disaster to Cyprus as a unitary state came in 1974. Greece's military junta launched a pro-Enosis coup against President Makarios. Turkey promptly invaded and Cyprus has been divided ever since.

Turkish troops in tanks during their 1974 invasion of Cyprus

was a 'Peace Operation' that saved them from the attentions of terrorists bent on their annihilation.

Now Cyprus is a member of the European Union, and with the opening of the border in 2003 showing that both sides can interact peacefully, there is growing international pressure for a solution to the Cyprus problem. As the line of division becomes increasingly porous there are grounds for optimism.

❏ 'Cyprus is the common home of the Greek Cypriot community and the Turkish Cypriot community. Their relationship is not one of majority and minority, but one of two communities in the state of Cyprus.'
—From a statement by former UN Secretary-General Javier Pérez de Cuéllar, February 1990 ❏

Nicosia

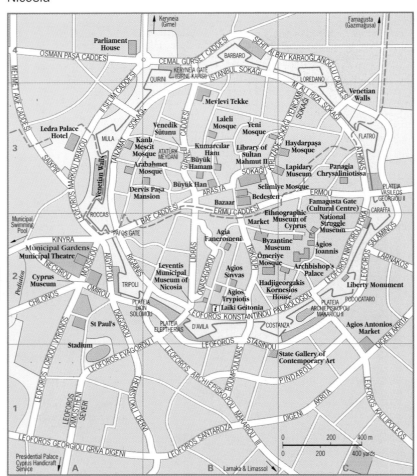

Ömeriye Mosque (left), originally St. Mary's Church
All in a day's work at a workshop near the Green Line (far left)

►►►CITY HIGHLIGHTS

NICOSIA (LEFKOSIA/LEFKOSA)

Cyprus's capital is a place apart. No sea breeze or mountain tang reaches here, only the heat-shimmered air of the Mesaoria (Mesarya) Plain at the island's heart. To a Greek Cypriot the city's name is Lefkosia; to a Turkish Cypriot it is Lefkoşa (not much difference there, you might think); to the world at large it is Nicosia. From 1974 to 2003 it remained frozen, locked in a 30-year time-warp, its Greek and Turkish halves interfacing only in what had become the traditional Cypriot manner: with barbed wire, oil-drum barricades and sandbagged sentry posts.

The Green Line, the United Nations-patrolled buffer zone, separated the two communities completely. Across the divide, each side taunted the other with prominently displayed flags. The barrier was as much psychological as physical: Cypriots trying to imagine what life was like 'on the other side' came up with a picture of grim-faced men ready to storm across at a moment's notice. Tourists and others who had visited both sides—as most Cypriots could not—knew better.

Nicosia

Much has changed since 2003, which saw the opening of
the Green Line at the UN's Ledra Palace Hotel checkpoint
in Nicosia. Nicosians in particular, and Cypriots in
general, have got to know each other better. But the
barrier, though peacefully breached in ever more places,
still remains.

GROWING FAST Thankfully, Nicosia and its 210,000
inhabitants add up to more than an object (or abject) lesson in human folly. The Greek Cypriot sector is a vibrant
demi-city, semi-surrounding the old Ottoman core.
Propelled by the impetus of a booming economy, this half
of the capital has been expanding rapidly, swallowing up
hapless villages in its path and making shapeless suburbs
of them. Housing, industrial and business developments,
and the road links they require, have combined to make
part of the outskirts a giant construction site.

By contrast, the old city within the Venetian walls is a
bright collage of narrow streets lined with houses, workshops, cafés and shops, interrupted occasionally by a
smart shopping or dining area. The workshops, concentrated along the Green Line, form an enclave of busy dens.
The workshops and Green Line together form an unlikely
yet popular tourist attraction.

Some sections of the inner city are falling down, some are getting ready to, others either have been or are being refurbished. In the case of the Laïki Geitonia district ('Popular District' in Greek), an attractive if somewhat twee and touristy taverna-and-gift-shop area is the result.

BRIDGING THE GULF Everything moves a little slower on the Türkish side. Traffic is less intense, office and apartment blocks fewer, the pace of redevelopment less hurried. Some things don't change on this side of the divide, however: The summer heat is equally hard; hospitality carries the same weight; and the workshops beside the Green Line churn out the same abundance of gadgets.

Sheer necessity in the area of vital public services, as well as a new awareness that the two communities share a common city, has led to a growing amount of official contact across the line of division. Sliced in two as it is by the 'Cyprus problem', Nicosia has its own underlying unity which may yet outlast the guns and the barbed wire fortifications. Seen from the air, the old city is a perfect circle delineated by the defensive perimeter of the Venetian walls. Until recently defensive mentalities have reigned supreme, but there is now new hope that the circle of reconciliation can be squared.

NAME GAMES II
At the time of independence, it was agreed that places should have two names: Greek and Turkish. Paphos (now Pafos) was Baf in Turkish, and Episkopi was Piskobu. Since the partition of 1974, only Turkish names have been used in the Turkish Cypriot zone. Instead of Keryneia and Ammochostos (Famagusta), road signs refer to Girne and Gazimağusa. In addition, some of the existing Turkish names were changed. Greek Cypriots complain, and their complaint is upheld by the UN, that such changes are illegal. The reality on the ground and on maps, however, is that Greek names are never used in the North.

45

Murals fill the interior of Agios Ioannis (St. John's Cathedral) in the monumental heart of Nicosia

46

*Richly decorated Agios
Ioannis is Nicosia's most
important Greek
Orthodox church*

Greek Cypriot (South) Nicosia

▶ Agia Faneromeni
(Church of St. Faneromeni)   42B2
Odos Faneromenis
Open: irregularly. Admission free
In 1821 the Ottoman governor of Cyprus ordered a series
of executions on the off-chance that the victims might be
contemplating rebellion. Among those who paid the ultimate penalty in this pre-emptive strike were the head of
the Cypriot Church, Archbishop Kyprianos and several
bishops, who lie buried under this 19th-century church
close to the Green Line. The diminutive Arablar Mosque
stands nearby.

▶▶▶ Agios Ioannis (St. John's Cathedral)   42C2
Plateia Archiepiskopou Kyprianou
Open: Mon–Fri 8–12 and 2–4, Sat 8–12. Admission free
Compared with the great European cathedrals, Nicosia's
Orthodox cathedral is a dinky little place. Completed in
1662 on the ruins of the Lusignan-era Benedictine abbey
church of St. John the Evangelist, which had been sacked
by invading Mamelukes in 1426, it is much too small to
accommodate the tour groups that descend upon it for a
snatch of tour-guide exposition amid a multilingual
babble. It was not built with tour groups in mind, of
course, and its size reflects its abbey origins rather than
any assessment of its worth. For Agios Ioannis is splendid
and justifies the superlatives the tourist guides lavish
upon it, but you should go early, before the guides start
their rounds.
Situated beside the Archbishop's Palace, Agios Ioannis
has become the state church, with an ornate throne for His
Beatitude and special places for Their Excellencies the

president of the republic and the Greek ambassador. The abundant murals on its ceiling and walls, mostly dating from the early 18th century, depict scenes from the Christian history of Cyprus, such as the evangelizing mission of St. Paul and St. Barnabas in AD45. Icons, gilt decoration and multicoloured lamps sparkle in the otherwise gloomy interior. The pulpit is graced with a magnificent but sinister-looking double-headed eagle, the emblem of Byzantium.

▶ Agios Trypiotis (Church of St. Michael Trypiotis)   42B2

Odos Solonos
Open: irregularly. Admission free

Evidence for its former status as the top people's church in Nicosia is seen in the silver-chased icons and other offerings donated by the well-heeled faithful in times past. The church's solid 17th-century bulk is lightened by some earlier Byzantine touches, like the carved lintels on some doorways.

▶▶ Archbishop's Palace   42C2

Plateia Archiepiskopou Kyprianou

Officially described as neo-Byzantine, the palace looks suspiciously neo-Venetian but in any case dates from 1960 and seems oddly uninspired. The modest private apartments of its first occupant, Archbishop Makarios, the late head of the Cypriot Orthodox Church and first president of the Republic of Cyprus, are occasionally open to the public for organized visits (*Admission free*). A gargantuan bronze sculpture of the archbishop obstructs the otherwise light and delicate lines of the palace's facade.

▶ Bayraktar Mosque   56C1

Costanza bastion of the Venetian walls
Open: irregularly. Admission free

The restored Standard Bearer's Mosque, which dates from 1820, is in the Constanza bastion at the point where a Turkish soldier planted the Ottoman colours on the Venetian walls during the final assault of the 1570 siege. He was shot down and his remains now lie in this mosque. Gardens that once surrounded the mosque were truncated in favour of a bus station.

▶▶▶ Byzantine Museum and Art Galleries   42C2

Plateia Archiepiskopou Kyprianou (tel: 22430008)
Open: Mon–Fri 9–4.30, Sat 9–1
Admission: moderate

Part of the monumental complex beside the Archbishop's Palace, this museum and art gallery features the largest and most impressive icon collection on the island, although there are individual pieces of greater worth in other locations. One part of the collection, which spans a thousand years, is given over to items—such as the sixth-century religious mosaics from the Panagia Kanakaria church at Lythrangkomi (Bolta 1) in the North—looted from the Turkish area after 1974, and bought back at great expense by the Greek Cypriot government when they turned up on the international black market and even at legitimate art sales. Other floors of the museum house paintings, most of which are undistinguished.

Controversial and colossal, the statue of Archbishop Makarios stands outside the Archbishop's Palace

47

NOW AT THRONI - TOMB OF MAGARIOS

BUILDING ON MUD
In the area around the Archbishop's Palace are many old Ottoman-style houses built using traditional mud-brick construction methods. Many have been restored in a campaign to preserve the city's original appearance as far as possible.

GUARDED 24HRS BY SOLDIERS/ POLICE

Elegant street lamps in Plateia Archiepiskopou Kyprianou

Terracotta figures in the Cyprus Museum

48

The Aphrodite of Soloi takes pride of place in the museum

▶▶ Cyprus Handicraft Centre 42A1

186 Leoforos Athalassis (tel: 22305024)
Open: Mon–Fri 7.30–2.30, Thu also 3–6 (except Jul–Aug)
Admission free

The pristinely modern workshop of the Cyprus Handicraft Centre on the edge of Nicosia seems a strange place for preserving the endangered folk arts and artisanal skills of simpler times—a bit like making flint tools aboard a space station. Yet there is no question that such a venture is needed, as modern technologies and changing social habits sweep away the knowledge of generations. Each traditional Cypriot village handicraft has its place here: basket-making, pottery, weaving, iron-working, lace-making, wood-carving and more. You can watch the craftsfolk at work. The finished products are sold in the centre's shop.

▶▶▶ Cyprus Museum 42A2

1 Leoforos Mouseiou (tel: 22865888)
Open: Mon–Sat 9–5, Sun 10–1. Admission: moderate

The modest dimensions of this museum will please those more familiar with the blister-inducing museums of countries that like to think they not only invented culture but retain a monopoly on it still. This unassuming style begins with the almost perfunctory neoclassical portico. The real surprise, however, is inside, where the cultural harvest of 10,000 years seems comparatively thin until you realize that much of Cyprus's heritage has been siphoned off (the word 'stolen' also springs to mind) to various museums and private collections all over the world.

Nevertheless, the museum contains much that is downright surprising as well as merely interesting. To follow the progression of displays is to make a journey forward in time.

The first faint traces of human occupation appear in the neolithic period, with discoveries from the aceramic (literally, 'without pottery') settlements at Khirokitia (Choirokoitia) and Kastros, represented by stone figurines and simple implements of bone and flint. A great array of Bronze Age exhibits includes 2,000 votive terracotta figurines, most of them crudely made, uncovered at the sanctuary of Agia Eirini (Akdeniz) in the Turkish Cypriot zone.

Even minus her arms and legs, the superb Aphrodite of Soloi (Soli) still charms visitors, who gather around the marble sculpture as though awaiting some words of ineffable wisdom. The goddess is also represented by a conical stone, an archaic symbol of her worship. Keeping Aphrodite company is a superb, larger-than-lifesize bronze nude statue of the Roman emperor Septimius Severus.

The 12th-century BC 'horned god', found at Egkomi (Enkomi) near Famagusta (Gazimağusa), and an ornamented bronze cauldron uncovered at Salamis are equally memorable.

►► Ethnographic Museum of Cyprus *42C2*

Plateia Archiepiskopou Kyprianou (tel: 22432578)
Open: Mon–Fri 9–5. Admission: moderate
Housed in the refurbished Old Archbishopric, the Ethnographic Museum has a folk art collection that includes 19th-century costumes, tapestry, embroidery, pottery and wood-carvings from all over Cyprus.

►► Famagusta Gate (Pyli Ammochostou) *42C2*

Caraffa bastion of the Venetian walls, Leoforos Athinon (tel: 22430877)
Open: Mon–Fri 10–1 and 4–7 (Jun–Aug 5–8, Sat 9–1). Admission free
The coming and going of art exhibitions has replaced the to and fro of people and goods through this robust, tunnel-like gateway in the city walls, one of three inserted by the Venetians when they built the walls between 1567 and 1570. The structure had fallen into disrepair until it was restored and reopened as the Nicosia Municipal Cultural Centre. The Famagusta Gate is not only popular in its own right, but it also helps to support a nearby enclave of smart cafés and restaurants. Its restored passages and side-chambers are usually in use for exhibitions, conferences, lectures and performance art.

► Freedom Square (Plateia Eleftherias) *42B2*

Between Odos Lidras and Leoforos Evagorou I
Greatly oversold as Nicosia's principal square, Plateia Eleftherias consists of little more than a bridge over the moat around the Venetian walls, with some office blocks and cafés at either end. Not even the adjacent D'Avila bastion and the Town Hall add greatly to the attraction. The square is a popular meeting-point, however.

►► Green Line *42B2*

A line of artisans' workshops follows this man-made scar that runs east–west across the middle of old Nicosia. Here Greek Cypriot troops face their Turkish opposite numbers across a band of destruction while United Nations peacekeepers man the thin blue line in the middle. In some places the opposing forces are only a few metres apart and incidents occasionally take place, ranging from insults to fatal shootings. The more usual profile along the Green Line, however, is one of suffocating boredom.

ART OF PEACE
Art often has a resonance that transcends the petty calculations of politicians and others interested in preserving the status quo, however demeaning. One show at the Famagusta Gate cultural centre caused controversy and hope in equal amounts through featuring contemporary works by both Greek Cypriots and Turkish Cypriots.

49

GREEN EXCURSION
For an interesting stroll in Greek Cypriot Nicosia, start at either the Pafos Gate or the Municipal Gardens and walk beside the Venetian walls on Leoforos Markou Drakou. Continue towards the UN base at the Ledra Palace Hotel and the Green Line crossing point there.

Colourful detail of graffiti on a section of the Green Line which divides the Republic of Cyprus from the Turkish North.

The career of Archbishop Makarios encompassed a dramatic period in the history of Cyprus. For the first time in a thousand years the island had a government of its own choosing. Yet by the time of his death it was a divided island wrestling with a bitter legacy of bloodshed and hatred.

DEAR COLONELS...
Makarios despised the military junta that seized power in Greece, the fountainhead of democracy, in 1968. In turn, the Greek colonels hated Makarios and tried to eliminate him. In July 1974, Makarios wrote to them in protest at such unneighbourly behaviour: 'I have more than once so far felt, and in some cases I have almost touched, a hand invisibly extending from Athens and seeking to liquidate my human existence.' Two weeks later the junta launched the coup aimed at the archbishop's overthrow and assassination.

Memorials to the archbishop-president are ubiquitous

MAKAPIOC Γ
ΕΘΝΑΡΧΗΟ ΚΑΙ

Rites of passage High in the Troodos Mountains, on a hill above the great monastery of Panagia tou Kykkos, Greek Cypriot soldiers form a guard of honour standing watch over the tomb of Archbishop Makarios III: sometime novice at Kykkos; priest, bishop and head of the Cypriot Church; revolutionary and first president of the Republic of Cyprus. His black-robed figure became a familiar public presence from the 1950s to the 1970s, not only on the strife-torn stage of his own country but to a worldwide audience as a leading light in the Movement of Non-Aligned States.

For one whose love of his homeland was all-consuming, the view from his last resting-place could scarcely be bettered. The island is laid out around the memorial like some vast exercise in geography, all its savage beauty encompassed in a single sweep, and none of its pain. For good or ill, almost everything that may be said of modern Cyprus can be placed at the portals of that tomb on Throni hill.

Ideals in action Makarios Mouskos was born in 1913 into a poor farming family in the village of Pano Panagia in the western Troodos foothills. He was educated within the proud cloisters of Kykkos, where the fires of Hellenism and the memory of the Christian empire of Byzantium were kept alive during centuries of foreign oppression. It was a potent cocktail, this mix of religion and nationalism, and when its ingredients were thrown together during the fading years of Britain's empire they combined with explosive force.

While Colonel Grivas led EOKA in a terror campaign against the British and those Cypriots who opposed Enosis (union with Greece), Makarios provided the spiritual staying power. 'Cyprus is Greek', the ethnarch later proclaimed. 'Cyprus has been Greek since the dawn of history and it will remain Greek. Greek and undivided we have taken it over, Greek and undivided we shall preserve it. Greek and undivided we shall deliver it to Greece.' With his charisma and the mystical nature of his call, he united the Greek Cypriots behind his ideal. In 1960 Cyprus achieved independence from Britain, but not union with Greece. Makarios was elected president.

On the way If Makarios had been content with independence, Cyprus might now be a model of intercommunal calm, a flourishing and united island. But to think so is to mistake the forces that were at work. Makarios himself saw independence as only a half-way house, a forward position from which new advances could be made towards the ultimate goal of Enosis. With the British out of the way, the main obstacle to achieving Cyprus's destiny was the island's Turkish community.

It has been said that Greek Cypriot policy during the Makarios years was made purely on the basis of his intuition or whim. The outcome was that the Turkish Cypriots withdrew into enclaves—whether in fear of their lives or as a deliberate effort to sabotage the new republic is a fiercely contested issue of modern Cypriot history.

Final recognition After the Greek-inspired coup of 1974 that almost killed Makarios (see panel opposite) and led to the Turkish army's occupation of northern Cyprus, the ethnarch appeared to regret the harsher aspects of the pro-Enosis drive and to reach out to the Turkish Cypriots for a solution that recognized their rights. Too late. He then focused his efforts on dealing with the post-partition humanitarian crisis among his own people and in pressing for an end to occupation and division.

Makarios died in 1977. The Greek Cypriots who pay their respects at his tomb on Throni hill come to honour his achievements even as they must live with the consequences of his failings.

COLOSSAL MISTAKE
A 10m (33ft) high, 20-ton statue of Archbishop Makarios has been a source of controversy among Greek Cypriots ever since it was placed in the grounds of the Archbishop's Palace in Nicosia (see page 47). General opinion seems to be that it is a monstrosity, though few go so far as to suggest that the archbishop should be melted down and sold for scrap.

Archbishop Makarios, President of Cyprus, sitting in his office

51

Inside the house of Hadjigeorgakis Kornesios, who was executed by the Turks in 1809

►►► Hadjigeorgakis Kornesios House   *42C2*

20 Odos Patriarchou Grigoriou (tel: 22305316)
Open: Mon–Fri 8.30–3.30. Admission: inexpensive
Georgakis Kornesios was a *dragoman*, a Greek official appointed by the Sublime Porte in Istanbul to be the 'interpreter' between the Ottoman court and its Greek Cypriot subjects. Kornesios's job combined opportunity and danger in equal measure, evidenced by the elegant wealth of his mansion and his execution in 1809 for failing in the balancing act between his own people and the ruthlessly suspicious Turkish authorities.

The restored 18th-century mansion, housing the Ethnological Museum, encloses a courtyard containing a Turkish *hamam*, or bath. Its upper level has rooms decorated in the style appropriate to a wealthy Ottoman official, including a divan-lined reception room, a living room and bedroom. Downstairs are the servants' quarters and storage rooms. Colonnades and fine Ottoman woodwork add to the mansion's graceful aspect.

►► Laïki Geitonia   *42B2*

Adjacent to Odos Lidras and the D'Avila bastion
An area just inside the city walls near Plateia Eleftherias, Laïki Geitonia is a model of urban restoration and renewal. An attractive, crumbling quarter of traditional houses and shops has been totally refurbished and lined with trees. Boutiques, artisanal workshops, tavernas and souvenir shops have opened, and the area teems with life throughout the day and into the small hours. A small **Jewellery Museum** is worth a quick inspection, and the Leventis Municipal Museum (see below) a longer one.

►► Ledra Palace Hotel   *42A3*

Leoforos Markou Drakou
Formerly Nicosia's most elegant hotel, the Ledra Palace was damaged in the intercommunal fighting of the 1960s and 1970s and now stands in UN territory inside the buffer zone as a UNFICYP base. You cannot visit the hotel itself, except on official business, but outside it is Nicosia's 'Checkpoint Charlie', the principal crossing-point between the still divided city's two zones.

► Ledra Street (Odos Lidras)   *42B2*

This popular pedestrian-only shopping street runs north from Plateia Eleftherias up to the Green Line, where it ends abruptly in concrete barriers and Greek Cypriot sentry posts. The incongruity of Nicosia's (and indeed Cyprus's) division seems encapsulated here, in an otherwise ordinary shopping street that ends in what is virtually a war zone. For the best possible view over the still-divided city, visit the Ledra Museum-Observatory on the 11th floor of the Shakolas Building, on the corner of Odos Lidras and Odos Arsinoïs.

►► Leventis Municipal Museum of Nicosia   *42B2*

17 Odos Ippokratou, Laïki Geitonia (tel: 22661475)
Open: Tue–Sun 10–4.30. Admission free
Housed in a restored mansion in the renovated Laïki Geitonia district, this museum is an interesting evocation of Nicosia in days gone by. European Museum of the Year in 1991, it documents the city's history from the

GREEN SOLUTION
The term Green Line was coined in 1964, when a British officer of the pre-United Nations peace-keeping force in the capital, negotiating the separation of the city's battling Greek and Turkish communities, used a green chinagraph pencil to draw a line across his map of Nicosia, thereby establishing the dividing line between their two sectors.

7th century BC, when it was the city-kingdom of Ledra; Greek, Roman, Byzantine Leukos; the medieval Lusignan period, when it was named Nicosia and became the island's capital; Venetian, Turkish and British rule; independence and Nicosia's subsequent doleful distinction as Europe's only formally divided city. Paintings, photographs, household items and costumes recall the time when Greek and Turkish Cypriots lived in harmony.

▶ Liberty Monument
42C2

Podocataro bastion of the Venetian walls
Cypriot civilians emerge rejoicing from the dungeon of British oppression into the bright sunshine of freedom, as gallant EOKA fighters raise the bars on their prison cell. This marble-and-bronze memorial to Cyprus's struggle against colonial rule has a symbolism that may be standard government-issue patriotism, but its execution raises the quality of the Liberty Monument's sculpture group beyond this predictable mould.

▶▶ Municipal Gardens
42A2

Leoforos Mouseiou
Although not the only patch of green in Nicosia, these gardens near the Pafos Gate, are the most attractive and accessible of the city's parks. Flowers and trees provide a blessing in the fierce heat of summertime Nicosia. The open-air Garden Café Restaurant stands beside the neoclassical **Municipal Theatre**, which presents plays.

FINEST COMPLIMENT
Laïki Geitonia's success, both in restoration and commercial terms, has spawned imitators, not only in Greek Cypriot towns such as Limassol, Larnaka and Polis, but also to a certain extent across the divide, in Turkish Cypriot Nicosia, Keryneia (Girne) and Famagusta (Gazimağusa).

The Liberty Monument recalls the struggle for independence

53

54

►Municipal Swimming Pool   42A2
Leoforos Louki Akrita (tel: 22781155)
Open: Jun–Aug daily 10–8; Sep–May daily 10–7. Admission: moderate
An unpromising name disguises one of Nicosia's most useful places: an open-air complex of wonderfully cool water in extravagant quantity. Its pools mimic the azure blue of the sea and its sunbathing areas are the stuff of which dreams are made after a sticky expedition along Nicosia's cultural trail.

► National Struggle Museum   42C2
Plateia Archiepiskopou Kyprianos (tel: 22305878)
Open: Mon–Fri 8–2 and Thu also 3–5.30 Jul–Aug).
Admission: inexpensive
This museum records the more favourable aspects (from a Greek Cypriot point of view) of the conflict between 1955 and 1959 to free Cyprus from British rule and attain union with Greece. For this cause EOKA (the National Organisation of Cypriot Fighters) waged a terror campaign, and the museum's exhibits are grim—educational but scarcely entertaining.
    Pride of place goes to a reproduction of an execution cell complete with rope and trapdoor, the mechanisms of martyrdom for EOKA fighters convicted of murder by the British.

► Nicosia Municipal Arts Centre   56C2
Odos 19 Apostolou Varnava (tel: 22432577)
Open: Tue–Sat 10–3 and 5–11, Sun 10–4 (closed until Jan 2007). Admission free
This important cultural centre (also called the 'Power House' as it is housed within the city's old power station) stages art exhibitions on different themes and is home to an art reference library.

The minaret of the Ömeriye Mosque soars above the divided capital

►► Ömeriye Mosque   42B2
Odos Trikoupi
Open: daylight hours. Admission free
Greek Nicosia's Muslim population is small, consisting of diplomats, businessmen and tourists, but the Ömeriye Mosque remains open to serve them and is, in addition, a point of general tourist interest. It was formerly the Latin Church of St. Mary, dating from the 14th century, until the victorious commander of the 1570 Ottoman invasion, Lala Mustafa Paşa, ordered its conversion to a mosque. Its tree-shaded entrance leads to a cool interior and, on payment of a fee, to a superb view of Nicosia from the balcony of the minaret.

► Pafos Gate
(Pyli Pafou)   42A2
North end of Leoforos Mouseiou
One of the three historic openings in the Venetian walls, the Pafos Gate is the one most affected by the division

A proud priest (above) watches over his church, the superb Panagia Chrysaliniotissa (left)

of the city, as the Green Line runs within a few metres of it, and the Roccas bastion, which overlooks it, is flag-festooned Turkish Cypriot territory. The gate itself is unaffected, but traffic moving into the old city has to swing hard right immediately to avoid the barricades.

▶▶ Panagia Chrysaliniotissa (Our Lady of the Golden Flax) 42C3

Odos Odysseos
Open: irregularly. Admission free
Although slightly off the beaten track, this 15th-century church is worth the extra distance, being perhaps unique in its calm, age-worn evocation of the religious sentiment described as 'sacred' or 'holy'. The church stands amid a part of old Nicosia that has emerged from the neglect of recent decades.

▶ State Gallery of Contemporary Art 42B1

Leoforos Stasinou (tel: 22304947)
Open: Mon–Fri 10–4.45, Sat 10–12.45. Admission: moderate
The collection comprises sculptures and paintings by Cypriot artists, dating from about 1930 onwards. Inevitably, the quality of the work shown is variable, but at least the items represent a change from the often unvarying diet of religious art in other Cypriot collections.

▶▶▶ Venetian Walls 42A3

In the years preceding the 1570 Ottoman invasion, the Venetians knew it was only a matter of time before the Turks attacked. The Lusignan walls were too extensive and puny to be defended, so the Venetians demolished them, along with churches, palaces and houses, to build a powerful, tighter defensive system around the old city. All their work was in vain, as the overwhelming Ottoman army stormed the walls and subjected Nicosia to an orgy of looting, burning, rape and murder (an estimated 20,000 inhabitants were killed).

EQUAL SHARES
The British officers who established the Green Line in 1964 were scrupulous in sharing out the 'Venetian walls', 11 bastions spaced equally around the circuit. So that neither side could complain of a 'bastion gap', the strongpoints were shared out 50:50. Caraffa, Podocataro, Costanza, D'Avila and Tripoli are entirely in the Greek sector; Roccas, Mula, Quirini, Barbaro and Loredano in the Turkish; and Flatro in the UN buffer zone.

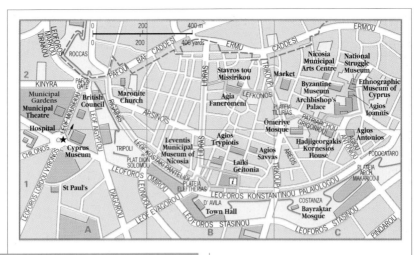

Walk

Greek Cypriot Nicosia

This walk through Greek Cypriot Nicosia includes part of the Venetian walls and the Green Line. It could take four hours if you visit the various sights mentioned, or one hour if you choose to do it quickly. The sights on the walk are covered in more detail on pages 46–55.

The Garden Café Restaurant in the **Municipal Gardens**►► is a good place for a coffee or soft drink before starting out. Cross Mouseiou Avenue to the excellent **Cyprus Museum**►►►.

Note the United Nations and Cyprus National Guard military positions near the **Venetian Walls**►►► at the **Pafos Gate**►. Although spectacular as an ensemble, some sections of the walls have lost much

The Lion of Venice stands guard at the Cyprus Museum

of their former glory. The Tripoli bastion is now used for parking.

From Plateia Eleftherias you can make a detour to **Laïki Geitonia**►► before turning into **Odos Lidras**►, which ends abruptly at a roadblock just short of the Green Line. Odos Nikokleous and Odos Faneromenis lead, via the courtyard of **Agia Faneromeni Church**►, to Odos Lefkonos. Turn right into Odos Trikoupi, where the **Ömeriye Mosque**►► is open to the public.

A short walk via Odos Tillirias, Odos Patriarchou Grigoriou and Odos Isokratous brings you to the monumental heart of Nicosia, Plateia Archiepiskopou Kyprianou in the handsome area known as the Archbishopric, with the **Archbishop's Palace**►► and **Agios Ioannis**►►►, as well as the **Byzantine Museum and Art Galleries**►►►, **National Struggle Museum**► and **Ethnographic Museum**►►.

Turkish Cypriot (North) Nicosia

▶ **Arabahmet Mosque**   *42A3*
Salahi Şevket Sokağı
Open: irregularly. Admission free
Built in 1845 and named after an Ottoman governor, the mosque stands amid a grove of cypress trees. In the surrounding graveyard are the white marble tombstones of various notables, including that of Kamil Paşa, four-times grand vizier to the Ottoman sultans. The mosque contains an important relic: A hair said to have come from the beard of the Prophet Muhammad.

▶▶ **Atatürk Meydanı (Atatürk Square)**   *42B3*
Southern end of Girne Caddesi
In British times, this elegant little square was bordered by government offices and was a centre of the island's administration. Now it is more of a commercial hub. At its heart stands a Venetian column, which was once topped by a sculpted lion of St. Mark. The Turks made short work of the lion, as was only fair, seeing that they had made equally short work of the Venetians. The British placed a burnished copper globe atop the marble shaft, and although the sun has long since set on the empire symbolized, the globe sits there still, presumably in default of inspiration for some other uplifting emblem.

The lofty minaret of the Arabahmet Mosque rises above a large dome

57

▶ **Bazaar (Belediye Pazarı)**   *42B3*
Opposite the eastern end of Arasta Sokağı
Open: Mon–Fri 6–3, Sat 6–1
This big bazaar stands opposite the Bedesten and Selimiye Mosque. The covered shopping area, although more Westernized than its counterparts in Turkey, offers the kind of bargain buys that are the unique selling point of any bazaar.

▶ **Bedesten**   *42B3*
Opposite the eastern end of Arasta Sokağı
Generally closed
Ruined walls and arches are the most obvious attributes of this former Orthodox cathedral of Venetian times which to the conquering Ottomans in 1570 was well suited to be a grain store and later a covered market (hence the name 'Bedesten'). It stands next to the Selimiye Mosque, a fact that apparently precluded its continuation as a Christian religious foundation. This building is a hybrid, featuring Byzantine, Gothic and Renaissance elements from the remains of two side-by-side churches dating from the 12th to the 16th centuries, and incorporating some later Ottoman elements. Scrambling around in the rubble is not as rewarding as it ought to be, although there are some interesting gargoyles and other carved pieces still to be seen.

DOWNHILL SLIDE
The Venetians were far less kind to Nicosia than the Lusignans, viewing it primarily as a fortified base. Even so, at the time of the Ottoman conquest in 1570 it was still a cosmopolitan city of 50,000 people. Three centuries later, when the British took over, Nicosia was all but derelict, with fewer than 12,000 inhabitants.

Fruit and vegetables in the bazaar

Nicosia

The tiny mosque in the courtyard of the late 16th-century Büyük Han

58

NORTH AND SOUTH

Citizens of European Union member states can cross the border freely between north and south. At the time of writing there are five crossing points (two of them in Nicosia) and a sixth (also in the capital) is being prepared. Non-EU citizens visiting the Turkish Cypriot north cannot cross to the Greek Cypriot sector, but non-EU citizens may cross into the Turkish Cypriot sector from the south.

Hexagonal chimneys line the Büyük Han's roof

▶▶ Büyük Hamam (Great Bath)   42B3

Mousa Irfan Sokağı
Open: summer daily 7.30–1 and 4–6; winter daily 8–1 and 2–6.
Admission: expensive
There are some doubts about the origins of this building, but they don't seem important inside the marvellously evocative, steam-suffused Turkish bath. A nail hammered into the wall shows the height the Pediaios (Kanlı) River reached in 1330, when 3,000 people drowned.

If the photographs on the wall are anything to go by, the attendants are particularly adept at massage—'Try and you feel well', writes one satisfied client. These bone-cracking massages, a touch of the old camel-hair-glove treatment and even self-service are all available. Fridays are reserved exclusively for women.

▶▶▶ Büyük Han (Great Inn)   42B3

Arasta Sokağı
Open: Mon and Wed–Thu 8–8, Tue and Fri 8am–midnight, Sat 8am–3pm. Admission free.
Open again after major restoration, this caravanserai was built by the Turks in 1572, just one year after they completed their conquest of Cyprus, an indication of how important such places were in the Ottoman scheme of things. The main entrance is big enough to take a loaded camel and rider; a smaller door in the wall—the 'eye of the needle'—was used either by vertically disadvantaged camels or by people only.

A caravanserai was more than a place of accommodation with parking for camels. It was a social centre, trading-place, warehouse and business services centre for merchants on the move. Inside the slab-sided edifice is a courtyard surrounded by 68 rooms on two levels, with lodgings ranged along the upper floor and storage space below.

Every room of the inn had a fireplace, and their hexagonal chimneys can still be seen in a line around the roof. The fort-like set-up was admirable for defensive purposes. In the middle of the courtyard stands a small octagonal mosque reached by a stairway.

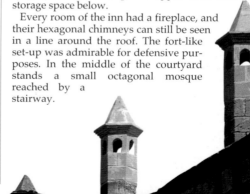

►►► Dervis Paşa Mansion 42B3

Belig Paşa Sokağı
Open: summer daily 9–7; winter 9–1 and 2–4.45
Admission: moderate

Once the residence of a wealthy Turkish publisher, this mansion near the Green Line was in a disastrously dilapidated state before restoration began in 1979. Today, the mansion, dating from 1807, has had all its Ottoman grace restored and functions as the Ethnographic Museum. It can be compared in some respects to the Hadjigeorgakis Kornesios House in the Greek Cypriot zone (see page 52).

Dervis Paşa was the publisher and editor of the first Turkish newspaper in Cyprus, *Zaman* (Time), which hit the streets in 1891. Journalism could clearly be a lucrative profession in those days, and Dervis Paşa lived in style. The museum re-creates that style room by room, beginning with the servants' quarters on the arcaded ground floor and continuing upstairs to the wood-panelled luxury of his family's living quarters. Divan-lined rooms combine with display-cases featuring a myriad items, such as inkpots and pens, jewellery, ornamental scimitars, ceramics, embroidery, lamps, clothes, a beautifully ornamented hookah and rugs.

►► Green Line 42B2

Nicosia's self-inflicted wound seems little different when seen from this side of the west–east line than from the Greek Cypriot side, except that the Turkish army keeps people further away.

Otherwise there is little to choose between the two in terms of their devoted attention to barbed wire, booby traps and rifles. The workshops along the line are perhaps more interesting on this side, even if the noises and smells emanating from some make them seem like the anterooms of hell.

The **Mula bastion** of the Venetian walls overlooking the buffer zone and the UN-occupied Ledra Palace Hotel has been equipped with a little memorial park and benches. The adjacent street, Tanzimat Sokağı, boasts some fine old Ottoman houses which had been falling down until a restoration project was begun.

ELUSIVE CITY
The Bronze Age settlement of Ledra, over whose remains Nicosia was built, remains one of the most elusive ancient sites in Cyprus. Fragments of foundations and an occasional rock-cut tomb uncovered during excavation work for new buildings are all that have come to light so far.

QUIET WAY
Walking from the Selimiye Mosque along Kirlizade Sokağı, past the Lapidary Museum, the Haydarpaşa Mosque (now the HP Gallery) and the Yeni Mosque, and returning by way of Eski Saray Sokağı, makes a quiet and interesting stroll through a traditional quarter of old Nicosia.

59

Quiet back streets in the city's atmospheric old Turkish quarter

The former Turkish Cypriot leader did not officially exist. Despite this, he always cut a larger-than-life figure within Turkish Cyprus, where he was simply the village headman on a grander scale. His retirement from office in 2005 might have opened the door to a settlement.

ACID TEST
'Turkish Cypriots have to be convinced that the people...on the other side...are people who have changed in heart and who really seek peace, people who are not furthering their policy of Hellenizing Cyprus by hook or by crook.'
– From an address by Rauf Denktaş to the UN Security Council

60

TRYING TIMES
Denktaş was banished from Cyprus in 1964 by the government of Archbishop Makarios. In October 1967, he attempted to return clandestinely from Turkey. His boat came ashore at the wrong place and he was arrested by the Greek Cypriot police. Plans to try him for offences against the state were abandoned in the face of strong international pressure and he was re-exiled instead.

Populist approach The old harbour at Keryneia (Girne) is one of the highlights of Cyprus. An old saloon car may occasionally be seen heading towards its elegant horse-shoe of waterfront restaurants. The harbour is a pedestrian zone, so the driver parks nearby and walks the rest of the way, stopping frequently to chat or shake hands with acquaintances. Now in his 80s, he might have retired from the presidency, but Rauf Denktaş is still the ordinary man's politician.

It is, perhaps, as well that his friends and voters recognize Denktaş, for no government on earth, save that of Turkey, ever did. As president of the self-proclaimed Turkish Republic of Northern Cyprus (TRNC), Denktaş may not have been exactly an international pariah but his claims on behalf of his people, by turns emotional and analytical, elicited little response from a world community that continued to call for the withdrawal of Turkish troops and a settlement of the Cyprus problem that offered justice to the Greek Cypriots who lost their birthright in 1974. Born in 1924 at Paphos (as it was spelt then), Denktaş himself knows the pain of separation from his roots.

School of hard knocks Denktaş's emotion came from his experience of combating the Greek Cypriot drive for union with Greece, and the traumatic experience the Turkish Cypriots suffered in their isolated, surrounded and harassed enclaves. The analysis (cold calculation some would say) came from his lawyer's mind—he trained at Lincoln's Inn in London. His motives were suspected, although this is a common enough situation for any politician. Did he use the crisis to advance his own position? Greek Cypriots believed so and labelled him intransigent.

Denktaş's life as president was an odd mix of playing at the highest level in international politics and handling the routine affairs of a small, mainly agricultural society. Secretary-generals of the United Nations, leaders of the Security Council, NATO and various Islamic organizations all weighed his words carefully, calculating the chances for a settlement that everyone agreed was overdue. Yet there was no movement. Denktaş stood firm: If the price of a settlement was a deal that put Turkish Cypriots back even part of the way to pre-1974 conditions, and if the penalty of being labelled intransigent was greater isolation, he blocked the settlement and chose isolation. Yet it was Denktaş who opened the border in 2003.

Rights stuff Listening to Denktaş, one sensed his yearning for people to understand the situation of the Turkish Cypriots. He quoted often from the American Declaration of Independence and added that if all men have the right to life, liberty and the pursuit of happiness, then the right to life must come first. He proposed compromises on the territorial issue—the return of areas adjacent to the demarcation line to the Greek Cypriots. These proposals were rejected as inadequate, yet stirred up protest from extremist elements on his own side.

The TRNC's presidential palace within the Quirini bastion of Nicosia's Venetian walls was formerly allocated to the vice-president of the Republic of Cyprus, a post reserved for a Turkish Cypriot under the 1960 constitution and once held by Denktaş's friend and mentor, the late Dr Fazil Kuçuk. It is a modest and informal affair for an international statesman. For a photographer, however, it was quite respectable and the former president is a keen amateur photographer. Denktaş now maintains his own office on the outskirts of the walled city, from where he monitors and comments on Cyprus developments. He is writing his memoirs.

Opposite and below: Members of the press watch as Rauf Denktaş leaves UN discussions in Geneva, 1974

61

The courtyard of the Kumarcılar Hanı (Gamblers' Inn)

SHADED SPOT
A tiny patch of ornamental garden just outside the Keryneia Gate represents one of the few patches of greenery in the Turkish Cypriot sector of the old city. It makes a shaded place to rest, or to wait for a bus.

Modern art displayed at the converted Haydarpaşa Mosque, now the HP Gallery of Modern Art

► **Haydarpaşa Mosque**   *42C3*
Kirlizade Sokağı
Open: Mon–Fri 9–1 and 2–5, Sat 9–1. Admission free
The 14th-century Latin church of St. Catherine joined the long parade of churches used by the Ottomans as mosques. Still an outstanding Cypriot example of the Gothic style, it has now embarked upon an interesting new career as the HP Gallery of Modern Art.

►► **Kumarcılar Hanı (Gamblers' Inn)**   *42B3*
Asma Alti Sokağı
Courtyard accessible. Admission free
A smaller and altogether more precious—in the stylistic sense at least—cousin of the Büyük Han, this late 17th-century caravanserai is being restored. The antiquities staff don't seem to mind people wandering into the *hanı's* flower-bedecked courtyard, which makes a good place of escape from a hot and busy part of the old city.

► **Keryneia Gate (Girne Kapısı)**   *42B4*
Between the Quirini bastion and Barbaro bastion of the Venetian walls
In high summer, the Keryneia Gate in the Venetian walls, dating from 1567–1570, may be the best sight in Nicosia. For it is here that the main road leads out of town to the Pentadaktylos (Beşparmak) Mountains and to the coast around Keryneia (Girne), with its cooling sea breezes.

► **Library of Sultan Mahmut II**   *42B3*
Zuhtizade Sokağı
Open: summer daily 9–2; winter daily 9–1 and 2–4.45. Admission: inexpensive
A delightful little place, the domed library was built for Sultan Mahmut II and opened in 1829. It contains 1,700 books in Turkish, Arabic and Persian, including antique copies of the Koran, some as much as 700 years old.

► **Lapidary Museum**   *42C3*
Zuhtizade Sokağı
Open: summer daily 9–2; winter daily 9–1 and 2–4.45; key from Library of Sultan Mahmut II. Admission inexpensive
This museum of carved stonework contains various bits and pieces including sarcophagi, gargoyles and a pulpit ,,salvaged from old churches and wealthy private homes. The 15th-century Venetian mansion which houses the museum is appealing in its own right.

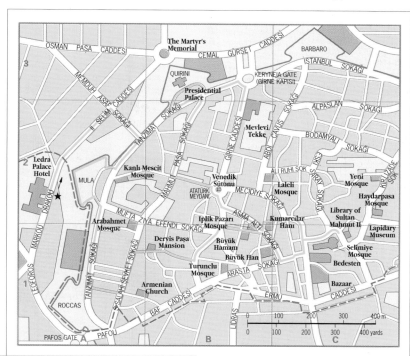

Walk

Turkish Cypriot Nicosia

Like its Greek Nicosia counterpart, this walk covers city walls, the Green Line, monuments and ordinary streets. Designed to be completed in an hour, it takes longer if you visit the places mentioned. The sights are covered in more detail on pages 57–65.

Begin at the Ledra Palace checkpoint, overlooked by the former **Ledra Palace Hotel**, now UN territory. Pass through the city walls, turning right on to Tanzimat Sokağı. The **Mula bastion** has been converted into a memorial park, and there is a fine view from here of the Ledra Palace Hotel and over the Green Line. Farther along, once battered Ottoman houses have been restored.

Turn left on to Salahi Sokağı. The **Dervis Paşa Mansion**▶▶▶ is on the right. Next, turn right along Mufta Ziya Efendi Sokağı, which leads to an area rich in historic buildings: the **Büyük Hamam**▶▶, the **Büyük Han**▶▶▶, the **Kumarcılar Hanı**▶▶; the **Bedesten**▶, the **Selimiye Mosque**▶▶▶, and the **Library of Sultan Mahmut II**▶.

Take Asma Alti Sokağı to pleasant **Atatürk Meydanı (Atatürk Square)**▶▶, the business and commercial heart of Turkish Cypriot Nicosia. Mahmut Paşa Sokağı leads to the Quirini bastion, within which lies Turkish Cyprus's modest **Presidential Palace**. Near the adjacent **Keryneia Gate (Girne Kapısı)**▶ is the **Mevlevi Tekke**▶▶▶, once the home of Nicosia's 'whirling dervishes' and now a museum.

The Library of Sultan Mahmut II

Nicosia

Mementoes (right) in the Mevlevi Tekke, where whirling dervishes once danced

64

►►► Mevlevi Tekke   42B3

Girne Caddesi
Open: summer daily 9–2; winter daily 9–1 and 2–4.45.
Admission: moderate

This is the Cyprus foundation of the legendary Mevlevi dancers, the 'whirling dervishes' who danced the mystic rites of the Sufi sect until Kemal Atatürk banned such practices as part of his drive to secularize Turkey in the 1920s, a policy also adopted in Cyprus. The spinning symbolized the motion of the heavenly spheres and the dancers' stance, one palm upraised and the other pointing downwards, man's position as a 'bridge' between heaven and earth, with God's blessings flowing from one to the other. Islamic scholars have written approvingly of the 'saintliness' of Jalal al-Din al-Rumi, called Mevlana (Master), the 14th-century Sufi adept who formed the rituals of the brotherhood.

A *tekke* was a kind of Islamic monastery and this one, founded early in the 17th century, was the only Mevlevi monastery in Cyprus. Located next to the Keryneia (Girne) Gate, the building now operates as the Ethnographic Museum. The disco-style dance-floor, where the dervishes whirled themselves into religious rapture, can still be seen, along with marvellous old photographs which show them in action. Among the museum's exhibits are an old HMV (His Master's Voice) gramophone donated by the wife of former president, Rauf Denktaş. More interesting historically are Koran reading-desks inlaid with mother-of-pearl, prayer rugs, books, ornamental scimitars and traditional costumes. One wing of the *tekke* contains the tombs of the sheiks who ran the Mevlevi order in Cyprus.

► Presidential Palace   63B3

Quirini bastion of the Venetian walls
The unpretentious 'White House' of the Turkish Republic of Northern Cyprus was formerly the vice-presidential palace of the government of the united island. It can be seen (but not visited) near the Keryneia (Girne) Gate.

►►► Selimiye Mosque   42B3

Selimiye Sokağı
Generally open: dawn–dusk. Admission free
Formerly the 13th-century Cathedral of St. Sophia (the Holy Wisdom), this was one of many Latin churches which the Ottoman Turks converted into mosques after their 1571 conquest. The twin minarets remain the most distinctive landmarks of the divided city, and are visible from a long way off across the Mesaoria (Mesarya) Plain. The mosque takes its name, though only since 1954, from Sultan Selim II, the Ottoman ruler who ordered the invasion of Cyprus.

The cathedral's foundation is dated to 1209 and its consecration to 1326, quite a rapid construction rate for those days, perhaps because the income of the diocese was lavished upon it to an extent that drew a papal rebuke. Although the Cathedral of St. Sophia was damaged when Nicosia was sacked by the Genoese and the Egyptian Mamelukes, repairs still left its treasury attractive enough for the Venetians to be moved to pocket the lot.

All of the cathedral's human and saintly images were removed, and all other Christian decoration covered up, as required by Islamic tradition. The *mihrab* (prayer niche indicating the direction of Mecca) stands in the former chapel of the Virgin Mary. Today the mosque seems better patronized by young Turkish army conscripts than by Turkish Cypriots.

► **Turunçlu Mosque**   *63B1*
Baf Caddesi
Open: irregularly. Admission free
Dating from 1825, this mosque has clearly taken its inspiration from the Cypriot church architecture of the period, a reversal of the usual conqueror-to-conquered flow in cultural ideas. The 19th-century **Iplik Pazarı Mosque** stands near by in the quarter of the same name, which was once the Ottoman-era cotton market.

OFFICE BOYS
Today the limp hand of Ottoman-inspired bureaucracy seems to be taking a firm grip on the Turkish Cypriot sector. A complex of extravagant new office blocks has been built near the outskirts of northern Nicosia to house the pen-pushers in a style appropriate to their pretensions, if not to the governance of a tiny agrarian statelet.

The cool interior of the Selimiye Mosque, once a 13th-century Gothic cathedral

65

Nicosia

OLD SOLDIER

Before it was taken over by UNFICYP, the Ledra Palace Hotel inside the Green Line near Pafos Gate was one of the island's principal hotels, with a long and elegant colonial history. Damaged in the intercommunal fighting, it awaits the day when, perhaps, it can be returned to its original function.

COOL TIP

Some hotels in Nicosia have a swimming pool, but if yours is not one of them, there are several public pools in the city. It may be wise to choose a hotel near one of the municipal pools. When you consider the intense summer heat, the dust and the sweaty tours of museums and churches you will probably face, this proximity might turn out to be welcome.

Hotels are thin on the ground in Nicosia, but they do exist

Accommodation

In an island where tourism reigns supreme, Nicosia takes second place to the resorts in terms of quantity and, to some extent, quality of hotel accommodation. However, business people and a growing number of independent travellers for whom a package holiday is anathema will find that choice in the capital is limited but growing and that quality is improving all the time.

ROOM AT THE INN Despite the fact that Nicosia is the capital of Cyprus, hotels and other forms of tourist accommodation are not its strong suit—compared with the coastal resorts at any rate. Where the latter are knee-deep in hotels, self-catering apartment units, and villas in all quality, style, and price categories, Nicosia is a poor relation. Primarily this is because it is not a tourist destination. Nicosia International Airport, once the island's sole air gateway, is now a mouldering ruin, the principal base of UNFICYP (the United Nations Force in Cyprus), and a pawn in negotiations between Greek and Turkish Cypriots over the island's future.

The capital is a mainly business and political destination, with day trips to the city as an optional extra for visitors, although it has much of history, culture and style to offer—much more than many places to which the sun-seekers rush headlong. It is a real city, a real community, and offers a taste of the real Cyprus that is as genuine in its way as the most typical mountain village. (More precisely, due to the Green Line, which has been only partially opened in the last few years, it is still two cities: one Greek Cypriot, the other Turkish Cypriot.) The business exists thanks to growth in tourism, offshore financial and other services, agriculture, shipping and light engineering sectors; the politics arises from Cyprus's role as a focal point of international diplomacy, and the island sees a steady stream of mediators, negotiators, ambassadors and advisers doing their bit to promote reconciliation.

NO ROOM The **Cyprus Hilton** in Greek Cypriot Nicosia is the jewel in Nicosia's crown, an assertion with which Turkish Cypriots would surely not quibble. Its star status is an indicator of the capital's place in the scheme of things. None of the successful indigenous hotel groups have built

a flagship hotel here, although the development of the Cyprus International Conference Centre is beginning to change this. Nicosia is, however, one of the few locations on the island where the independent traveller has much choice, all other places being given over almost entirely to package tourists. Recent years have seen an increase in the number of good mid-range hotels, while those at the budget end are undergoing upgrades and renovations.

A swimming pool to beat the heat at the top-rated Hilton Park Hotel

AREA CODES The choice of location in Greek Cypriot Nicosia falls into two areas: inside the Venetian walls or outside. As a rule, those inside are in older buildings, which by and large have been renovated or rebuilt to modern standards. Outside the old centre, the Greek Cypriot half of Nicosia fades away, through the business and commercial district, into suburbs for which 'characterless' is a charitable description. On the whole, hotels in this part of town share this lack of character but compensate with modern facilities and easy access.

  Turkish Cypriot Nicosia does not have the same suburban problem, but then it does not have many hotels in the first place. In this respect it shares Turkish Cyprus's less developed tourist infrastructure, which is partly due to the international isolation that followed the 1974 conflict. The Saray Hotel is Turkish Cypriot Nicosia's nearest equivalent to the Hilton, and mid-range hotels are thin on the ground. Cyprus is, however, a popular destination with mainland Turks, and hotels that cater for them are usually friendly and inexpensive.

Nicosia Cyprus Hilton is generally considered to be the capital's best hotel

Ice cream provides a welcome antidote to the sweltering summer heat

Food and drink

Nicosia's eateries are mostly designed to satisfy the city's own diners, with few of the visitor-orientated places that crowd the coastal resorts. This means that genuine local taste, in all price ranges, is easier to find. Yet visitors who require a tourist diet can find menus to fill the bill.

FAST FOOD As befits an industrious city, Nicosia is full of fast-food eateries designed to get people back to work quickly with something filling under their belts. This may not sound appetizing, but in fact it helps visitors enjoy Nicosia's status as a 'genuine' Cypriot town. Ordinary Cypriots pop into the snack-bars for an instant coffee, which goes under the generic name 'Nescafé'; as brewed in these bars, the resulting beverage is an odds-on favourite for the accolade of 'world's worst-tasting coffee'. As an accompaniment to the coffee, your choice may be a cheese-filled pie or a cheese-and-ham 'toastie', often using the slightly bitter *halloumi* cheese.

On a more substantial level, there are cafés, the most typical being those that serve lunch to workers from the many small workshops along the Green Line. The cafés are largely unused by tourists, because they tend to look rather rough and ready. The cooking, however, is simple, nourishing and tasty, the atmosphere is usually convivial, and the prices are user-friendly.

REAL DISHES In several distinctive areas of the old city better restaurants are concentrated in mutual-support enclaves, with a few individual gems scattered among them. The most important of these areas as far as the visitor is concerned is **Laïki Geitonia**, an atmospheric warren of cobbled streets mostly holding boutiques and souvenir shops, but with an extensive alfresco restaurant quarter at its heart. Lunch is the popular time, yet in the evening, when Laïki Geitonia glows with lantern and candle light, the ambience and the food are at their best.

Nicosians can be sniffy about Laïki Geitonia, seeing it as a tourist trap. The 'in' crowd are more likely to head for the **Famagusta Gate**, where off-beat bars and cafés mingle with restaurants. The latter are smarter and tend to be more expensive than average, yet not to the

extent of overcharging customers for the privilege of resting on their seats. This is dining out with a touch of Cypriot style, in streets that rub shoulders with the Green Line to lend an air of unreality to the proceedings. An aspect of the city's increasingly cosmopolitan air is the trend towards a more adventurous dining scene and sophisticated cuisine, represented by the homegrown new Cypriot booking, as well as by ethnic and international restaurants and places that serve fusion dishes.

TURKISH TASTE The Turkish Cypriot zone is similar in many respects to the Greek Cypriot, although there are fewer restaurants and less choice. The snack-bar end of the market is complemented by a greater number of shish kebab outlets, and the succulent smell of grilling lamb can be savoured in the air as well as tasted at the counter. Along the Green Line runs a string of working-class cafés whose attributes perfectly complement those a few metres away on the other side. Freshly-squeezed fruit juice makes a wonderfully thirst-quenching drink on a typically sultry day, and kiosks dispense masses of the stuff.

Adjacent to the Selimiye Mosque and Bedesten are some tourist-orientated open-air restaurants little different from those of Laïki Geitonia in the Greek Cypriot sector. These establishments are clean and friendly, and the atmosphere bustling and lively; the food has not been too far compromised in order to cater to international tastes. On the downside this is a miniature tourist ghetto, leavened with a handful of well-dressed Turkish Cypriots, which won't necessarily appeal to those seeking genuine Turkish Cypriot taste.

Small eateries with terraces are common

69

HOME COOKING
The best introduction to Cypriot cuisine may come if you are lucky enough to be invited to a Cypriot's home for dinner. Fresh fruit and vegetables from the market are sure to be on the menu, as are a few 'secret' recipes, handed down from mother to daughter in the manner of old village traditions.

Coffee and water, the essential ingredients of a quick break

Shopping

Although not exactly world-renowned as a shopping mecca, Nicosia is the principal place in Cyprus for this popular activity.

NO PARADISE Nicosia's increasing prosperity and sophistication has brought it closer—though by no means all the way—to being a chic European shopping capital. Limassol and Keryneia (Girne) offer tough competition when it comes to price tags and the range of goods available, but Nicosia does represent the island's main concentration of shops and markets.

In Greek Cypriot Nicosia, the most important shopping areas are Odos Lidras and Odos Onasagorou within the city walls; both are well known for their department stores, clothing and footwear outlets, as well as for electrical goods. The adjacent tourist-orientated Laïki Geitonia district is the place for souvenirs of all kinds, from postcards and key-rings to hand-made lace and jewellery. Archiepiskopou Makariou III Avenue, outside the Venetian walls, is another principal shopping artery, noted for its department stores, and side-streets off it are the places for chic specialist stores.

CRAFT VIRTUES Handicrafts are big business, pushing the finest products from traditional centres in the hinterland. The excellent **Cyprus Handicraft Centre** at 186 Leoforos

TOP PEOPLE'S CATALOGUE
Some famous shoppers have in the past taken advantage of Cyprus's reputation for quality products: King Agamemnon, for example, who Homer describes in the *Iliad* as wearing a cuirass (body armour) of Cypriot copper; and Alexander the Great, whose favourite sword was made in Cyprus. Neither of them is known to have visited the island, however, so they must have done their shopping by mail-order.

Scent of a bargain at an antique shop in the Turkish sector

Athalassis (see page 48) in the southern outskirts is a workshop that gives an excellent introduction to various handicraft types and styles, all under one roof, as well as the chance to buy items in its shop. Products recognized by the parent Cyprus Handicraft Service are labelled 'CHS' and are also on sale in Limassol, Larnaka and Pafos. This is not the only outlet, and prices are likely to be keener in shops such as the **Craft Box** (430 Odos Stasikratous)' where commercial considerations take precedence over preserving threatened folk arts.

Among craft-produced fabrics to watch out for are the unsurpassed hand-made Lefkara lace, or *lefkaritika*; *pafitika* loom embroidery; *lefkonika* towels, aprons and placemats; *alatjia* silky-smooth striped cotton; and hand-crocheted lace and wool. Pottery from Kornos and Foini is particularly fine, although the grand traditional clay pots called *pitharia* are on the large side for souvenirs. Leatherwork has a diminished range, but handbags and jackets are good value. Copper is no longer commonplace, but exquisite ornaments and even cooking pots can still be found. Gourds are transformed into plant-pots, vases, carafes and the like, while reeds are used for basket-weaving and light furnishings. Finally, Cypriot forests provide the basic raw material for an exhaustive range of wood-carvings.

ORIENTAL COOL Turkish Cypriot Nicosia boasts many of the same products, although sales are on a smaller scale and include items with a more oriental touch, such as hookahs and *kilims*. Visitors used to Turkey, where haggling is a way of life, will discover that it is not so in Turkish Cyprus, even in the bazaars; this is just one of many ways in which Turkish Cypriots are more European than their cousins on the mainland. Shops in the Turkish sector are somewhat scattered, although there is a smart enclave around Atatürk Meydanı and a more popular one adjacent to the Selimiye Mosque in the centre, while outlying streets such as Mehmet Akif Caddesi have modern shops.

Both parts of the divided city share a mirror-image district of dingy old workshops that run alongside the Green Line. Some of these are craft workshops which produce a variety of metal and woodwork items to order.

Pots such as these may tempt the souvenir-hunter

71

MARKET PLACES
Markets in Nicosia are neither as numerous nor as extensive as Cyprus's vast range of fresh products and handicrafts would suggest. Yet the weekly fruit and vegetable market and the permanent markets and bazaars on both sides of the Green Line are sources of unrivalled value as well as much local colour.

A fruit-seller offers his wares at the Municipal Market

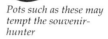

Nicosia

Nightlife

Compared with the tourist resorts, nightlife in Nicosia is more scattered and less easily defined. In compensation, it is also less artificial, appealing much more to local people than to hyped-up holidaymakers. In the Greek Cypriot sector especially, there is much of the exuberance and style appropriate to a capital city.

GETTING THE RHYTHM The Greek Cypriot half of Nicosia works and plays hard. Friday is the big release, when the dance clubs, cafés and restaurants start buzzing for the weekend; Saturday is the hottest time; by Sunday, the spirit is still willing though the flesh has grown weak; on Monday, people go out, but more from a sense of duty than real enthusiasm; Tuesday is reserved for rest and recuperation; everyone perks up a bit on Wednesday and maybe makes a brief mid-week foray; and Thursday is taken up by more R&R. Nightlife in Nicosia follows the pattern of the city's differences from the coastal resorts in other regards, with tourist-orientated attractions almost non-existent and the emphasis firmly on what appeals to Greek Cypriot and permanent residents' sensibilities.

Dancing is the big diversion, with a sharp divide between discos and nightclubs in terms of age. The discos are filled with sultry and stylish fashion-demons who, during the day, are ordinary fresh-faced schoolchildren. The nightclubs, on the other hand, form a kind of hip senior citizens' home for the over-19s, where live music alternates with disco and traditional Greek and oriental favourites.

LAID BACK More restrained entertainment is on offer to those who seek it. The **Municipal Theatre** on Odos Mouseiou is an elegant place where classical and modern plays in both Greek and English are performed. Experimental theatre often takes place at the **Famagusta Gate Cultural Centre**, an area of fashionable cafés and restaurants that have become popular meeting-places of the city's young and stylish looking for something more sophisticated than their local taverna. The **British Council**, 3

A DJ mixes on the decks while clubbers party

Leoforos Mousieou, features chamber music and other events, as does the **Goethe Institute** at 21 Leoforos Markou Drakou. In venues around town, the **US Embassy's cultural section** does likewise. The city's seven cinemas screen international films, mostly American but also Greek and other European movies, in their original soundtrack, with Greek subtitles where appropriate. As well as the Cultural Centre, the Famagusta Gate is at the heart of an adjacent area of trendy cafés, some with live music, which are popular with the smart set and open into the small hours.

INFORMATION SOURCES Information on entertainment can be found in the Cyprus Tourism Organization's free *Monthly Events* and from the free *Nicosia This Month,* produced by the municipality. Both are available from tourist offices and usually

73

from hotels, conference centres and tour operators. During the summer, Cyprus Broadcasting Corporation (CyBC) broadcasts *Welcome to Cyprus* on 498m in English, French and German, giving news and 'what's on' information.

Traditional music is still popular, especially as an accompaniment to eating out

QUIETER TIME Turkish Cypriot Nicosia is altogether more restrained, so much so that many Nicosians decamp to nearby Keryneia (Girne) at the coast for the town's dance clubs, nightclubs, casinos and cafés, and for the all-important 'atmosphere' that makes going out at night more than a chore.

Those who stay in the capital are more likely to concentrate on going out for a meal, although the restaurant may well feature some live music, even if only from a singer with a synthesizer, and, at weekends, possibly a belly dancer. The **Saray Hotel** does, however, have a casino and also features live music performances. Chic bars and restaurants, aimed at a younger, more cosmopolitan clientele, are springing up along the southern end of Mehmet Akif Caddesi and in the shadow of Selimiye Mosque in the heart of the old city.

FUEL FOR DANCING
Greek Cypriot Nicosia's nightclubs are usually crowded by 10PM, although the action may not start for an hour or so after this. They play their share of Western dance music, but the real moments of audience participation come when Cypriot and Greek music, both modern and traditional, are performed.

Public transport is generally good, but a moped or bicycle is ideal for getting through old Nicosia's cramped backstreets

Practical points

One half of Nicosia is exclusively Greek Cypriot, the other Turkish Cypriot. But within each zone there is the contrast between the old city, inside the Venetian walls, and modern business and residential districts.

FLYING IN Greek Cypriot Nicosia is served by Larnaka International Airport, about an hour away by road; and Turkish Cypriot Nicosia by Ercan International Airport. The latter is not recognized by the International Air Transport Association (IATA), is served only by Turkish and Turkish Cypriot airlines, and is considered an illegal port of entry by the Greek Cypriot authorities.

GREEN LINE The main stumbling-block to getting around remains the UN buffer zone, called the Green Line in Nicosia, which separates the Greek Cypriot sector in the south from the Turkish Cypriot in the north. The only crossing-point in the city between the Greek Cypriot sector and the Turkish Cypriot sector is for pedestrians who pass through the border at the Ledra Palace Hotel checkpoint. There is also a vehicle crossing-point on the western edge of the city at Agios Dometios (Metehan) and, at the time of writing, the possibility of a second city centre pedestrian crossing at Odos Lidras/Ledra Street (Lokmacı Barikatı). Since Cyprus's EU entry, citizens of the union's member states may cross freely between the two sectors.

PHOTOGRAPHY Taking pictures of the Green Line, UN personnel and installations, the Greek Cypriot National Guard and the Turkish army is strictly forbidden.

GOOD DIRECTIONS
Guided walking tours of historic Nicosia (in the Greek Cypriot zone) leave from the Tourist Information Office on Odos Aischylou in the Laïki Geitonia quarter. These offer a good introduction to the city, with access to churches which are otherwise frequently locked, and with a well-informed and enthusiastic commentary. Leaflets giving timetables and itineraries are available from the office.

ON FOOT Old Nicosia, within the Venetian walls, is a small and not frantically busy place, so walking is a good way to get around. The only proviso to this is that it can get desperately hot, particularly when the sun is overhead and there is less chance of 'shade-hopping' from point to point. Outside the walls, walking can be a traffic-tormented, heat-infested nightmare, particularly as distances are great and points of interest few and far between.

CAR Outside the walls the going by car is a lot easier than it looks, although the one-way system may require you to take roundabout routes to your destination. Nicosian drivers are relatively tolerant of tourists driving the distinctive rental cars with red licence-plates and an initial letter 'Z', though if irritated by too much indecision their response can be explosive. Parking ought to be a problem, given the busy traffic and lack of spaces, but Nicosians 'solve' the problem by parking wherever they like, whatever the consequences. Driving is on the left in both sectors. Drivers can travel between the two sectors at the Agios Dometios (Metehan) crossing point. Cars rented from some companies in the Greek Cypriot south may be taken into the Turkish Cypriot north, provided special insurance is purchased, but at the time of writing cars rented in the north may not be taken into the south.

Taxis are plentiful, metered, and not too expensive

75

TAXIS Booked in advance by telephone, flagged down, or picked up from one of the ranks scattered around the centre, taxis are fairly inexpensive and efficient. In addition, a small group can hire a taxi for the day to tour either half of the divided city. This is cost-effective and relaxing, with the added benefit that you will have a guide—the driver—who will normally speak some English at least.

BUSES Metropolitan bus services in both sectors are adequate. Anyone on a short visit will be unlikely to unravel the routing and timetable complexities enough for them to be useful, although services to and from the centre for visitors staying at an outlying hotel may prove convenient. In the Greek Cypriot sector, a free service on yellow buses is available around the old town and local environs. The main bus stations are at Plateia Dionysos Solomos and outside the Costanza bastion. In the Turkish Cypriot sector, the principal interchange point for buses are at the Keryneia Gate (Girne Kapısı) and the bus terminal about 1km (0.5 miles) to the north.

PEOPLE MOVERS
Anyone planning to stay in the city for an extended period may find it worth-while to invest in a moped, which offers a fast and efficient way of getting around, and can be sold at the end of your stay. Of course, a bicycle is equally effective and more environ-mentally friendly, though it is harder on the legs.

The main highway from Nicosia is the one that leads out to the coastal resorts

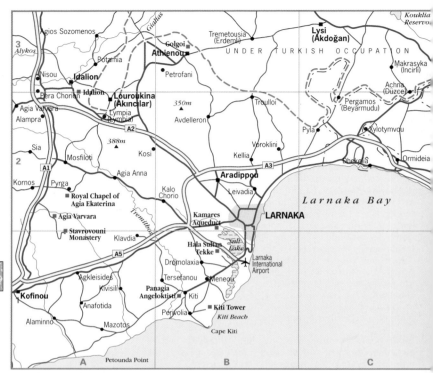

Famagusta
(Ammochostos, Gazimağusa)

Famagusta

Bay

Acheritou
(Güvercinlik)

Agios
Nikolaos
Reservoir

Varosha
(Maraş)

Deryneia

Frenaros

Avgorou

Panagia
Chordakiotissa

Sotira

Paralimni

Agia Trias

Pernera

Liopetri

Profitis
Ilias

Fig Tree Bay

Protaras

Xylofagou

Makronisos

Agia Napa

Potamos

Agia
Thekla

Nissi
Bay

Agioi
Anargyroi

Cape Pyla

Cape Gkreko
(Akr Gkreko)

———— See Drive pages 94–95

— · — British Sovereign base

| 0 | 5 | 10 | 15 km |
| 0 | | 5 | 10 miles |

D   **E**

THE SOUTHEAST From Nicosia, Cyprus's main highway runs southwards, skirting the edge of the Mesaoria Plain, a fast track to the bustling resorts that line the island's southern and western shores. In the past, before partition, this was the direction most holidaymakers would have taken from Nicosia Airport.

Based on the gateway city of Larnaka, the southeast region covers a great arc of coastline, and a wedge of hilly country that can be considered as foothills of the Troodos Mountains, if only because the Troodos are so dominating that any hills within reach can be so considered. That 'within reach' helps define an important characteristic of the southeast: It is important to understand that not everywhere that is visible is within reach.

The region is unnaturally cramped on its eastern flank, but this has nothing to do with geography even if it is a physical reality on the ground. Instead, the legacy of the Turkish invasion in 1974 presses hard on this corner of the island.

The long-running division between Greek and Turkish Cyprus is ever present in the demarcation line against which the area abuts. The line can now be crossed at several points, but it retains some of the limiting character of a meandering river with only a few bridges.

Villages in this area have expanded rapidly in the past 30 years or so, not just because of the pressure of the burgeoning tourist industry but also to accommodate the Greek Cypriot refugees who poured in from the Turkish-occupied zone after the invasion.

Looking out from the quiet, cloistered court-yard of the 16th-century Agia Napa Monastery (left)

▶▶▶ **REGION HIGHLIGHTS**

Cape Gkreko *page 81*
Foinikoudes Promenade *page 88*
Hala Sultan Tekke *page 82*
Panagia Angeloktisti (Our Lady Built by Angels) *page 83*
Pierides Foundation Museum *page 88*
Potamos Creek *pages 92–93*
Salt Lake *page 96*
Stavrovouni Monastery *pages 96–97*

SUNNY STORY
The 3,300 hours of sunshine per year that attract people to beach resorts such as Nissi Bay and Protaras also provide them and the local population with free hot water. Solar heating systems on the roofs of Cypriot houses are almost universal, and the companies making them have established lucrative export markets in the Middle East. In summer the water can be heated to 84°C (185°F), a temperature that may fall to 35°C (77°F) in winter.

ON THE BEACH From a point near the demarcation line at Deryneia, you can look across to the hotel blocks and beaches of Famagusta (Gazimağusa), on the other side. Yet the contradictions of Cyprus are such that one of the Mediterranean's most vigorous holiday and clubbing resorts is located only a few kilometres away. Agia Napa is as artificial a construction as it can be. It exists purely and simply to offer the place of escape that attracts many tourists to Cyprus in the first place, and it does so with total commitment and some style.

Even in the resort's immediate surroundings, life goes on much as it did in the past. This is the Kokkinochoria, or 'red villages' country, where the vivid rust-coloured soil can produce no fewer than three potato crops every year so long as it is well irrigated, which it is. Moving away from the thin commercial carapace along the shore is to move into a different kind of Cyprus.

It would be hard to get further from traditional Cyprus than in the British Sovereign Base Area at Dhekelia. The base permits no commercial development. Military development is something else, and although more than half its area is freely accessible, part of the coastline here is not.

OUT FROM LARNAKA In Larnaka the southeast hosts a fast-expanding small city, a growth that's mainly been due to its having Cyprus's busiest airport, which serves

the coast from Agia Napa to Limassol and inland to Nicosia, and its second-busiest port. Larnaka contains more elements of intrinsic interest than Limassol, as well as being conveniently located for exploring the coastline and the line of hills that lies between it and Nicosia.

Unlike the Agia Napa area, the shoreline from Cape Kiti west as far as Governor's Beach is not much developed, and there are some stretches of wild and uninhabited coast. This has as much to do with the lack of golden sands as with any commitment to conservation, but the effect is the same for anyone in search of peace and quiet.

Between the main motorways linking Limassol, Larnaka and Nicosia lies a triangular 'island' of land, an intriguingly isolated piece of countryside. There are only a few points of tourist interest—Agia Ekaterina Chapel and Stavrovouni Monastery (see page 96), for example—and a handful of villages. Mostly the dusty trails lead seemingly nowhere and, in the scorching heat of summer, the deserted landscape takes on an almost lunar quality. In a way this area encapsulates all that is southeast Cyprus: You can have the fast track if you want it, but the alternative is never far away. In fact, because of the rapid and relentless development of previously tranquil western Cyprus in the past decade, you now have a better chance of getting away from it all in the Southeast—provided you keep away from the resorts.

MARCH OF PROGRESS
The red soil of the Kokkinochoria ('red villages') district around Agia Napa would be less rich were it not for constant irrigation. In the past, water was brought up from underground aquifers with the help of windmills, many of which still dot the landscape. Nowadays diesel-powered pumps do the work, but some windmills are being restored and brought back into service.

79

Time to relax on a spectacularly sited bench overlooking Cape Gkreko

The Southeast

HOT TO TROT

In recent years Agia Napa became one of the hottest summer clubbing resorts in the Mediterranean, with big name DJs from western Europe jetting in to pump up the volume for masses of primed-to-party young people.

This brought in its tow something of a wild party atmosphere, not to mention a surge in drunkenness, pill-popping, and unruly behaviour, that didn't sit too well with the families that were the resort's bread and butter. It did, however, bring good business for the 'orgy boats' that now float beside the tour boats and glass-bottom boats in the harbour.

With the police now cracking down on the noise and illegal and anti-social activities associated with the clubs, the spark and the cachet seem to have gone out of the scene.

Above: Agia Napa Monastery is an oasis of calm in the busy resort

After a hard day's sunbathing, Agia Napa knows how to let its hair down

▶▶ Agia Napa   77E2

What Agia Napa lacks in cool sophistication—and it lacks a lot—it makes up for with its single-minded commitment to being a successful holiday resort, with all that implies in terms of cafés, shops, nightclubs and the like. The resort's own beaches lie on either side of the harbour and incorporate a cluster of sea caves—they are not particularly large but they are complemented by those of nearby Nissi Beach and Makronisos (see page 92). All are thick with sunbathers at peak times.

One point of historical interest in Agia Napa is a monastery, to which the town clings like a poor relation hoarding an inherited jewel. **Agia Napa Monastery**▶▶ (adjacent to Plateia Seferi. *Open* daily dusk–dawn. *Admission free*) is a 16th-century monastery, and with its Orthodox church these were once all there was to Agia Napa. Now they look lost, engulfed and surrounded by the glitter of the new resort.

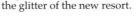

However, it is not to see Byzantine monasteries that people go to Agia Napa. The formerly deserted shoreline in and around the town has become Cyprus's holiday playground, as the tourist industry reacted to the loss of some of its best resorts after the 1974 invasion.

Although overwhelmed by tour boats and private yachts, the harbour and marina retain elements of local colour in the fishing boats that discharge their marine cargoes here. Glass-bottom and other tour boats leave from here for cruises in the direction of Cape Gkreko and Larnaka. Behind the harbour, the tiny waterfront chapel of **Agios Georgios** now looks sadly out of place.

The **Tournaritis-Pierides Marine Life Museum**▶▶ (25 Odos Agias Mavris, tel: 23723409. *Open* Mon–Fri 9–2, Sat 9–1. *Admission inexpensive*) has displays and dioramas.

▶ Agia Thekla   77D2

This small whitewashed chapel beside the sea, a short distance to west of the busy Nissi Bay resort area, overlooks another, but smaller, tourist beach. It is easy to miss the original chapel hewn into the rockface beside the beach, its gloomy interior and a few icons illuminated by a single oil lamp. The quiet, rough road that runs between the sea and the main highway along this section of the coast makes a fine place for a walk or a bicycle tour.

▶ Agioi Anargyroi   77E2

Another of the small, whitewashed chapels scattered at intervals along this stretch of coast, the building makes a visual contrast with the blue of the sea. Agioi Anargyroi's main claim to fame is that it lies at the end of a shaded pathway and is one of the few easily accessible points of interest that can draw sunbathers from the beach.

▶▶▶ Cape Gkreko (Akr. Gkreko)   77E1

The scenic, undeveloped peninsula east of Agia Napa makes a welcome change from the hotels more usual in the area. Forming the sharp point of a peninsula, the cape's tip is unfortunately out of bounds because of the presence of military and civilian radio installations and a lighthouse. The surrounding waters are excellent for snorkelling and scuba-diving (but only when the sea is calm), and cliffs provide dramatic views of the rugged coastline in both directions, as well as windy vantage points for flying kites and birdwatching. Dirt-bike riders favour some of the trails in the area, and walkers can enjoy the paths through the low-growth groves of the Cavo Gkreko National Forest Park (390ha/960 acres).

▶ Deryneia   77D2

This village lies so close to the demarcation line that it even has a café with a viewpoint from where pictures can be taken (this is usually forbidden elsewhere) of the UN observation towers and the fortified military positions of either side, with Famagusta (Gazimağusa) and its resort suburb of Varosha (Maraş) beyond. Deryneia is blessed with a modern Orthodox church of such extravagant size and domed magnificence that it seems to have been designed to send some kind of religious or political message to the Turkish Cypriots across the way.

ODD ATTRACTION
Boat trips leave from Agia Napa bound for various scenic attractions along the coast. One of these trips goes around Cape Gkreko and along the coast towards Varosha (Maraş), a resort suburb of Famagusta (Gazimağusa) that has been entirely abandoned for more than 30 years (see page 249). The UN buffer zone extends out to sea, so the boats cannot get too close, but the sight of the town's crumbling holiday hotels and apartment blocks is still astonishing.

81

RADIO WAVES
A transmitter of Radio Monte Carlo stands beside the sea on the point of Cape Gkreko, relaying French-language programmes to the Middle East.

Tough decisions— whether to swim in the azure waters of the sea or stick to the hotel pool?

Hala Sultan Tekke—a little piece of Arabia on the shores of Larnaka's Salt Lake

GOLDEN AGE
Archaeologists are still excavating a middle to late Bronze Age settlement near Hala Sultan Tekke. A treasure trove of 23 gold objects recovered from the site has not yet been released for display by the Department of Antiquities.

PILGRIM'S WAY
The Hala Sultan Tekke on the shores of Larnaka's Salt Lake is reputed by Cypriots to be the third most important shrine of Islam, after the mosques of Mecca and Jerusalem. During important Islamic festivals it becomes a place of pilgrimage for Muslims travelling from far and wide.

▶ Dhekelia 76C2

This is the heart of the British Sovereign Base Area (one of two on the island), which, among other things, snoop on telecommunications traffic in the Middle East. The extent of military installations which are inaccessible to the public is less than half the base area. Police checkpoints on the road at either end and an armed sentry at the main entrance are usually the only obvious formalities.

▶▶▶ Hala Sultan Tekke 76B1

Open: Jun–Aug daily 7.30–7.30; Apr–May, Sep–Oct daily 9–6; Nov–Mar daily 9–5. Admission: free; donation expected
Tucked away in a grove of palm trees on the shore of Larnaka's Salt Lake (see page 96), the mosque is a rare monument to the period of Arab raids and conquests during the seventh and eighth centuries. With its dome and minarets, it looks like a scene from *The Arabian Nights* set in the Cypriot countryside. The interior of the dome is decorated with medallions inscribed with the names of Allah, Muhammad and the first six caliphs of Islam: Abu Bakr, Umar, Uthman, Ali, Hussein and Hassan.

Although the mosque dates from the early 19th century it enfolds the tomb of the Hala Sultan, also known as Umm Haram, an aunt of the Prophet Muhammad, who died here in AD649 (year 28 of the Islamic calendar) after falling from her mule. Her sepulchre, covered by green cloths of mourning, can also be visited. The stone surmounting it is said to have flown miraculously from Mount Sinai in Egypt to protect the tomb, and Muslim ships sailing within view of the shrine would dip their colours in honour of the illustrious lady. The grandmother of the late King Hussein of Jordan, who died in Cyprus in 1929, is also entombed in here. The mosque has been undergoing a UN-sponsored renovation and is now often visited by Turkish Cypriot pilgrims from the North.

▶▶ Kiti

76B1

This attractive but otherwise ordinary village west of Larnaka boasts one remarkable monument in its heart, as well as points of interest in the countryside, all of which are worth a detour. Fishing for trout is allowed with a permit in the small freshwater **Kiti Lake**▶ a short distance north of the village, where the Tremithos River has been dammed as part of Cyprus's extensive reservoir system.

The misleadingly named **Kiti Tower** is not actually in the village of Kiti itself but beside the sea at rugged Cape Kiti, several kilometres distant. The tower is a simple, fortified stone observation post, which was built by the Venetians as part of their vain attempt to fend off an invasion of Cyprus by the Ottoman Turks in the 16th century. A lighthouse overlooks the sea and the steep cliffs along this coast, which is dotted with beaches.

In addition to its more or less routine (for Cyprus, that is) panoply of murals, icons and gilt iconostasis, the church of **Panagia Angeloktisti (Our Lady Built by Angels)**▶▶▶ (tel: 24424646. *Open* daily 8–12 and 2–4 (Jun–Aug 6pm). *Admission free*.) rebuilt in the 12th century on the foundations of a fifth-century church, has a beautiful mosaic in the domed roof of the semicircular apse behind the iconostasis. The mosaic depicts the Virgin Mary carrying the infant Jesus and flanked by the winged archangels Gabriel and Michael. The mosaic can be lit up for visitors on request. The style and workmanship of the mosaic, with its tiny tesserae of coloured and precious stones, stand comparison with the famous 6th-century mosaics of the Emperor Justinian, Empress Theodora and the Byzantine court at Ravenna in Italy.

It seems that the Panagia Angeloktisti mosaic was the work of an imperial craftsman from Constantinople at a time when Byzantine mosaic art was at its height. And therein lies a mystery: Why are there not more mosaics of this calibre in Cyprus, given the wealth and influence of the Cypriot church at that time? They are roughly contemporary with the somewhat cruder mosaics from the Panagia Kanakaria church at Lythragkomi (Boltaşı) in the North, which are now displayed at the Byzantine Museum and Art Galleries in Nicosia.

83

The ornately decorated iconostasis at Panagia Angeloktisti church in Kiti

Cyprus has no shortage of that essential ingredient for marine sports: sea water. No point on the island is much more than an hour's drive from a sea that is warm and of a blue so inviting as to encourage even the most timid.

POINT OF VIEW
Glass-bottom boats, which sail from harbours in or near all the main resorts, offer certain undeniable advantages over scuba-diving when it comes to observing the local marine life: even inexperienced practitioners can breathe without the aid of cumbersome mechanical devices; you can share observational data in real time (in other words, chat) with your companions; and the picnic sandwiches don't get soggy—unless it rains, of course!

84

The term 'marine sports', just about all of which are practised around the island's shores, covers a multitude of sins. Simplest of all is swimming at the beach, and even the most determined of land-bound sunworshippers may make a discovery that changes their whole vacation: The sea is warm! From there the sky's the limit.

Adventure lines At all popular beaches a line of coloured buoys parallel to the shore indicates the safe bathing area watched over by lifeguards, and which power-boats are not allowed to enter. There are plenty of companies eager to introduce beginners to sailing, paragliding, water-skiing, jet-skiing and windsurfing, though none of these activities is inexpensive. Experienced practitioners will find the conditions for these sports enjoyable, if not overly challenging. Sea-kayaking is rare, even though conditions appear perfect for it.

Paragliding is common and may seem risky, but it is quite safe—and a satisfying experience to soar high above the crowded beaches and turquoise sea.

Snorkelling and scuba-diving are popular, thanks to crystal-clear waters and rocky sections of coastline. Submarine cliffs and valleys, coral colonies, sea-anemones, and sponges, fish, and sea-shells in exotic shades offer plenty of interest for divers, but note that it is illegal to remove antiquities and sponges from the seabed. Experienced divers can even visit the '*Titanic* of the Mediterranean'—the *Zenobia*, a vehicle ferry that sank just off Larnaka in 1980 on her maiden voyage to Syria, after a computer errror added too much ballast to one side. Despite all this,

Windsurf rigs lined up and ready to go at Nissi Beach

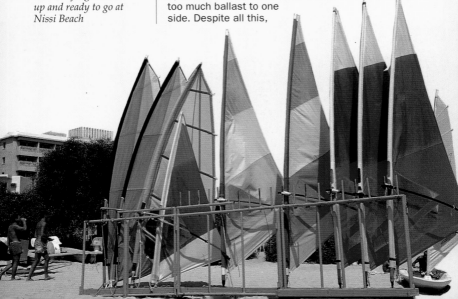

the island is no scuba-diving paradise in terms of the range of marine life that can be encountered. Sharks may occasionally be sighted but rarely come inshore, and although some 260 different fish species frequent the waters off Cyprus, they do so only in low numbers.

Amateur sportsfishing is limited due to the lack of big game fish, although it is possible to go out with a commercial swordfishing boat. Spear-fishing, angling and fishing with vertical lines or trolling lines with a maximum of 100 hooks and with up to three fish-traps are the only permitted sea-fishing methods; nets and other commercial gear are not allowed. Sea bream, grouper, amberjack and sea perch are among the species that may legally be caught. A permit issued by Fisheries Department district offices (see page 105) is required for spear-fishing with an aqualung, and is issued only to certified divers.

Sporting zones The main marine sports locations are: Agia Napa–Protaras; along Larnaka Bay; around Limassol and Lady's Mile Beach, where windsurfing is particularly good; at Pafos and Coral Bay; the Polis–Lakki area; Keryneia (Girne) and Famagusta (Gazimağusa). The waters off the Karpasia (Karpaz) Peninsula are a maritime exclusion zone, and there are other restricted areas along the Turkish Cypriot coastline.

For most, the areas listed above will offer all the possibilities they need during a two- or three-week holiday. Serious practitioners may wish to use a four-wheel-drive vehicle to reach the many isolated coves. An alternative route to out-of-the-way places is by speedboat. These can be rented at the main resorts without the need for a special licence, or you can rent a fishing boat with skipper. Even if you only want to swim *au naturel* in a deserted bay, your own speedboat is a great way to get there.

85

GOING UNDER
There are numerous sub-aqua clubs, diving centres and underwater safari companies at the principal resort areas: Agia Napa–Protaras, Larnaka, Limassol, Polis–Lakki, Pafos, Keryneia (Girne) and Famagusta (Gazimağusa). Tuition and guided tours are widely available. Further information is available from the **Cyprus Federation of Underwater Activities** (a member of the World Federation of Underwater Activities), PO Box 21503, Nicosia, tel: 22755246.

Paragliding off the beach at Agia Napa

LIVING LEGEND
The French city of
Marseilles also claims
Lazarus as a former
bishop in competition with
Larnaka. Either possibility
would surely make him
the most widely travelled
former corpse in antiquity.

►► Larnaka 76B2

When Nicosia International Airport was closed by the
Turkish attack of 1974, Larnaka developed as Cyprus's
main international gateway. Partly as a result, the city of
60,000 inhabitants has become an important tourist destination in its own right. It could be argued that its intrinsic
merits do not entirely justify this, but Larnaka has numerous points of interest and an atmospheric old town that
compensate for the haphazard development which has
crowded in on the city. In addition, Larnaka is a good
base for exploring the coast and the eastern Troodos
Mountains, and is less than an hour by road from Nicosia.

IN THE CENTRE Agios Lazaros (Church of St. Lazarus)►►
(Plateia Agiou Lazarou, tel: 24652498. *Open* Apr–Aug daily
8–12.30 and 3.30–6.30; Sep–Mar daily 8–12.30 and 2.30–5.
Admission free) is a cathedral-like 17th-century Orthodox
church with a fabulous gilt iconostasis, a fabulously ugly
chandelier and a soaring baroque tower. It is best known
for its association with that Lazarus who, as the New
Testament declares, was raised from the dead by Jesus. The
next time Lazarus died he was not so lucky, and legend has
it that he was buried in Larnaka (at that time called Kition).
The original church was built here when the saint's supposed sepulchre was discovered in the 9th century. The
sepulchre can still be seen, but the saint's remains were
removed to Constantinople by the Emperor Leo VI.

In the grounds of the church is a small **Byzantine
Museum►** (tel: 24652489. *Open* Jun–Aug Mon–Sat 8.30–1,
4–6.30 (not Wed and Sat); Sep–May Mon–Sat 8.30–1,

*The church of Agios
Lazaros, a prominent
Larnaka landmark, has a
fine Byzantine Museum*

Larnaka's extensive beach runs alongside the seafront promenade

87

4–5.30 (not Wed and Sat). *Admission: inexpensive*), in which are gathered some outstanding examples of ecclesiastical art: icons, Bibles, chalices, bishops' mitres and robes. Every year on the feast day of St. Lazarus, eight days before the Greek Orthodox Easter, the saint's icon is paraded through the town.

The 16th-century **Al-Kebir Mosque**▶▶ (*Open* daily. *Admission free, but donation expected*), which is still in use, is an interesting place to visit if only to compare the simplicity of its cool, columned interior with the intensely decorated churches then favoured by the Christians.

The **Laïki Geitonia**▶ area of Larnaka is a smaller version of Nicosia's district of the same name, and has been restored to create a pedestrian area with cafés and restaurants, and a certain amount of style and atmosphere. This is mostly evident in the evening, however, as Larnaka's Laïki Getonia has not been anything like as successful as the capital's version at attracting daytime hustle and bustle.

WATERFRONT ATTRACTIONS Larnaka Fort▶▶ (tel: 24304576. *Open* Jun–Aug Mon–Fri 9–7; Mar–Apr, Sep–Oct Mon–Fri 9–6; Nov–Feb 9–5. *Admission: inexpensive*) is possibly Larnaka's premier attraction. Rusting pre-World War I artillery pieces manufactured by Krupps of Germany stand hub to hub in the 16th-century fort's lower level, part of which is surrounded by gardens and used as an open-air theatre. The topmost level, with its turreted battlements, offers a view over the harbour and the maritime approaches to Larnaka. In its time, the fort would have been a particularly tough nut to crack for any would-be invader, and Turkish gunners manning the artillery of an earlier era must have prayed for something hostile to sail within range of their well-sited pieces. The fort also houses The **District Medieval Museum**▶, displaying suits of armour and other objects of the era.

Cabin-cruisers, yachts, glass-bottom boats and excursion cruisers line up side by side in the busy marina. Situated north of Larnaka Fort, it is an important draw for boat-owners in this part of the Mediterranean.

Palm trees and ornamental lamp-posts run the length of the reconstructed **Foinikoudes Promenade►►►**, which follows the seafront south from the marina and makes a fine place for a stroll. The beach is usually busy, although its imported sand is certainly not the stuff of desert island dreams.

Across the way, Larnaka's efforts to improve its facilities are encapsulated in the smart-looking hotels and restaurants that have replaced pubs and tavernas. A bust of the Athenian hero Kimon, who led a fleet to recapture Persian-occupied Kition in 450BC and perished in the failed attempt, stands in a place of honour on the promenade.

MUSEUMS Larnaka owes the outstanding collection of ancient Cypriot objects in the **Pierides Foundation Museum►►** (Odos Zinonos Kitieios, tel: 24817868. *Open* Mon–Thu 9–4, Fri–Sat 9–1. *Admission: moderate*) to the 19th-century scholar and archaeologist Demetrios Pierides, who ensured that many finds were not spirited off the island. Housed in a handsome 19th-century mansion owned by the Pierides Foundation, the collection includes pottery, ornaments, statues and the like, dating from the neolithic period to the classical era. Particularly interesting are the many delicate items of Roman glassware, and a funerary offering from 750BC depicting a lounging nobleman.

Despite being up against some stiff competition from the Pierides Foundation Museum in the Cyprus ancient history stakes, the **Larnaka District Archaeological Museum►** (Odos Kalograion, tel: 24630169. *Open* Mon–Fri 9–2.30 and, except Jul–Aug, Thu 3–5. *Admission :inexpensive*) pulls together a noteworthy legacy from nearby sites such as Kition and Khirokitia (Chorokoitia). There are archaic terracotta figurines, ceramics from virtually all stages of Cyprus's history, jewellery, amulets, seals, bronze implements and weapons, coins, statues and funerary monuments. In the pleasant garden around the museum there is a jumble of pediments, columns and stelae. The only shortcoming is a lack of 'star' exhibits.

The **Tornaritis-Pierides Palaeontology Museum►** (Plateia Evropis, tel: 24628587. *Open* Tue–Fri 9–2, Sat–Sun 9–noon, except Jun–Aug. *Admission free*) is a trip down evolution's memory lane. Housed in the Municipal Cultural Centre, its dinosaur dioramas and other reptilian resources are the kind of culture that children can get to grips with.

The bust of the Athenian hero Kimon on Foinikoudes Promenade

SEASIDE STROLL
The waterfront Foinikoudes Promenade offers the most stylish stroll in Larnaka, running as it does from the marina, past a multitude of café terraces and on to Larnaka Fort. At night it is also one of the liveliest parts of town.

ANCIENT MONUMENTS With all due respect to the 4th-century BC philosopher Zeno, whose birthplace it was, ancient **Kition►** (off Leoforos Archiepiskopou Kyprianou. *Open* Mon–Wed, Fri 9–2.30, Thu 9–2.30 and 3–5 except Jul–Aug. *Admission: inexpensive*) must be a strong contender for the accolade of 'world's most boring archaeological site'. Kition's decline and fall have been almost total, and the few pitiful remnants of this once important Phoenician, Greek and Roman city mostly lie under fast-expanding Larnaka. Kition moved in the fastest circles of its day, with Mycenaeans, Phoenicians and even the Assyrians taking an interest in its progress. An 8th-century BC basalt stela found at the site bears an inscription of the Assyrian King Sargon II.

Thirty three arches remain of the **Kamares Aqueduct►**. Built by the Turks in the 18th century, the aqueduct was in use until as recently as 1939.

BACK TO NATURE The city's **Municipal Park►** is a modestly sized triangle of trees, plants and grass located beside one of the main roads out of town. Larnaka, like other Cypriot cities, is short of parks, making the ones that do exist doubly valuable.

Inside the Municipal Park, the recently established **Natural History Museum►** (tel: 24652569. *Open* Jun–Aug Tue–Sun 10–1 and 4–6; Sep–May Tue–Sun 10–1 and 3–5. *Admission: inexpensive*) offers visitors an interesting collection of dioramas featuring scenes from the natural world in Cyprus, such as the pink flamingos that gather every winter in the salt lakes near Larnaka and Akrotiri.

WHO'D BE A STOIC?
Zeno's philosophy, Stoicism, taught that everything is predetermined and there is no sense in struggling against fate. Emotion should be suppressed; only conscientious pursuit of duty is important. This appealed to Republican-minded senators during the Roman Empire, particularly those who opposed tyrants like Nero. Ironically, Stoicism reached its apogee of influence with the Emperor Marcus Aurelius (reigned AD161–80), a kind of Stoic saint whose reign was marked by barbarian invasion and plague, and whose *Meditations* on his life of duty remain influential to this day.

The elegant facade of the Pierides Foundation Museum

Walk

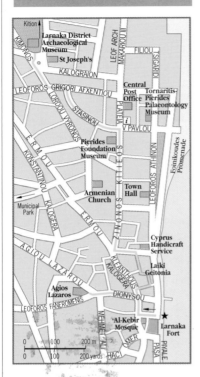

Larnaka city centre

Although not especially attractive or interesting, Larnaka does have several points of interest which are grouped fairly close together; this one-hour walk connects most of these sights, which are covered in more detail on pages 86–89.

From the turrets of **Larnaka Fort**▶▶ look out over Larnaka Bay, the palm tree-lined seafront promenade and the city's beach. Cross Odos Kamil Kenan to the **Al-Kebir Mosque**▶▶, open outside prayer times.

Cross to Odos Dionysou and continue along it through the old Turkish quarter, its narrow streets occupied by workshops and coffee shops which have been taken over by Greek Cypriots. At the end is **Agios Lazaros Church**▶▶.

Return along Odos Dionysou and turn left on to Odos Leanthous Kalogero; to its right lies **Laïki Geitonia**▶, a restored area now given over to shops and cafés.

Follow Odos Zinonos Kitieos to the end for the **Pierides Foundation Museum**▶▶, a mid-19th-century building housing a large collection of historical objects.

Then turn left on to Odos Stasinou, left again on to Leoforos Grigori Afxentiou and then right on to Odos Lordou Vyronos (Lord Byron) Street. Right across the square at the end there is the **Larnaka District Archaeological Museum**▶, where you can see many of the objects that have been excavated in the area.

The Pierides Foundation Museum

90

Few countries have had as many interesting visitors as Cyprus during the past 5,000 years. Just about every empire that ever dipped its toes in the Mediterranean decided it liked the island's many and varied charms so much that it wanted them all to itself.

Mycenaeans, Egyptians, Phoenicians, Persians, Greeks, Romans, Byzantines, Lusignans, Venetians and Turks: The parade has been continuous, and each has left a little piece of itself behind, providing employment for archaeologists for generations to come. One such is Marina Ieronymidou, a Cyprus Department of Antiquities archaeologist responsible for the Byzantine and medieval period. She expects that it will take her whole career to uncover all the secrets of the 16th-century Venetian sugar mill she is excavating at Episkopi. Budgets are painfully tight, allowing her only four weeks of digging each year, and Cyprus's legacy of historic sites is so rich that its handful of full-time archaeologists is drastically overstretched.

Big attraction Archaeology involves much more than 'just' uncovering the tomb of a king or an ancient temple, says Marina, and her work on the sugar mill, part of an estate owned by the last queen of Cyprus, provides valuable insights into the Cypriot economy shortly before the Ottomans took over, and into the lives and working conditions of ordinary Cypriots. Worthy as these goals are, it is still the ancient cities and their temples to pagan gods that attract the tourists: places such as Kourion, Pafos and Amathous in the Greek Cypriot zone, and Salamis in the Turkish Cypriot zone. Both sides have their problems. Projects in the Greek Cypriot zone get reasonable support and international backing, but commercial considerations sometimes take precedence. Some historic sites in the Turkish Cypriot zone have suffered from neglect as well as lack of resources and international backing. Despite all this, Cyprus retains a remarkable heritage, which can be experienced either free or inexpensively for a remarkable voyage of the imagination all the way back to the glory days of Greece, Rome and Byzantium.

GOING UNDER AGAIN
Archaeologists in Cyprus are beginning to think they may have to rebury some of their excavated sites. This is in order to preserve historic treasures from the deterioration that sets in as soon as they are exposed to the elements for what may be the first time in thousands of years.

91

*Mosaic floor (top) at Kourion
The ruins of ancient Kourion (below), overlooking the sea, are among the finest in Cyprus.*

The golden sands and azure waters of Nissi Bay attract multitudes of sunworshippers

TEETHING TROUBLES
Sharks are occasionally seen off the Cypriot coast—this is the Mediterranean, after all—but fortunately these magnificent creatures rarely come inshore. If you are worried about having your toes nibbled while you're swimming in the sea, take heart: There are no reliable reports of sharks being sighted in hotel swimming pools.

► Liopetri   77D2

Villages of the red-earth Kokkinochoria district have a reputation for basket-weaving, with many of the baskets being used for carrying the potatoes which are equally characteristic of the area. Liopetri is one of the main producers of these baskets, and local people can often be seen working on them in the shade. The village's cafés and shops make for a quieter and simpler experience than those of the nearby resorts.

► Makronisos   77D2

A westerly extension of the Nissi Bay tourist area, Makronisos is notable for its headland enclave of Hellenistic and Roman rock-cut tombs in an area otherwise dominated by beach cafés and hotels. Nevertheless, it was these local businesses that funded the excavation of the burial chambers in the late 1980s. Items from the site can be seen at the Cyprus Museum in Nicosia and in the Larnaka District Museum.

► Nissi Bay   77D2

The whole panoply of a modern beach resort is spread along this and the adjacent sandy bays (one of which is actually called Sandy Bay), just west of Agia Napa. Golden sands, turquoise seas, guaranteed sunshine; what more could anyone want? Peace and quiet are not to be expected—except possibly during a midnight swim—in an area where a small square of beach space is worth its weight in golden suntan oil.

► Ormideia   76C2

The village's heyday, such as it was, dates from the 19th century when it was a summer retreat for officials from Larnaka. Nowadays, Ormideia is an averagely interesting village just off the main road from Larnaka to Agia Napa.

► Paralimni   77E2

Once a village, Paralimni has now grown into a small town under the pressure of the nearby tourist resorts. Its **Church of the Panagia (Our Lady)** is impressively built but not otherwise particularly noteworthy. The town seems to be one of those many places where nothing much happens (although it was struck by an earthquake in 1941), yet Paralimni is the source of a rather grotesque delicacy, ambeloboulia; this is a tiny migratory songbird that is (illegally) captured around the town, pickled and then eaten whole by devotees.

On the town's western edge is **Paralimni Lake**, once a proper lake that was drained on account of its malarial mosquitoes. The lake bed still fills with water in winter but dries out to a mud flat in the heat of summer.

►►► Potamos Creek   77D2

This narrow creek, just outside the village of Xylofagou, is the picture-postcard image of a Mediterranean fishing harbour, with blue-painted boats coming and going from the fishing grounds, a jumble of nets on the crazily leaning wooden jetties where they tie up, and swarthy fishermen downing a beer in the harbourside café. Almost everywhere that fishing boats dock in Cyprus, they are virtually squeezed out by tourist craft and

certainly dominated by tourist hotels and tavernas. Potamos is an exception, which is doubly welcome because it occupies such an attractive and surprising location. Near the harbour is the small chapel of **Agios Georgios**, and the rocky coastline in this area makes a pleasant change from the crowded beaches elsewhere.

Paralimni's Church of Our Lady

▶ Protaras   77E2

A no-nonsense beach resort that's popular with families with small children, whose primary assets are sand, sunshine and a sea that is pleasantly warm in summer. Watersports are the main concern of those beachgoers who can be persuaded to raise themselves up from the sand. The nearby resort of **Pernera**▶ adds up to more of the same and the two are connected by the fine sandy beach of **Fig Tree Bay**▶, which is packed wall to wall with sunbathers at peak times.

WAY OF PEACE
The coastal track that runs between the main coast road and the sea from Makronisos to Potamos Creek is little used, since almost all traffic sticks to the main road. This makes the track a surprisingly peaceful place for walking or cycling.

▶▶ Pyla   76C2

Minefields, police posts and a UN watchtower over the village coffee shop tend to detract from the carefully cultivated image that all is well in this village, jammed up against the demarcation line, where Greek and Turkish Cypriots still live together more or less in harmony. For all that Pyla is overlooked by a ridge bristling with military positions, the main business of the village—buying duty-free from the Turkish shops that import their goods from the Turkish Cypriot zone—continues, despite being illegal.

Ready for the morrow: Fishermen's nets at Potamos Creek

The experiment in living together is hopeful, even if disputes between the two communities can sometimes break out over, for example, repairs to the mosque or the placing of Greek emblems outside the coffee shop.

Drive

See map on pages 76–77

Agia Napa to Deryneia

This short route (20km/12.5 miles) begins at one of Cyprus's busiest resort areas, traverses the Kokkinochoria district, and ends at a viewpoint overlooking abandoned hotels in the Turkish Cypriot zone. Allow a full morning or afternoon to stop off for sunbathing and swimming at the small coves that dot the coast. The sights on this drive are covered in more detail on pages 80–97.

The 16th-century **Agia Napa Monastery**►► and its Orthodox church look a little lost surrounded by the brash glitter of Agia Napa, but locals still go there to kiss the icons, light candles and pray.

Head east for the two approaches to **Cape Gkreko**►►►; the first one leads along a rough track to a high cliff with a dramatic view of the cape, festooned with military and civilian radio masts on one side and looking back towards Agia Napa on the other. The second approach, about 200m (650ft) beyond the first, leads to the cape—or as close as you can get (a fence denies access to the point itself). Adjacent rocky inlets are favoured by cabin-cruiser skippers and scuba-divers, while land-bound folks may instead decide to settle for an ice cream from the van that is usually parked on the shore.

Agioi Anargyroi►, a white-washed chapel beside the sea, lies at the end of a rough track from the main road. A

*Chapel (above) near Fig Tree Bay
Basket-weaving (left), Agia Napa*

walkway leads from there to a beach bordering shallow Konnos Bay, less than a kilometre (half a mile) to the north. The beach is probably best reached from a rough and very dusty track just before the Grecian Park Hotel, a little farther along the main road. It consists mostly of sand and is a safe place to swim.

Despite—or perhaps because of—its colourful name, the narrow stretch of sand at **Fig Tree Bay▶** is likely to be packed with sunbathers lying in regimented rows under beach umbrellas. There is no lack of cafés and tavernas for anyone who needs a break or sustenance.

Between Protaras and Pernera, on the left-hand side of the road, up the cliffside, the small church of Profitis Ilias is reached by climbing a stairway.

Pernera▶ is a modern resort, distinguished only by its beach, tiny harbour and seafront tavernas.

At the crossroads where the main road turns left towards Paralimni, a right turn leads to **Agia Trias▶**, a pleasant sandy bay which takes its name from a small shoreside chapel and which has some reasonable seaside tavernas.

Formerly a village, **Paralimni▶** has grown into a substantial town under the twin pressures of nearby tourist development and an influx of refugees from the north during the 1970s. Its inner core retains some character, further enhanced by the stone-built Panagia Church.

From a café—called appropriately Viewpoint Café—on the northeastern edge of **Deryneia▶** and reached by a side-road with signs indicating the way, you can look beyond the Greek Cypriot, UN and Turkish military outposts to the city of Famagusta (Gazimağusa) and its abandoned suburb, the once thriving resort of Varosha (Maraş).

Panagia Church in Paralimni

95

Greek Orthodox monk taking his ease at Agia Ekaterina

▶ Royal Chapel of Agia Ekaterina   76A2

Open: irregularly. Admission inexpensive

In the dry season, the track that leads from the main road near Pyrga to the 'Chapelle Royale' of Agia Ekaterina must be one of the dustiest in Cyprus. The church is notable as much for its isolated location and scenic outlook as for its intrinsic interest and its remains. The latter are undergoing restoration and are likely to appeal mainly to specialists. Built during the Lusignan era, which accounts for its French name and Gothic style, the Royal Chapel's vaulted interior contains some murals, including one of Queen Charlotte of Bourbon.

▶▶ Salt Lake   76B1

Like its cousin on the Akrotiri Peninsula near Limassol, Larnaka Salt Lake is filled with shallow salty water in winter but dries out to leave a hard crystalline crust in the summer. The salt used to be exploited commercially, but growing pollution has brought this to an end. Indeed, when seen from a distance the dried-up lake bed appears a dazzling white; from close up, however, the salt is encrusted with hydrocarbons and dirt. Pink flamingos, presumably unworried by the pollution, are among the birds to winter here, but their number has been declining.

▶ Sotira   77D2

The village name means 'salvation', and certainly there are enough Orthodox churches in and around it almost to guarantee this happy outcome. The best known is the **Church of the Metamorfosis (Transfiguration)**▶, rebuilt in 1533 on an older foundation, and with a finely carved iconostasis and Byzantine eagle emblem. **Agios Mamas** is several centuries older and features some reasonable murals. Just outside the town is the partially restored **Panagia Chordakiotissa**, formerly a Latin monastery. All three sights open irregularly (*Admission free*). The nearby village of Frennaros takes its name from the French for the Friars Minor (Frères Mineurs), Franciscan monks who once occupied it.

▶▶▶ Stavrovouni Monastery   76A1

Open: Apr–Aug daily 8–12 and 3–6; Sep–Mar daily 8–12 and 2–5. Admission free. Women not allowed; dress respectfully

This is one of Cyprus's most emblematic historic places, a monastery perched on a 700m (2,300ft) high peak on the edge of the Troodos Mountains, commanding a spectacu-

SALTY TALE

St. Lazarus, to whom Larnaka's church of Agios Lazaros is dedicated, is also associated with the Salt Lake. Legend tells that Lazarus asked a woman from Larnaka for some of the grapes she was carrying. She replied that there was more chance of the soil yielding salt instead of wine than of her parting with any of her grapes. Lazarus replied, 'Then let it be so; from henceforth the soil shall produce salt, not the fruit of the grape.'

lar view across the Mesaoria (Mesarya) Plain to Nicosia in one direction and to the Mediterranean at Larnaka in the other. Of course, the founders of the 'Mountain of the Cross' monastery in AD327 were not so concerned with the view—unless it was the equally fine view of heaven from such a vantage point.

The mother of Emperor Constantine the Great, the future St. Helena, kept herself busy in Cyprus, between introducing snake-hunting cats (see panel on page 103) and establishing monasteries. At Stavrovouni she apparently did both, bequeathing the new foundation a relic of the True Cross which she had come across on a trip to the Holy Land. Ironically (since the mountain-top was sacred to Aphrodite in ancient times), women can go no further than the visitors' car park.

Stavrovouni has been destroyed and rebuilt so many times through the centuries that only its reputation—and the superb views—are really note-worthy, the 17th-century buildings being best described as 'solid'.

The venerated relic of the True Cross, hanging beside the iconostasis in the monastery church, is lavishly cov-ered in gold leaf and set within a silver-ornamented wooden crucifix.

At the foot of the mountain is the small **Agia Varvara Monastery**, where the monk Kallinikos paints highly prized icons.

▶ Voroklini

76B2

This village north of Larnaka has developed a reputation for its hand-woven baskets, which can be bought in local shops and indeed all over southern Cyprus. The village is one of several in this area that has been forced to grow too rapidly, due to an influx of refugees from the 1974 conflict and some tourist development associated with the nearby coastal resorts along Larnaka Bay.

▶ Xylofagou

77D2

A Venetian watchtower stands in glorious isolation on the shore near here, reached along tracks that traverse an intensely farmed district on the edge of red-soil country. The village itself is quite attractive.

97

Christ Pantokrator at Stavrovouni

CROSS CONNECTION
In 1553 the Englishman John Locke recorded his impressions of climbing Stavrovouni: 'Upon the sayd hill is a certain Crosse, which is, they say, a Holy Crosse. This Crosse in times past did, by their report of the Island, hang in the ayre, but by a certain earthquake, the Crosse and the Chappell it hung in were overthrowen, so that never since it would hang in the ayre.'

The stunning view from Stavrovouni

Moniatis
Saittas
1092m
Vasa
Omodos
Pera Pedi
Koilani
Kouka
Silikou
873m
1210m
Zoopigi
Trimiklini
Agios Mamas
Kalo Chorio
Agios Konstantinos
810m
Odou
Melini
Potamiou
Vouni
Lofou
Silikou
Laneia
Kapileion
Louvaras
Arakapas
Eptagoneia
Akapno
Vik
Pachna
Agios Amvrosios
Monagri
Limnatis
Korfi
1001m
Dierona
Kellaki
Sanida
Gerasa
Apsiou
Prastion
Apaisia
Pano Kivides
Alassa
476m
Spitalli
Palodeia
Fasoulla
Mathikoloni
Akrounta
692m
Germasogeia
Lake
Foinikaria
Parekklisia
Pyrg
Moni
Sotira
Kantou
Germasogeia
Armenochori
Mouttagiaka
Agios Tychon
Sanctuary
of Apollo
Ylatis
Kato Polemidia
A1
Mesa Geitonia
Amathous
Erimi
Kourion
Kolossi
Ypsonas
Episkopi
Kolossi Castle
LIMASSOL
(LEMESOS)
Trachoni
Fassouri
Asomatos
Episkopi Bay
Akrotiri
Salt Lake
Peninsula
Lady's
Mile
Beach
Akrotiri
Bay
Akrotirion
Agios Nikolaos ton Gaton
Akrotiri Airfield
Cape Zevgari
Cape Gata

A   B   C

Varatsinia
Syrgatis
939m ▲
Ora
Kornos
Delikipo
Pyrga
Royal Chapel of
Agia Ekaterina
Agia
Varvara
Stavrovouni
Monastery
A1
Pano Lefkara
Kato Lefkara
Lageia
Vavla
Kato Drys
Agios Minas
Agkleisides
A5
Vasa
Vasilikos
Skarinou
Kofinou
**Khirokitia (Choirokoitia)
Neolithic Village**
Choirokoitia
Anafotida
Alaminno
Asgata
Tochni
Agios Theodoros
Kalavasos
Monagroulli
Psematismenos
Pentakomon
Maroni
Mari
Mesovouni
Maroni
ios Georgios A1
Alamanos
Governor's
Beach
Zygi
Dolos
Point

99

— See Drive pages 118–119
-- · -- British Sovereign base

0 .... 5 .... 10 .... 15 km
0 .... 5 .... 10 miles
D .... E

THE SOUTHWEST

THE SOUTHWEST Southwest Cyprus covers an area based on the port city of Limassol (Lemesos). The region is an important commercial and industrial hub, having developed rapidly as a replacement for Famagusta (Gazimağusa) after the Turkish invasion of 1974.

As is so in much of Cyprus, the sea and the mountains are never far from any point in the southwest. Another defining geographical feature of the area is the great wedge of the Akrotiri Peninsula jutting into the Mediterranean west of Limassol, with its Salt Lake in the middle. Here is one of Britain's two military Sovereign Base Areas in Cyprus, a factor that has saved the peninsula from the unrestrained development characteristic of other coastal regions, at the price of having some of its

The contrast of sleepy villages (far left) backing the busy port of Limassol (below)

▶▶▶ REGION HIGHLIGHTS

The Southwest

NOISE POLLUTION
The fragile atmospherics of ancient sites such as Kourion and the Sanctuary of Apollo Ylatis can easily be shattered by the arrival of a fleet of tour-buses. Not only is noise generated by the influx of people, but the drivers generally leave their engines running to keep the air-conditioning working. This is yet another reason for getting to such places early, before the crowds.

The age-old Cypriot way of life is still to be found in villages like those in the foothills of the Troodos

most scenic stretches placed out of bounds. Although the southwest coastline is the most popular in concentration of numbers of visitors, and many of its businesses are owned by Greek Cypriot refugees from the Turkish Cypriot area, it has had a hard time replacing the 'lost' beaches of Famagusta and Keryneia. Had the replacements been of comparable extent and quality, Limassol and its environs would no doubt have been equally popular in the past.

Some notable stretches aside, much of the coastline is rocky and those beaches that do exist can be busy. A surprising exception is the excellent Lady's Mile Beach on the eastern shore of the Akrotiri Peninsula, but as this looks out on the less than scenic installations of Limassol harbour, and is on the terrirtory of a British military base, its relative emptiness may be understandable.

THE HILLS ARE ALIVE You can't get away from them—all of southwest Cyprus is dominated by the great bulk of the Troodos Mountains looming against the sky. Many people on holiday at the coast are sufficiently tempted by the sight to get up off the beach and head for the hills, yet they usually rush directly from the coast to the peaks, passing through the foothills that lie between in a rush. This is a mistake, for the whole southern edge of the Troodos is filled with sleepy little villages, as far in spirit from the close-packed beaches as it is possible to imagine, even though they may be little more than 10–20km (6–12 miles) distant.

The secret of discovering the best of these villages is to get off the main roads and slow down to idling pace, both mentally and physically. Take time to stop by the wide pools of silvery water lying amid the dry summer landscape, where dams have been established and rod-and-line fishermen take advantage of the trout on offer.

A great swathe of the southern Troodos is given over to vineyards, and with Limassol being the main area for

wine production in Cyprus, traffic can be heavy at harvest time; however, as 'heavy traffic' in much of this area means two lorries on the road at the same time, the hardship is not too great. Cycling and walking are generally easier here than higher up in the mountains, and the wonder is that so few people choose to practise them.

CLASSIC TIMES The southwest has some of Cyprus' finest and most important historical sites. The ancient coastal cities of Amathous and Kourion definitely fall into this category, especially the latter, with its dramatic clifftop location and romantic Greek theatre built into the side of a steep slope. Near Kourion are the remains of the Sanctuary of Apollo Ylatis, the woodland god. It seems a fortunate privilege that so much of this once sacred place remains for the modern visitor to appreciate.

The region thus encompasses all of Cyprus' virtues: the sea, mountains, village life and history; it even has a city for those who cannot do without the urban touch.

Graeco-Roman remnant of Kourion, bathed in romantic Mediterranean light

IMPERIAL BOOST
Limassol developed at the expense of nearby Amathous partly because a Roman emperor gave his name to a new port built on an earlier settlement called Lemesos. At the end of the fourth century, Theodosius the Great, the last to rule over a united empire, named the settlement Theodosias. This act more or less guaranteed the town's prosperity, and in the 20th century Limassol went back to the future and reacquired its earlier name of Lemesos.

GETTING THE MESSAGE
During the period of British rule, so the story goes, the *muktar* (headman) of Agios Tychon village near Limassol had been pressing the authorities to build a bridge over a nearby stream, but to no avail. Then the district officer arrived on an official visit and, while he was crossing the stream where the bridge was needed, his horse slipped, pitching him headlong into the water. A bridge was soon forthcoming.

FOSSIL BONES

Discovered in 1961 by David Nixon, the schoolboy son of a Royal Air Force serviceman from the Akrotiri air base, the late Pleistocene sea-cliff site of Akrotiri Aetokremnos has been controversial ever since. Bones of the extinct Cypriot pygmy hippopotamus (*Phanourious minutus*) and pygmy elephant (*Elephas cypriotes*) were found among stone implements and other indications of human occupation. Radiocarbon measurements date the bones to around 9000BC, 2,000 years earlier than the previously accepted earliest date for human habitation on Cyprus.

102

Descendants of snake-fighting cats bask in the glow of victory at Agios Nikolaos ton Gaton Monastery

▶ Agios Amvrosios · · · · · · · · · · · · 98A3

This is an attractive village in the heart of Cypriot wine country, best known for the organic wine produced here from grapes grown without chemicals or pesticides. The finished product is likewise free of artificial flavouring or colouring (see pages 152–53).

▶ Agios Georgios Alamanos Convent · · · 99D2

Open: daily. Admission free
Standing at the coast midway beween Amathous and Governor's Beach, this convent is a tranquil place, an attractive and bright modern construction founded on an original 12th-century cloister. Icons and honey, both produced by the resident nuns, can be purchased here. A nearby trail leads to the sea at the Agios Georgios Café, a simple eatery with a campsite beside the rocky coast.

▶ Agios Minas Convent · · · · · · · · · · · 99D3

Open: Mon–Fri for group visits only; May–Sep closed 12–3; Apr–Oct closed 12–2. Admission free, donation welcome
Lying in a peaceful valley between Vavla and Kato Drys, this 15th-century convent is dedicated to St. Menas the Glorious, a third-century Egyptian martyr. The nuns of this immaculately maintained convent, a tranquil religious retreat (except when it is visited by a tourist bus) make and sell icons and honey noted for their quality.

▶▶ Agios Nikolaos ton Gaton Monastery · · 98B1

Open: daily. Admission free
'St. Nicholas of the Cats' owes its fame as much to the felines of its title as to the sainted Nicholas. The cats referred to are those reputedly introduced to Cyprus by St. Helena, mother of the Roman Emperor Constantine the Great, to rid the island of poisonous reptiles (see panel). There are still plenty of cats at Agios Nikolaos, which was indeed founded during Constantine's reign (AD324–37), although the present structure represents the partially, but quite handsomely, restored remnants of a 13th-century abbey abandoned to the invading Turks in 1570.

Today the religious peace is subject to disturbance from military jets operating from the nearby British air base.

▶▶▶ Akrotiri Peninsula · · · 98B1

The Akrotiri Peninsula, a thick wedge of land jutting into the Mediterranean just west of Limassol, is occupied almost entirely by one of the two British Sovereign Base Areas in Cyprus. Although most of the peninsula is freely accessible, the military installations around Akrotiri Air

Base at its tip, including the promontories at Cape Zevgari and Cape Gata, are closed to the public. See also Agios Nikolaos ton Gaton Monastery, page 102; Episkopi, page 104; Fasouri Plantations, page 105; Kolossi Castle, page 108; Lady's Mile Beach, page 111; and Salt Lake, page 116.

▶▶▶ Amathous

98C2

Open: Apr–May and Sep daily 9–6; Jun–Aug 9–7.30;
Nov–Mar 9–5. Admission: inexpensive

The ancient city of Amathous is the subject of intermittent excavation, with archaeologists uncovering harbour remains from the Phoenician period and elements of the later Graeco-Roman city. Occupied from around 1000BC, Amathous chose to stick by the Persians during the Greek revolt 500 years later, but sided with the Greeks when Alexander the Great came on the scene. Despite being small, the site (overlooking the sea 6km/4 miles east of Limassol) is atmospheric yet suffers from an absence of information, beyond the simple label 'Agora' (market place), to add to visitors' understanding of its significance.

In addition to the market-place—an open area of white stone surrounded by the vestiges of colonnaded porticoes—there are indications of an early Christian basilica, baths, and, on the hill rising to the east, the acropolis and parts of the defensive walls. There were temples to Hercules, Adonis and Aphrodite.

Much archaeological work remains to be done on what was an important city-state; although it declined in influence under the Romans and Byzantines, the former used it as a district capital. In the late sixth century Amathous was the birthplace of St John the Almsgiver, later patron saint of the Knights Hospitaller.

Little remained of the city's glory by the time King Richard I of England, the 'Lionheart', landed near here in 1191 on his way to the crusades, and its stones were later used as a convenient quarry for buildings in Limassol, as well as for more distant projects such as the Suez Canal.

ÉLITE FIGHTERS
There are frequent historical references to Cyprus being overrun with poisonous snakes. Snake-fighting cats were bred at several locations, including Agios Nikolaos ton Gaton. If the small numbers of remaining poisonous vipers are anything to go by, the feline special forces were victorious, so no one should blame the cats of today for their self-satisfied airs.

103

Complex spiral patterns can be seen on some of the ruined columns at ancient Amathous

The Southwest

▶ **Arakapas**   98C3

This averagely pretty hill village, with an attractive open square, is most notable for the small 16th-century church of **Panagia Iamatiki** adjacent to a modern church of the same name with a baroque bell-tower. The latter has taken over the duties of Our Lady the Healer, and miraculous cures are attributed to her intercession, a tradition the village celebrates with a festival each September.

▶▶▶ **Episkopi**   98A2

There are really two Episkopis. The original one, now little more than a village, was settled by refugees escaping from nearby Kourion (ancient Curium) in the 7th century AD and grew to importance as the seat of an archbishopric. The other is 'settled' by personnel and their families from the British Sovereign Base Area's Episkopi Barracks, located a short distance to the west of the old village.

Episkopi Barracks is a little piece of Britain set down beneath the warm sun next to the blue Mediterranean, and is more like an English garden suburb, with typically British street names. The old coast road from Limassol to Pafos runs through here, and generally the only formality is to stick to the speed limit when passing the police checkpoints at either end of the base.

Housed over the foundations of a building devastated in the earthquake of AD365, **Kourion Archaeological Museum**▶▶▶ (tel: 25232453 *Open* Mon–Fri 9–2.30; Thu (except Aug) 3–5. *Admission: inexpensive*) is an excellent collection of discoveries from excavations on the site of Kourion and the nearby Sanctuary of Apollo Hylates. There are pottery, oil-lamps, coins, ornaments, *amphorae*, sculptures and little votive figurines.

Most poignant of all is a group of three skeletons huddled against the sudden blow delivered by nature to their city and lives: A young man tries vainly to shelter a woman, who is surely his wife, while she in turn attempts to protect an 18-month-old child. They all died together when the earthquake's powerful tremors demolished Kourion.

Water captured from winter streams fills Germasogeia Lake

Fishermen mending their nets on the black sands of Governor's Beach

105

▶ Fasouri Plantations   98A1

Citrus groves form a dense forest around Fasouri village just to the west of Limassol, at the base of Akrotiri Peninsula. The company operating the plantations offers guided tours, but it may be enough simply to drive or cycle around the orchards on leafy roads shaded from the sun by overhanging cypress trees, breathing in the scent of oranges, lemons and limes. Walking tends to be less pleasant because traffic moves fast on roads that are narrow and have no proper pavements.

▶ Foinikaria   98C2

The small village of Foinikaria, tucked away in the hills northeast of Limassol, is a pleasant enough place for taking a quiet coffee break in the shade, but its main attraction is the nearby shimmering **Germasogeia Lake▶**. Fishing for trout and other species is permitted in the lake, which is fed by springtime surges in the Germasogeia river. A permit is necessary and may be obtained from the Cyprus Fisheries Department's district office at Limassol (near the old harbour entrance; tel: 25305470).

▶▶ Governor's Beach (Akti Kyvernitou)   99D2

This fine, and popular, stretch of sand at the end of a rough track, east of Limassol, has only one potential drawback: The sand is almost black and soaks up vast quantities of solar heat, releasing it into the soles of unsuspecting barefoot sunworshippers.

▶ Kalavasos   99D2

A pretty enough but otherwise unremarkable hill village, Kalavasos features a narrow-gauge train, comprising engine and freight cars, parked on a bridge over the Vasilikos River. Used up to the 1960s to serve iron and gypsum mines, the train is now derelict, although it is surrounded by a tracery of fairy lights. Mining history around Kalavasos reaches back almost 4,000 years to when copper was first extracted here. South of the village, the neolithic cemetery of **Kalavasos-Tenta** (*Open* Mon–Fri 9–4. *Admission: inexpensive*) is evidence of one of the earliest known permanent sites of human habitation on Cyprus.

ARCHAEOLOGIST'S DREAM
The rough countryside of the Vasilikos river valley around Kalavasos is an archaeologist's dream, or nightmare, with Cypriot and international teams facing a mountain of excavation work in several hundred identified sites dating from as far back as 6500BC.

Cyprus has seen military bases come and go from its earliest days. Where once there were Greek and Roman triremes, then Venetian and Turkish galleys, today there are Royal Air Force jet-fighters. The two British bases on the island fulfil much the same role as their predecessors, projecting military power into an area still considered vital to Western interests.

SUNSHINE SOLDIERING
Although the base authorities are reluctant to admit it openly, perhaps fearing that the taxpayers will take a dim view of it, most British service personnel in Cyprus seem delighted to be there. They may have to work hard but they can play in the sun, which is more than can be guaranteed at bases in Britain and Germany.

106

A squadron of Royal Air Force Tornado bombers, a dozen jets returning from a live-fire exercise somewhere over the Mediterranean, shatters the calm of early morning above the Akrotiri Peninsula. Amidst a deafening concussion of noise they touch down out of sight at the airfield beyond the security fence. The scene is both routine and familiar at Akrotiri, one of Britain's two Sovereign Base Areas (SBAs) in Cyprus (the other is at Dhekelia, east of Larnaka—see pages 82 and 102).

Britain's role dates back to the end of its colonial era in Cyprus in 1960, when it bowed to the violently expressed will of the Greek Cypriot people and gave up its domination of the island. In agreement with the new government of independent Cyprus, however, Britain retained two bases as important staging posts and as convenient 'watchtowers' for keeping an eye on the former Soviet Union and the unstable, oil-rich lands of the Middle East. They have been employed in this role during the Gulf Wars of 1991 and 2003 and to support the subsequent military operations in Iraq.

The bases are called Sovereign Base Areas because they remain British territory and are not part of the Republic of Cyprus. Her Majesty's Government does not own most of the land on the SBAs—some 57 percent of their total area of 250sq km (100sq miles) is privately owned by Cypriots,

British military radar installation at the summit of Mount Olympos

and SBA law is closely aligned with Republic of Cyprus law. The bases' irregular boundaries are accounted for by the need to exclude civil centres of population as far as possible.

OUT OF BOUNDS The only contact most visitors are likely to have with the SBAs is when they pass through on the public highways that traverse them and an occasional spot-check of traffic by police officers or base security personnel. A more annoying side-effect of their presence is that some interesting areas, located in or near military installations, are out of bounds to the public. These include the tips of the Akrotiri Peninsula and Cape Gkreko, as well as the summit of Mount Olympos, the highest mountain in the Troodos range, which is crowned by the geodesic dome of a military radar.

Some compensation for these restrictions is that only small-scale commercial activity is allowed in the SBAs, a ruling that has undoubtedly helped preserve the natural environment from destruction at the hands of developers who would otherwise have filled it up with hotels and apartments. Archaeological sites on base territory, of which there are many including the ancient city of Kourion and the sanctuary of Apollo Ylatis, remain the responsibility of the Cyprus Department of Antiquities.

LIVING STANDARDS Inside the living quarters of the bases, with their street names reminiscent of an English suburb, life goes on as normal for the 4,000 service personnel and their families. They have their own houses, shops, churches, banks and hospitals, as well as sporting facilities such as cricket fields and polo pitches. When off duty, the troops take advantage of the many sea and mountain sports that Cyprus offers all of its residents.

The SBAs represent an important asset to the island's economy, from direct and indirect expenditures as well as through offering employment, but many Cypriots are unhappy about their existence, and a vociferous minority engages in sometimes violent demonstrations against them.

It is logical to wonder how long Britain will want to retain these military bases. The answer probably lies in how long Cyprus continues to be a convenient stepping-stone to an area considered vital to Western interests. A casual glance back through the pages of history suggests the stay could be a long one.

LIQUID ELEMENT
In Cyprus, where water is a scarce commodity and its misuse is frowned upon, travellers passing through the British barracks at Episkopi may be outraged to note the lush green of a well-irrigated cricket field and other sports grounds in what is called Happy Valley. Aware of this, the base authorities are at pains to point out that the occupants provide the irrigation themselves, so to speak, by reusing water from the base's sewerage system.

107

Going shopping in a little slice of Britain at the Dhekelia base

Remains of Stone Age houses at Khirokitia Neolithic Village

▶▶▶ Khirokitia (Choirokoitia) Neolithic Village   99D2

Tel: 24322710. Open: Jun–Aug Mon–Fri 9–7.30; Apr–May and Sep–Oct daily 9–6; Nov–Mar daily 9–5.
Admission: moderate

The historic site of Khirokitia Neolithic Village (dating from around 5800 to 5500BC) is next to the modern village of Choirokoitia in the foothills of the Troodos Mountains. Khirokitia's round, stone-built dwellings, heaped in close profusion, climb the slopes of a steep promontory around which curls a loop of the Maroni River. The geography provided isolation and protection for the agricultural community here; the complex construction of the huts indicates that a high degree of social organization existed.

Excavations revealed that the people of this aceramic (literally 'lacking pottery') culture buried their dead under their cramped huts. High infant mortality and a lifespan of between 25 and 40 years ensured that there was no shortage of occupants for this village of the dead. For the living, however, life is thought not to have been too bad: The conditions for farming, livestock and hunting were favourable, while warfare seems not to have been a problem. The nearby village of Choirokoitia was the scene of a battle in 1426 in which Egyptian Mamelukes defeated the Cypriot forces of the Lusignan kings.

▶▶▶ Kolossi Castle   98A2

Tel: 25934907. Open: Jun–Aug daily 9–7.30; Apr–May, Sep–Oct daily 9–6; Nov–Mar daily 9–5. Admission: inexpensive

A romantic castle in bright stone, with a fine view over surrounding orchards from its turreted battlements,

Kolossi was a place of refuge for crusader knights fleeing from their latest abortive mission to the Holy Land. An original structure on the site was granted to the Knights Hospitaller (the Order of the Hospital of St. John of Jerusalem), or the Knights of St. John, who located their Commandery here after being driven definitively from Palestine in 1291. The Hospitallers engaged in a tug-of-war over the Castle with the equally footloose Knights Templar, the dispute being resolved, to the Hospitallers' satisfaction at any rate, when their rivals were proscribed by papal decree in 1312. The present structure was built by the French Grand Commander of the Hospitallers, Louis de Magnac, around 1454.

Kolossi's romantic ruins make it easy to imagine crusader knights striding around in flowing capes emblazoned with the Holy Cross. Its stout walls must have given its defenders confidence to make fun of Genoese and Mameluke besiegers, discounting the unlikely chance of their breaking in. The Hospitallers concentrated mostly on peaceful pursuits, accepting the bounty of their wheatfields, cottonfields, sugar-cane plantations and vineyards. The latter are recalled in Commandaria, a sweet red dessert wine.

In addition to the central keep, there are the remains of a basilica, sugar-cane factory and aqueduct. The fleur-de-lis symbol can be seen carved on walls and fireplaces, and the entrance hall has a medieval mural of the Crucifixion, damaged by time and 20th-century vandals.

Crusaders found life at Kolossi Castle easier than fighting in the Holy Land

109

► Kornos   99E3

Although noted for its production of ceramics, and especially the large traditional Cypriot pots called *pitharia,* which are shaped by hand rather than being turned on a wheel, little evidence of this activity is to be seen by the casual visitor. The village is otherwise unremarkable and scarcely worth diverting for.

►►► Kourion   98A2

Open: Jun–Aug daily 8–7.30; Apr–May, Sep–Oct daily 8–6; Nov–Mar daily 8–5. Admission: moderate

Architects of the ancient world had an advantage over their modern counterparts when it came to designing cities: the best locations were all freely available. Kourion's builders made full use of this and the ruined city occupies a stunning clifftop setting overlooking the Mediterranean west of Limassol.

HISTORY According to Herodotus, Kourion was founded in the 14th century BC by Greek colonists and became an important city-state. The 12th-century BC Egyptian pharaoh Ramses III wanted Kourion to come under his dominion, and its kings later paid homage to Assyria.

The Romans brought Kourion (Curium in Latin) to the peak of its prosperity and, as with the rest of Cyprus, it soon embraced Christianity. An early bishop, Philoneides, was martyred during persecutions by Emperor Diocletian at the end of the third century AD. Kourion was shattered by the earthquake of 365 and, although rebuilt, was abandoned following Arab raids during the seventh century.

SOLE MATES
The remains of a neolithic settlement contemporaneous with that at Khirokitia has been found at Kastros, at the very tip of the Karpasia (Karpaz) Peninsula in the Turkish Cypriot zone.

TURNCOAT CITY
Kourion played a pivotal, if shameful, part in the Greek revolt against Persia in 498BC. In his *Histories,* Herodotus wrote that its king, Stasenor, changed sides, abandoning the Greek cause and helping to deliver Cyprus into Persian hands.

The last rays of the sun illuminate the stone benches of Kourion's theatre

SIGHTS The ruins of Kourion that can be seen today are dealt with in order from east to west. For the adjacent Sanctuary of Apollo Hylates, see page 116.

'Enter for the good luck of the house' was the inscription that welcomed visitors to the imposing patrician dwelling known as the **House of Eustolios**▶▶. It takes its name from one Eustolios, praised in an inscription dating from the end of the fourth century AD for not leaving his fellow citizens in 'abject misery', but who donated his baths and an annexe of the house for the relief of the earthquake-stricken city. The Christian nature of the house is attested by another inscription, referring to the 'venerated signs of Christ', and a mosaic of a young woman with the Greek legend KTICIC, symbolizing the Creation.

Built into the side of a steep gully overlooking the sea, the **Theatre**▶▶▶ must have presented its audiences with a dilemma: to concentrate on the show or on the magnificent view, a difficulty that continues to this day now it again puts on theatre, dance and music performances (see panel). Originally built during the Hellenistic era for presenting Greek plays, the theatre was transformed into an arena by the Romans to satisfy their passion for bloodletting as a spectator sport, before being restored to theatrical use in the Christian era. At its best when the late afternoon sun showers its white stones with rosy light, the theatre is a spectacle in itself, conjuring up the ancient world by the sheer drama of its setting.

The 5th-century **Early Christian Basilica**▶▶▶ complex includes on its clifftop site the main church, a chapel, sacristies, annexes and the bishop's palace, testifying to the power of the Christian Church less than a century after it had become the official religion of the Roman Empire. Bishop Zeno, who represented the Cypriots at the Council of Ephesus in AD431, is thought to have been responsible for the basilica's construction.

The **Roman Forum**▶▶ is the subject of continuing excavation, with numerous constructions coming to light, including medieval lime-kilns. In this jumble of stone behind the basilica are a Hellenistic-era water reservoir, a Roman nymphaeum (which seems to have been Kourion's main water distribution centre) and other public and private structures.

The **Achilles Mosaic**▶▶ is a damaged mosaic in a second-century AD public building near the main road.

The mosaic depicts the dramatic moment when Odysseus unmasks Achilles—who had been disguised as a girl by his mother to prevent him going to the Trojan War—by producing a sword and shield which Achilles cannot resist grasping. Near by is the **House of the Gladiators►►**, a large private dwelling undoubtedly owned by a wealthy patrician. The house takes its name from the mosaics depicting gladiators in combat found there.

Located 3km (2 miles) west of the main excavation site, the elongated **Stadium►** (*Open* permanently. *Admission free*) was an arena for track and field events, with an estimated capacity of 6,000 spectators. Little remains of the stadium apart from the lower courses of its exterior wall.

►► Lady's Mile Beach   98B1

This fairly good stretch of beach not far from Limassol, just outside the closed area of the Royal Air Force base at Akrotiri, was named for the place where the colonel's wife's horse was walked during the balmy days of the British Empire. Generally all but deserted, the beach is supposed to be popular with service personnel from the base, and some of its cafés will serve you only if you are, or at least look like, one of the troops. Frequent strong winds in this area make it an excellent place for windsurfing, but the view across to the cranes of Limassol harbour can hardly be described as scenic.

►►► Lefkara   99D3

There are two Lefkaras, about 1km (0.5 miles) apart, thanks to the common Cyprus practice of having a 'Pano' (Upper) version of a village and a 'Kato' (Lower) one.

Lace is the attraction here, the traditional local style called *lefkaritika* (see page 113). This cannot be described as a pattern as such because no designs are ever repeated, each being a unique creation of one of the village women who sit outdoors in the shade painstakingly stitching the intricate work, usually backing them on to pieces of Irish linen. Silverware and *loukoumia* (Turkish, or Cypriot, delight) are the other specialties of the two villages.

Kato Lefkara is a particularly attractive mountain village, with pastel-painted houses giving a picture of idyllic charm. Although it clearly thrives on its lace sales the approach is low key, making a stroll around the village a pleasant experience. Pano Lefkara has much more of a tourist infrastructure in the way of shops, tavernas and parking places, so inevitably it gets thronged at peak periods. The manufacture of *lefkaritika* has spilled over into the neighbouring village of Kato Drys (the birthplace of the 12th-centruy Cypriot St. Neofytos), where the houses are being handsomely restored.

111

Kourion's ruins (left) crown the top of a cliff overlooking the sea

Above: Petra tou Romiou, better known as the Rock of Aphrodite

Boat trip

Limassol to Aphrodite's Rock

This trip can be taken either on one of the excursion boats that leave from Limassol harbour, or by renting a boat at the harbour, with or without a crew. The time spent depends principally on the kind of boat you have, but it is as well to allocate a whole day.

Leaving Limassol's busy Old Harbour, you pass the even busier commercial port, the principal maritime gateway to Cyprus, with a constant procession of cargo ships coming and going. From there you run alongside the sandy stretch of **Lady's Mile Beach**►► on the eastern flank of **Akrotiri Peninsula**►►►, with the **Salt Lake**►►► visible behind. Not much

can be seen of the military facilities at the Akrotiri air base behind its screen of dunes and vegetation—presumably this is how the Royal Air Force likes it—but you may see Tornado or Harrier jets heading out for live-fire exercises. Rounding Cape Gata, then Cape Zevgari, you sail along the western arm of Akrotiri Peninsula. Keeping close inshore guarantees a spectacular view of the cliffside at **Kourion**►►► where the ruins of the Graeco-Roman city bask in the sun (see pages 109–111).

Pissouri Bay►► makes a fine place to come close inshore and perhaps moor to enjoy the sandy beach.

The best way to approach **Petra tou Romiou**►►►, otherwise and more famously known as the Rock of Aphrodite (see page 177), is from the sea. This was the same route the goddess herself took when she was born in the foam and borne ashore by the gentle west wind. More mundanely, with only stony beaches in the area, it is generally a reasonably quiet destination, however you approach it.

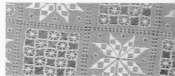

Making lace by hand in the twin villages of Pano Lefkara and Kato Lefkara is a generation game, mothers passing on their skills to their daughters. Lefkara lace is sought after by royalty and by the many humbler visitors who come here.

The women sit outdoors in the shade, chatting, while their fingers move nimbly and with painstaking care over pieces of linen. Their needles seem to have a life of their own as they pull the thin strands of mercerized cotton. Delicate patterns—naturalistic or abstract—slowly take shape. These exist only in the mind of their creator, and might never again be repeated. 'How long will it take to make?' a visitor asks a woman working on a particularly intricate piece. 'A year,' she replies.

Lace has been made in Lefkara for centuries, even before the village became a retreat for wealthy Venetians seeking relief from the heat of summer. The Venetian women brought embroidery with them and worked on it while the village women worked on theirs. The legacy of these two embroidery traditions is now in demand the world over.

MILANESE PIECES
Leonardo da Vinci is said to have visited Lefkara in 1481 to obtain lace hangings for Milan Cathedral. No evidence exists to substantiate this claim. Leonardo might never have been to Lefkara, but he should have!

113

Man's work The men were no doubt quite content that their womenfolk were gainfully employed. As time passed, the gain from this employment exceeded that from the men's farms, and Lefkaran men became sales representatives for the graceful products made by their wives, mothers, sisters and daughters, travelling abroad with samples while the women remained at home stitching.

Generation game The tradition of mothers passing on their skill to their daughters has been partially disrupted by modern social and employment trends. Visitors to Lefkara can, however, still watch several generations of the same family working through their repertoire of stitches: buttonhole stitch, stem stitch, back stitch, satin stitch and so on. Watch the patterns unfold from the needle points: geometric motifs and a characteristic zigzag called 'the river'. Natural patterns are also employed—butterflies and flowers are popular.

A Lefkaran woman practising the painstaking art of making lace

114

Limassol's 13th-century castle was later strengthened by the Venetians

▶▶ Limassol (Lemesos) 98B2

Although the largest and most popular tourist centre in Cyprus, as well as its key industrial and commercial hub (thanks mainly to its excellent port facilities), it takes quite a stretch of imagination to describe this city of 165,000 as 'attractive', even if it does consider itself to be the 'Paris of Cyprus'. Yet Limassol has its points of interest as well as being a good base for exploring the southern coast and the Troodos Mountains. In addition, the city has an active and occasionally sophisticated nightlife scene, which is an important contributory factor to Limassol's popularity.

OLD TOWN SIGHTS Occupying a commanding position near the Old Harbour, **Limassol Castle▶▶** (tel: 25305419. *Open* Mon–Sat 9–5, Sun 10–1. *Admission: moderate*), which dates to the Lusignan era in the 13th century, with later modifications by the Venetians, Turks and British, provides present-day visitors with an excellent viewpoint from its battlements. Its main claim to fame now, however, is that it houses the **Cyprus Medieval Museum▶** in a series of Gothic-arched halls deep in its interior. The museum complements this gloomily atmospheric setting with exhibits that consist mainly of funerary monuments.

The higgledy-piggledy houses of the former Turkish Quarter are all clustered around Limassol Castle, making it an excellent district in which to wander.

The quietly distinguished little Orthodox church of **Agios Antonios▶** is in this part of the city. Also notable is the adjacent **Cami Kebir** mosque. In this area is a modern multimedia attraction, the

Time Elevator (*Open* May–Oct Mon–Thu 9.15–8.30, Fri–Sun 9.15–9.15; Nov–Apr daily 9.15–7.45; shows every 30 minutes. *Admission: expensive*) which takes you on a virtual tour of Cyprus's history and is housed in an early 1900s carob mill.

A fairly sleepy corner compared with the frenetic activity of the modern commercial port, the **Old Harbour** retains elements of colour in the many fishing boats tied up gunwale to gunwale. Private yachts and cruisers are also moored here, and this is the starting-point for cruise excursions up and down the coast. The seafront promenade starts from near the harbour and makes for a pleasant, shaded stroll beside the Mediterranean.

TO THE NORTH Heading north from the Old Town along Agiou Andreou Street will take you to the **Folk Art Museum▶** (253 Odos Agiou Andreou, tel: 25362303. *Open* Jun–Sep Mon–Wed and Fri 8.30–1.30 and 4–6.30, Thu 8.30–1.30; Oct–May Mon–Wed and Fri 8.30–1.30 and 3–5.30, Thu 8.30–1.30. *Admission: inexpensive*), housed in a fine 19th-century mansion. The museum displays an interesting and varied collection of typical objects, ornaments and costumes of everyday use in Cyprus during the more recent past, as well as wedding dresses which point to the importance of these special occasions.

Lounging around on the beach is a popular way of life at Limassol

Continuing along this street and then turning right on to Odos Tornariti will take you to the **Municipal Gardens▶**. Although not especially big, the gardens represent a welcome patch of greenery and shade, being almost unique in Limassol in this respect. They contain the Municipal Open Air Theatre and the increasingly straggly looking Municipal Zoo. The Limassol Wine Festival takes place in the park during September and is a great open-air party, with free wine flowing and throngs of people taking full advantage of the opportunity.

Limassol Zoo, inside the shaded oasis of the Municipal Gardens

To the north of the Municipal Gardens is the **Limassol District Archaeological Museum▶** (corner of Odo Kanningos and Odos Vyronos, tel: 25305157. *Open* Mon–Fri 10–5, Sat 10–1. *Admission: inexpensive*). The museum is well placed for sources of exhibits—Amàthous and Kourion both lie near Limassol—and its extensive collection of ceramics and pottery dating from Mycenaean to Roman times is well worth a visit. Highlights are a bust of Aphrodite and statues of Egyptian and Phoenician gods.

TO THE SOUTH Since 1974, Limassol has developed as the island's premier port, growing to keep pace with the economy's rapid development. All the activity of a major port can be seen to the south of town towards Lady's Mile Beach, with merchant ships coming and going constantly.

EVERGREEN PLEASURE
Greenery is conspicuous by its near absence in Limassol, so if you want to take advantage of what little there is, combine it in a short stroll. Walk through the Municipal Gardens to the seafront, and then continue south along the palm tree-shaded promenade.

In summer, the Salt Lake dries out to a hard crystalline sheen before filling up when the rains come again

Partially restored column and pediment from the temple which dominates the Sanctuary of Apollo Ylatis

▶▶▶ Salt Lake   98B1

For half the year this is more salt-flat than salt lake, but come November rains the shallow basin fills, attracting the first of many migratory birds, including pink flamingos. Feeding on small crustaceans in the salty water, the birds present quite a spectacle—a pink splurge of motion in the middle of the lake (see panel opposite). During the dry season, the glittering salt-flat in the heart of Akrotiri Peninsula makes for a fine cross-country run if you have a four-wheel-drive or dirt-bike. The Salt Lake is just outside the closed area of the British base. As with the lake near Larnaka, the salt is no longer fit for human consumption and the number of flamingos has been declining.

▶▶▶ Sanctuary of Apollo Ylatis   98A2

Tel: 25997049. Open: Jun–Aug daily 9–7.30; Apr–May, Sep–Oct daily 9–6; Nov–Mar daily 9–5. Admission: moderate

Strabo, a Greek geographer writing early in the first century AD, referred to a promontory near Kourion 'from which they hurl those who have touched the altar of Apollo'. Fragments of the altar are strewn in a pile of rubble at the heart of the sanctuary, 3km (2 miles) west of the main Kourion site (see pages 109–11). This was one of the classical world's most sacred places. Broken walls mark the house of the priest of Apollo. The temple's roof has vanished into the Mediterranean sky; yet the wonder is how much remains.

Apollo's sanctuary, in continuous use from the seventh century BC until the end of the fourth century AD, when classical pagan cults were abolished in favour of Christianity, has completed its journey through the centuries in a remarkable state of preservation. Originally there were two entrances, the Kourion Gate and the Pafos Gate, with the modern entrance lying between them. The dormitories and display halls can clearly be identified, as can a *palaestra* (gymnasium), a baths complex, the remains of the priest's house, and the strongroom which held the temple treasury.

The heart of the sanctuary consists of some remarkable monuments: the archaic *temenos*, or precinct of the god; the Temple of Apollo, partially restored and reached by the long, narrow Sacred Way; and votive pits into which were thrown masses of surplus offerings, many of which can be seen in the island's museums. One monument is unique in the Mediterranean: a circular area of rock pitted with holes that archaeologists speculate was the scene of ritual dances around a cluster of trees and bushes sacred to Apollo.

SHOCKING PINK
Most European flamingos migrate to Africa for the winter, and sizeable flocks regularly stop over on Cyprus at the salt lakes near Akrotiri and Larnaka; they are eagerly awaited by both serious birders and casual observers. The shallow brine lakes are among the most important feeding areas in the eastern Mediterranean for this bird, which filters minute organisms from the water with its bill—the pink colouring comes from the prawns the flamingos consume. Other species that can be seen at the lake at various times between October and April include the black-winged stilt, dunlin, ruff, little stint, marsh sandpiper, little egret, grey heron and little-ringed plover.

117

At the end of the Sacred Way, the Temple of Apollo retains the romance of antiquity

DOWN THE PIT
Pilgrims came from all over the Mediterranean to the famed Sanctuary of Apollo Ylatis at Kourion, particularly during the Roman Empire. They left so many votive offerings at its altars that the priests were forced constantly to clear them out to make space for new ones. This they did by depositing less valuable items in a specially dug pit on the sanctuary grounds. Archaeologists have since been recovering thousands of these, most of them small terracotta figurines representing people and animals. A selection can be seen at archaeology museums in Nicosia, Limassol, Pafos and Episkopi.

▶ **Zygi**   99D2
This little coastal village between Limassol and Larnaka has developed a reputation as a seafood centre, popular with visitors and Cypriots alike, with many of its fish restaurants lined up along the shore and on the main street. Unlike many such places in Cyprus, the seafood here is mostly fresh rather than frozen. At some tavernas, such as Apovathra, you choose your own fish and eat it right beside the water, although the nearby electricity plant and concrete factory may put you off.

Agios Minas Convent

Drive

See map on pages 98–99

Limassol to Lefkara

This 50km (31 mile) route begins at the coast and winds into the foothills of the Troodos Mountains. Passing through some attractive villages on the way, the drive route terminates at one (or rather two) of Cyprus's most interesting villages. The sights on this drive are covered in more detail on pages 103–117.

Limassol's major attraction, from the point of view of this drive, is that it is fairly easy to escape from towards the east. The quickest route out of town is via the A1 motorway, but the B1 coast road is more attractive: In the long term its sea view seems certain to be sacrificed to a sea-wall of hotels.

Loukoumia *(above)*, or *Turkish delight,
from Lefkara
The church and village of Pano Lefkara
(below)*

The ruined ancient city of **Amathous►►►** lies alongside the coast road just beyond the sprawl of Limassol's beach-hotel district. Its air of rather forlorn majesty and the on-going excavation of its Phoenician harbour and Greek acropolis make for a fascinating stroll through history.

Beyond the undistinguished village of Parekklisia the road climbs steadily, opening up a superb view over terraced hillsides to the distant Mediterranean. Some of the rocky landscape has been partially reafforested, and the intermittent green canopy of leaves adds to its attractiveness.

The church of Agios Georgios in **Kellaki►**, ensconced like a miniature Parthenon on a rocky outcrop at the summit of the village, has a fine gilt iconostasis and a priest who is happy to show it off to visitors. By now you are into 'hairpin bend' country, which is characteristic of much of Cyprus as you move away from the coast.

Zoodhokos Pigi►, the 'Monastery of the Life-giving Spring', sits on a spur outside Eptagoneia, visited seemingly by no one despite its handsome modern aspect.

A popular place for a break with tourists travelling between Limassol and Nicosia, **Agios Minas►►** is well worth the stop. The convent is beautifully maintained and the nuns are welcoming to visitors.

Kato Drys►, an attractive mountain village with narrow streets crowded with typical old houses, some painted blue, as well as with some fine villas, is the home village of the late Cypriot-British millionaire Sir Reo Stakis, who made his fortune in restaurants, hotels and casinos. Just beyond it is the Plane Tree Restaurant, whose owner is the proud possessor of what he claims is the largest plane tree in Cyprus, planted by one Mr. Cavecas in 1906.

The twin villages of **Lefkara►►►**, separated by only a kilometre/half a mile (they are also connected by a steep, narrow road which is more interesting and challenging than the main road), are particularly famed for their lace and silverware.

119

The Troodos Mountains

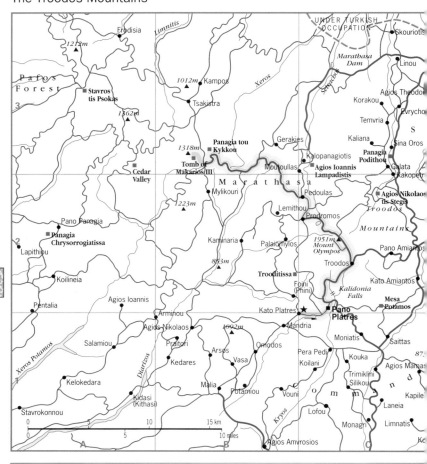

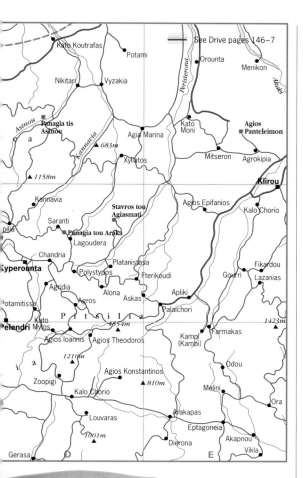

See Drive pages 146–7

THE TROODOS MOUNTAINS It is not a great exaggeration to say that, geographically, Cyprus consists of the Troodos Mountains and a few other fragments. The range dominates the western half of the island, a citadel that guards well its treasures of nature, religion, agriculture and human life.

From all but the most distant points of Cyprus the mountains are unmissable. They rise up virtually from the shoreline in a steepening swell that gathers momentum the higher it reaches, until it crests on the 1,951m (6,400ft) high Mount Olympos, the fittingly named abode of Aphrodite (not to be confused with its namesake in Greece where the Olympians dwelt). The summit is a military base, but the slopes attract skiers in winter.

Of course, the mountains date from a far earlier era than classical antiquity. Long before the island existed in its present form, the mountains were there, the product of volcanoes that erupted tens of millions of years ago. Erosion has been working on them ever since, wearing them down slowly but inexorably to remnants of their former glory; even so, the Troodos will be around for some time to come.

Page 120: Mountain sunset seen from a point near the Archbishop Makarios III tomb on Throni Hill
Right: Typical village house, Koilani

WORLD CLASS

UNESCO has included ten historic Byzantine churches in the Troodos Mountains in its World Cultural Heritage classification. They are:

- **Agios Ioannis Lampadistis** (page 132).
- **Agios Nikolaos tis Stegis** (page 124)
- **Archangelos Michaïl** (page 148)
- **Metamorfosis tou Sotiros** (page 140)
- **Panagia tis Asinou** (page 141)
- **Panagia Podithou** (page 126)
- **Panagia tou Araka** (page 140)
- **Panagia tou Moutoulla** (page 135)
- **Stavros tou Agiasmati** (page 149)
- **Timiou Stavrou** (page 148)

COOL STUFF

Throughout southern Cyprus, heading for the Troodos is the answer if you want to escape the scorching summer temperatures elsewhere. While the temperature in Nicosia can soar above 40°C (104°F), and 35°C (95°F) is not uncommon around the coast, Mount Olympos rarely goes higher than 27°C (84°F). The average temperature in the high mountains is 15°C (59°F) lower than that of Nicosia.

Forestry Department information sign

122

At a more mundane level, the Troodos are the subject of much head-scratching over road maps. Roads that lead to the mountains often become twisting byways or rough trails that add hours to any cross-island journey, although in recent years a scheme to improve the mountain roads has seen most of the through-routes improved and even some of the trails macadamized. Yet there the mountains are. Look up at them from a prone position on any beach and you will see them staring straight back down at you, cool, green and imperious, masters of all they survey. Sooner or later most visitors to Cyprus ask themselves: 'I wonder what it's like up there...?'

What it's like is a breath of fresh air, as the sultry Mediterranean zephyrs are magically transmuted by altitude into cool, sharp-edged breezes. Cypriots knew all about this before

ΝΟΠΑΤΙ ΠΡΟΣ (ΝΤΟΛΦΙΝ)
ΡΙΣΤΙΚΟ ΠΕΡΙΠΤΕΡΟ ΤΡΟΟΔΟΥ
ΟΤΡΑΤΗ ΤΟ (DOLPHIN)
ΟDOS TOURIST PAVILIO

the tourists, of course, and a hard thing for them to bear is the way the visitors have pursued them to their mountain hideaways. Even the environs of the president's summer residence is the target of tramping tourists whose curiosity has got the better of them.

High times There is enough room in the Troodos for everyone, provided they stay away from the choke-points where the few good trans-mountain roads converge. Hiking trails, which are both educational and scenic, have been marked out by the Forestry Department at several locations around the upper reaches, and in most places there are no obstacles, apart from obvious physical ones, to striking out into the forests on deep-penetration hiking expeditions.

Today's forests are relative newcomers to the Troodos. The Forestry Department is continuing the task begun by the British to restore the tree cover laid low by centuries of over-felling. Restoration has more than an aesthetic value, because the Troodos range is the island's principal watershed, the reservoir of a precious resource diminished by forest loss and erosion. Cyprus's main rivers rise here. Fed by the heavy winter rains, they plunge wildly downhill before running into as many dams as the authorities can muster to capture the flow before it disappears in summer's drought.

Sporting life Sport is a big attraction in the Troodos—even if most people get sufficient exercise staring out their car or tour-bus window at the passing view. As well as hiking, both bicycling and mountain-biking are challenging possibilities. Their difficulty on steep gradients and rocky paths, aggravated by altitude and heat, should not be underestimated, yet why go to the mountains if not to get closer to nature? In winter there is even skiing (always assuming there is snow).

Considering how many people head for the hills to find a different Cyprus, it is ironic that the Troodos Mountains first gained popularity for their isolation from the coast. Orthodox monks, in particular, chose this path to escape the temptations and dangers of the plain, with its worldly towns and threat from invaders and pirates. When the stars crowd into the night sky like jewels scattered on a black velvet background, framed by tree-covered peaks, it seems as if the monks chose wisely and that heaven is not far away.

MOUNTAIN TIME
'The country we traversed is charmingly picturesque, a series of plains sloping gently towards the hills, all beautifully green. Above the hills rises a chain of high mountains, whose summits are crowned with snow.'
—*Travels of Ali Bey* (1806)

123

Selling the famous Marathasa Valley cherries

Agios Nikolaos tis Stegis, one of the finest of the Byzantine mountain churches

▶▶▶ Agios Nikolaos tis Stegis   *120C2*

Open: Tue–Sat 9–4, Sun 11–4. Admission free

Like several other historic Troodos Mountain churches, this small 11th-century edifice 5km (3 miles) south of Kakopetria has two roofs: an outer one that protects the church from heavy winter snowfalls, and an inner one in the classic domed Byzantine style. Indeed, the 'tis Stegis' part of its name means 'of the roof'. A combination of its age, construction, and, especially, the suite of superb religious frescoes in its interior has given Agios Nikolaos the status of a UNESCO World Cultural Heritage Site.

Dating from the time of the church's construction to the 17th century, the frescoes depict some of the key moments of the Christian faith, including the raising of Lazarus from the dead, Christ's entry into Jerusalem, and the Assumption of the Virgin. In addition, there is a finely rendered Christ Pantokrator gazing down from the dome—always a vital Orthodox symbol—and a painting of St. Nicholas, for whom the church is named. The situation of Agios Nikolaos tis Stegis in the shadow of the mountains along a narrow side-road in the scenic Solea Valley, as much as the stellar quality of its decoration, attracts frequent visitors.

▶▶ Agios Theodoros   *120C3*

Easily one of the most picturesque of Cypriot villages, Agios Theodoros has become both a subject for artists and an artists' retreat. The rugged Pitsilia region forms the painterly backdrop, its forested peaks rising above the village's own 1,000m (3,300ft) hilltop altitude. The fine villas dotting the vineyard-studded surroundings testify to the wealth that can be gleaned from agriculture and local business, as well as art. The 16th-century church of the **Panagia▶** (Our Lady) (*Open irregularly. Admission free*) contains a superbly preserved iconostasis of the following century, with a silver-gilded icon of Our Lady, prayers to which are said to be efficacious whenever rain is needed—in Cyprus that means just about always.

FROM THE ROOFTOPS
Some Troodos villages can be disappointing to look at from a distance, because their houses lack the red-tiled roofs that fit so well the image of a rustic lifestyle and complement the green of hills and forests. From close up it can be seen that many roofs are made of corrugated iron, an entirely romance-free material but one that is practical in an area of heavy snowfall.

▶ Agros   121D2

Various kinds of liquid inducements exist for making a visit to Agros. There is a choice of three for which the village is world famous, in Cyprus at any rate: rose-water, mineral water and wine. Agros is both well sited and handsome, its inhabitants doing their best to keep it a living, and even flourishing, entity.

▶ Arsos   120B1

The houses of Arsos with their red-tiled roofs hug the side of a valley on the southwestern Troodos slopes. This is a Krassochoria (wine district) village, famed for its deep-red wines as well as the fiery *zivania* spirit, and is characteristic of the smaller villages of the area. Most of the younger people have moved to jobs in the cities and at the coast, so Arsos gets by on the hard work of its old folk. Legend gives Arsos a romantic beginning: It was reputedly named after Cleopatra's younger sister, Arsinoë, who was banished from Egypt by Julius Caesar in 47BC.

▶▶▶ Cedar Valley   120A3

In times past, the phrase 'cedars of Lebanon' was a household expression and a romantic image of that country. The cedars of Cyprus may not have attained such popular acclaim, but there is no doubting the romantic appeal of this valley on the western slopes of the Troodos, filled with serried ranks of the distinctive trees. Many of the routes to Cedar Valley, from any direction, are sufficiently rough for it to be as well that both the journey and the final destination are scenic enough to make the experience worthwhile.

The variety of cedar, *Cedrus libani brevifolia*, is indigenous to Cyprus. Most of the island's 50,000 or so cedars are here in the **Tripilos-Mavroi Gremmoi Nature Reserve▶▶▶**, between Kykkos Monastery and Stavros tis Psokas in the Pafos Forest, alongside pine, plane and golden oak. They stand tall and proud, their symmetrical branches rising in horizontal order and their cylindrical green cones standing straight up.

WILD AT HEART
A reserve for the rare and previously endangered moufflon has been established in Cedar Valley, although these wild mountain sheep may also be found higher up in the Troodos. Cyprus Airways has adopted the moufflon as its emblem.

Call of the wild in Cedar Valley

125

Cedars of Cyprus are the attraction in this rugged valley

The Troodos Mountains

KEY QUESTION
Acquiring the keys to the Kingdom of Heaven can present little greater difficulty than finding the keys to one of Cyprus's Orthodox churches that contains icons and other historical treasures visitors want to see. These might well be locked, and the key-holder, usually the priest, is nowhere to be seen. The first port of call should be the nearest *kafeneion* (coffee shop); even if the priest is not there the locals may know where he is and will often volunteer to fetch him. It it as well, however, to be prepared for a long wait.

Not all the Orthodox churches in the Troodos are of venerable age. This one at Galata is modern

▶▶▶ Commandaria Region   *120C1*

A narrow sliver of the southern slopes of the Troodos is given over to the production of grapes, from which are made Cyprus's distinctive Commandaria sweet red dessert wines. There is little, besides its slightly higher altitude, to distinguish this area from the nearby Krassochoria wine district in terms of landscape or climate, but the tradition of its unique suitability for Commandaria is fixed. See Focus on Wine, pages 152–53.

▶▶ Foini   *120B2*

This small village nestles in the bottom of a valley near Kato Platres. Its steep-sided streets boast several traditional pottery-makers; in times past the village was an important producer of the large *pitharia* pots, but now it specializes in smaller pieces. There is a small but interesting **Pylavakion Museum▶** (*Open* irregularly. *Admission: inexpensive*), in which exhibits recall the village's pottery-making history.

▶▶ Galata   *120C3*

Just off the main road from Nicosia, at the point where it climbs through the Solea Valley towards the Troodos peaks, Galata is a pretty village, consisting of a cluster of white-painted houses set down on the green valley floor. Its restored Ottoman-era **Hani Kalliana Inn** is of interest.

Agios Sozomenos▶ in the village centre dates from the early 16th century, and its post-Byzantine frescoes make for an interesting comparison with the much older ones in churches elsewhere in the Troodos. Similarly, among the fields just outside the village, is 16th-century **Panagia Podithou▶▶**, a UNESCO-recognized site particularly notable for its triangular rendering of the Crucifixion and its superb Our Lady as the Queen of Heaven in the narthex. The small timber-roofed church of **Archangelos Michaïl** (also known as Panagia Theotokos)**▶▶**, nearby, has simpler but still impressive post-Byzantine frescoes. Finally, there is **Agia Paraskevi▶**, a small 16th-century church situated on the old road from Galata to Kakopetria (All four of these churches are open irregularly. *Admission free*).

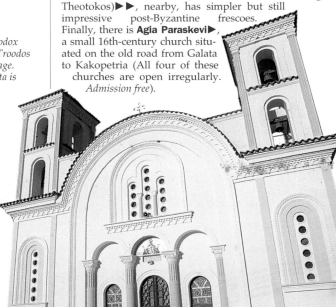

►►► Kakopetria   *120C3*

On the road to Troodos from Nicosia, Kakopetria is the first indication that you are entering a totally different environment. As the road begins to climb you can turn off towards the village, the historic and somewhat ramshackle old heart of which is considered so typical of Cyprus that it is being preserved and restored. Kakopetria is a fast-growing resort, with a view over fertile valleys, and well equipped with hotels and restaurants. The village is on the northern edge of the mountains, but is close enough to explore them.

► Kaliana   *120C3*

Certain small villages seem, in an unforced, unrestored way, to be characteristic of the old way of life in Cyprus. This one, situated in a narrow side-valley on the western edge of the Solea Valley, is in addition representative of the area's agricultural richness, surrounded as it is by orchards, vegetable plots and vineyards. Nothing much ever happens in Kaliana: It is a charmingly tranquil little place. The 16th-century church of **Agioi Joachim ke Anna** (*Open* irregularly. *Admission free*) is its most notable asset, containing some murals from the same period.

►► Kalidonia Falls   *120C2*

Visions of a Cypriot Niagara must be put firmly out of mind. Indeed, a dispassionate observer looking at this diminutive cascade tumbling all of 20m (65ft) into a shallow pool might even wonder if the description 'waterfall' is overdone. These objections noted, however, Kalidonia Falls is still a worthy phenomenon, if only for its uniqueness in being fed by a perennial stream, known as the Kryos Potamos. The signposted 2km (1 mile) Kalidonia Trail follows a pretty route through the forest to the falls from a point near Troodos resort.

Kakopetria village

GOING WITH THE FLOW
Virtually all of Cyprus's rivers originate from the snow and rain that falls on the Troodos watershed. Apart from the waters that flow over Kaledonia Falls, however, few survive much beyond the spring. Yet in the past the streams had a more abundant and long-lasting flow. Cyprus's first regular supply of electricity came from a hydroelectric plant at Kakopetria.

Kaledonia Falls

As long as your chosen sport does not depend on white water, Cyprus is surely an outdoor sports enthusiast's paradise. Trails through the Troodos and Pentadaktylos (Beşparmak) mountains allow serious hikers and mountain-bikers to push themselves hard, while gentler routes around the coast cater for the more easy-going.

Hikers (above) in the Troodos.
Soaring above the coast near Kition (below)

128

Active holidays are said to be getting more popular by the minute, although this does not seem to be the case if you compare the numbers of mountain-bikers in the Troodos to those of sun-worshippers at Fig Tree Bay. Mountain-biking in the Troodos is no picnic: The hills are high, the trails rough, the sun hot and any effort to overcome these difficulties involves perspiration in disheartening amounts. Cycling along the coast is at least easier, although caution is needed on the busy coast roads, and cyclists should stick to the less frequented coastal tracks. Facilities for renting touring bicycles are available in all main resorts, and mountain-bikes can be hired at Pano Platres in the Troodos. Further information on the island's bicycling possibilities is available from the **Cyprus Cycling Federation**, 20 Ionos Street, PO Box 24572, 1301 Nicosia, tel: 22663344.

Walking away Many of Cyprus's outdoor activities are free: hiking, for example, or even just walking and admiring the flowers and the scenery. Several nature trails have been established by the Forestry Department around Troodos village, Pano Platres and Mount Olympos in the Troodos Mountains, and in the wild and lonely Akamas Peninsula on the northwest coast. They range in length from 3km (2 miles) or so to over 20km (12 miles). In the Pentadaktylos (Beşparmak) Mountains there are also numerous trails. One runs across the spine of the mountains from Voufaventon (Buffavento) Castle to the Halevga (Alevkaya) Forest Station. All involve some huffing and puffing, but for an averagely fit person it would be an overstatement to call them hikes.

Real hiking is all about going in search of moufflon in the Pafos Forest, with a compass, a large-scale map (these can be obtained from some bookshops, although some of the highly detailed military survey maps are unavailable for security reasons; in the Turkish Cypriot zone no such maps are available), and a good supply of food and water. The Akamas has almost equally difficult terrain but is more popular with walkers because of its proximity to a beautiful section of the coast. The experience of traversing such hard-boiled landscapes, knowing that few other people

Rock-climbers near Trooditissa Monastery

are willing to do so, may be satisfaction enough. In summer, clothing should be light but offer adequate protection against the sun, and footwear should be sturdy at all times of the year.

Assisted passages Horse-riding may be preferable to cycling or walking, since the horse does most of the work. Cross-country trekking is available at all of the main resorts, at some places in the interior, and outside Nicosia; tuition is offered by various local horse-riding centres. Further information is available from the **Cyprus Equestrian Federation**, PO Box 14043, 2153 Nicosia, tel: 99973333.

Dirt-bikes can be hired in all the holiday resorts. All across Cyprus there is rough non-agricultural country where dirt-bikes come into their own. Some of the rugged trails in the Akamas Peninsula and the Troodos Mountains are ideal—but not for the little mopeds that most riders hire.

Fishy pursuits Cyprus has compensated for diminished rainfall by damming its rivers. Freshwater lakes have been created and stocked with trout, carp, catfish, silver bream and perch. At some dams, these reservoirs can be fished year-round. A permit from the local Fisheries Department district office in Limassol, Larnaka, or Pafos is required (see page 105). Further information is available from the **Ministry of Agriculture, Natural Resources and Environment Fisheries Department**, 13 Odos Aiolou, 1101 Nicosia, tel: 22807862.

WALK OF LIFE
Inasmuch as walking can be considered an outdoor sport, an excellent account of walking in Cyprus is given in Colin Thubron's book, *Journey Into Cyprus*, recording a 1,000km (620-mile) tour of the island he made on foot in 1972, before partition.

129

FOOTBALL GLORY
The Cypriots' own sporting passion is reserved almost exclusively for football (soccer), introduced by the British. Each season, the Greek Cypriot First Division alone accounts for the equivalent of one ticket sold for every man, woman and child in the country. The sport is organized by the Cyprus Football Association, which controls the four top divisions and 12 minor divisions. Turkish Cypriots are no less fanatical about the game.

A sea-angler tries his luck near Agia Napa

By bike

Through the Troodos

Fresh air and marvellous views are among the attractions of the Troodos Mountains, and what better way to experience them than from the saddle of a bicycle? This 40km (25 miles) round-trip is demanding and you should be confident of your fitness and stamina before attempting it.

Several shops in Pano Platres hire mountain-bikes, advertising that they do so on their windows. Numerous trails lead off road for any particularly

Testing time for mountain-bikers high in the Troodos

keen mountain-bikers, although some sections of the road are tough enough to make this seem superfluous. Individual sights on this tour are covered in more detail on pages 126–150.

Going downhill at the start of the trip means that the last leg will also be downhill—which may be an important consideration if you are on your last legs by then. Starting from **Pano Platres▶▶▶**, head downhill towards **Kato Platres▶**, passing the church of **Faneromeni** on the way.

Still heading downhill, you enter the strikingly situated small village of **Foini▶▶**, which is noted for its pottery production—both traditional Cypriot ware and modern varieties— and which also has a small pottery museum, **Pylavakion Museum▶**. Beyond Foini the road begins to climb up through open countryside.

The experience of cycling uphill in the thin mountain air, under the strong Cyprus sun, will provide an insight into the exertion required to complete the whole route; if you decide this is not for you, take the track which runs off to the right at the chapel as this will drastically shorten the trip.

This trail leads to **Trooditissa Monastery▶**. On its rough surface, even the few downhill stretches seem like uphills (though they are not quite as physically demanding as the uphills), so it is not necessarily an easy option.

If you choose not to take the short cut, continue on the main road, now lined with woodland, towards Timios Stavros village, or detour to the left through the steeply sited village of Agios Dimitrios. In this segment you emerge from the forest cover and the true impact of the Troodos range can

The church at the scenically sited Trooditissa Monastery

be seen, as the view opens up across forest-covered peaks and down into open valleys with tiny villages pinned to their slopes.

If you are so fit that the route so far has seemed like no more than a jaunt, you may wish to push things farther by detouring to the left at Lemithus, down into the church-dotted valley and the hamlet of Treis Elies. Otherwise, it's best to stick to the main road.

Climbing again, you move back into the forest cover in the direction of the Troodos summit, but turn away from it at the high-altitude village of **Prodromos►**. A Forestry College and Agricultural Station near Prodromos show the importance attached to both

activities in this area. If the route so far has seemed hard, relief is close at hand: Forestry Department picnic sites along the way make ideal places for a break and the road soon begins to head downhill. A short diversion, to the right this time, again leads to Trooditissa Monastery, overlooking a steep gorge.

The final stretch is an exhilarating downhill run on a sharply curving road all the way to Pano Platres. Because this road slices past the village and joins the main road 1km (0.5 miles) below the town, be sure to follow the signs for Platres and not race past them; otherwise the final stretch will be an unwelcome uphill one.

A mosaic at the entrance to the Trooditissa church

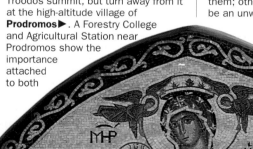

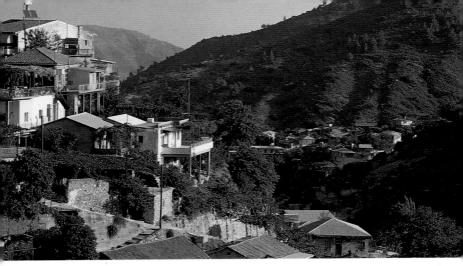

Looking towards the village of Kalopanagiotis

FIRE RISK
Fire can be a serious hazard in the mountains, particularly when the long, dry summer creates tinder-box conditions in the forests. The consequences of a blaze can be devastating to the reafforestation effort. It ought to go without saying that no one travelling in the Troodos should take the slightest risk of setting off a fire.

Relaxing in the shade of a café terrace at Kampos

▶▶ **Kalopanagiotis**   *120C3*

This village, in the heart of the Marathasa Valley on the northern slopes of the Troodos, used to be a noted spa resort thanks to its sulphur springs. Nowadays its closest connection with water is in the **Kalopanagiotis Dam** just outside the town. The village still attracts visitors, however, who come to see the former monastery of **Agios Ioannis Lampadistis**▶▶▶ *(Open* Jun–Nov Tue–Sun 8–1, 2–7; Mar–May Tue–Sun 8–1, 2–7; Dec–Feb Tue–Sun 8–1, 2–4. *Admission* church *free,* museum *inexpensive),* whose remarkable church, really three churches in one, is a UNESCO World Cultural Heritage Site.

The three churches stand side by side under an outer snow-roof. Each is painted with frescoes depicting the saints and the life of Christ and the Holy Family. Those of the domed central church, 11th-century Agios Irakleidios, have faded drastically with time, but the remaining two, a 12th-century Orthodox church and a 15th-century Latin chapel, both with vaulted ceilings, have retained their frescoes more or less intact. A small museum holds items relating to the history of the monastery and the churches.

▶ **Kampos**   *120B3*

The northwestern corner of the Troodos takes some beating as a rough-country area traversed by some very poor roads. This apparent disadvantage can be seen as a positive advantage, however, if you are looking for isolation and wilderness. Not many tour buses make the mountain-goat trek into this quarter. Kampos village is

one of the few centres of any size in the area, with a hotel, tavernas and coffee shops, and marking a divide between the rugged higher ground and the gentler lower slopes. The surroundings are dotted with ruined Byzantine churches, and with forest stations and picnic areas.

►► Koilani   120C1

A charming small village in the heart of the grape-growing, wine-making district on the southern Troodos slopes, Koilani has not allowed its commitment to Bacchus to divert it entirely from the path of righteousness. Proof of this lies in the **Koilani Ecclesiastical Museum►** (*Open* irregularly; ask at village *kafeneion*. *Admission: inexpensive*). Given that a great deal of Cyprus's cultural heritage rests on its Byzantine and Orthodox religious tradition, a museum like this helps put some perspective on an otherwise potentially bewildering array of churches and treasures. Its collection includes icons spanning six centuries (from the 13th through to the 19th), religious vessels and ornaments (including some outstandingly crafted in silver), and antique prayer books.

► Kyperounta   121D2

This small village lies in rough country off the eastern face of the Troodos at an altitude of 1,080m (3,543ft), and makes an interesting diversion for travellers touring the environs of the upper mountains. Its small 16th-century church of **Stavros (The Holy Cross)►** (*Open* irregularly. *Admission free*) has some restored frescoes and a group of paintings depicting the discovery of the True Cross.

► Louvaras   121D1

For *aficionados* of Byzantine mural art, the village's 15th-century **Agios Mamas►** church (*Open* irregularly. *Admission free*) boasts some frescoes by the noted artist Philip tou Goul, from what is now Lebanon, who achieved renown in Cyprus for his work at the time of the Lusignan kings (see panel on page 149). Goul was also responsible for important works at Stavros tou Agiasmati church near Platanistasa (see also page 149).

► Mandria   120B1

Mandria is best known as a crossroads village for visitors descending from the mountains and seeking a more scenic route to the coast. It is also a market-gardening centre in an area of large farms. Taking the right fork here leads to Pafos, while the left fork leads to Limassol. Apart from the road, tiny Mandria itself is so peaceful sometimes that all its inhabitants seem to have tiptoed away.

►►► Marathasa Valley   120B2

While much of the Troodos Mountains consists of wild and rugged country, there are several valleys of almost fairy-tale charm, besides providing important access routes to the high mountains. One of these is the Marathasa Valley, set in a green, fertile landscape dotted with agricultural villages on the northwestern slopes of the Troodos. Marathasa is renowned for its cherry harvest.

LONESOME PINE
Driving the rough trails of the Troodos Mountains can be intimidating for the novice, particularly as a single mistake could send a car, its driver, and passengers tumbling over a precipice. This is not really likely, but maintaining concentration during a long, hot, dusty and bumpy drive is hard, and the margin of error on the narrowest trails can be small. Part of the thrill of being in the mountains comes from getting away from everyone else, and the roughest trails are the ideal places for this. The question each driver must ask is whether the isolation is worth the effort.

133

Honey is just one of the products of the Marathasa Valley

134

▶ Mesa Potamos Monastery   *120C2*

About halfway along a rough track between Pano Platres and Kato Amiantos are the ruins of the 14th-century Mesa Potamos Monastery, with rebuildings from later centuries. It overlooks a steep gorge where the Mesa Potamos riverbed plunges downhill (the river also plunges down, but only in winter). This trail makes for an enjoyable, if by no means easy, mountain-biking expedition from Pano Platres, where the bicycles needed for such an undertaking can be rented.

▶▶▶ Mount Olympos   *120C2*

Military bases, both old and new, occupy some of Cyprus's finest locations. However, it does seem particularly cruel that the 1,951m (6,400ft) summit of the island's highest mountain, Mount Olympos (also known as Mount Khionistra), should be out of bounds. The white geodesic dome of a British radar installation is the *trompe-l'oeil* occupying a position once sacred to Aphrodite. Tyre-traps, security fences and guards complete the dismal picture. Occupying the high ground has always been a military priority, but too many of Cyprus's recent priorities have been military ones.

Elsewhere around the summit, there is a Cypriot army bunker, a fire-watch observation tower, and red-and-white-painted television masts. In between it is just possible to enjoy the benefit of Olympos' altitude in the superb view across the surrounding mountains. The 7km (4-mile) **Artemis Trail**, a signposted nature trail established by the Forestry Department, begins at a point a little way downhill from here and describes a circumference of the summit, featuring information panels that point out interesting examples of flora, geology, and geography on the way (see page 137).

Some heaps of rubble off the western summit are thought to indicate the ancient settlement of **Palaia Choria**. The stones were apparently piled up to form a defensive wall by Venetian troops planning a last-ditch stand against the 16th-century Turkish invaders, who had already captured Famagusta (Gazimağusa) and Nicosia. Not much came of this do-or-die resolution, however, and the Turks were soon in control of the entire island.

In winter the snows of Olympos create a skier's playground, with several ski-lifts serving the pistes.

A television tower takes advantage of Mount Olympos's towering altitude

The restored and revitalized main street in Omodos

►► Moutoullas 120C3

In the Marathasa Valley, Moutoullas is an attractive village noted for the frescoes and handsomely carved doors of its tiny 13th-century Byzantine chapel of **Panagia tou Moutoulla►** (*Open* irregularly. *Admission free*), one of the ten historic churches in the mountains acclaimed by UNESCO. A key is available from the adjacent house.

►► Omodos 120B1

This, the largest of the Krassochoria wine villages, has taken some fairly shrewd steps to preserve its traditional character, while cashing in on the tourist boom that has otherwise tended to pass the mountain villages by—as well as contributing to the drain of their young people to the resort towns. Part of the village centre has been restored and developed as a street-stall and café centre, while some residents invite visitors in for a guided tour of their traditional homes, albeit for a fee.

It seems mean-minded to question the restoration effort, which included replacing the asphalt in the village square with cobbles, but the outcome for this otherwise attractive place appears to be neither fish nor fowl, a split-personality village unable to decide which way it wants to go. Nevertheless, Omodos's new-found vigour causes the Cypriot authorities to count it a success story in the restoration and preservation drive.

Among the goods for sale are the local lace (called *pipilla*) and the ring-shaped bread called *arketana*, a speciality of Omodos that is now sold all over the island. The restored house interiors, hung with gourds and kitchen utensils beside the traditional oven, also have a cellar where the large earthenware pots called *pitharia*, formerly filled with wine, are stored. In addition, among the rustic and traditional items in the village's **Folk Museum►** is a restored 15th-century wine press.

Omodos's **Stavros Monastery►** (*Open* daily. *Admission free*) was founded in AD327 by St. Helena, mother of the Roman Emperor Constantine, who donated a golden cross said to hold hemp fibres from the ropes that bound Jesus to the cross, and another said to contain a fragment of the True Cross. The monastery, most of which is 19th century, also houses a museum of EOKA, the Greek Cypriot guerrilla group that fought the British for union with Greece during the 1950s.

Cherries ripen through the lazy days in the Marathasa sun

135

CHERRIES BLOSSOM
Cherries, such as those grown in the Marathasa Valley, are a relatively recent Cypriot product, but one which has caught on quickly. Roadside tables, market stalls and shop counters throughout Cyprus, but particularly in the valley, groan under the weight of this top-quality fruit during its short spring and early summer season. Most of the cherries are eaten fresh, though some are used in preserves.

LIFE FROM DEATH
Dead and rotting trees are prized almost as much as live ones in the sparse forests around Mount Olympos. This is because rotting trees provide a food source for microbes and other organisms, which play an essential role in forest ecology and, therefore, in the reafforestation process.

The monasteries of Cyprus are storehouses of Greek Cypriot tradition and the Orthodox faith. Ironically, these religious foundations, intended as refuges from the world, are now among the island's foremost tourist attractions.

OH, WHEN THE SAINTS...
Name days, the feast days of the various saints for whom most Cypriots are named, take the place of birthdays in Greek Cyprus (although celebrating birthdays is increasingly popular). Monasteries are often 'hosts' of name-day feasts, with stalls and entertainments in their grounds. Some examples:
● **Agios Antonios** (St. Anthony), 17 January
● **Agios Neofytos** (St. Neofytos), 24 January
● **Agios Georgios** (St. George), 23 April
● **Agioi Petros ke Pavlos** (Sts. Peter & St. Paul), 29 June
● **Agios Ioannis Lampadistis** (St. John Lampadistis), 4 October
● **Agios Loukis** (St. Luke), 18 October

Detail (top) of the iconostasis, Panagia Chrysorrogiatissa. Christ Pantokrator, Panagia tou Kykkou (below)

More so than even the churches, the monasteries are the fountainhead of the faith. Their fortunes have ebbed and flowed with the tides of history, but their commitment to Orthodoxy, to the memory of Byzantium and to the emotional claims of Hellenism has never wavered. A visit to those monasteries that have not been turned into museums will show that the fires of faith still burn bright.

Throughout Greek Cyprus, 2,000-year-old Orthodox traditions are being maintained in work and prayer. Icons are being painted; hymns, church music, and prayerbooks written; and monastery estates tended. And, because the religious men and women reconcile differently the requirements of hospitality and tranquillity, visitors are either being welcomed or fended off. The monasteries' ageless atmosphere is no accident; they have taken the worst that the ravages of time and the hand of man could impose, and yet they are still there.

High society A constellation of proud foundations holds the traditions in trust: Panagia tou Kykkou (page 142) and Trooditissa (page 150) high in the Troodos Mountains; Machairas (page 190) amid the foothills of Pitsilia; Stavrovouni (page 96) on the heights above Larnaka; Panagia Chrysorrogiatissa (page 176) in the Pafos Forest; and Agios Neofytos (page 158), with its cliffside chambers, overlooking Pafos. There are the humbler, more human convents, where nuns make honey and tend their flowers: Agios Nikolaos ton Gaton (page 102), overrun with pampered cats; reclusive Agios Georgios Alamanos (page 102); flower-bedecked Agios Minas (page 102); and deeply spiritual Agios Irakleidios (page 188).

In the Turkish sector of Cyprus, the last monks have departed from glorious Apostolos Varnavas (page 232) near Salamis, now an archaeological museum; rustic Agios Mamas in Morfou (Güzelyurt—see page 216) is also a museum; and the most spectacular of all, that of Apostolos Andreas (page 230), beside the rocky cape of the same name and with its blessed spring, drifts towards the same end.

A dying tree (above) marks a milestone along the Artemis Trail

Walk

The Artemis Trail

Named after the goddess of the forest, this marked trail circles the upper reaches of Mount Olympos, where the Forestry Department is working to restore Artemis's realm. At just over 7km (4 miles), the walk can be completed in about two hours, although with more time you will be better able to enjoy the view and the flora.

Black pine trees are the main constituent of the forest, with some of the plant species around them—barberry, St. John's wort and catmint, for example—being identified on information panels. Other points of interest along the route are mineral formations. Panel 6 points to a group of black pine trees that have been struck by lightning.

Other species that can be seen are fir trees and, around panel 11, where reafforestation is under way, cedars of Lebanon. Shortly after that there is a test quarry for chromite. The 'Walls of the Old Town' at panel 22 coincide with the site of **Palaia Choria**, and are said to have been used by Venetian soldiers planning a last-ditch stand against the invading Ottomans in the 16th century.

The slopes are steeper here and show the effects of erosion that is proving difficult to reverse. Panel 29 indicates a giant black pine.

The views from beyond the ski-lift look out across the plains around Morfou (Güzelyurt) in the Turkish Cypriot zone. From here the trail soon returns to its starting point.

Imagine a chill wind in your face, the swish of skis on snow, and an exhilarating downhill rush through a white-painted world. Cyprus's winter charms stretch a long way from the doubtful warmth of the beach, to the ski slopes of the Troodos Mountains.

Skiing in the morning, swimming in the sea in the afternoon. This tempting and, on the face of it, surprising prospect is possible in Cyprus, although it may involve a fair amount of driving and some wishful thinking about snow and warm seas. The Mediterranean island, with its 300 or so days of sunshine every year, may not be the obvious destination for a skiing holiday, yet in the Troodos Mountains, specifically on the uppermost slopes of 1,951m (6,400ft) high Mount Olympos, skiing is eminently possible and skiing in the sun an odds-on probability.

In a good year (or a bad one, depending on how you look at it) there may be enough snow to permit skiing from December to April, but more usually the season lasts from January to March. Given their altitude, the slopes are frequent candidates for snow, but given their latitude, rain is at least as likely. Nevertheless, the snows of Olympos do exist and can reach a depth of up to 3m (10ft), although a good deal less than that is more usual, yet still adequate.

Allowances needed At such times enthusiasts get their skis on and head for the pistes. The Troodos Mountains are not the Alps, however, and the facilities in terms of lifts, runs, equipment hire, on-site refreshment and après-ski are limited. In the 40 years that skiing has been

138

COOL IDEA
During the Ottoman era (and doubtless before then as well), the snows of Olympos were put to a more practical use than as a medium for swift motion. Snow was transported to Nicosia and other towns to be used as a cooling agent for drinks and food. In effect, the mountains became a giant ice-making machine.

Practising those all-important turns

practised in Cyprus, it has been growing steadily in popularity, and genuine enthusiasts will happily make allowances for the minimal possibilities so long as they have an opportunity to ski at all. In any case, there are cafés located near by with log fires, mulled wine, and the other essentials after a day on the pistes.

There are four ski-lifts on Mount Olympos, serving the runs at Sun Valley and the North Face, which are clearly signposted on the approach roads. The former offers downhill stretches more or less corresponding to beginner and intermediate levels, while the latter features more testing descents of between 1 and 1.5km (0.5 and 1 mile). Instructors from the Cyprus Ski Federation are on hand for beginners and intermediate-level skiers who want to get started or improve their technique. Several cross-country trails snake through the scenic pine forests from Sun Valley. Lift passes come with either seasonal or temporary membership of the Cyprus Ski Federation, obtainable on site, while you can rent equipment such as skis, poles and boots, or buy accessories at Sun Valley.

Alpine breaks Given that the distance to Mount Olympos from the coast is not great, the only problem in getting there is that most of the roads are poor. Driving in winter during sudden snow showers can be particularly difficult, but in fine weather and when the roads have been cleared it presents few problems. It is also possible to stay in the mountains and thus combine an alpine break with skiing. The main resorts are Troodos, which is also the closest to the pistes, and Pano Platres, a little farther down on the southern slopes. Both of these are important year-round resorts, and Pano Platres in particular has plenty of accommodation, restaurants and other facilities.

An international skiing competition takes place in February, with top skiers from other countries taking part, and several lower-level competitions as well. There are other attractions to being in the mountains at this time of year: tobogganing, for example, or taking part in snowball fights. Hiking, surrounded by Christmas-card scenery, is another kind of Cyprus treat.

WINTER CAMOUFLAGE
With names like Edelweiss and Vienna, the hotels and chalets of Platres can have one reaching for the map, just to check which country this is. These alpine-style names work well enough in winter, but in summer they do seem a mite strange.

139

Skiing in the morning and swimming in the afternoon is the Cyprus promise

Tranquil Panagia tou Araka Monastery in the Troodos foothills

HILL STATIONS
The British, in their colonial heyday in India, loved their 'hill stations', little pieces of the motherland parked atop breeze-cooled heights to which they would withdraw before the withering heat of a real Indian summer. Being of fixed habits, they simply translated the institution to Cyprus. Pano Platres (see page 143) developed as just such a mountain retreat in the late 19th century, initially for convalescent soldiers, then for genteel society seeking relief from Nicosia. Cypriots followed the trend, so that Platres was a flourishing holiday resort long before anyone thought of dipping their toes in the Mediterranean.

▶ **Palaichori**   *121E2*

Seen from the head of the mountain pass leading to it, the village of Palaichori, with its white-painted houses and red-tiled roofs, looks like a frozen avalanche suspended in the act of tumbling down the steep hillside on which it perches. Close up the image is less alarming, but the Byzantine-era village is no less pretty. Orchards, vineyards (which produce a fine red wine), almond trees and vegetable patches form its backdrop, softening the rough contours of the surrounding hills. These are irrigated by water from the nearby Palaichori Dam, which is filled on a seasonal basis by the poplar-lined Peristerona stream.

On a slope just above the village stands the newest member of the Troodos constellation of UNESCO churches, the early 16th-century church of **Metamorfosis tou Sotiros (Transfiguration of the Saviour)** (*Open* irregularly. *Admission free*, but donation welcome; key from neighbouring priest's house). It has the steep-pitched roof and unremarkable outer walls typical of the mountain churches, and was added in 2001 to the original nine churches for its frescoes by an unknown artist somewhat after the style of Philip tou Goul, and others from later periods. Look for the mural of the tax-avoiding St. Mamas of Morfou, bearing a 'look-no-hands' expression while he happily rides along on his lion; and, naturally enough, one of the Transfiguration, in which Christ appears in radiant glory on Mount Tabor (or Mount Hermon) to his awestruck disciples Peter, James and John.

▶▶▶ **Panagia tis Asinou**
(Our Lady of Asinou)   *121D3*

Open: summer daily 9–5; winter daily 9–4.
Admission free, donation welcome

Also known as Panagia Forviotissa, this is among the most tranquil mountain churches, thanks to its forest location near **Nikitari** village. Dating from the 12th-century, Panagia tis Asinou is considered the finest Byzantine church in the Troodos, heading the list of UNESCO World Cultural Heritage Sites.

The tiny church is filled with dazzling frescoes representing the zenith of Byzantine religious art. Some date from 1105, including those depicting the Last Supper and the Ascension, painted by artists from Constantinople. The classic Orthodox image of Christ Pantokrator, who looks down from the dome as if from a window in heaven, has one of its noblest representations here. Repainting and restoration has been carried out through the centuries, most recently in the 1960s.

►►► Panagia tou Araka
(Our Lady of the Pea)   *121D2*
Open: daily 10–4. Admission free, donation welcome
The 12th-century Byzantine monastery, named after the local wild peas (or vetch), is in no sense a grandiose affair. Its modest bearing is enhanced by the trellised verandas overlooking its courtyard and its hilly situation near **Lagoudera** village in the eastern reaches of the Troodos.

Yet UNESCO has granted World Cultural Heritage status to the establishment, principally for the unparalleled frescoes (dating from 1192) that adorn its church. Artists were commissioned from Constantinople, capital of the Byzantine Empire. The Christ Pantokrator gazing down from the dome of heaven is particularly fine, with an expression that seems sadly resigned to human weakness, and eyes that appear to follow the observer, their gaze penetrating to the soul.

Other scenes include an image that imparts both great tenderness and wonder at the birth of the Saviour: A midwife washes the holy infant as Mary looks on. In an Annunciation scene, the Archangel Gabriel steps down from a heaven that looks like a Byzantine palace to deliver to Mary his message of the miraculous birth.

LODES OF UMBER
Mines in the Troodos supply a material that has been highly prized by artists, from ancient Egypt through the Italian Renaissance to modern times. The material is umber, an iron oxide mineral pigment, and Cypriot lodes are reckoned to yield among the best quality in the world. Umber is found at the interface between a layer of sedimentary chalk formed over millions of years and underlying solidified lava. Several locations in the Troodos produce umber from the so-called Pera Pedi Formation.

141

The tiny church of Panagia tis Asinou plays host to a superb suite of religious frescoes

Modern mosaics provide an indication of the wealth of imagery in Panagia tou Kykkou monastery

▶▶▶ Panagia tou Kykkou (Our Lady of Kykkos)

120B3

Open: Jun–Oct 10–6; Nov–May 10–4. Admission free; museum admission: moderate

Photography is emphatically not permitted in the church of this proudest and richest of all Cyprus monasteries, which is dedicated to Our Lady.

Visitors who sneak a quick snapshot of its icons and glittering ornamentation, expecting at most to be admonished by the guardian, are liable to find themselves grabbed by the scruff of the neck and bundled unceremoniously out of the door. Kykkos is as impressive as its haughty self-image implies, and, as with the Kingdom of Heaven, entry is dependent on good behaviour.

The present structure dates from the 19th century, previous foundations since its establishment in the 10th century having succumbed regularly to fire. It might have made the monks humble to wonder why their venerable institution has so often been burnt to a crisp, but it doesn't. In any case, their most treasured possession, an icon of the Virgin Mary said to have been painted by St. Luke, and donated to Kykkos by the 12th-century Byzantine Emperor Alexius I, has come through all the blazes intact. Enclosed in tortoiseshell and mother-of-pearl, it stands on the iconostasis.

Most of the monastery's wealth is invested in land, much of it donated by the faithful as a means of avoiding Ottoman inheritance taxes in previous centuries. The **Kykkos Museum** displays some of the monastery's movable assets: ecclesiastical vessels, ornaments in gold and silver, and intricately embroidered vestments. Modern icons and murals are characteristic of Kykkos, particularly on the outside walls, and it remains to be seen how well these withstand the challenge of time. Kykkos is renowned throughout the Orthodox world, and has temporal power also, having been instrumental in maintaining Greek Cyprus's Hellenism through centuries of foreign occupation. Archbishop Makarios, the republic's first president, was a novice at Kykkos, and the monastery's counsel still reaches deep into the heart of Greek Cypriot government.

▶ Pano Amiantos

120C2

This village on the eastern face of the Troodos should be notable for little more than its pleasant character, an unremarkable place and no doubt happy to be so. Between here and its sister village **Kato Amiantos** farther down the mountain, however, is a 'monument' of which no village could be proud: A lifeless landscape that looks like the dark side of the moon. The installations of the Amiantos asbestos mine are unused now, crumbling into mementoes of industrial archaeology, but the mountain will take a long time to recover, if ever, from the depredations wrought across its surface.

▶▶▶ Pano Platres   120C2

The principal resort of the mountains, Pano Platres is an alpine-style village at an altitude of 1,100m (3,600ft). It was formerly a mainly Cypriot holiday hideaway, but has become popular with foreign visitors as they search for something more exciting than the traditional beach holiday. The result of these two streams of visitors, plus the village's position at an important crossroads, means it gets busy at peak times, up to and including the unwelcome phenomenon of traffic jams. Still, it never quite loses its charm even then. At calmer times, in the magical early morning for example, the mountain stillness is interrupted only by the sound of rushing water, as the Kryos Potamos stream goes charging downhill.

All the amenities of 'civilization'—hotels, restaurants, cafés, shops, supermarkets, banks, exchange bureaux, a petrol station, a tourist information office, a police station—can be found in Pano Platres, most of them lined up along the steeply curving main street. These may be welcome to anyone who has been hiking along the hot and dusty mountain trails around the village, particularly in those areas where forest cover has not been re-established and there are no shading branches to ward off the sun. Day-old European newspapers are available for anyone who can't stand to be out of touch.

The main tourism role of Pano Platres is as a base for exploring the mountains. For those who take the time to do it properly—by mountain-bike or on foot—the way may be hard but the rewards are great. When the tourist buses and day-trippers in jeeps have pulled out for the night, groping their way down the narrow, twisting roads back to the resorts along the coast, Platres belongs to those who live there, however temporarily. The sharp-edged mountain air invigorates, and the substantial Cypriot food and crisp Cypriot wine taste all the sweeter.

DROPPING A LIGHT
A large tract of the forest running downhill to the west from Kykkos is quite visibly of more recent origin than its surroundings. This is because although warnings about the dangers of summer fires are widespread, no one thought to inform the Turkish air force, which in August 1974 dropped napalm on the forest, incinerating an enormous area and setting the re-afforestation programme back by a generation.

143

TROODOS CENTRAL
There are no attractions as such in Pano Platres. Rather, it is the village, its character and location in the mountains that attract visitors. Pano Platres lies at the heart of the mountain web. Trails from here climb up through the forest to Kaledonia Falls, and beyond to Mount Olympos; downhill, following the course of the Kryos stream, to the Pera Pedi Forest and Pera Pedi Lake; and eastwards, under the 1,629m (5,344ft) high South Shoulder, towards Mesa Potamos Monastery. Mountain-bikes can be hired in several shops along the main street for tough expeditions along forest trails or steep mountain roads.

Catering for visitors to Panagia tou Kykkou, this shopkeeper does a heaven-sent trade

In both the Greek and Turkish Cypriot sectors the process of reafforestation begun by the British continues today. Not only do local industries, wildlife and water supplies benefit, but visitors find among the trees a ready-made shelter from the sun and a holiday experience far different from the traditional beach model.

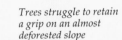

Trees struggle to retain a grip on an almost deforested slope

Cyprus's forests are among the island's glories. In the dog days of summer, when heat smothers the plains, the forests of the Troodos and the Pentadaktylos (Beşparmak) Mountains act like magnets, drawing people upwards to the cool scent of eucalyptus, cedar and pine. So extensive are the forests in both ranges, and so rugged the terrain on which they grow, that they represent the last great place of escape on the island. No other country in the Levant boasts such wide-ranging and dense forest cover, yet the green canopy shading the mountains is but the straggly remnant of its former glory.

The main tree varieties on Cyprus are Aleppo pine, black pine, cypress, eucalyptus, juniper, plane, oak and cedar, the latter most notable at Cedar Valley in the Pafos Forest. In addition, cultivated trees not generally found in the forests include walnut, olive, carob, almond, citrus (orange, lemon, grapefruit and tangerine), fig, pomegranate, loquat, mulberry, apricot, damson, date palm and banana.

Fallen giants In ancient times the fame of Cyprus's forests spread far and wide—and people came from far and wide to chop them down. Cypriot trees went into the fleets with which Phoenicians, Persians, Greeks and Romans dominated the Mediterranean, and into copper smelters to fuel Bronze Age civilization. Natural regeneration was unable to keep pace with demand, yet even as late as the Ottoman period the island's forests covered not only the mountains but extended to the coastal plains. Excessive felling, over-grazing by goats of young shoots that would have

replaced the fallen giants, clearance for agriculture and fires all conspired to lay the forests low.

The British were horrified at the destruction and took steps to reverse the process. They created the first forestry station, at Stavros tis Psokas in the western Troodos in 1884, to re-establish the Pafos Forest, which is still at the forefront of the reafforestation scheme. In 1907 Winston Churchill, then a junior government minister, visited Cyprus and determined to aid the work with additional funds. It was not merely a question of aesthetics: Loss of trees led to soil erosion and to climate changes. Streams dried up in summer and underground aquifers were depleted, a serious problem that remains.

Extreme devastation High in the Troodos Mountains, the traveller may suddenly come upon a scene that looks like the end of the world. Around the villages of Pano and Kato Amiantos the forest vanishes and a great swathe of mountainside lies desolate. The Amiantos asbestos mine is no more, but its legacy has permanently scarred the mountain, an extreme example of the devastation wrought by ill-considered exploitation. Not far away is the Forestry College at Prodromos, where students learn the skills of replanting and caring for the trees.

There is no equivalent to this level of devastation in the Pentadaktylos (Beşparmak) Mountains of North Cyprus, although there are quarries in the foothills and the legacy of wildfires are burned forest. Woodcutters are active enough in the higher reaches, but the exploitation is on a small scale and the forests seem well able to cope. In any case, even more so than the Troodos, the Pentadaktylos are sparsely populated and have only minimal tourist facilities. Reafforestation continues in both the Greek and Turkish Cypriot sectors, with determination but with a long way to go. It may be that Apollo Ylatis, the woodland god whose sanctuary stands on the coast between Pafos and Limassol, would be mollified by knowing that the glory of his realm is being re-created, tree by tree.

FOREST STATIONS

There are forest stations scattered all over the Troodos Mountains, covering not only the high peaks, but reaching all the way to the lowest foothills in all directions. The Stavros tis Psokas Forest Station (see page 179) in the western Troodos foothills has a guest-house, and most have information panels, and picnic and barbecue areas. Some have nature trails, such as the Artemis Trail on Mount Olympos (see page 137).

The Pentadaktylos (Beşparmak) Mountains of North Cyprus have a network of similar forest stations. A forest trail runs from Agios Ilarion (St. Hilarion) Castle to Kantara Castle, and there is an important forest station at Halevga (Alevkaya), with a restaurant and a forestry museum.

145

GOING UP

Awareness of trees has been particularly acute in Northern Cyprus since the wildfire of June 1995 which incinerated a 40km (25-mile) swathe of forest on the northern slopes of the Pentadaktylos (Beşparmak) Mountains. Since then, fire prevention and fighting measures have been stepped up and millions of saplings have been planted by the authorities, local businesses and community groups.

Athalassa Forest near Nicosia: a nursery for the reafforestation effort

Panagia tou Kykkou

Drive

See map on pages 120–121

Kato Platres to Throni

This 50km (31 mile) drive is spiritually soothing, both for the lofty outlook and champagne air of the high mountains and for the emblematic Byzantine monastery at its end. Two hours of leisurely driving would complete it, but you should savour the experience and explore some of the side-trails. The sights on this drive are covered in more detail on pages 124–151.

Take the road north out of Kato Platres and, as the open slopes of the

Troodos Mountains' southern approaches give way to thick pine forests, you arrive at **Pano Platres**▶▶▶, boasting a plethora of hotels and restaurants which have not, however, detracted overmuch from its alpine charm. At the first T-junction on the edge of Platres turn right for Troodos, then left at the second T-junction.

You may think it's a little early in the itinerary for walking, but if not, the short trek to the **Kalidonia Falls**▶▶ is recommended for its immersion in the forest air, with perhaps a free shower under the trim little waterfall as well; a **trout farm** is situated beside the Psilodhendro restaurant at the start of the walk. At the next junction follow the sign for Troodos.

Still climbing, you pass a cluster of government lodges on the left, and somewhere off to your right, hidden among trees on the steep eastern slope, the president's summer palace. Shortly afterwards there is the first of several picnic areas that dot the route. **Troodos**▶▶ resort is not exactly idyllic, with its souvenir shops and fast-food outlets, but its popularity depends on precisely those assets. At the far end of the resort turn left, following the sign for Prodromos.

A subsequent left turn puts you on the short diversion to **Mount Olympos**▶▶▶. The summit is out of bounds, but the outlook from nearby viewpoints is spectacular, which compensates for the limited view obtained from the tree-lined road up to this point. Return to the main road and turn left for Prodromos.

Now head downhill, passing the Hera ski-lift to the left, followed by the Prodromos reservoir. This rectangular, stone-lined basin of water is not especially grand, but its banks make for a pleasant enough picnic site. At the hairpin bend at the entrance to Prodromos either carry straight on to explore the village or bear right towards **Pedoulas**▶, a busy yet attractively sited village. As forest gives way to open countryside, the views into the rugged valleys become more spectacular.

Note the colossal **Holy Cross of Pedoulas** to your right. From here the road to Kykkos widens, following a winding course into the eastern fringe of Pafos Forest.

The great bulk of **Panagia tou Kykkou**▶▶▶, with its church and extensive outbuildings, dominates the landscape when seen from a higher viewpoint, but as you arrive along the road it emerges suddenly and unexpectedly from behind the forest cover. All the power and glory of Cyprus's Orthodox Church is evident in the imposing foundation of its most powerful monastery.

From here continue uphill towards Throni for the **Tomb of Archbishop Makarios**▶▶, the final resting-place of the nation's first president. At the summit of 1,318m (4,325ft) Mount Kykkos, the tomb amply fulfils Makarios's desire to look out across the land he led to independence.

147

Head for the hills...

▶ Pedoulas
120C2

Early summer brings a fabulous harvest of cherries to this village in the Marathasa Valley. Roadside stalls are filled with the dark fruit, piled up in baskets like heaps of precious stones. The village's small 15th-century church of **Archangelos Michaïl▶** (*Open* irregularly. *Admission free*), a UNESCO World Cultural Heritage Site, has a sloping roof and some interesting frescoes, while a short distance along the road to Kykkos is the modern **Holy Cross of Pedoulas**, a huge cross visible from a long way off.

148

The tower and dome of Pedoulas's lavish, modern church in the heart of the village

▶ Pelendri
121D2

Somewhat off the beaten track to the east of the upper mountains, Pelendri overlooks the greener lower slopes from its 880m (2,887ft) vantage point. It was once a royal estate, the property of Jean de Lusignan, son of the 14th-century king of Cyprus, Hugh IV. It is distinguished for its church of **Timiou Stavrou▶▶** (*Open* irregularly. *Admission free*), a UNESCO-classified site. Dating from 1360, the church has a suite of fine frescoes depicting a wide range of biblical scenes.

▶ Pera Pedi
120C1

Dominated by the **KEO winery**, which is conveniently sited for processing the grapes that are the key element of the local economy, Pera Pedi lies south of Platres.

Just north of the village, the **Pera Pedi Dam** on the Kryos river makes a fine target for a walking excursion and a scenic picnic site on arrival. Its churches of **Agios Nikolaos** and **Agios Ioannis** have some interesting 16th-century icons.

▶▶ Pitsilia
121D2

This vaguely defined but large area on the eastern flank of the mountains is the wild side of the Troodos, with few specific points of tourist interest. Scattered villages hanging on its slopes make their living from vineyards and almond and hazelnut orchards. The best roads in the Troodos either stop, as if in fright, when they hit Pitsilia or bypass it. This makes it perfect for aimless wandering.

▶ Prodromos
120C2

Perched at an altitude of 1,390m (4,560ft), Prodromos commands a spectacular view across the Troodos Mountains. Indeed, it offers a better panorama than can be gained from many points higher up, mainly because of its position overlooking a constellation of tiny villages on the western slopes in an agricultural area that has not been heavily forested. The sense of greater vision is no doubt helpful to students of the Cyprus Forestry College at Prodromos.

▶▶▶ Solea Valley   121D3

Also known as the 'valley of apples', on account of the preponderance of orchards in its agricultural make-up, the Solea Valley carries the main road from Nicosia via Peristerona into the Troodos Mountains. It is a sad fact that the lines of traffic making this journey generally bypass the valley, as if the end of the road were more important than the attractions en route. It is worthwhile taking the time to visit some of the valley's small agricultural villages, such as Evrychou and Kaliana, which are characteristic of an older way of life on Cyprus. Bordered by the **Adelfoi Forest**▶▶ and watered, in winter at any rate, by the Karyotis stream, the Solea forms a green carpet across the steadily climbing landscape.

▶▶ Stavros tou Agiasmati   121D2

Open: irregularly. Admission free

Located 8km (5 miles) by road from the village of Platanistasa (4km/2.5 miles of them along a dusty track), this little mountain church has developed into something of a minor village industry, as groups of tourists scour the coffee shops for the keyholder. Any initial disappointment on arriving at the drab-coloured, strikingly situated structure is soon dispelled. The 15th-century frescoes, some by the Lebanese artist Philip tou Goul (see panel), which fill the Church of the Holy Cross, recount just about every significant episode from the New Testament, with a few from the Old Testament thrown in as well. The beautifully rendered Virgin in the half-dome behind the iconostasis might alone have persuaded UNESCO to include the church in its list of World Cultural Heritage Sites.

MURAL-MAKER

An inscription in the church of Stavros tou Agiasmati near Platanistasa dates its frescoes to 1494 and records the name of their creator as Philip tou Goul, a Lebanese Christian whose family achieved wealth and influence in Cyprus under the Lusignan kings and whose name derived from the old French word *gueules*, a heraldic term meaning 'red'. Goul's work employs a lively palette, of which red is indeed the most vibrant colour. His cycle of frescoes at Stavros tou Agiasmati is considered the finest surviving example from the 15th century in Cyprus. Goul's contemporaneous work, from 1495, also graces the church of Agios Mamas at Louvaras (see page 133).

149

Magnificent frescoes in the remote church of Stavros tou Agiasmati

HOT TIP

Throni hill, on which the tomb of President Makarios stands, may be spiritually warming for the archbishop's admirers but it can be a chilly place even in summer from which to watch the dramatic sunset. Warmth can be obtained from the little chapel at the top of the hill; the walls soak up the sun's heat during the day and send it out in a satisfying glow at twilight.

TESTING TIMES

The Cypriot government lists Prodromos as the highest village in Cyprus. Yet Troodos is higher than Prodromos. Question: Which is the highest village in Cyprus? Answer: both. Prodromos can safely claim to be the highest village because Troodos is not considered by the government to be a village, since it has no permanent residents.

Village time moves at its own leisurely pace in the mountains

▶▶ Tomb of Archbishop Makarios III   120B3

Open: daily 9–3. Admission free

On Throni hill, 2km (1.5 miles) from Panagia tou Kykkou, the first president of the Republic of Cyprus, Archbishop Makarios III, who died in 1977, rests in a tomb surmounted by a black marble slab and watched over by an honour guard of the Cyprus National Guard. It was Makarios's wish that he be buried here, at the top of a mountain that commands an unparalleled view across the island. A simple and not especially attractive modern chapel dedicated to him stands at the summit of the nearby hillside, amply fulfilling his wish to look out in eternity across the land he loved. Mountains march away into the haze, rimmed by the silver gleam of the sea.

▶ Trooditissa Monastery   120B2

Rarely open for visitors

Trooditissa is alpine in character, thanks to its design and location among the pine forests overlooking a steep gorge some 5km (3 miles) from Pano Platres. The present buildings date from the 1700s, and the church boasts a priceless icon, a silver-gilt work of the Virgin and a leather belt decorated with silver medallions, which is reputed to cure infertility.

▶▶ Troodos   120C2

Troodos is one of those rare tourist resorts which, considering it consists mostly of gift shops, tavernas and car parks, should not be attractive, yet is. Perhaps the reason for this is its situation near the forested roof of the mountains and the feeling of well-being imparted by the fresh air; or perhaps the obvious pleasure that the tourists take from being among a crowd as a reward for the loneliness of the mountain trails. Two nature walks, the 9km (5.5-mile) **Atalanta Trail** and the 3km (2-mile) **Persephone Trail**, leave from Troodos, taking different trajectories through the forests around the village.

During the British period Troodos was a mountain resort and an army summer base for colonial administrators and troops, influenced by the British tradition in India of fleeing to the mountain 'hill stations' to escape the scorching heat of the plains. The governor's summer residence (now belonging to the president of the republic; closed to the public) is hidden away in steeply sloping, dense forests just south of Troodos.

▶▶ Vasa
120B1

A wine-making village in the Krassochoria district, Vasa is a red-roofed crown on a hilltop in the southwestern Troodos, below Omodos. Wine is not the only drink for which Vasa is renowned; mineral water from the village's excellent spring is bottled here.

The village once belonged to the Catholic Knights Hospitaller, whose commandery was at Kolossi (see page 108); the village's church of **Agios Georgios** was apparently built in the 14th century by Orthodox monks who had been expelled from their monastery by the Hospitallers. Roman-era tombs in the area suggest that this may have been a mountain hideaway some 2,000 years ago; their treasure of coins, jewellery and *amphorae* can be seen in Nicosia's Cyprus Museum. The house of the Cypriot poet Lipertis, who died in 1937, has been restored and can be visited.

▶ Vouni
120B1

Like many of the mountain villages, Vouni had, until recently, known better and richer times—not richer in terms of money, but richer in the life of a community whose young people had not yet drifted away to the towns in search of jobs. And like many of them still, it whiled away the drowsy hours of the long summer days, as if dreaming of those better times. Now, with preservation orders, art and craft workshops and outside investment coming in, Vouni has awoken from its sleep and is taking action to break the cycle of decline. Red-tiled roofs and cobbled streets maintain the feel of its past.

RIMBAUD TOO

The French poet Arthur Rimbaud was employed as foreman during construction of the British governor's (now the president's) summer residence at Troodos. Rimbaud arrived in Cyprus in 1879 and worked in a quarry at Potamos Creek near Agia Napa. Typhoid forced his return to France in May the following year. A year later he was back, in Troodos. In a letter home he complained: 'It is always necessary to travel by horse; transport is terribly difficult, the villages very far away, the food very dear.' He complained of cold and of feeling ill, but admitted 'the air is very healthy'.

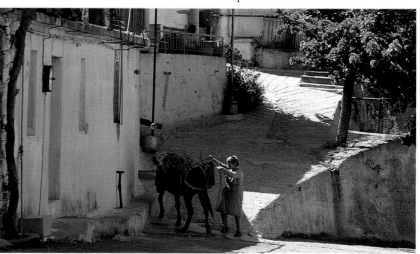

▶ Zoopigi
121D1

One of the villages that produces the Commandaria dessert wine, Zoopigi is a brightly coloured village, surrounded by vineyards, in a dazzlingly green area far off the main slopes of the Troodos. Dotted with villas and pretty villages, the grape-growing country has an ambience reminiscent of classic European wine-producing regions such as Tuscany and Rioja.

In Zoopigi village, a donkey still carries the weight

Cypriot wines were renowned for their quality in ancient times. Today wine is once again one of Cyprus's most important exports, with great stretches of land given over to viticulture.

VINTAGE CHAMPAGNE
Cypriots say that it was from their vines that the Champagne grape was first grown, and that these were taken from Cyprus at the time of the crusades, when Count Thibaud of Champagne visited his cousin, the Lusignan Queen Alice, in Cyprus.

152

It is a late afternoon in autumn, and golden light washes over the vineyards that carpet the southern and western foothills of the Troodos Mountains. Thick bunches of ripened grapes weigh down the vines, awaiting the picker's hand. The whole village has turned out, it seems, pickers of all ages bent double under the sun and piling up grapes in bags ready for collection. Soon Cyprus's narrow roads will be busy with lorries moving vast quantities of grapes to the wineries. 'Next year's wine is the sweetest,' goes the Cypriot expression, but this year's seems sweet enough.

Wine is among Cyprus's most important exports, with both production and sales growing by leaps and bounds. Britain is the principal overseas market, but sales in continental Europe are growing, even in such wine-producing citadels as France and Italy. Cyprus wines draw on a reputation that reaches back to ancient times, when they were commended by Homer. King Solomon, too, had a way with words that are music to a modern wine-marketing executive's ears: 'My beloved is unto me as a cluster of Cyprus grapes in the vineyards of Engadi'.

Producer's choice Georgios Yiallouros looks more like a Viking warrior than a Cypriot wine-grower, but that has proved no disqualification for owning one of Cyprus's most interesting wineries. His Ecological Winery at Agios Amvrosios in the southern Troodos produces, as its name implies, ecologically sound wines from its organically grown grapes. They also taste good. Georgios, who is a welder by profession, and his wife Joanna, set up their winery in the late 1980s, initially supplying only friends and neighbours. The business developed quickly and is today a

Georgios Yiallouros (right), owner of the Ecological Winery at Agios Amvrosios, displays the fruit of his natural talent

respectable cottage industry producing up to 100,000 bottles a year in five brands: Ambelidha, a dry white; Oenanthi, a rosé; and three reds, Agravani, Agrambeli and Cabernet Sauvignon.

Monks also have their feet in the wine press. Panagia Chrysorrogiatissa monastery, near Pano Panagia, has won respect for its high-quality Monte Royia wines. An estimated 30,000 families (mostly in the Greek Cypriot section of Cyprus) are involved in grape production, with nearly 10 percent of the island's surface area given over to this crop. Yet, although production from small independent wineries like the Ecological Winery and Panagia Chrysorrogiatissa is growing fast, the bulk of wine-making is dominated by four giant wineries based in Limassol: KEO, ETKO, LOEL and SODAP.

Vineyards near Pafos are the source of a light, fruity wine

Festival time Limassol is the scene of the industry's showcase, the Limassol Wine Festival, held in the city's Municipal Gardens in September. This can turn into quite a riot, as all the island's wineries are present and all give away free wine as fast as their staff can fill up festival-goers' plastic cups. Not much considered oenology gets done at this event, but everyone has a high old time. Cyprus wines run the gamut from light, sparkling whites to full-bodied reds, with most popular attention being focused on the former as they go so well with the climate and with an alfresco taverna dinner.

153

CYPRUS WHISKY
The villager's waste-not-want-not philosophy has provided Cyprus with a distinctive product, *zivania*, or 'Cyprus whisky'. Made from the grape remnant after wine fermentation, and distilled in a copper pot called a *kazani*, it is an alcohol so fiery that Cypriots drink it in frugal moderation, and even employ it as rubbing alcohol for soothing aches and tired muscles. The alcohol is used in the production of local gin, sherry and brandy, and much of it is exported. Zoopigi and Kalo Chorio are important village producers of *zivania*.

Cypriot wines: all bottled up and ready to go

Just desserts A wine that has experts reaching for their superlatives is Commandaria, the heir to a wine that was drunk in ancient times at festivals in honour of Aphrodite. In its 'modern' form it originated in the 13th century with the crusader Knights Hospitaller, who produced it at their Grand Commandery, the estate they owned and operated from Kolossi Castle, west of Limassol. A dark, ruby-red, sweet dessert wine, Commandaria is made from grapes picked at the last possible moment, then sun-dried, from vineyards above 1,000m (3,300ft) around the villages of Zoopigi, Agios Konstantinos and Kalo Chorio.

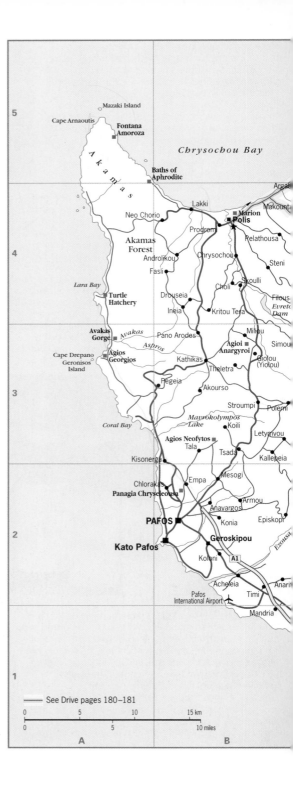

Mazaki Island

Cape Arnaoutis

Fontana Amoroza

Chrysochou Bay

A k a m a s

Baths of Aphrodite

Argat

Lakki

Makount

Neo Chorio

Marion

Polis

Prodrom

Relathousa

Akamas Forest

Androlikou

Chrysochou

Steni

Fasli

Skoulli

Lara Bay

Drouseia

Choli

Filous

Evreta Dam

Turtle Hatchery

Ineia

Kritou Tera

Avakas Gorge

Avakas

Pano Arodes

Mihou

Aspros

Agioi Anargyroi

Simou

Cape Drepano
Geronisos Island

Agios Georgios

Kathikas

Giolou
(Yiolou)

Theletra

Pegeia

Akourso

Stroumpi

Polemi

Coral Bay

Mavrokolympos Lake

Koili

Letymvou

Agios Neofytos

Tala

Tsada

Kalleheia

Kisonerga

Empa

Mesogi

Chlorakas

Panagia Chryseleousa

Armou

Anavargos

PAFOS

Konia

Episkopi

Kato Pafos

Geroskipou

Koloni

A1

Ezousa

Acheleia

Anari

Pafos
International Airport

Timi

Mandria

— See Drive pages 180–181

| 0 | 5 | 10 | 15 km |

| 0 | 5 | 10 miles |

A   B

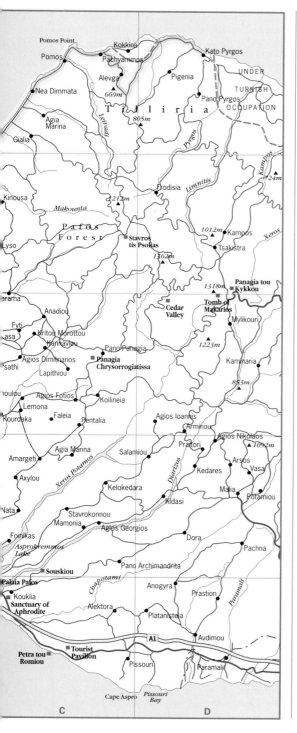

155

ROAD SENSE
Many roads between the coast and the Troodos Mountains are of sufficient width only for one-and-a-half vehicles to pass each other; two vehicles (a more usual combination) won't fit. This leads to some interesting situations, particularly as Cypriot farmers have learned that by driving their pick-ups straight at tourists' Z-registration hired cars they can, as if by magic, be left with the whole road to themselves. It is as well to be cautious.

THE WEST From the sun-gilded lower slopes of the Troodos Mountains where grapes ripen in profusion during the long summer days, to the wild shores of the Akamas Peninsula, western Cyprus has a romantic quality scarcely matched anywhere else on the island. This, after all, is where Aphrodite was born, carried ashore by the west wind at the rock called Petra tou Romiou. Her favourite haunts are dotted all over the region and here her spirit lingers still.

In Pafos, the west boasts Cyprus's fastest-growing resort area, thanks to the opening in 1984 of Pafos International Airport as a spur to developing this section of the coast. Sadly, many of the lessons that should have been learned from older resorts have pretty much been ignored at Pafos. The town retains some elements of its original charm and has its own intrinsic merits as a holiday resort, despite the complaints of those who react sniffily to the slightest hint of commercialism. It must be said, however, that tourism development and conservation have fought it out here—and development has won.

Coral Bay, north of Pafos, is one of the best beaches on the island

RISK FACTORS The battle lines in this debate have shifted northwards, to the coast at Polis and Lakki, to the ruggedly beautiful Akamas Peninsula, and to the beach at Lara Bay where endangered sea turtles come ashore to lay their eggs. At Lara, the development offensive has been slowed, if not halted. The government's tourism policy is effectively on trial in this area, which many people, Cypriots and tourists alike, consider to be the last refuge of the natural world along the coast. The omens are not good, though, and the government's proposal, taken in 2000, to permit 'mild and controlled' development in the Akamas Peninsula—an area that was supposed to become a national park—set alarm bells ringing among Cypriot and international environmentalists. This followed an earlier ruling approving a 'relaxation' of zoning regulations to allow a company owned partly by the family of a government minister to build a giant resort hotel on the edge of the peninsula.

Trying to redress the balance, Friends of the Earth's Laona Project sponsors 'low-impact' tourism in villages bordering the Akamas, allowing local people to benefit financially from tourism without ruining their villages' traditional character. Though there is powerful opposition, locally and nationally, to any attempt to slow the development juggernaut in the Akamas area, the project at least offers an alternative. This and the long-delayed establishment of an Akamas Peninsula National Park, seem the only way to secure the survival of what has been called 'the last truly Homeric landscape in the Hellenistic world'.

History has left its mark in the west. Pafos was an early capital of the island, and the seat of the imperial governor during the Roman Empire and into the Byzantine period. The ruins of its patrician houses and public buildings have yielded a remarkable harvest of archaeological finds. At Old (Palaia) Pafos, now the village of Kouklia, the excavated walls of an earlier city still bear scars from Greek wars with Persia; here also are the moving vestiges of the Sanctuary of Aphrodite. Byzantine monasteries and churches are thick on the ground.

ROUGH COUNTRY The sweep of little-developed coastline from Polis to the demarcation line at Kato Pyrgos is a glimpse of Cyprus before tourism. Between the coastal plain and the mountains the picture is similar: Those lime-green hills bathed in lemon light look deceptively mild from a distance, but contain some of the roughest tracks on the island, and the moufflon (wild sheep) roams an area now being painstakingly reafforested.

Sunset belongs to the west, and an appreciative audience is always on hand to watch it. As the sun touches the shining surface of the sea, casting a shimmering red light across the waves and setting the sky aflame, it is easy to believe that the Mediterranean remains the realm of gods and heroes, and that the wind still sighs in the rigging of a triple-banked galley sailing just over the horizon.

Smooth sea, rough country: the distinctive signature of the Akamas Peninsula

157

GOING BANANAS
The climate and soil of western Cyprus are ideal for the production of bananas. You can see the remnant of once extensive plantations along the coast north of Pafos, easily identifiable even to the agriculturally challenged by the many bright blue plastic bags in which bunches of bananas grow. Smaller than their Caribbean cousins, Cypriot bananas have a strong local following, and after the harvest you are sure to be given them at the end of a taverna meal.

Sky and sea form the stage for the sunset's daily spectacle

SWEET-TOOTHED BUFFALO
Cyprus' sugar is said to have been so sweet that Egyptian buffaloes, who had somehow acquired a taste for that delicacy and also discovered where it came from, were apparently in the habit of swimming across the sea just for a nibble.

MOIST ZEPHYRS
Rainfall in the west is higher than in the rest of the island, which accounts for the noticeably lusher vegetation hereabouts. This is a result of Homer's 'moist west winds' hitting the barrier of the Troodos Mountains, causing the clouds to unload their cargo of water. The difference in average precipitation may be discernible to meteorologists, but the average visitor is unlikely to be deluged.

Agios Neofytos Monastery, founded by the ascetic hermit St. Neofytos

▶ Acheleia　　　　　　154B2

Until competition from the Caribbean began to overwhelm it during the Venetian period, western Cyprus had an important sugar industry, with processing plants in villages from here to Episkopi exporting their product all over Europe.

Acheleia's sugar connection is no more, and its two Byzantine churches— the 12th-century **Agios Theodosios**, modernized in the 1930s, and the 16th-century **Agios Georgios**—are its only points of special interest for visitors; there are some faded murals in the former and icons in the latter. The village is in the heart of a government-sponsored cluster of experimental farms aimed at improving yields and broadening the range of products in cultivation. Several such farms are indicated on road signs around Acheleia.

▶ Agioi Anargyroi　　　　　　154B3

Closed for renovations
The sulphur springs near this village are reputed to be efficacious in cases of arthritis, and following renovation to the thermal baths, due to be completed in 2006, should be even more so. Beside the springs is a modern hotel with swimming pool. The nearby village of **Giolou** is known for its rich farmland surroundings and an Onion Festival in July.

▶▶ Agios Neofytos　　　　　　154B3

Open: Apr–Oct daily 9–2 and 2–4; Nov–Mar daily 9–4.
Admission: monastery free; museum and Encleistra: inexpensive
The tiny 12th-century cave church of Agios Neofytos Monastery near the village of Tala is crammed with spectacular murals. Its founder, the ascetic would-be hermit St. Neofytos, could be described as a failed recluse. Having side-stepped an arranged marriage, he carved himself a cave in the Melissovouno hill overlooking Pafos, but instead of having a quiet hermitic life, he became a

religious superstar, his writings attracting followers from all over the Orthodox world. The *encleistra* (enclosure) carved into the cliff-face by the 12th-century saint is covered with murals.

►►► Akamas Peninsula
154A5

This wild, lonely peninsula is frequently cited as the last piece of genuine wilderness left in Cyprus—an indication of the anti-development passions this area arouses. It is beautiful indeed, a rugged coastline bordered by azure waters and a backbone of forested hills.

Difficult to access, to put it mildly, its terrain is so testing for four-wheel-drive vehicles, mountain-bikes and dirt-bikes that few people chance it (although it is possible to cross the tamer parts in an ordinary car). As a result, its ecology has remained largely intact until now, and it is possible that a national park will be created to protect at least part of it (see pages 162–163), although there is powerful opposition from the government, local communities and commercial interests.

The fruit of a reafforestation scheme, **Akamas Forest►►** is spreading through some of the roughest terrain on the peninsula. It is, however, traversed by a fairly good trail, beginning at the coast about 6km (4 miles) north of Lara Bay and ending at Neo Chorio (or vice versa), which makes it easier to get to grips with its rugged charms.

Fontana Amoroza►, the 'Fountain of Love', is no more than a muddy pool near the tip of the peninsula. Its association with Aphrodite is tenuous but tantalizing, since anyone who tastes its water will immediately fall in love. Wrote Italian Renaissance poet Ludovico Ariosto: 'Thanks to the goddess, young people and old experience the ardour of love to the last hours of their lives'. Aphrodite gives the ultimate compliment to her own gender: 'In this place, every woman and girl is more desirable than in any other place on earth'.

Steep and narrow, the roads of **Neo Chorio►►** village witness some interesting moments when four-wheel-drive vehicles heading into and out of the Akamas encounter one another. The villagers seem quite used to traffic snarls (sometimes involving three or even four jeeps) and are always ready to leave their café tables to assist. If Neo Chorio has something of the feel of a frontier town, it is hardly surprising, for the Akamas Peninsula is, after all, the wild west.

The bay near Fontana Amoroza, source of legendary love

COUP DE FOUDRE
Visitors to the Fontana Amoroza in the Akamas Peninsula might wish to be careful about who they go with, as legend has it that anyone who drinks from the pool will fall instantly head over heels in love with the first person they see.

Selling fresh-picked oranges in the Akamas Peninsula

160

The Baths of Aphrodite, sacred to the goddess of love

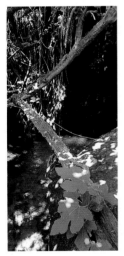

▶▶ Avakas Gorge   154A3

Hikers need to get their boots on for this spectacularly jagged gorge, which slices inland from a point between Cape Drepano and Lara Bay and makes testing ground for a stroll. In the rainy season the Avakas river comes charging through the gorge, and rain and wind may dislodge rocks from the cliff sides.

▶▶ Baths of Aphrodite (Loutra tis Afroditis)   154A5

Open: permanently. Admission free
Near the start of the Akamas Peninsula, this tiny freshwater pool half-hidden by a cave and trees is five minutes' walk from the parking area. Ordinary mortals are forbidden to enter the cool waters of the spring-fed pool where the goddess of love is said to have bathed. As its waters are said to confer eternal youth, this is disappointing.

▶ Cape Drepano   154A3

Uninhabited **Geronisos Island**, lies just off Cape Drepano's rocky shore; there are faint remains of a Roman-era settlement from the time of Cleopatra. Cape Drepano itself is a scenic spot, with a small fishing harbour overlooked by the domed church of **Agios Georgios** (*Open* daily. *Admission free*), built in the 1920s, and a rocky shore favoured by sunbathers. The area appears to have been quite important in Roman times, and archaeologists have uncovered rock-tombs and scattered traces of monumental architecture. The Christians picked up where the pagans left off, and Agios Georgios has a predecessor, dating from the 6th century, now jumbled on a nearby excavation site.

▶ Chlorakas   154B2

On the shore amid hotels, stands a museum containing the Grivas Boat. The Greek army Colonel (later General) Grivas landed here in 1954 to form EOKA and lead the struggle against the British for Enosis (union of Cyprus with Greece). The caique here is similar to the one Grivas used

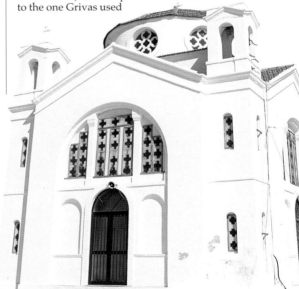

Modern Agios Georgios basks in the sun at Cape Drepanon

▶▶ Coral Bay   154A3

Situated just to the north of Pafos, this bay has one of the longest and finest stretches of golden sand in the area. Because of this, a resort has grown up around it and the beach can get very busy at peak times. Out of the main season it is quieter and remains a good spot for bathing. There's not much else of interest among the slew of bars, tavernas, hotels, villas and apartments that have chewed up the area's once handsome olive goves and vineyards. But on a headland between Coral Bay beach and the neighbouring Corallia beach, stands the partly excavated Bronze Age Mycenaean site of **Paleokastro-Maa▶**, dating from around 1200BC. The site's small Museum of the Mycenaean Colonization of Cyprus (*Open* Mon–Sat 10–4. *Admission: inexpensive*) has a few objects from the excavations—and an aerial photograph of the area taken in the 1970s, that alone is worth the admission for its view of a then entirely undeveloped coastline.

In the hills overlooking Coral Bay is the fast-expanding village of **Pegeia**, which is recorded in a Cypriot folk song thanks to its village spring, To Vrysi, and is notable for half a dozen excellent tavernas in and around its square. Dull villa developments have taken over the once-handsome farmland betweeen here and Coral Bay.

▶ Geroskipou   154B2

This village has come a long way since it was the Sacred Garden of Aphrodite, and the journey has been mostly downhill. Aphrodite relaxed here after amorous adventures, in a garden watered by a spring. Flowers, olive trees and fruit trees, including pomegranate trees, which were sacred to Aphrodite, grew there. Nowadays myth has to deal with the reality of a nondescript, fast-growing village, virtually a suburb of Pafos.

Geroskipou is reputed for pottery and *loukoumi* (Turkish delight, or, as it is known in these parts, Cypriot delight—see panel). The five-domed church of **Agia Paraskevi** (*Open* Apr–Oct Mon–Sat 8–1, 2–5; Nov–Mar Mon–Sat 8–1, 2–4. *Admission free*) dating originally from the 9th century but frequently rebuilt, is a rarity simply for those five domes, and contains an important icon of the Virgin besides. The **Museum of Folk Art▶** (tel: 26306216. *Open* Jul–Aug Mon–Fri 7.30–2.30; Sep–Jun Mon–Wed, Fri 9–2.30, Thu 9–5. *Admission: inexpensive*), in the house of Hadji Smith (a Cypriot the British appointed as their vice-consul in 1800), displays a moderately interesting collection of period domestic items and costumes.

CYPRIOT DELIGHT
This is really Turkish delight, but Greek Cypriots find it hard to look on any-thing Turkish with much delight, hence the name change. Whatever the name, it is a still-delightful confection of jelly, almonds and sugar, dunked in icing-sugar. It is sold in a variety of colours and flavours, and tastes as good as it looks—but perhaps a dental appoint-ment is a wise precaution if over-indulgence is intended.

161

SILKEN THREADS
As recently as the 1950s, the area around Geroskipou was thick with mulberry trees, and a mill in the village itself produced that most noble of materials—silk. Cyprus was selected as a centre of silk production during the Byzantine Empire after monks smuggled silkworms out of China in the 6th century, in the reign of the Emperor Justinian.

A shepherdess leads her flock to pastures new

The wild and wonderful Akamas Peninsula is nature's last stronghold in Cyprus. Isolated, rugged and beautiful, it is a treasure even more valuable than the Troodos Mountains. Many people believe that granting the peninsula national park status is the only chance to preserve some vestige of the island's natural heritage.

NAKED TRUTH
The virtually unfrequented beaches of the Akamas, although mostly composed of pebbles or rock, are among the best places in the island for sunbathing and swimming in the tradition of Aphrodite and Adonis. The only drawback to going nude—apart from binocular-equipped hikers admiring the peninsula's wildlife and scenery—is that some of the rocks just under the surface are razor sharp. The more remote beaches are best reached by power-boat, which can be hired in Lakki.

Diving off the Akamas Peninsula

Manoeuvring a four-wheel-drive vehicle in the Akamas can be as much a test of human nerve as of mechanical endurance. The slopes you tackle at times seem vertical, and the rock-fields you negotiate may seem as sharp as razor-blades to your tyres.

Nature protects herself with formidable defences in the Akamas Peninsula, a thick wedge of rock jutting out into the sea in the far west, and until now humans have not mounted the kind of full-scale commercial assault needed to break down the walls and sack the citadel. If the increasingly vocal, not to say desperate, environmental lobby in Cyprus has its way, they never will. The idea of creating an Akamas Peninsula National Park was mooted in 1986 and has since had the support not only of Friends of the Earth and Greenpeace, but of the World Bank and the European Union. Despite this, the Cypriot Council of Ministers decided controversially in 2000 to recommend 'mild and controlled' development in the peninsula. In addition, they proposed to reduce the area of any eventual national park from 230sq km (90sq miles) recommended in a 1995 World Bank/EU report to about 70sq km (27sq miles). In 2005 the government had yet to decide on the Cypriot Council of Ministers recommendations or to initiate legislation. Clearly a crucial decision has to be made, one whose outcome will determine not only where Cyprus stands on conservation, but also the fate of the peninsula which takes its name from Akamas, son of Theseus, and a hero of the Trojan War.

Back to nature Some 530 plant varieties, almost one-third of Cyprus's indigenous species, call the Akamas home, and in springtime the colours are those of a giant impressionist palette. Forests of Aleppo pine mixed with Phoenician juniper bushes crown the rough range of hills that runs along the peninsula's spine. Birds, too, are numerous, with some 168 species having been observed in the area. Snakes and other reptiles get along just fine, and butterflies add their dash of colour.

Explosive company Britain's armed forces used to conduct live-fire exercises in the Akamas and a large part

of the peninsula was out of bounds when the red flags that denoted a military exercise were flying. Under a 1999 agreement, the shooting has been transferred to Cyprus National Guard ranges elsewhere on the island, but there is still a danger of undiscovered unexploded ordnance lying around. The warnings not to pick up unidentified objects that 'might explode and kill you' are still in force.

For the time being, however, tranquillity and the Akamas still go together like peaches and cream, and the best way to experience this blissful reality is to load up a small backpack with a picnic and water and walk. There are a few specific points of interest: the Baths of Aphrodite, Fontana Amoroza, Pyrgos tis Rigaenas, Neo Chorio village, the Akamas Forest, the ancient necropolis of Agios Konon and the wreck of a grounded boat on the northern shore. In addition, the Cyprus Forestry Department has established two nature trails, the Aphrodite and the Adonis, which range across interesting geology and flora in the setting where the goddess and the golden shepherd boy carried on their ill-fated romance. There are many unmarked trails to follow, and no reason for not pushing into the rough countryside. To hike as far as the mystic blue of the sea at Cape Arnaoutis is quite a trek, but the sense of peace and immersion in wilderness is ample compensation.

COUNTING SPECIES

Of Cyprus's 128 endemic plant species, 39 are to be found in the Akamas, and 530 species in all have been identified. These include: Aleppo pine, cypress, Phoenician juniper, spiny broom, thorny burnet, bramble, carob tree, lentisk, terebinth, myrtle, virgin's bower, kermes oak, gorse, caper, headed thyme, Cyprus thyme, Cyprus woodruff, marjoram, sage, wick weed, Spanish hedge-nettle, fig tree, royal oak, alaternus, storax, olive tree, eucalyptus, strawberry tree, oleander, gromwell, golden drop, rock roses and various *Cistus* species.

Of fauna, 168 bird, 12 mammal, 20 reptile and 16 butterfly species have been identified. Birds to look out for include: Eleonora's falcon, turtle dove, crested lark, Cyprus warbler, Cyprus pied wheatear, Bonelli's eagle and Scops' owl.

Tranquillity and the Akamas Peninsula go together hand in glove—at least until the effects of the decision to authorize development make themselves felt

LIVING DOLL
The legendary Pygmalion was said to have ruled over Palaia Pafos. He was both king and sculptor, and fell in love with the statue of a beautiful young woman he had created; the goddess Aphrodite brought the statue to life and Pygmalion married the woman, named Galatea. The child of their union was named Paphos.

CLOSE SHAVE
It doesn't fit with Aphrodite's image of celestial beauty, but there is a suggestion that she may have been worshipped as a bearded goddess, Aphroditos, at several locations in Cyprus, including Amathous. The fifth-century AD Roman antiquarian Macrobius wrote in his *Saturnalia*: 'There is in Cyprus a bearded statue of the goddess with female clothing but with male attributes, so it would seem that the deity is both male and female.'

▶▶ Kato Pyrgos   *155D5*

Although only some 60km (37 miles) from Nicosia as the crow flies, Kato Pyrgos is one of the most inaccessible locations on the whole island, thanks to the conflict of 1974, which cut it off from easy communication with the capital. The direct road now runs through some of the roughest sections of the Troodos Mountains, and visitors from Nicosia prefer to go the long way, via Limassol, Pafos and Polis. Its isolation, one of the village's attractions, saved it from being overwhelmed by tourism. Tranquil little Kato Pyrgos is favoured by Cypriot holidaymakers, and there are several reasonable hotels, cafés and tavernas to serve them.

▶ Koloni   *154B2*

Cyprus is not noted for its pottery, with the exception of the giant, hand-thrown red pots called *pitharia* which were popular in the past and can still be found, usually filled with flowers, today. Nevertheless, a pottery tradition does exist, and has been carried on to a certain extent. At this village south of Pafos you can see pottery being made, and you can buy what you see.

▶ Kouklia   *155C1*

This would be an otherwise ordinary Cypriot village were it not surrounded by the fragmentary remains of an ancient city and the most important temple of Aphrodite, the goddess who made Cyprus her own. Pausanias, a second-century AD travel writer, attributed the founding of **Palaia (Old) Pafos▶▶** to King Agapenor, a legendary hero of the Trojan War. Its vestiges date from the Bronze Age to the end of the Roman Empire's pagan era. At the Marcello hill outside Kouklia, archaeologists have uncovered part of the ancient city walls, revealing a dramatic scene from the Cypriot rebellion against Persia in 498BC: a Persian siege mound reaches up to the walls in preparation for troops to storm them; the defenders tunnelled desperately to undermine the mound and there was heavy fighting. Herodotus wrote that the Persians retook all the rebel cities, and the fate of their inhabitants can only be guessed at.

Mosaic of Leda and the swan at the Sanctuary of Aphrodite, near Kouklia

One's sense of expectation on entering the **Sanctuary of Aphrodite►►►** (tel: 26432180. *Open* daily 9–4. *Admission: inexpensive*) cannot quite survive the reality of finding its remnants sparse and hard to interpret. An impossible effort of imagination is needed to fill the spaces between vanished walls and broken columns with glimpses of the scene to which ancient writers allude: youthful handmaidens of Aphrodite giving themselves willingly to visiting pilgrims, who arrived in colourful processions, dancing, singing and wearing garlands of narcissus and myrtle. This was the shrine of the goddess of love, Homer's 'golden Aphrodite', whose *temenos* (sacred precinct) and incense-burning altar were renowned across the ancient world.

The temple comprised two halls, connected by porticoes and rooms for administration and guests. One part of the complex dates from the late Bronze Age around 1200BC, the other from the Roman period, until the Emperor Theodosius abolished the pagan cults near the end of the fourth century AD. Evidence from images on coins, analysis of the remnants and commentaries from antiquity prove that this was not a temple in the traditional Greek style, like the Parthenon in Athens, but was more like an oriental shrine consisting of an open enclosure, of which the archaic sanctuary was only a small part.

Holes gouged in the walls of the *temenos* have no obvious purpose, and it is speculated that they were made by robbers searching for the 'treasure of Aphrodite'. A shallow basin in the floor was probably filled with holy water and used by worshippers for ritual ablutions. The later hall shows the interest the Romans took in the shrine. The Emperor Titus dedicated an altar in AD69, and in the next century Trajan repaired earthquake damage.

The on-site museum is housed in a Lusignan manor called the Château de Covocle, which was itself incorporated into a Turkish-era farm called the Chiftlik. Several important finds from the sanctuary are on display, including a conical stone which is thought to have been the archaic cult idol of Aphrodite.

Inside the museum of Palaia Pafos, where remains from the Sanctuary of Aphrodite can be seen

NAUGHTY GIRL
Aphrodite's extra-curricular activities frequently landed her in trouble. In the *Odyssey*, Homer tells how, upon her release after being caught *in flagrante* with her lover Ares by her husband Hephaestous, 'laughter-loving Aphrodite [fled] to Paphos (Pafos) in Cyprus, where she has her sacred precinct and an altar fragrant with incense. There the Graces bathed her and anointed her with the imperishable oil that the immortals use. And when they had decked her out in her lovely clothes she was a marvel to behold.'

The West

Lara Bay, home to endangered turtles

FATAL ATTRACTION
Newly born turtles emerge from their nests at night and head instinctively for the sea, attracted by the luminescent glow of the water. A tragic aspect of tourism development at many of Cyprus's beaches is that the neon lights of nightclubs are brighter than the sea's luminescence. The effect is that the young turtles head instinctively for the nearest disco. For them, it is a fatal attraction.

▶▶▶ Lakki   154B4

Formerly a sponge-diving centre, until the sponge supply ran out some years ago, the last resort on the northern road into the Akamas Peninsula is growing fast. That growth may have to be curtailed if the Akamas is to remain the largely unspoiled wilderness it is today. Lakki attracted visitors who consider themselves more enlightened than their fellow holidaymakers soaking up the sun on the beaches of, say, Agia Napa. Alas, even enlightened visitors appear to need hotels, restaurants, gift shops, fizzy drinks with ice, suntan lotion, cars, jeeps and motorcycles—and that in the end makes them seem not quite so enlightened after all. The development versus preservation contest is at its sharpest here, and the outcome is still in doubt. Hotels are, so far, restricted in number and capacity but villas and apartments are mushrooming.

Taken on its own merits, however, Lakki is an attractive and colourful place, its newly expanded fishing harbour the liquid gateway to the Akamas, and beautifully situated in the heart of sweeping Chrysochou Bay. Scuba-diving is popular in the area, with several schools teaching the art to beginners, not so much at the village itself but along the rocky Akamas coastline. A fringe of mostly excellent tavernas specializing in seafood graces the harbour, and the adjacent beaches are popular with visitors getting their suntans in order before striking out on hiking expeditions into the Akamas.

▶▶▶ Lara Bay   154A4

Located between Pafos and the western shore of the Akamas Peninsula, sandy Lara Bay is the next logical item on the tourism development agenda. This will be bad news for the endangered green and loggerhead turtles if environmentalists lose their battle to prevent the development scenario being enacted. Female turtles will only come ashore to lay their eggs on open, quiet beaches, of which few now remain in Cyprus—or indeed anywhere in the Mediterranean. A conservation scheme, the Lara Turtle Project, has been established by the Cyprus Fisheries Department on the Lara Reserve to protect the turtles' nesting grounds and to

As might be expected of a village with a busy fishing harbour…

MAKING CHARCOAL
The rugged area of the Troodos foothills, called Tilliria, running south from Pachyammos, is noted for its production of charcoal. Indeed, in the past, almost all Cyprus's charcoal was produced in Tilliria, thanks to its proximity to the Pafos Forest and the suitability of its soil (baked soil was used to line the kilns and was a major determinant of the charcoal's quality). Nowadays, iron kilns are used and charcoal can be made in two days instead of the previous one or two weeks. Cyprus's excellent grilled food depends on charcoal for its taste.

ensure the highest possible rate of survival of fledgling turtles.

Lara is not exactly hard to get to, but the track that takes over from a tarmacadamed road is bumpy and dusty enough to discourage casual visitors, who are not in any case greatly desired at the site during the nesting and hatching season. Mesh fences are placed in the sand around the trenches dug by female turtles to house their eggs. A public information tent containing display cases of baby turtles being prepared for release has also been established to help explain the project to visitors and, it is hoped, to gain their co-operation in keeping the nesting site undisturbed.

The coast on either side of Lara Bay is a mixture of rocky and stony beach, and is also part of the Lara Reserve. In the reserve area sunbeds, beach umbrellas, caravans, tents and the like cannot be taken on to the beach, and visitors cannot stay on the beach after sunset. Also banned are fishing, other than with a rod and line, using or anchoring a boat without a permit, and driving any vehicle onto the beach. The 'Turtle Protected Area' extends to a distance of 90m (300ft) from the shore, and to a depth of 20m (65ft) in the water.

▶ Mavrokolympos Lake   154B3
Trout may be on the menu after a successful fishing expedition to the lake, created by a dam on the Mavrokolympos River a short distance inland from Coral Bay. Fishing is permitted here, for trout and other species, with a permit issued by the Cyprus Fisheries Department (see page 105).

▶ Pachyammos   155C5
The pocket-handkerchief-sized beaches are the main attraction of this tiny village on the northern coast, near the point where the the coast road begins its spectacular climb into the lower peaks of the Troodos Mountains to avoid the fortification-ringed Turkish Cypriot enclave at Kokkina (Erenköy).

...seafood is high on the menu at most tavernas in Lakki

The icon is the principal religious art form of the Orthodox faith and the very image of Byzantium, the Christian empire whose capital was Constantinople (today's Istanbul). For almost 2,000 years icons have transmitted to the faithful their message of the holiness of the saints and the glory of God.

PICTURES AND EXHIBITIONS

Icons can be seen at many places on Cyprus, mostly in churches. Among the best are:

- **Agios Trypiotis** (page 47)
- **Panagia Chrysaliniotissa** (page 55)
- **Agios Lazaros** (page 86)
- **Stavrovouni** (page 96)
- **Panagia tou Kykkou** (page 142)
- **Agios Irakleidios** (page 188)
- **Machairas** (page 190)

The museums with the best icon collections are:

- the **Byzantine Museum** (page 47) in Nicosia
- the **Byzantine Museum** (page 172) in Pafos

In the Turkish Cypriot zone:

- the **Icon Museum** (page 213) in Keryneia (Girne)
- **Apostolos Andreas Monastery** (page 230)
- **Apostolos Varnavas Monastery** (page 232)

Cyprus's Orthodox churches are treasure chests of icons

As the wellsprings of the thousand-year-old classical civilization dried up in the fourth century AD and the Roman Empire staggered into its decline and fall, a new force rose to the forefront. Christianity, formerly the reviled superstition of slaves and the ignorant poor, became the official state religion of the new Byzantine Empire. In art, the classical preoccupation with the human form gave way to stylized images of the introspective, spiritual dominion of the new religion. Man was no longer the measure of all things; the Christian God and his saints held the keys to the kingdom of heaven and eternal life.

The icon, from the Greek word *eikon* (image), is the perfect mirror of this change. Representations of Christ, the Virgin Mary, angels and saints, and scenes from liturgical history are venerated, not—at least in theory—for themselves, but as aids to devotion and channels of God's blessing. The traditional medium used by Byzantine painters was egg tempera on gesso over wood; oils are a comparatively recent introduction from Western Europe. Sometimes gold leaf is employed, and intricate gold or silver covers are placed over the images.

Venerated symbols Cyprus's importance in the history of icons lies in the number and quality of its surviving images and the island's role as a sanctuary for icon-makers during periods of 'iconoclasm', notably in the 8th and 9th centuries, when doctrinal disputes based on the second commandment's prohibition of the worship of images flared up and icons were destroyed in vast numbers. Icons are not the only signs of the faith: Domed churches, murals, mosaics and ecclesiastical garments and vessels also have their place. But they are the most important in the eyes of many of the faithful, and kissing the icons is a key element in the rituals of the Orthodox Church.

It is this element of loving veneration that the secular or non-Orthodox tourist is most likely to lack. To view an icon purely as a work of art is to remove all sacred content from it, leaving it a surface impression only. Of course, there is a hierarchy of aesthetic worth among icons and the church authorities are well aware of the value of the pieces they hold. In this they are not alone: International art thieves are as devoted to icons as the most pious churchgoer.

Images of eternity Perhaps the most obvious characteristic of icons is the immobility of the subjects. Although the painters must reach deep into their own spirituality to transmute paint into an image of transcendent faith, following centuries-old patterns, there is little of ordinary humanity in the result. Christ, the Virgin and the saints, who were all at one time human, are captured frozen in eternity, gazing far beyond the everyday world to the celestial city of God. The occasionally more naturalistic example is all the more refreshing for its rarity.

Cyprus's churches are great storehouses of icons in all sizes and from all periods of Byzantine history. Some are faded almost beyond recognition; some have been disastrously 'restored'; others, particularly precious or sacred, are hidden away from sight. The iconostasis, an often elaborately carved and gilded screen separating the nave of the church from the inner sanctuary, is the main 'exhibition area'. Icons still pour forth from monasteries, convents and churches, the motive for their creation being the same as impelled the evangelist Luke, 19 centuries ago, to paint the first examples, one of which is said to rest in the church of Panagia tou Kykkou monastery (see page 142): the veneration of God and his holy saints.

ICONS AS WEAPONS
Icons play a part in the war of words between Greek and Turkish Cypriots over the island's cultural patrimony. Following the Turkish invasion of 1974, it is clear that icons were looted and destroyed. This seems not to have been a deliberate Turkish policy but rather the result of fighting, undisciplined actions by troops, and the work of art thieves—who have also struck in the Greek Cypriot sector. The Greek Cypriots have been forced to buy icons taken from monasteries and churches in the north and sold on the international black market.

169

FROM RUSSIA...
Basil Grigorovich Barsky visited Panagia tou Kykkou in 1727 and reported the monks' comments on the miracle-working icon: 'The icon, so it is said, is painted on some rare wood from the Tree of Paradise, but not by modern methods. Rather it is done with a sort of wax and mastic. This is impossible to verify because of the silver covering...They carry the icon up to the mountain-top in times of drought and reveal her face upon which rain miraculously falls.'

This superb rendering of Christ can be seen at Panagia Chrysorrogiatissa, near Pafos

CONFLICT OF THE GODS
Some scholars have interpreted the mosaic of Apollo and the musical shepherd in the House of Aion at Pafos as a pagan allusion to the inevitable triumph of the old gods over the Nazarene who had brought Christianity to the world. If this analysis is correct, the pagans were soon to be proved mistaken.

LENT
CAMELING
IN
LARNACA

▶▶▶ Pafos   154B2

Pafos remains, in many respects, the most attractive of Cyprus's major holiday resorts, despite the frenzied development that is overwhelming the coast on either side. Its historic resonance dates back to the Roman Empire, when it was the island's capital, ruled by a governor whose palace has been uncovered. So rich is the site of ancient Nea Pafos in cultural treasures that it is included in UNESCO's list of World Cultural Heritage Sites. The spelling of the town's name has been changed officially from Paphos to Pafos; there is Kato (Lower) Pafos, where the main tourist area is located near a picturesque harbour, and Upper (Pano) Pafos, better known as Ktima.

Ancient sites The **Mosaics of Pafos**▶▶▶ (tel: 26306217. *Open* Jun–Aug daily 8–7.30; Sep–May daily 8–5. *Admission: moderate*) were discovered in a cluster of buildings of the Roman period, principally the third century AD. They form a major historical treasure, with a range of subject matter and quality of workmanship that alone would guarantee their worth. Their vigorous treatment of pagan myths contradicts the belief that the wellsprings of classical art dried up as Christianity gained the ascendancy. The mosaics are in four main locations, reached through a neoclassical entrance.

The **House of Dionysos** makes for a dazzling journey through pagan mythology: Narcissus, who fell in love with his own reflection in a pool of water; Dionysos in triumphal procession; the twin heroes Castor and Pollux, offspring of the union of Leda and Zeus; the tragic tale of Phaedra and Hippolytos; Ganymede being carried off by Zeus; the love between Pyramos and Thisbe; Neptune and Amymone; and Apollo and Daphne. Also discovered, at a lower level, was a third-century BC mosaic pavement made from black and white pebbles instead of tesserae.

The **House of Orpheus** is named for a mosaic depicting Orpheus playing his lyre, surrounded by wild beasts enchanted by the music. Hercules appears in the first of his labours, where he fights the lion of Nemea. An Amazon is also shown.

The **Villa of Theseus** is undergoing further excavation for mosaics which are undoubtedly there to be uncovered. This seems to have been the palace of the Roman proconsul (governor) and bids fair to be the richest of all. Mosaics showing Theseus battling the Minotaur; Poseidon, god of the sea, riding the waves on a sea monster, accompanied by Amphitrite; and the first bath of the infant Achilles, give some idea of the marvels to be expected.

The **House of Aion**, next to the Villa of Theseus, has yielded a five-panelled mosaic showing Leda being approached by Zeus in the shape of a swan; the infant Dionysos being handed to his future tutor Tropheus; a beauty competition between Cassiopeia and the nereids, watched over by Aion; Dionysos leading a procession of maenads and satyrs; and Apollo condemning the flute-player Marsyas to death for daring to challenge him to a musical contest.

Although the second-century AD **Odeion**▶, close to the mosaics, suffers from comparison with the larger and more spectacularly sited theatre at Kourion, it retains considerable charm within its semicircle of limestone

Taking the camel trail in Pafos

In the Tombs of the Kings

blocks—enough to be in use still for summer musical and theatre performances after 18 centuries. Ticket information is available from the Pafos Tourist Information Office. Next to the auditorium, though not easily recognizable, are the remains of the agora, the main public square of ancient Pafos.

The **Tombs of the Kings**▶▶▶, (tel: 26306295. *Open Jun–Aug daily 8–7.30; Apr–May, Sep–Oct daily 8–6; Nov–Mar daily 8–5. Admission: inexpensive*), beside the sea at the northern end of Kato Pafos, is a complex of rock-cut tombs, where leading citizens of Pafos (not royalty) were interred during the city's Hellenistic and Roman periods (third century BC to thirrd century AD). Their carved steps

BATTLE OF WORDS
During the 1974 conflict, Turkish warplanes rocketed the archaeological zone beside the harbour in Pafos, damaging some of the priceless mosaics in the process. Opinions naturally differ as to whether this was a case of the pilots simply missing their intended targets (vessels in the harbour bringing military supplies from Greece) or a deliberately vandalistic strike against an important Greek cultural monument.

171

leading down to the burial chambers were indeed the pathway to the underworld. Archaeologists are still busy, and will be for many years to come, uncovering the *tumuli* (mounds) that have accumulated over the tombs and digging down to the graves. Several tombs have impressive *atria* (courtyards) surrounded by Doric pillars, and were decorated with paintings and other ornamentation.

A late pagan mosaic in the House of Dionysos

Excursions leave Pafos southwards to Aphrodite's Rock and northwards to the Akamas Peninsula

MUSEUMS Given the rich archaeological harvest of the Pafos area and western Cyprus, **Pafos District Archaeological Museum**▶▶ (tel: 26306215. *Open* Mon–Fri 9–5, Sat 10–1. *Admission: inexpensive*) has no shortage of treasures, dating from prehistoric to Venetian times. These include pottery, sculpture, coins and jewellery. That the Romans found Cyprus chilly in winter is shown by a set of moulded clay hot-water bottles.

Near the bishop's palace, the **Byzantine Museum**▶ (tel: 26931393. *Open* Mon–Fri 9–4, Sat 9–1. *Admission: inexpensive*) concentrates on Orthodox religious art, particularly icons, dating from the 12th to the 18th centuries. There is a fine gilt statue of the Virgin and Child.

The **Ethnographical Museum**▶ (tel: 26232010. *Open* May–Sep Mon–Sat 9–1 and 3–7, Sun 9–1; Oct–Apr Mon–Fri 9–1 and 2–5, Sat 9–1. *Admission: inexpensive*) contains a diverse, although not extensive, range of exhibits, from neolithic tools and ancient funerary sculptures, to local costumes and everyday household objects. This small, privately operated museum is in Pano Pafos (Ktima).

Pafos Aquarium▶ (Dionysou Street, tel: 26953920. *Open* spring and autumn daily 9–7; summer daily 9–8; winter daily 9–6. *Admission: moderate*) makes a good place to give children a break. Its display tanks mainly feature Mediterranean marine life but include colourful saltwater and freshwater creatures from around the world.

Churches The church of **Panagia Chrysopolitissa**▶ is a 13th-century construction standing amid the ruins of a colossal early Christian basilica, the largest on the island. Long-term archaeological research is being conducted on the site so it is frequently closed to the public, a great disappointment to many who wish to see St. Paul's Pillar, where the apostle is said to have been scourged with 39 lashes during his evangelizing visit to Cyprus in AD45—presumably before he converted the Roman proconsul, Sergius Paulus, to Christianity. **Panagia Limeniotissa**▶ is a ruined and partially excavated

SCHOOLBOY FIGHTERS
The modern gymnasium (high school) on the outskirts of Pafos, although not a tourist 'attraction' as such, is an impressively grand (or grandiose) construction, a symbol of the classical foundation that still inspires Greek education. A relief in the schoolyard depicts a young boy attacking a lion with a stone; many of the EOKA guerrillas who fought, and died, for union with Greece against the British in the 1950s were, literally, schoolboys, and the monument honours their struggle and sacrifice.

fifth-century Christian basilica near the seafront. Our Lady of the Harbour proved to be conveniently sited in the path of seventh-century Arab raiders, who laid it low.

Today a damp and mysterious underground chamber, the catacomb of **Agia Solomoni▶** (*Open* permanently. *Admission free*) was once a refuge for early Christians. A sacred tree, said to have the power to cure disease, stands near the entrance.

The **Theoskepasti Church▶** is modern and stands where there was once an early Christian church of the same name, which means 'veiled by God'. A miraculous fog apparently shrouded the church, making it invisible to Arab raiders, who made do with destroying less favoured Panagia Limeniotissa at the other end of the harbour.

THE HARBOUR AREA The harbour is everyone's ideal Mediterranean fishing port, with gaily painted craft tied up in rows, private yachts, glass-bottom boats, and cruisers joining them. Taverna terraces stretch to the water's edge and the scene is animated all day. Remains of the ancient breakwater are at the harbour's eastern end.

Pafos Fort▶ ▶ (tel: 26932841. *Open* Jun–Aug daily 10–6; Sep–May 10–5. *Admission: inexpensive*), with turrets and gloomy halls, was rebuilt by the Ottoman Turks to protect the harbour. It is similar to Limassol and Larnaka forts, but smaller and it stands on the site of the earlier castles built by the Byzantines, Lusignans and Venetians.

Also known as the Byzantine Castle, **Saranda Kolones▶ ▶** (*Open* permanently. *Admission free*) takes its principal name from the Greek for '40 columns', a reference to the many ruined columns found near by. The castle, close to the Odeion and the complex of Roman-era houses where the mosaics were found, was built during the Lusignan period in the 12th century on the foundations of a Byzantine fortification. The Lusignans had scarcely finished the place when an earthquake struck in 1222 and destroyed it again. Byzantine, Lusignan, or just plain ruined, the castle makes a fine place for scrambling over walls and battlements.

There are two **Municipal Gardens▶** in the town, one in Kato Pafos and one in Ktima.

173

HARBOUR STROLL
Unquestionably the most atmospheric place for a stroll in Pafos is around the old harbour, with its colourful fishing boats. Start at the fort and continue past the former harbour warehouses, now waterfront tavernas, towards the souvenir shops at the eastern end.

The catacomb of Agia Solomoni, shaded by a tree decked with votive offerings

Walk

Historical sites of Pafos

As capital of Cyprus during the Roman Empire, Pafos developed a brilliant urban lifestyle. The walk traverses some of the excavated highlights and, if visits to the sights are included, lasts about four hours. The sights themselves are covered in more detail on pages 170–173.

Begin at the end of the pier. Across the harbour are the remains of the ancient breakwater, and adjacent are the scant ruins of an early fort. The harbour is devoted to fishing boats and pleasure cruising. As you walk towards the town you pass **Pafos Fort**▶▶, which replaced the earlier one near the end of the mole.

Turn right along the seafront promenade (Leoforos Apostolou Pavlou), then left along the lane behind the cafés. To your left is the ruined early Christian basilica of **Panagia Limeniotissa**▶, and to your right the modern **Kyklos Art Gallery**▶. Continue to the end of the lane where

Pafos Fort, built by the Ottomans, was declared an ancient monument in 1935

four Roman-era buildings contain the **Mosaics of Pafos**▶▶▶, one of the island's most marvellous ancient scenes. The four buildings, all excavated ruins, are the Houses of Aion, Theseus, Orpheus and Dionysos. From the House of Dionysos, walk east along the lane called Sofias Vembo Street (or Kyriakou Nikolaou Street on local maps). A short detour to the left leads to the **Odeion**▶. Continuing straight ahead, you pass the ruined Byzantine Castle, or **Saranda Kolones**▶▶, on your left. Turn left on to Leoforos Apostolou Pavlou, then first right to the early Christian basilica and **Panagia Chrysopolitissa**▶▶. Finally, return to Leoforos Apostolou Pavlou and turn right for the **Agia Solomoni**

Christendom's white wedding retains elements of fairy-tale—even if its solemnly sworn vows are often honoured more in the breach than the observance. Cyprus's divorce rate is rising, but couples still get married with the best of intentions and a certain unforgettable style.

Your first sight of a Cypriot wedding can be an irritating experience. You may be driving along a deserted road far from anywhere when, suddenly, you find yourself stuck in the mother of all traffic jams. When Cypriots wed, they like as much of Cyprus to be there as possible.

During the church service the bride will be required to fear her husband, an undertaking she appears to forget pretty quickly. The duties expected of a couple entering into the holy state of matrimony having been agreed to, the bride and groom move to the icing on their wedding-cake, otherwise known as the traditional Cypriot wedding feast. They start out married life as they aim to continue: happily ever after. One participant who probably has a tough time celebrating is the bride's father, who has had to shell out for his daughter's dowry; a house is generally considered acceptable.

Fertile imagination Fertility is assured by the 'spreading of the mattress', when the married women sew the bed linen to it and a baby boy is rolled along it. The feast itself is the product of at least a day's cooking by the women guests—after all, the whole village has been invited. Feasting, singing and dancing are the order of the evening, along with various good luck rituals. 'Pinning on the money' is one of the final rituals, when the bride and groom dance alone and their parents, relatives and friends pin banknotes to their clothes. No doubt Aphrodite watches over the proceedings with great satisfaction.

Wedding portrait at Kourion Theatre

BIG DAY
In previous years weddings could only take place on a Saturday, but that regulation has now been relaxed and Sunday weddings are becoming more common.

Wedding-day bliss, or blues: marriage is a serious business

Monk on the move, Panagia Chrysorrogiatissa monastery

►► Pafos Forest   155C4

Winston Churchill took a hand in the creation (or re-creation) of this vast forest northeast of Pafos. In 1907, while a junior minister with responsibility for colonial affairs, Churchill began the process of reafforestation that has continued to this day, with the Cyprus Forestry Department slowly restoring to a huge area the tree cover that vanished into the shipyards and foundries of the ancient world. In summer, fire is a permanent threat to the tinder-dry forest. See also Cedar Valley, page 125 and Stavros tis Psokas, page 179.

► Panagia Chryseleousa   154B2

Open: irregularly. Admission free
In the village of Empa, near Pafos, this restored church dates from the 11th century. A noteworthy fresco of Christ Pantokrator gazes down from its dome.

►► Panagia Chrysorrogiatissa Monastery 155C3

Open: daily dawn–dusk. Admission free
'Our Lady of the Golden Pomegranate' monastery is one of the most dramatically sited in Cyprus. Its flower-bedecked courtyard and its fine view over the surrounding forests caught the attention of the young Makarios Mouskas, living in the village of Pano Panagia just below; the boy would grow to fame and glory as Archbishop Makarios. The monastery also commands a certain amount of fame and glory for its Monte Royia winery's high-quality wines, particularly the red Ayios Andronicos, and for an icon of the Virgin found by St. Ignatius in the 12th century, and now kept in a silver case.

►► Pano Panagia   155C3

The late Archbishop Makarios (see pages 50–51), first president of the Republic of Cyprus and a figure of international reputation in the non-aligned movement, was born and raised in this isolated mountain village overlooked by the monastery of Panagia Chrysorrogiatissa. His plain family home has been preserved and maintained as a shrine in honour of this complex and controversial figure, who saw no contradiction between his religion and his politics, and who is revered by many Greek Cypriots as the father of the country.

Heavenly view across the country from Panagia Chrysorrogiatissa

▶▶▶ Petra tou Romiou (Rock of Aphrodite)

155C1

Aphrodite's Rock, a place of pilgrimage for romantic couples

This unusual rock formation standing in shallow sea water beside the Limassol–Pafos road must be the most famous spot in Cyprus. The name means 'Rock of Romios' and comes from the legend of the Byzantine hero Dighenis, who hurled enormous rocks at Arab invaders and destroyed their fleet.

However, the rock's fame stems from a more ancient and timeless myth, for it was here that Aphrodite, goddess of beauty and love, first set foot in the world, as recounted in the Homeric *Hymn to Aphrodite*:

> I will sing of stately Aphrodite,
> gold-crowned and beautiful,
> whose dominion is the walled cities
> of all sea-set Cyprus.
> There the moist breath of the western
> wind wafted her over the waves
> of the loud-moaning sea.

This favourite child of Zeus was met on the shore by her handmaidens, the Horae (Hours), who received her with joy, decked her out with precious jewels, set on her immortal head a crown of gold and gave her earrings of gold and copper. Botticelli's diaphanous *Birth of Venus* (Venus was the Roman equivalent of Aphrodite) is undoubtedly the best-known image of the moment when the goddess was borne ashore on a seashell. Petra tou Romiou is a virtual place of pilgrimage for romantic couples, particularly at sunset when a gentle breeze ruffles the surface of the 'loud-moaning sea'.

Aphrodite came to Cyprus as an adaptation of the Phoenician Astarte, who was a soul-sister of the Assyro-Babylonian Ishtar. When she could spare time from her primary duties, she was also Aphrodite Pelagia, goddess of the sea; Aphrodite Pontia, of seafarers; Aphrodite Euploia, who guaranteed prosperous voyages; and Aphrodite Gelenaia, goddess of fair winds. She was happiest playing the sweet game of love as Aphrodite Urania: Her raunchier side showed through in Aphrodite Pandemos and Aphrodite Porne. Finally she settled down as Aphrodite Nymphia, the protector of marriage.

ACTING THE GOAT
The insatiably nipping teeth of the humble goat have taken much of the rap for deforestation in Cyprus, presumably because humans prefer to blame a dumb animal rather than look too closely in the mirror. One (rather pompous) authority on the subject wrote: 'Goats and reafforestation are irreconcilable; and the authority of some tribunal should intervene to sentence them not only to legal separation, but to irrevocable divorce.'

TRAUMATIC BIRTH
The early Greek writer Hesiod provided an earthy account of the birth of Aphrodite in his *Theogony*. The goddess was created, he wrote, when Cronos castrated his father Uranos and cast his genitals into the sea, where they floated to the surface to produce a white foam, from which arose Aphrodite.

ROUGH NEIGHBOURHOOD
In 1879 the British colonial administrator for the Pafos district lambasted the people of the area in and around Polis for the extraordinarily high number of thieves and cut-throats among them. Fortunately their descendants have turned to more benign pursuits and the chance of having one's throat cut in Polis today does not seem excessive.

The main square in Polis is bordered by shops and cafés

▶▶ Pissouri Bay   155D1

On a stretch of the coast where sandy beaches are few and far between, Pissouri Bay's golden sands guarantee its popularity. Reached via a long side-road from the main Limassol–Pafos coast road, Pissouri is basically a beach and very little else, although there are some reasonable tavernas around the bay. In the countryside behind, where tasteful tourist and expatriate accommodation is being developed, vineyards still hold sway.

▶▶▶ Polis   154B4

The principal resort north of Pafos, Polis is still essentially a big village that has taken on the role of a resort without surrendering itself to it entirely. It is a laid-back sort of place, with lots of old-fashioned nooks and crannies in addition to a central pedestrian area, centred on Plateia Dimarcheiou, mostly given over to tavernas and shops. If the scarcely developed northwest coastline has a metropolis, Polis is it, and its size and leisurely pace are a welcome sign of just how different things are in this part of Cyprus.

Arriving at Polis from the south, you are presented with a choice: Turning left leads to the wild Akamas Peninsula and its mythological associations with Aphrodite; turning right takes you along the all-but deserted northwest coast, around the broad sweep of Chrysochou Bay, towards the Turkish Cypriot enclave of Kokkina (Erenköy) and the main demarcation line beyond Kato Pyrgos.

Polis's ancient predecessor, Marion, founded by Ionian Greeks in the seventh century BC, was an important Greek port city, thanks mainly to its proximity to rich copper mines. Destroyed in 312BC by Ptolemy I of Egypt, Marion was rebuilt as Arsinoë by his son Ptolemy Philadelphus. The future holds a great deal of work for archaeologists

CAMEL TRAIN
In the area south of the Pafos Forest, camels used to transport copper from the Troodos mines to the sea at Pafos. It was the Venetians who established the Camel Trail through this exceedingly rough terrain and who built bridges over the rivers to carry it.

Life in the fields is not always idyllic

charged with separating the story of Marion-Arsinoë from the tangle of undergrowth in which its remains are embedded. Preliminary work has uncovered a Hellenistic necropolis as well as the remains of public and private dwellings, but not much is visible to reward the visitor who goes searching for it. You can see some of what has been collected from the site at the **Marion-Arsinoë Archaeological Museum▶** (tel: 26322955. *Open* Mon–Wed and Fri 8.30–2, Thu 8–2, 3–6 (closed pm Jul–Aug), Sat 9–5. *Admission: inexpensive*).

▶▶ Pomos   155C5
This attractively located fishing village on the hilly northwest coast is flanked by Pomos Point, a small but sharp-edged peninsula jutting into the sea. Pomos is a little oasis of cafés on this quiet stretch of the coast.

▶ Souskiou   155C2
The church of Souskiou is modern, and its silvered icon of Christ on the Cross disappeared during a time of troubles, only to turn up in nearby Ariminou. The latter's devout inhabitants blithely maintain that the icon travelled to their church under its own steam. There is a chalcolithic-period cemetery near the village, with faint traces of early human habitation.

Polis is on a user-friendly scale—even its churches are of modest dimensions

▶▶ Stavros tis Psokas   155C4
Reaching this abandoned 18th-century monastery in the Pafos Forest (see page 176) could break the hearts of all but the most determined; even its monks pulled out in the 19th century. Some of the tracks that connect the monastery to the outside world add new dimensions to the word 'rough'. If you desire solitude, it is worth the journey, for Stavros tis Psokas is now a forest station with a restaurant and guest-house surrounded by wilderness.

▶ Timi   154B2
Near Pafos International Airport, this might be the best place to pick up a last consignment of *haloumi*, the traditional cheese of Cyprus, which is particularly tasty when grilled. The village's **Agia Sofia** church represents a rare instance of a mosque being transformed to Christian use in the aftermath of the 1974 Turkish invasion.

Drive

See map on pages 154–155

Polis to Kato Pyrgos

The attraction of this drive is that there is not much to see in an area largely free of the mass tourism that reigns elsewhere, and there are no 'sights' in the conventional sense. Covering some 40km (25 miles), it could be raced through in less than an hour, but that would be to miss out on the spirit of the coast.

The few sights encountered on the drive are covered in more detail on pages 164–179.

Polis▶▶▶ is a town with a choice to make. The outcome will determine if it is to retain any elements of the down-at-heel charm, which up to now has made it a welcome place of escape for lovers of the 'real' Cyprus, or if it will grasp the nettle of mass tourism and give up its identity in the process. The signs are mixed, but the pressure to open up another resort area for Cyprus is heavy and Polis has already changed enough to persuade 'purists' to pass it by.

The main road eastwards out of Polis hugs the long eastern sweep of Chrysochou Bay, with fine views to the west towards the Akamas Peninsula and, in clear weather, Cape Arnaoutis at its tip. A short way out of town is a disused pier.

A worthwhile diversion is to **Makounta** village, on a road that climbs up through orchards and olive groves. The dusty track on the left, about halfway to Makounta, ends at a small dam.

Back on the coast road, the next village is a coastal extension of the small inland village of Argaka—a kind of Argaka-on-Sea, dominated by the looming mass of the Troodos Mountains. The beaches on either side of Argaka are stony, with rough brown sand; they are not the stuff of picture postcards, yet they have charm in a sense that nature is at work on its own agenda here, not merely acting as an adjunct to a tourist brochure.

Continuing northeast along the coast road, in an area dotted with

Looking towards the sweeping curve of Chrysochou Bay

The coastline near Polis

small seaside churches and farms with fields reaching almost to the water's edge, the coastal hamlets, smaller cousins of inland villages, are more notional than real—blink and you'll find you've already passed through.

With so many near-deserted beaches, swimmers may take the opportunity to do a little nude bathing. However, there are some parts of the coastline that are spoiled by piles of abandoned rubbish.

The small fishing village of **Pomos**▶▶ is one of the prettiest on the coast, which is now more rocky, leading to the distinctive hump of Pomos Point. Fishing boats and an occasional cabin-cruiser make lazy circles in the shallow turquoise waters just off shore.

At **Pachyammos**▶ you can visit the modern, seaside church of Agios Rafaïl and see its extensive covering of contemporary murals inside. Beyond this, the sad realities of modern conflict intrude on an otherwise idyllic scene and force the traveller away from the coast. Cyprus National Guard, United Nations and Turkish army positions climb into the hills around the Turkish Cypriot enclave of Kokkina (Erenköy). Photography is forbidden just where the spectacular scenery would otherwise persuade you to reach for your camera. Nevertheless, the enforced detour is a memorable one, and there is no law preventing you from stopping to admire the view.

A busy and dusty little resort, **Kato Pyrgos**▶ is much favoured by Greek Cypriot holidaymakers seeking an escape from the foreign visitors who have taken over every other resort on the island.

A walk on the wild side of Cyprus can turn up a surprising variety of both indigenous and visiting fauna. Some species have to be protected if they are to survive the loss of habitat brought on by a fast-growing economy.

DONKEY WORK
The once universal donkey, that long-suffering symbol of traditional Mediterranean village life, is as rare now as baggy breeches on its owners. Yet donkeys may still be seen in remoter areas, although any villager rash enough to display such a venerable symbol of local colour is liable to be mobbed by strangers with video cameras. Meanwhile, wildlife biologists are researching the 'wild donkeys' of the Karpasia (Karpaz) Peninsula in the Turkish Cypriot zone, an alarming sounding creature that, if not mythical, is surely the stuff of which nightmares are made.

182

It is a sight that could make a conservationist out of the most hardened cynic: baby loggerhead turtles, tiny bundles of frantic energy and haste, scrabbling over the sand on their first journey. The turtle-ettes don't know it but they have a guardian angel, a host of guardian angels in fact, who have protected and nurtured them and now watch with delighted satisfaction as their little charges obey the dictates of evolution and leave them for the warm embrace of the sea.

Time was when such creatures did not need the help of the Lara Bay Turtle Project to make their way in life; but time also was when the golden sands lay deserted under the sun and beach hotels were a nightmare of the future. Nowadays female turtles will not even come ashore at most of their favourite beaches on the west coast to bury their eggs: Water-skiers, swimmers, sunbathers and cafés do not make for the required tranquil birthplace. As a result, the loggerhead turtles are on a fast descent to oblivion. The Lara Project aims to reverse their slide.

Protection racket On Cyprus, the animal kingdom is retreating before the spreading tide of humanity and all its works, penned into ever-diminishing scraps of habitat, until they eventually go the way of the extinct Cyptus pygmy hippopotamus and pygmy elephant. Not all Cypriots, nor tourists, are willing to accept that the island's wildlife heritage must be sacrificed on the altar of economic progress. The battle to save the turtles is one example of their commitment. There are others.

While driving through the western slopes of the Troodos Mountains, it is a good idea to stop

The rarely sighted mouflon (top). Newly hatched turtles (below) head across the sand towards the sea at Lara Bay

from time to time, turn off the engine and listen. There may be nothing to hear but the chirp of birdsong and the wind sighing through the pine branches; but there may be the sharp clatter of rocks tumbling down scree-covered slopes, signifying that a moufflon is trying to put as much distance between itself and you as its legs will permit.

This wild mountain sheep is the star of Cyprus's wildlife show. A shy, retiring creature, its less-than-flattering attitude to humans is: if you can see me, you're too close. Travelling normally in pairs, they head north like, well...like the proverbial mountain goat, taking the punishingly steep hills in their stride, stopping only to check whether you can still see them before disappearing among the trees. Spotting a moufflon is a memorable experience—while it lasts.

Wildlife parade Cyprus has much to delight on its wildlife roster. Griffon vultures soar on updrafts in the Pentadaktylos (Beşparmak) Mountains; pink flamingos crowd the salt lakes at Larnaka and Akrotiri when winter rains restore their waters;

Southern festoon butterfly, one of many species that take full advantage of Cyprus as the 'island of flowers'

183

monk seals, although rarely seen, cavort off the Akamas Peninsula; green and loggerhead turtles nest on protected beaches. More than 55 butterfly species, including the painted lady, speckled wood, brown argus, Cleopatra and two-tailed pasha, have been identified.

Migrating birds can't seem to pass Cyprus by: the swallow, swift, little ringed plover, Eleonora's falcon, beeeater, hoopoe, Cyprus pied wheatear, masked shrike and black-headed bunting are just a few of the species that either pause on their migration route or remain to breed.

The venomous blunt-nosed viper should ideally be avoided, but most snakes are non-poisonous and anyway are rarely seen.

SERPENTINE ROADS
Snakes, such as three varieties of whip snake and the Montpelier snake and viper, are most likely to be observed flat as pancakes and dried to a crisp after being caught under the wheels of passing cars while attempting to cross the road. This is a sad sight which even the Roman Emperor Constantine's mother, St. Helena, who introduced snake-fighting cats to Cyprus, would surely have abhorred.

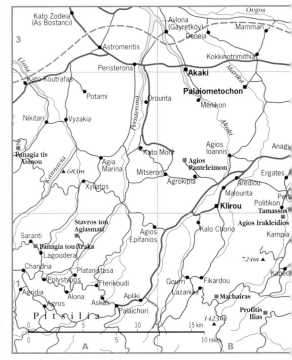

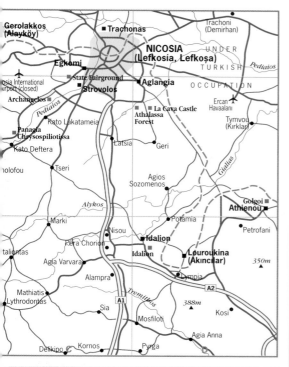

Gerolakkos (Alayköy)
Trachonas
Trachoni (Demirhan)
NICOSIA (Lefkosia, Lefkoşa)
UNDER
Egkomi
TURKISH
Pediaios
osia International airport (closed)
State Fairground
Aglangia
OCCUPATION
Strovolos
Archangelos
Ercan Havaalanı
La Cava Castle
Athalassa Forest
Pediaios
Kato Lakatameia
Tymvou (Kırklar)
Panagia Chrysospiliotissa
Latsia
Geri
Kato Deftera
iholofou
Tseri
Agios Sozomenos
Gialias
Alykos
Golgoi
Athienou
Marki
Nisou
Potamia
Petrofani
Pera Chorion
Idalion
taliontas
Idalion
Louroukina (Akıncılar)
350m
Agia Varvara
Alampra
Lympia
A2
Mathiatis
Lythrodontas
Tremithos
388m
Kosi
Sia
A1
Mosfiloti
Agia Anna
Delikipo
Kornos
Pyrga

185

The products of irrigation and good land (left) The desert-like central plain (far left) in the summer heat

THE CENTRE

Central Cyprus may seem like the bit left over when all the more popular places have been covered, but it has its own quiet charm—a quality some of those other places have traded for modernity and prosperity, and the bustle and hassle that go along with them.

Yet outside Nicosia this is the region most affected by Cyprus's division. In normal circumstances it would form a squashed circle around the capital, reaching north towards the Pentadaktylos (Beşparmak) Mountains and south to the Troodos, taking a bite out of the Mesaoria (Mesarya) Plain to the east and the Morfou (Güzelyurt) Plain to the west. Instead, the circle is slashed in two by the barbed-wire scar of the demarcation line that cuts across the island's middle. And although openings have now

Handicrafts on sale in a restored traditional dwelling

appeared in the line, the reality of division remains.

Time was when all roads running through this area led to Nicosia. Now most of the highways have been amputated; central Cyprus is filled with roads that lead nowhere, or at best to a checkpoint manned by a bored but determined sentry. With no sun-hallowed beaches or sharp-tanged mountain air to commend it, central Cyprus is left with only its farms and workaday villages to distract the senses and divert attention from that dismal line.

REAL THING Well, not quite. Amid the constellation of farming villages, which in any case share the characteristic restful welcome of most Cypriot villages, there are enough bright stars to more than justify pulling off the main highway from Nicosia to the coast. Because this area is not one for which tour guides and tourist brochures employ the nearest handy superlatives, it is in some respects far closer to the 'real Cyprus' than many places more favoured.

The immediate vicinity of Nicosia is filled with a mess of suburbs and, more poignantly, permanent refugee villages: Hastily built housing projects for Greek Cypriots who got out of the north just one step ahead of the advancing Turkish army in 1974. A little farther away, however, is a bewilderingly large and all-but-deserted landscape that rolls and wanders to nobody's whim but its own.

Finally, the central area butts up against the Troodos foothills and the coastal plains, and hands the torch on to its competitors.

ROAD WITH A VIEW
The main road west from Nicosia through Peristerona to the Troodos Mountains runs alongside the UN buffer zone for most of its length, providing a good view of 'the other side'. You can see across the fertile Morfou Plain to the town of Morfou, a centre of the citrus industry, and beyond it to the dark mass of the Pentadaktylos Mountains.

GETTING LOST Travel this area by the main roads and you pass through as if in a bubble, traversing familiar-looking fields and villages, and insulated from its true impact. Turn off the main roads on to the narrow side-roads, then stony tracks and dusty trails, and a new experience awaits, one that has little to do with route maps and easily followed itineraries. In other words, you're going to get lost. Count on it. Of course, getting lost in Cyprus is a relative concept: It rarely takes long to get found again.

Yet to drift through this sometimes barren, often dusty region is to glimpse another Cyprus, one as distinctive in

its own way as parts which are better advertised.

It may be just as well that the ridges and valleys of the central region offer enough of interest to the casual transient, because the traditional tourist 'attractions' are thinner on the ground than elsewhere. The package does, however, include an ancient city or two (thoroughly ruined of course), some venerable monasteries and surprising old Byzantine churches.

The closer you get to the mountains, the more rugged the landscape becomes, but paradoxically also more green and fruitful thanks to underground water sources and reservoirs. The heartland has its moments too.

Houses at Fikardou conservation village, shuttered against the sun

DUST DEVIL

The kind of dry and dusty tracks that the Troodos foothills specialize in hold a special peril for the occupants of open-topped jeeps, which otherwise can take most obstacles in their stride. The dust gets everywhere, so that not only do the occupants need frequent showers, but so does the inside of the jeep.

PLAYING WITH FIRE

In the farming country around Nicosia it is not uncommon to see miniature 'wild fires', as farmers clear and prepare the land for the next crop. This can pose a danger to traffic, as thick smoke reduces visibility to zero. It can also pose a danger to the farmers' own houses, if a wind pushes the flames in an unintended direction.

Machairas Monastery, one of the principal seats of the Orthodox faith in Cyprus

Murals depicting saints at Agios Irakleidios Monastery

▶ Agios Irakleidios Monastery 184B1

Open for group visits only, Mon, Tue, Thu 9–12. Admission free
The nuns of this monastery used to be among the most relaxed towards visitors in all of Cyprus, which was perhaps just as well, seeing that they got so many of them. Too many, as it turned out, and they have now restricted both the numbers of visitors to their bougainvillea-bedecked cloister and the time when they are permitted to visit. They have their treasures to display: the whitened bones of St. Irakleidios's hand, and his head too, the latter mercifully placed out of eyeshot inside an ornate gilt reliquary.

Of notable icons and murals the monastery church has an elegant sufficiency, and in a smaller adjoining chapel there is a Roman-era tomb which is thought to be that of the saint. Irakleidios was an early bishop of nearby Tamassos and a martyr for the faith.

The present foundation dates from the 18th century, although a monastery has existed on the site since the fifth century, having been destroyed and rebuilt a number of times.

▶ Agios Panteleimon Monastery 184B2

Rarely open for visitors. Admission free
This simple, flower-bright, 18th-century monastery is set in good farming country near the village of Agrokipia in the low foothills of the Troodos Mountains. The villages around here stand between two of the important secondary routes from the mountains to Nicosia, which make for interesting alternatives to the main road through Peristerona and Kakopetria.

▶ Agios Sozomenos 185D2

Wide open countryside around this village southeast of Nicosia is mainly given over to sparsely populated farmland, eventually jutting up against the demarcation line. Abandoned hamlets in a state of shell-scarred dereliction are eerily empty reminders of the island's troubled recent history and that even now Cyprus is not all sweetness and light.

HELD AGAIN
In the buffer zone (and therefore unreachable) some 8km (5 miles) west of Nicosia is a UN base at St. David's Camp, a former British army installation. In the aftermath of World War II, Jewish survivors of the Holocaust who had been intercepted while trying to reach Palestine were interned here by the British colonial authorities.

► Archangelos Michaïl Monastery   *185C2*

Open: daily. Admission free
Dedicated to the Archangel Michael, this monastery is a very short drive from Nicosia and makes for a pleasant quick excursion from the city. The palm tree-bordered foundation dates back to the Byzantine era, but was rebuilt in the 18th century, since when it has been owned by the wealthy and influential Kykkos Monastery of the Troodos Mountains.

►► Athalassa Forest   *185D2*

Something doesn't quite add up with this nature park just outside Nicosia. It is attractive enough and certainly welcome in the environs of a hot and busy capital not noted for its wealth of green spaces. But a military base, a weather station and an agriculture and forestry research institute take up a fair part of the available area, and access to the public space is far from simple. Nevertheless, shaded walks and picnics are possible and there is an artificial lake, while the research institute creates enough pleasant scents from its range of exotic plants to mask at least some of the city's diesel fumes.

Buffer Zone   *185D2*

While it may be in poor taste to consider this a tourist attraction—and certainly no Cypriot would consider it so—it exists and exercises a peculiar fascination, just as the Iron Curtain once did. In any case, it is hardly possible to get there before being stopped by a warning notice, or Greek Cypriot or United Nations checkpoint (a determined attempt to get into the zone may lead to arrest—or worse—and should not be attempted).

The array of observation posts and flag-decorated defensive positions looks toy-like and innocuous from a distance, an image enhanced by the fact that Greek Cypriots farm right up to the limit of what is permissible—and occasionally, to the distress of the UN, beyond.

NO PICTURES PLEASE
The UN shares the picture-shyness of the Greek Cypriot, Turkish and British troops on the island. Understandably, none of these forces wants to become a tourist attraction, and there are legitimate security reasons for restricting photography.

189

The tree-shaded grounds of Agios Panteleimon Monastery

▶▶ Fikardou 184B1

This attractive village, well out on the road towards the Pitsilia region of the Troodos Mountains, has been declared an ancient monument and conservation zone to preserve the wooden balconied houses dating from the Ottoman period and the general rustic charm of an entirely unspoiled Cypriot village. This folk architecture heritage brings the village under the gaze of Cyprus's Department of Antiquities, which may not please all of its inhabitants. It is one of a cluster of restored villages in the area, which include Gourri (see below) and Lazanias. You can visit two houses, the Katsinioros House and the Achilleas Dimitri House, which have been turned into a folk art museum (*Open May–Sep Tue–Fri 9–4.30, Sat 9–4, Sun 10–1.30; Oct–Apr Tue–Fri 9–4, Sat 9–3.30, Sun 10.30–2. Admission: inexpensive*).

▶ Golgoi 185D2

Located next to the military positions of the demarcation line, this ancient Greek colony of Corinth has itself settled into the rolling countryside southeast of Nicosia. Golgoi now awaits better days and fatter archaeological budgets before delivering up its secrets.

▶ Gourri 184B1

Although it has Ottoman-era houses with carved wooden balconies equal to those in nearby Fikardou, this village has not been declared a conservation zone and ancient monument.

▶ Idalion 185D1

The Bronze Age city-state of Idalion is one of many locations where the golden shepherd boy Adonis, who dallied once too often in pastoral idyll with Aphrodite, is said to have met his end at the tusks of a wild boar sent by the goddess's outraged husband, Hephaestous. It is difficult to relate soap-opera Greek mythology to the few stumps of Idalion that remain above ground at this location 19km (12 miles) south of Nicosia near the modern village of Idalion. Only minimally excavated, Idalion has nevertheless yielded traces of temples to Aphrodite and Athena, as well as great ashlar blocks from the walls which protected the city until its demise around 400BC.

▶▶▶ Machairas Monastery 184B1

Open: for group visits Mon, Tue, Thu 9–12. Admission free
This is a favoured location for capturing the mysterious romance of Cyprus's Greek Orthodox monasteries, which have borne the spirit of Byzantium

190

The highlight of Gourri village is its church

HOLY OLIVES
The olive trees around Idalion are said to have a holy provenance, having apparently sprung from olive-stones the future saints Paul and Barnabas spat out when they stopped to enjoy a spot of lunch.

The present structure of Machairas Monastery dates from the early 20th century

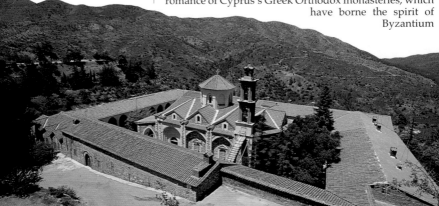

191

The pristine-looking interior of the Machairas Monastery

down through the centuries since the island was detached from the empire. Partly this is because it is a handsome-looking place, especially when the warm late-afternoon light washes its walls; partly because it commands magnificent views (in one direction reaching all the way to Nicosia); and partly because of its association with EOKA, the guerrilla organization that fought the British in an almost mystically inspired campaign to unite Cyprus with Greece.

Although the monastery's history stretches back to the mid-12th century, when an icon of the Virgin is said to have been found on the site, the present buildings date from the early 20th century, when the monastery was rebuilt after a disastrous fire ravaged the place in 1892. The result is an almost pristinely modern foundation which appears to re-create the graces of ancient Byzantium but without the patina of age that would make it look venerable as well. The church has, however, hung on to its important icon, covering it with a silver shell to add to the mystery.

Nicosia International Airport 185C3

This was once Cyprus's gateway to the world; now its only international connection is that it acts as the headquarters of the United Nations Force in Cyprus (UNFICYP). During the 1974 conflict, the airport was attacked by Turkish paratroopers who were repulsed by Greek Cypriot troops. UN sentry posts ring the base, and there are wrecked aircraft beside the runways.

The airport is one of the places whose reopening for business is regularly proposed by UN goodwill ambassadors as a measure to raise confidence between the island's divided communities, but the minimal level of confidence needed to get even the proposal, never mind aeroplanes, off the ground has never been forthcoming.

PRO PATRIA...
Grigoris Afxentiou, a deputy commander of EOKA in the fight against the British during the 1950s, was killed in a cave near Machairas Monastery. Brought to bay by British troops, he shot one of them, then died himself when the soldiers set fire to his hiding-place. The flag-bedecked cave is a popular place of pilgrimage for Greek Cypriots.

Eating out in Cyprus is a great social event, and traditional Cypriot cuisine lends itself to the experience. Lingering over an alfresco dinner in the scented evening air, or crunching into a village salad at lunchtime, can make the hard work of a holiday seem well worthwhile.

NET
WEIGHT
600 gr.

BRANDY SOUR
The recipe for this popular and refreshing Cyprus cocktail is: pour a liberal dash of angostura bitters into a tall glass, followed by a good measure of brandy and an equal amount of fresh lemon juice; add sugar and ice, fill the glass with soda and garnish with a slice of lemon.

192

If Cypriots thought eating and drinking had as their sole purpose the sustaining of life, they might give them up as a bad deal. As it is, they regard them as life-enhancing to an extent that it is hard to see how they find time for other things. This is most notable on family outings, especially if *meze* is on the menu—that avalanche of little dishes that cascades onto the table in a seemingly endless torrent, each one a traditional favourite to be savoured and discussed. With an unrivalled storehouse of fresh products to draw on from its farms and orchards, Cyprus can afford to pamper its collective stomach.

That doesn't mean diners always strike edible gold. In many holiday hotels the lowest common denominator is considered adequate, and in a multitude of tourist restaurants and tavernas the Cypriot touch has been left at the kitchen door. A new phenomenon is that of 'new Cypriot cuisine'. This catch-all term covers everything from places that merely tart up the 'old Cypriot cuisine' a little and stick a much higher price on it, to places that are genuinely trying to interpret the old standards in new ways and to a far higher standard than is usual, and others introducing elements of fusion and other trendy world-cuisine styles.

Good influence Cyprus stands at the crossroads of three continents and has absorbed culinary influences from all three,

This village salad looks as colourful as a still-life painting

but Greek and Turkish antecedents adapted to Cypriot tastes are the strongest. *Meze* provides the best possible introduction, with 20 to 30 dishes ranging from dips and raw vegetables to fish and meat in richly flavoured sauces. Such a meal is a test of appetite and endurance, another reason why Cypriots linger so long over it. A

restaurant which piles on the *meze* dishes, allowing some to get cold before they can be tasted, then follows up rapidly with the bill, is best avoided next time. Seafood and vegetarian *meze* are also available in some places.

Typical items on the Greek Cypriot *meze* list and as individual orders are: *haloumi* (goat's milk cheese flavoured with mint, which is often served grilled); *kolokithakia* (stuffed or plain courgettes); *koupepia* and *dolmades* (vine leaves stuffed with rice and meat); *lountza* (smoked pork which has been marinated in red wine); *tahini* (a sesame dip mixed with lemon, garlic and parsley); and *hummus* (an Arab-style dip made from chickpeas, garlic and lemon juice). Main dishes include such favourites as *afelia* (chunks of pork stewed in a red-wine sauce and sprinkled with coriander seeds); *keftedes* (fried meatballs); *kleftiko* (lamb or goat meat roasted in an earthenware oven); *souvlakia* (lamb or pork grilled on a skewer); and *moussaka* (a layered dish of aubergines or potato and minced meat in a béchamel sauce).

Turkish Cypriot variants of these and other dishes are available, the most important difference in the meat department being the absence of pork.

Desserts tend towards the sweet-toothed, liberally spread with honey. Fresh fruit of excellent quality is a standard item, but vegetables, despite their wondrous variety, take a back-seat to meat dishes.

Liquid refreshment Cypriot wines make an ideal accompaniment to a meal. Commandaria, a sweet red dessert wine with a history dating back to medieval times, is one of Cyprus's most notable products. In the Turkish Cypriot zone good-value labels from Turkey predominate. Fortified wine, too, is a local stalwart, while *ouzo* and *raki* are available on both sides of the divide. Cyprus's distinctive contribution to the world of cocktails is the refreshingly sharp brandy sour.

Take time to enjoy the good Cypriot food on offer in the island's cafés

FOOD FOR THOUGHT
While Turkish Cupriot cuisine shares much with that of the Greek Cypriots—with many dishes in common, including kebabs and *meze*—it is also marked by historical Ottoman and Turkish influences, which yield such dishes as *ımam bayıldı* (the priest fainted) and *hünkar beğendi* (the Sultan's delight).

SWEET TEMPTATION
A traditional Cypriot confection is *soujoukko*, which looks like a long waxy string of giant beads. Genuine *soujoukko* is made from almonds laced on strings and dipped repeatedly into heated grape juice until a thick covering congeals in layers around the almonds. The string is hung up in the sun to dry. Its taste and consistency are not unrelated to those of rubber, but it is surely more healthy than modern sugary confectionery.

▶▶ Panagia Chrysospiliotissa 185C2

Open: daily. Admission free

One of the strangest of all Cyprus's Orthodox churches, Panagia Chrysospiliotissa, some 11km (7 miles) south-west of Nicosia near Kato Deftera village, is one of the most attractive, with a simple charm. Our Lady of the Golden Cave stands halfway up a cliff-face in an enlarged natural cavern that recalls the catacombs of the persecuted early Christian churches; it may indeed have been used as such since the first century. The barely illuminated interior, reached by a steel stairway, is decked with votive offerings, including wedding dresses.

The votive-filled interior of the cave-built church of Panagia Chrysospiliotissa

▶ Pera Chorio 185C1

This small village near Idalion is noted for its 12th-century Byzantine church of **Agioi Apostoloi▶**, containing colourful frescoes, including a fine (but damaged) image of Christ Pantokrator in the dome.

▶ Peristerona 184A3

The village stands in orchard country near the demarcation line west of Nicosia on the road to Troodos. Peristerona is symbolic, in Greek Cypriot eyes at any rate, of the peaceful relations that used to exist in former times between the island's now divided communities. Two religious foundations, a 19th-century mosque, which is no longer in use, and a church, stand almost side by side in the centre, suggesting a solidarity that has now passed away. The church, the superbly multi-domed 10th-century **Agioi Varnavas ke Ilarion**, stands by the usually dry riverbed.

▶▶ Profitis Ilias 184B1

Some wild and wonderful forest trails criss-cross the country around this rustic monastery at the far end of a 6km (4-mile) track west of the village of Lythrodontas. There are views into a beautiful valley below, filled with

ANTIQUE VIRTUES
Strabo, in his *Geographica* (AD 23) wrote: 'Such then is Cyprus in point of position. But in excellence it falls behind no one of the islands: for it is rich in wine and oil, and uses home-grown wheat. There are mines of copper in plenty at Tamassos, in which are produced sulphate of copper and copper oxide useful in the healing art.'

cypress trees. The monastery, with its two-storey array of monks' cells and an old monastic church, is no longer operational, and a forest station occupies its grounds.

Apart from attending an occasional baptism in the church, few pilgrims make the journey for any reason other than to light a barbecue or enjoy a picnic in the cool glades around the monastery.

▶ Strovolos   185C2

Typical of the villages being swallowed whole by fast-expanding Nicosia, Strovolos still has a recognizable village centre and retains some country atmosphere despite the intense pace of new construction. This was the birthplace of Archbishop Kyprianos, a Greek Cypriot hero almost on a par with Archbishop Makarios. Kyprianos was executed by the Ottomans in 1821, along with many leading Greek Cypriots, when they were accused of conspiracy during the mainland Greek revolt against Turkish rule.

▶▶ Tamassos   184B2

Open: Tue–Fri 9–3, Sat–Sun 10–3. Admission: inexpensive

At first glance this appears to be one of those ancient Cypriot cities that have just barely survived their journey through the millennia and have come down to us as a seemingly indecipherable muddle of stones. A second glance tends to confirm that initial unpromising assessment, and it is unfortunate that neither the archaeological nor the tourism authorities have done much by way of providing information to fill in the details.

Tamassos has, however, a rich history, with references to its wealth dating back to Homer. The Roman poet Ovid also sang its praises as the 'best part' of Cyprus. The wealth was based, as was so often the case in ancient Cyprus, on the mining, smelting and working of copper.

Systematic excavation of the site began only in 1975, and since then a temple, thought to have been dedicated to Aphrodite, has been uncovered. Most notable of all and described by a leaflet available at the ticket office are two royal tombs with carved and decorated walls, dating from the 7th century BC. When the tombs were discovered in 1890 there were three of them, but local villagers, less impressed than archaeologists by Cypro-Archaic Period II royal tombs, destroyed one and used its stones for building materials.

GIFT OF APOLLO
In 1836 a local peasant found a life-size bronze statue of Apollo while ploughing a field near Tamassos. The man was so pleased with his windfall that he cut up the statue, which must have been priceless, and sold it for scrap.

195

The scant remains of ancient Tamassos, once an influential city

For 40 years, soldiers answerable to the United Nations secretary-general in New York have held the line between Cyprus's two communities. Their experience runs the gamut from boredom to death by hostile fire, a variety of sacrifice designed to give politicians as much time as they need to end the island's tragedy.

VOLVO SERVICE
It has not been all hardship for soldiers assigned to peacekeeping duties with the UN in Cyprus. Members of the Swedish contingent (which has since been withdrawn) were so well paid for their six-month tour of duty in Cyprus they called it the 'Volvo posting', because the first thing they would do when they went home was buy a Volvo with the money they had saved.

196

Sightings of Cyprus's peacekeepers are liable to be disjointed: a relaxed, blue-bereted sentry at the Pafos Gate checkpoint in Nicosia, who politely but firmly waves away all requests for a picture; a white-painted jeep sweeping through the countryside near the demarcation line, the UN pennant on its aerial snapping in the wind; observation towers in the buffer zone, calmly flying the UN flag between positions where Greek Cypriot and Greek flags engage in a kind of semaphore war with Turkish Cypriot and Turkish flags across the way.

Though few in number, the United Nations Force in Cyprus (known by the acronym UNFICYP) is ubiquitous. Its job puts it in harm's way between the two potential combatants. Its role is to defuse situations of tension long before the point where either side reaches for its holster. If the reality of the mission is that sunburn and tedium are more often a greater menace than flying bullets, that has not always been the case. Some UN soldiers have paid the ultimate price asked of them by the world community they serve and whose desire for peace in Cyprus they uphold.

UNFICYP armoured car on patrol along the Green Line in Nicosia

Out of control Four years after Cyprus gained independence from Britain, UNFICYP was set up. Power-sharing between Greek and Turkish Cypriots collapsed in 1963; fighting erupted in Nicosia, then spread throughout the island. British troops in the capital set up the Green Line separating the two communities there, but the island-wide situation was out of control. The UN authorized a peacekeeping force on 4 March, 1964 with troops from Austria, Britain, Canada, Denmark, Finland, Ireland and Sweden.

In its first 10 years, UNFICYP's complex task was to look after minorities threatened by the other side. In practice, as Turkish Cypriots withdrew into enclaves surrounded and occasionally attacked by Greek Cypriot forces, this usually meant protecting the Turkish Cypriots, which raised cries of bias against the peacekeepers.

In 1974 the situation changed drastically with a Greek-inspired coup against the Cypriot government—which President Makarios called an invasion of Cyprus by Greece—and the subsequent Turkish military intervention. Eight UN soldiers were killed and more than 60 wounded during the fighting that followed these events.

Observer status When the smoke of battle had cleared and the immediate humanitarian crisis of prisoners of war and refugees had been dealt with, UNFICYP's revised task, while no less onerous, was at least simpler. Its forces now man a series of observation posts in the UN buffer zone beween each side's ceasefire line, running from the Kokkina (Erenköy) enclave in the west and meandering across the island, through the Green Line in Nicosia, to a point south of Famagusta (Gazimaǧusa) in the east. Observers ensure that neither side intrudes militarily beyond its ceasefire line and that civilians do not enter the UN buffer zone.

As talks between the communities constantly failed to reach agreement, some governments grew disillusioned at the lack of progress and the cost and withdrew their contingents, although others took their place. The UN has many more serious problems in other parts of the world, and with the situation in divided Cyprus generally peaceful has focused its efforts elsewhere. UNFICYP strength has been declining, in line with Security Council decisions. The force has some 860 military personnel from Argentina, Britain, Hungary and Slovakia, 60 police officers, and about 150 civilians both Cypriot and international. A third of its annual $52 million budget is provided by the Republic of Cyprus.

UN Canadian troops patrol the Green Line that divides the Greek and Turkish areas of Nicosia

197

NOXIOUS WEED

A strand of seaweed may look like a dull, unintelligent creature but it knows enough to get a bunch of its pals together and head for the nearest beach. Some beaches, in particular those on the northern coast, attract great carpets of seaweed that can make any attempt to enter the water seem like a scene from *The Day of the Triffids*.

TO GO OR NOT TO GO...?

That is the question. In international law, the Turkish Cypriot zone is illegally occupied by the Turkish army. The Turkish Cypriots have their own side of the story to tell and there are strong touristic reasons for going there, but the salient fact of its occupied status ought not to be forgotten.

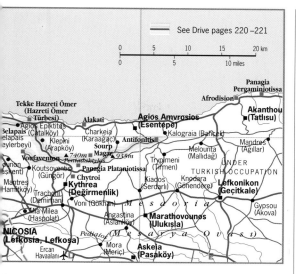

THE NORTH In this book, 'the north' refers only to the northern coast, the Pentadaktylos (Beşparmak) Mountains and the adjoining area. This is an imprecise geographical concept, not a political one. Nevertheless, for practical reasons the north lies wholly within the territory called by its inhabitants the Turkish Republic of Northern Cyprus, although it does not cover all of it (there remain the east and Turkish Cypriot Nicosia). Since the opening of the border in 2003, this area, and particularly Keryneia (Girne) has become easily accessible from the south.

With its friendly people, beaches, forest-clad mountains, castles, abbeys and churches, farming villages and fishing harbour, all northern Cyprus lacks is the kind of tourist overexploitation that has marred some other sections of the island. However, few visitors will complain about that.

Based on the handsome port town of Keryneia (Girne), the north lays claim to being the most beautiful and least 'spoiled' part of the island, with long stretches of glorious, unspoiled sandy beaches.

The long, jagged blade of the Pentadaktylos Mountains saws at the sky along much of the region's length. This range has an excessive number of names, being known also as the Beşparmak Mountains, the Keryneia Mountains and the Gothic Range (for the castles and abbeys dotting its slopes). The Castle and Harbour of Keryneia (Girne) are fascinating structures from the Byzantine era.

Keryneia (Girne)
Harbour (far left)
Packing charcoal (below
left) in North Cyprus

▶▶▶ **REGION HIGHLIGHTS**

Inside the ramparts of St. Hilarion Castle

WHAT'S IN A NAME?

Place-names, as well as being essential for letting people know where they are, may be a political statement. Official Greek and Turkish names exist for all localities on the island. Now only Greek names are used in the Greek Cypriot zone and Turkish in the Turkish Cypriot zone. The Greek-speakers accuse their Turkish-speaking neighbours of changing the names in their zone as part of a strategy to eliminate the Greek Cypriot cultural heritage there. The Turkish-speakers disagree, of course.

Coffee shop, Belapais

DURRELL COUNTRY Other writers have applied their pens to the history, culture and people of Cyprus, but few have illuminated them better—or at a more critical time—than the Englishman Lawrence Durrell. His book *Bitter Lemons* captures the moment when Greek Cypriots decided that violence would loosen Britain's hold on Cyprus and win union with Greece, while Turkish Cypriots determined that the former goal was undesirable and the latter unthinkable. Durrell's presence, by turns riotously funny and hauntingly sad, touches much of the north, particularly Keryneia (Girne), the mountains and the village of Belapais (Beylerbeyi), where he lived from 1953 to 1956.

The north is more than a tourist paradise or writer's creation, of course. Real people reside there, earning a living from the soil, sea and mountains. Many hail from southern Cyprus, refugees who made the doleful journey north in 1974 from homes that were too hard-pressed to retain, just as their Greek Cypriot counterparts were heading south. Others are immigrants from Turkey, poor Anatolian farmers for the most part, taking the chance for a better life, yet regarded with condescension by some Turkish Cypriots and with impotent fury by the Greek Cypriots. Despite this tragic background, however, the north is not fixated on the past.

BETTER TIMES The dazzling harbour at Keryneia is the jewel in the northern crown. In good weather (which means almost always), the semicircle of smart cafés and restaurants housed in its magnificent old warehouses spread their terraces on to the quayside. Customers flock to these cafés and restaurants, to the glittering constellation of casinos in and around Keryneia, and to the discos. Yet, despite its lively sense of fun, the town still manages to be a quiet place by the standards of most other resorts in the Mediterranean.

If you are seeking an even quieter time, then an even quieter time you can find. All along the windy heights of the Pentadaktylos Mountains are nature trails so lonely it seems as if the rest of the human race has packed up and left. And the Latin and Crusader castles and abbeys that give the mountains their Gothic tag are perched in places so far from being accessible that it is clear their builders never spared future tourists so much as a passing thought. Much of the long coastline is devoid of development of any kind, a living showcase of what the Mediterranean must have been like in the days when holidays abroad were the exclusive province of the idle rich. That's beginning to change now, but is still basically true.

The road leading out of Nicosia to Keryneia (Girne) passes the capital's Venetian Keryneia Gate (Girne Kapısı)

201

ON THE HORN
Anyone who has considered Cyprus's often vicious recent history might expect Cypriots to have horns—an accusation that was in fact made against them in ancient times. In reality, few people are more hospitable. This can be seen even at the sharp end of the divide, in the armed forces. Most Greek Cypriot conscripts are sun-wilted kids, pulling sentry duty while wondering how soon they can get away to the disco; tourists may be saluted by the Turkish military policeman turning them away from some restricted area.

LONESOME ROAD
The narrow road that runs along the northern coast from a point east of Agios Epiktitos (Çatalköy), very nearly *in* the sea for long stretches, is a delight to drive, cycle or walk. Little in the way of facilities of any kind will be encountered and the whole area retains a wild feel that speaks of former days in the Mediterranean.

The Peace and Freedom Monument, on Yavuz Çikarma

▶ Afrodision   199E2

Despite its intriguing name, this once-important Greco-Roman city has become one with the dung-covered fields hereabouts and awaits the belated attentions of - archaeologists. Just to the east on the coast lies the crumbling structure of the 12th-century Panagia Pergaminiotissa Church.

▶ Agia Eirini (Akdeniz)   198B2

In a ravine outside this agricultural village, fossilized bones of Cyprus' extinct pygmy hippopotamus were found. On the nearby shore are the remains of Palaia Kastro, an ancient temple site at which masses of terracotta votive offerings were discovered; they are now in the Cyprus Museum in Greek Cypriot Nicosia. Unfortunately, at the time of writing neither of these sites is accessible as they both lie within an extensive military zone, and the harsh sound of soldiers' whistles greets any attempt to penetrate the area.

▶ Agios Epiktitos (Çatalköy)   199D2

The church of St. Epictetus, dating from the 1830s and named after a 12th-century Christian hermit who took up residence in a cave near the town, is now a mosque. Large villas in the surroundings provide evidence of the village's popularity with well-heeled expatriates.

▶ Agios Georgios (Karaoğlanoğlu)   198C2

Renamed by the Turkish Cypriots for a high-ranking Turkish army officer killed during the 1974 invasion, this little seaside village west of Keryneia (Girne) was formerly noted for its fossils of Cyprus's extinct pygmy hippopotamus (see panel opposite). Just beyond the village, the beach of **Yavuz Çikarma▶**, where the Turkish invasion force came ashore, is marked by the rather grotesque concrete **Peace and Freedom Monument**, as well as a Turkish military memorial displaying Greek Cypriot tanks and other heavy weaponry knocked out during the operation. Ironically in view of its grim associations, the beach is also known as Bambi Beach. Off shore lies one of Cyprus's diminutive islets, Glykiotissa.

▶▶▶ Agios Ilarion (St. Hilarion Castle)   *198C2*

Open: summer daily 9–4.30; winter daily 9–1 and 2–4.45
Admission: moderate

Between Nicosia and Keryneia (Girne), and occupying a strategic position 700m (2,300ft) above the road, St. Hilarion is the picture-book image of a crusader castle—or was until the Venetians partially dismantled it in the 16th century. Nevertheless, more than enough remains intact for the picture to be scarcely affected. So powerful are the castle's layered defences that as recently as the 1960s Turkish Cypriot militiamen in occupation easily beat off determined attacks by the Greek Cypriot National Guard. The more romantic crusader and Lusignan period was the castle's heyday, when its cool mountaintop position made it an ideal summer residence for the Lusignan kings; the French knights called it the Dieu d'Amour (God of Love) Castle, perhaps in a misguided macho appreciation of Cyprus's very own Aphrodite.

This is the most impressive of the three crusader castles in the Pentadaktylos (Beşparmak) range, with three separate defensive systems of crenellated walls and towers culminating in a craggy redoubt. It was fortified in two major stages, beginning with the Byzantines in the 12th century. The castle was surrendered by the Byzantine usurper Isaac Komnenos to England's King Richard the Lionheart, while the latter was on his way to join the Third Crusade. Under several of the Lusignan kings, the castle was greatly strengthened during the following three centuries.

Entering the bailey (the courtyard enclosed by the walls), you climb past the stables and barracks of the garrison, and through another gate to the royal apartments, with a Byzantine church, a dining hall and more barracks. Still climbing, the final destination is the upper enceinte, with more apartments, a dining hall and kitchens. At the summit is a tower from which one aggrieved blue-blood, the Prince of Antioch, had his Bulgarian bodyguards pitched to their deaths for allegedly plotting against him.

▶▶ Alakati (Alagadi) Beach   *199D2*

Several fine beaches lie on either side of this one, 18km (11 miles) east of Keryneia , at what was a Mycenaean-era settlement. Farther east, one of these beaches has been put permanently out of commission by the eyesore of Turkish Cyprus's first, and badly needed, electric power plant (until it opened in 1994, all power had to be imported from the south, and cuts at peak times were a far from rare occurrence). In this area is also **Turtle Beach**, where Cyprus's rare loggerhead and green turtles come ashore to lay their eggs. Although some tourist developments—including a troops-only beach—have been established in this area, the coast is mostly wonderfully unexploited.

St. Hilarion Castle, perched high above the road

203

THEM BONES
At several points on the northern coast, including Agios Georgios (Karaoğlanoğlu) and Agia Eirini (Akdeniz), the fossilized bones of Cyprus's extinct pygmy hippopotamus have been found. Pious villagers got there before the palaeontologists, however, and, believing the bones to be those of St. Fanourios, ground them up, added the powder to water and drank the concoction for its supposed medicinal value.

WHITE KNIGHTS
St. Hilarion Castle is said to have provided the Walt Disney studio's animators with an inspirational model for the castle in *Snow White.*

With its varied landscape and climate, Cyprus offers much to interest both the scientist and the amateur botanist. The full range of flowers on the island has yet to be catalogued entirely, with more than 1,700 species already observed, 128 of these endemic. To the casual observer, the sheer quantity and variety of flowers is a truly unforgettable visual treat.

BLOOD AND TEARS
The legend of Aphrodite and Adonis is associated with the anemones that carpet great tracts of Cyprus in the spring. Red anemones sprang forth from the blood of the golden youth who was killed by a wild boar while hunting, and white anemones originated with the tears of Aphrodite at the death of her lover.

Spring is an early visitor to Cyprus. Already in January the first orchids are blooming, the prelude to a tidal wave of floral colour and fragrance that flows across the island for the next five months until it recedes under the intense heat of summer. Few of the island's flowers are adapted to the near-drought conditions that apply in summer, so they take their chance to bloom and seed when winter's rains have restored moisture to the soil. The burgeoning flowers create an astonishing display in fields, orchards and meadows, as well as in less promising locations, such as roadside verges and rocky slopes.

Cyprus in springtime merits its description as 'the scented isle'. March, April and May are the best months, when the species on display read like a florist's catalogue: tall white asphodels, poppies, chrysanthemums, tulips, hyacinths, narcissus, marigolds, irises, crocuses, peonies, cyclamens, anemones and many others, all of them in the wildest profusion. In *Bitter Lemons*, Lawrence Durrell wrote of the cyclamens and anemones around Klepini (Arapköy) in the Pentadaktylos (Beşparmak) Mountains 'glittering like young snow, their shallow heads moving this way and that in the sea-wind so that the fields appeared at first sight to be populated by a million butterflies'.

The Hottentot fig, now common throughout the Mediterranean, was originally introduced from South Africa

Hard times Even from July to the end of September, some hardier plants and flowers hold their own during the scorchingly hot and dry days. There are thistles in a rainbow of pastel tones, and the white flowers and purple stamens of the caper bush are no strangers either. These are joined in different locations by myrtle, pink-flowered oleanders and tamarisk. But the prevailing colour at this time of year is the brown of shrivelled-up plants and grass; delicately petalled things keep their heads down.

Flower power Some flowers have a connection with ancient mythology and actual historical events. Inside the stem of the giant fennel, whose yellow floral heads can reach up to more than 3m (10ft), Prometheus is said to have hidden and delivered to man the fire stolen from

heaven. Pafos, the 'flower town', celebrates all Cyprus's love-affair with flowers in its annual Anthestiria Flower Festival in May, whose antecedents reach back to the ancient floral rites in honour of Aphrodite and Dionysos. Nicosia, Larnaka, Limassol and Paralimni also hold flower festivals, a tradition that is spreading.

Orchid paradise Cyprus is a treasure trove of wild orchids, mostly growing in the Pentadaktylos Mountains and, to a lesser extent, in the Troodos, but with others at home in coastal areas. The sensuous orchid has acquired a collector's value almost on a par with the illegal trade in antiquities, even though some varieties are among the 'strictly protected floral species' designated by the Council of Europe. Venal collectors will often put their possession of a rare orchid ahead of the survival of the species, or even just of its natural beauty when alive and well in its own environment.

Of Cyprus's 45 orchid species, subspecies and varieties, three are threatened with extinction and survive in only a few locations, while others are in trouble as a result of loss of habitat to cultivation, reafforestation and tourist developments. Common lowland varieties are the yellow bee orchid, the wavy-leafed monkey orchid, the bug orchid and the holy orchid. High in the Troodos can be seen the eastern violet helleborine and other rare species. It goes without saying that none of these beautiful flowers should be picked or stepped on.

Bindweed

205

BEE LINE
It can be a fairly intimidating experience to turn a corner in the Cypriot countryside and encounter a heap of boxes buzzing like a squadron of World War II fighters on a strafing run. Bees are big business on the island, for between the flowering and fruiting seasons there is no shortage of pollen. Fortunately, the little critters have their own business to attend to.

Delicate oxalis

Vandalized and looted, Antifonitis Church and its unrivalled murals are mouldering away

►► Antifonitis Church

199E1

Generally open. Admission free

Getting to this highly symbolic place is no easy task—by the end of the trail even a jeep finds the going hard. Founded in the 12th century, the domed Byzantine church lies in a rugged valley near Agios Amvrosios (Esentepe), where the Pentadaktylos (Beşparmak) Mountains tail off towards the east. It is in a sad and grim condition that is little short of a scandal. If the tattered remnants of its frescoes are anything to go by, they must have been among the finest in Cyprus. Now, weeds flourish in the grounds. However, the worst is still to come: Its finest frescoes have been looted and the remainder vandalized.

The Turkish Cypriot authorities point out that much of the graffiti is in Greek and predates their control, and that the Greek Cypriots appropriate all international assistance, leaving them only their own limited resources on which they have too many demands.

At least they have made a start in cleaning up by sealing the windows and carting away the goat droppings that carpeted the floor. Any recovery, however, can by now be only partial at best. Antifonitis's 17th-century iconostasis has vanished, and the once-renowned frescoes of the Tree of Jesse and the Last Judgment can be admired only by the criminal who paid for their removal.

You can see the colours still glowing on the archangels Gabriel and Michael in the livery of Byzantine court officials. And you can turn your gaze into the dome, where the damaged image of Christ Pantokrator seems to bear an expression of bewildered sadness.

CULTURAL CONFLICT
Controversy over the treatment of cultural treasures such as Antifonitis is matched by Turkish Cypriot claims that 117 mosques were destroyed by Greek Cypriots between 1955 and 1974, as part of a determined attempt to eliminate their religious heritage.

The exterior of Antifonitis, overgrown and crumbling

►► **Belapais (Beylerbeyi)**   *199D2*

The village of Belapais, set among citrus groves high on the Pentadaktylos (Beşparmak) Mountains and overlooking the sea, is almost as emblematic of a vanished Cyprus as the sanctuary of Aphrodite. Here, the writer Lawrence Durrell lived from 1953 to 1956 among a memorable cast of characters whose island was just beginning its descent into tragedy, as recounted in his travel book *Bitter Lemons*. The Tree of Idleness is there, in the square in front of Belapais Abbey, as is Dimitri's café, where the villagers passed the hours. So too is the house 'made for some forgotten race of giants' that Durrell bought from the cobbler's wife, with assistance from the 'Turkish gentleman' Sabri (who was murdered in 2000).

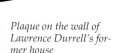

207

Were Durrell alive, he might recognize in today's villagers fellow spirits of those he portrayed with an affection that only now seems tinged with imperialist condescension. The denizens of Dimitri's café, lounging in the shade of the Tree of Idleness, 'whose shadow incapacitates one for serious work', were 'mostly grandfathers wearing the traditional baggy trousers and white cotton shirts...a splendid group, grey-bearded, shaggy-haired, gentle of voice and manner.'

But Belapais is now Beylerbeyi to its Turkish Cypriot inhabitants, many of them refugees from anti-Turkish pogroms in the south. Dimitri's café is a Turkish coffee shop, while a modern restaurant stands opposite the Tree of Idleness—although the identity of the tree is disputed, and some even maintain Durrell's original no longer exists. The steep, narrow streets through which Frangos chased his cows lead to Durrell's house, which sports a plaque recording his stay there but which has been vilely modernized. In a way, this is typical of the transformation wrought in village life by the passage of time to a more worldly age, with villagers being well aware of the commercial benefits to be gained from Belapais's situation.

Relatively small and personable holiday developments dot the surrounding hillsides: villas, cottages and restaurants. They cannot be said to overwhelm the atmosphere, but there is no doubt that Belapais has changed.

The magnificent 800-year-old ruined **Abbey of Belapais**►►► (*Open* summer daily 9–7; winter daily 9–1 and 2–4.45. *Admission: moderate*) could not so easily be changed by the passions of a few violent decades and still lies 'like some great ship at anchor'. ('Bellapaix', Durrell insisted, was the best modern approximation of its original name, Abbaye de la Paix: the Abbey of Peace.)

Plaque on the wall of Lawrence Durrell's former house

WRITE IMAGE
Belapais (Beylerbeyi) may be an object lesson in the mixed blessings that can accrue to a simple country village once a well-known writer has turned his or her pen on it. In the course of a brief visit, few places can live up to the picture created in one's imagination by a writer who has been inspired or seduced by it and its people. Belapais is still wonderful; but Lawrence Durrell's 'Bellapaix' exists beyond time and place.

Icons glow in the dimly lit church of Belapais Abbey

STONE CERTAINTIES
Belapais village owes its existence to Belapais Abbey in more ways than one: many of the stones used in building the village houses came from the abbey's ruins.

TREASURE TROVE
A hoard of 7th-century Byzantine silver plates was found in 1902 by villagers quarrying stone on the site of Lampousa. The plates, depicting scenes from the biblical story of King David, had been walled up in a niche, probably to protect them from Arab raiders.Some of the treasure is in the Cyprus Museum, Nicosia and the Limassol Medieval Museum; the remainder is in the British Museum, London and the Metropolitan Museum in New York.

Ruins of the great Gothic Abbey of Belapais

You enter Belapais Abbey via the ticket-booth beside the Tree of Idleness, through a once-fortified and moated gateway. To the right is the 13th-century abbey church, a tough-minded example of the French Gothic style. Icons glow amid the gloomy interior, which is often locked. The sacristy and chapter-house are to the northeast of the church.

Directly ahead through the gateway are the remains of the *cellarium* and kitchens, below which is the crypt, and at ground level to their right is the cloister. Four giant cypress trees stand centre-stage inside the cloister, of which only fragments remain of the ornately carved arches that supported the arcades where once monks strolled in contemplation. In the northwest corner of the cloister are two Roman marble sarcophagi at which the monks washed, apparently unconcerned by their original purpose.

The abbey's cloister is bordered to the north by the magnificent refectory, whose entrance is marked by the arms of the Lusignan kings. This enormous hall, its soaring vaulting still intact, is lit by six great windows commanding a superb view over the steeply sloping landscape (and the swimming pools in the gardens of villas farther downhill) all the way to Keryneia (Girne) and the sea. Stairs lead up to a carved pulpit, from which suitable texts would be read to the monks while they ate.

Outside again, more stairs lead up to the open sky, where once stood the dormitories in which the monks of St. Norbert had their cells—and to which they later brought their wives and children after succumbing to the worldly lures of Levantine life.

▶ Kalo Chorio (Kalkanlı)   *198B1*
The road from Keryneia (Girne) to Morfou (Güzelyurt), passes through this village and drops steeply away into the Morfou Plain. From the village's edge, a superb view is in prospect over the plain towards the distant Troodos Mountains.

▶ Karavas (Alsancak)   *198C2*
A cluster of historic sites lying on the coast just north of this village were, at the time of writing and clearly for some time to come, unreachable as they lie within a Turkish army base. These include the ancient city of **Lampousa**, apparently founded by Spartans in the 12th century BC (remarkable if true, as the Spartans, unlike other Greeks, were not noted colonizers). It continued into Roman and Byzantine times before it was wiped from the map by Arab raiders in the 7th century. Despoiled for building materials since medieval times, Lampousa cannot be visited at all, while the domed 12th-century **Achoiropoiitos Monastery** and the 15th-century **Agios Evlambios** church, both visible from the base boundary, look to be in miserable condition.

► Karavostasi (Gemikonağı)   *198A1*

On Cyprus's otherwise scenic northwest coast, the port of Gemikonağı presents an astonishing scene of industrial dereliction. Jetties with loading facilities where cargo ships once took on copper and iron ore now stand abandoned and rusting, and the hulk of an old coastal freighter is in a similar condition on the beach itself. The copper mines lie on the wrong side of the island's Greek–Turkish divide and are worked out anyway. The wasteland should, of course, be cleaned up, but while it remains it is worth seeing as an object lesson in decay.

► Karmi (Karaman)   *198C2*

Government-promoted renovation has made this one of the most attractive villages on the northern slopes of the Pentadaktylos (Beşparmak) Mountains. It has also made it popular with well-heeled expatriates, who appreciate its charm and fine location.

► Kormakitis (Koruçam)   *198B2*

The people of this village near Cape Kormakitis (Koruçam Burnu) are mostly ageing Maronite Christians of Lebanese origin. Many of the young people have left the Turkish Cypriot sector for better prospects elsewhere.

The small Orthodox church of **Panagia** on the edge of the village is dilapidated, but the Maronite **Agios Georgios►** church in the centre, dating from 1940, is alive and well, its decoration and statues of the Virgin and saints with illuminated haloes imparting an air of almost childlike innocence. From the needle-pointed cape itself, you can make out the Taurus Mountains of Turkey on a clear day.

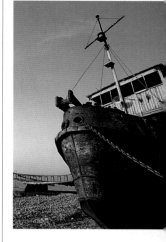

Derelict port installations spoil the shoreline at Karavostasi (Gemikonağı)

209

The church of Agios Georgios serves a small Maronite community at Kormakitis (Koruçam)

The map shows: Dome Hotel, KORDONBOYU, ERSIN AYDIN SOKAGI, Market, Archangelos Church (Icon Museum), Customs House, Harbour, Folk Art Museum, Cafer Paşa Mosque, Tower, Police, Town Hall, HURRIYET CADDESI, ATATURK CADDESI, Keryneia Castle & Shipwreck Museum, Marine Martyr's Monument, CUMHURIYET CADDESI, Fine Arts Museum

100 200 m
100 200 yards

The long sloping ramp that leads to the interior of Keryneia Castle

▶▶▶ Keryneia (Girne)   198C2

This little town (population 15,000) has a history stretching back to the Achaeans in the 10th century BC. In more recent times, it was common for residents of the then undivided capital to escape the scorching heat of a Nicosia summer by driving north over the Pentadaktylos (Beşparmak) Mountains to cool off in the town's harbourside cafés. Today, by way of a Saudi- and Turkish-financed highway, this excursion is popular once more. The drive from Nicosia to Keryneia takes just 20 minutes, well within the timescale even of tourists from the south crossing the Green Line on a one-day pass and taking a taxi to the coast. Thanks mainly to its characterful old harbour and Venetian castle, Keryneia would be among the front-runners in a contest for Cyprus's most picturesque town.

THE CASTLE Like most ancient military structures in Cyprus, **Keryneia Castle▶▶▶** (*Open* summer daily 9–7; winter daily 9–1 and 2–4.45. *Admission: expensive*) has undergone transformation at the hands of successive owners, driven by the need to update the fortifications to match developments in the craft of siege warfare. However, one thing that has never changed, even as recently as 1974, is that the castle controls the harbour.

The original Byzantine structure was a fairly simple one of four towers connected by curtain walls, elements of which were incorporated into the strengthened works constructed by the Lusignans. It was the Venetians who gave the castle its current look, by building massively thick walls intended to withstand artillery. They worked frantically to perfect the defences in the face of an expected Ottoman invasion, but then lamely surrendered in 1571 without a fight.

The entrance is in the northwest corner, where a 12th-century Byzantine church, St. George of the Castle, stands inside the walls to the left. Where once there was a simple drawbridge at the end of the moat, the Venetians created the elaborately protected entrance that you can see today, beyond the bridge that leads over the now dry moat. Towards the end of the tunnel leading up to the parade ground is the green-cloth-covered tomb of an Ottoman admiral, Sadık Paşa, who was killed during the conquest of the island. The parade ground is a wide open space surrounded by guardrooms, stables and visitors' quarters.

Ramps give access to defensive positions on the upper wall, and steps lead up to what were probably the Lusignan royal apartments and a small Latin chapel. In the other direction, downwards, are dungeons, storage rooms and powder magazines. Parts of the battlements are in fairly poor condition, so if you make a circuit of them you need to be cautious. The magnificent view over the harbour, the town, and the Mediterranean, as well as to the jagged peaks of the Pentadaktylos Mountains may make any potential risk seem worthwhile. You will find the Shipwreck Museum in the castle (see pages 212–213).

Coats of arms, Keryneia Castle

THE HARBOUR It is as well that **Keryneia Harbour►►►** is horseshoe-shaped, because at peak times in summer visitors need all the luck they can get to find a vacant seat at one of the waterfront café terraces. Keryneia aspires to being something that not much else in the Turkish Cypriot part of the island, mercifully you might think, cares a great deal about—chic. A little of what you fancy can go a long way, however, and the harbour area's style is possibly more welcome as a result of its rarity. The romantic atmosphere is enhanced by the knowledge that those (relatively) high-priced restaurants and bars were once carob warehouses, storage depots for the edible seed-pod of the carob tree, which, as a substitute for chocolate, was formerly a key Cypriot export.

North Cyprus is not a great yachting base, but what yachts there are inevitably find their way to the harbour at Keryneia, where they tie up alongside cruise boats and working fishing vessels, or in the new marina a short distance west of the castle. The harbour tower was part of the city's fortifications, from which a chain gate stretched across the old entrance, sealing it against hostile vessels. A customs house, breakwater, marina offices and the tourist information office complete the harbour's facilities.

OLD STYLE
Although 'Keryneia' is the town's official transliteration from Greek, on the ground in the Turkish Cypriot zone you are far more likley to see it written in the old way as 'Kyrenia' or in Turkish as 'Girne'.

211

BESIDE THE SEA
An evening stroll along the waterfront in Keryneia is the perfect end to a day, starting from a point near the Dome Hotel and finishing at a harbourside café terrace.

Boats moor alongside the waterfront café terraces in Keryneia Harbour

The North

Marine relic: the remains of a 2,300-year-old Hellenistic merchant vessel that once plied the seas between Greece and Cyprus

SHIP SHAPE
The Kyrenia shipwreck was the subject of a remarkable act of co-operation between the two communities, in the very aftermath of the devastating conflict of 1974. The Greek Cypriot authorities transferred to Keryneia temperature- and humidity-control equipment for the newly completed museum, without which the priceless recovered ship would have been in grave danger.

MUSEUMS Around 300BC, a trading vessel plied the coast of Asia Minor. The boat and its crew put in at Samos and collected a consignment of wine stored in *amphorae* (large pottery jars). They continued to Kos for a load of mill-stones; these were for sale but were also carried to provide ballast. The vessel's last port of call was Rhodes, where more wine-laden *amphorae* were added to the hold. Finally, the four-man crew pointed their ship's prow to the open sea and headed for Cyprus. They never arrived. Caught in a heavy storm, the wooden vessel foundered outside Keryneia harbour.

Thus do modern historians and archaeologists re-create the ill-fated final voyage of the Hellenistic merchant ship that is the remarkable star exhibit of the **Shipwreck Museum►►►**, inside the castle. For in a sense the 'Kyrenia ship' (as historians call it) did arrive, 2,300 years behind schedule, as the result of a massive marine archaeology recovery project during the late 1960s and early 1970s. The remains of the ship, which at this time was the world's oldest recovered ship, are a memorable and moving sight. A fair amount of the ship's 14.3m (47ft) long hull, made from Aleppo pine sheathed in lead, survived buried in sand on the sea floor and is displayed in a temperature- and humidity-controlled environment. More than 400 wine *amphorae* were brought up from the seabed, along with the millstones and four each of the simple utensils—cups, plates and spoons—the crew used.

A supply of 9,000 time-blackened almonds, intended for the crew's diet, were to be supplemented by fish caught en route. Radio-carbon analysis places the almonds at 288 BC (± 62 years) and the ship's timbers at 389 BC (± 44 years), suggesting that the ship may have been about 100 years old when it sank. The ship is a unique time-capsule, affording a glimpse of everyday life at sea shortly after the time of Alexander the Great; it should not be missed.

A moderately interesting collection of paintings and ceramics is about all the **Fine Arts Museum**▶ (*Open* summer Mon–Fri 9–2; winter Mon–Fri 9–1 and 2–4.45. *Admission: inexpensive*) has to offer, although its location in an old villa on the western edge of the town, overlooking the sea, suggests something more promising. More interesting is the **Folk Art Museum**▶ (*Open* summer Mon–Fri 9–2; winter Mon–Fri 9–1 and 2–4.45. *Admission: inexpensive*), housed in a converted carob warehouse with entrances on the harbourside and, one level up, in the street behind. This is one of the few buildings fronting the harbour that has not been turned into a café or restaurant. It contains a modest collection of traditional household goods, farming and milling implements, fabrics and clothing. These include an olive press, a primitive but effective threshing board, bridal chests and a traditional Ottoman bed. More interesting in a way is the building itself, which has not been prettified like all its neighbours and gives a good idea of the construction methods used in these warehouses.

The **Icon Museum**▶ ▶ (*Open* summer Mon–Fri 9–2; winter Mon–Fri 9–1 and 2–4.45. *Admission inexpensive*) was formerly the church of Archangelos Michaïl, built in 1860. Its tall baroque bell-tower, whitewashed steps and echoing courtyard were well known to Lawrence Durrell. Nowadays it has a different distinction: It is one of the monuments pointed to by the Turkish Cypriot authorities in reply to Greek Cypriot charges that they have destroyed the Christian heritage of this part of the island. The church is in excellent condition and its use as an Icon Museum is entirely appropriate. The iconostasis has been preserved, and many icons displayed have been brought from isolated churches for safekeeping.

CHURCH AND MOSQUE

Dating from the 10th century, the rock-cut Byzantine chapel of **Agia Mavra**▶ is almost lost in an area of jumbled rock and ruins east of the old harbour. Its neglected interior contains the sad remains of some ancient frescoes. Named after an Ottoman commander, the late 16th-century **Cafer Paşa Mosque**▶, with its ablutions spring, stands in a quiet backstreet above the harbour.

IN STYLE

Keryneia is where young and fashion-conscious Turkish Cypriots like to see and be seen. As prosperity spreads itself wider—even if only a little—this is also where the flashy cars and designer labels tend to gather. There is little that is chic about Turkish Cypriot Nicosia or Famagusta (Gazimağusa); Keryneia is the place to be.

213

Icons in the former Archangelos Michaïl Church, now Keryneia's Icon Museum

Above: Looking over the entrance to the harbour from the ramparts of Keryneia Castle

Walk

See map on page 210

Keryneia (Girne)

Keryneia is a small town. Even on foot you don't dare blink too often or you may miss it. What it lacks in size, however, it makes up for in charm. The sights on the walk are covered in more detail on pages 210–213.

Begin at the eastern end of the harbour and climb the steps to **Keryneia Castle▶▶▶**. A stroll around its battlements and bastions and a tour of the **Shipwreck Museum▶▶▶**, with its 2,300-year-old remains of a Hellenistic merchant ship and its cargo, form a vital part of the Keryneia experience. Exit from the upper level, pass the police station (marked Polis), and turn immediately right, to the green-painted entrance of the **Cafer Paşa Mosque▶**, before retracing your steps slightly and descending the alley on your left, to the harbour.

At the eastern end of the harbour a narrow causeway leads to the harbour tower, from which a gate once stretched to the western end, permitting or denying entrance to ships outside. Heading westwards along the sweep of the harbour, to the left are former warehouses, now converted into restaurants and cafés. Fishing boats, yachts and tour boats are moored at the quayside, filling the available space. You may occasionally see a sunken vessel beside the tower, victim of fierce northerly gales that blow in winter.

Midway along the harbourside is the **Folk Art Museum▶**, and at its end is the marina and customs house. The breakwater stretches out to cover the harbour from the north, with a beacon at its end.

Following the shore road west, you will see on your left the dazzling white bulk of Archangelos Michaïl Church, now the **Icon Museum▶▶**. The narrow streets of this area incorporate the old quarter, where much local colour can be seen. Below the Icon Museum, the Hotel Liman café terrace is shaded by the entwined branches of the 'Loving Trees'. Finally, the venerable Dome Hotel occupies the next headland along, and Kemal Atatürk's statue is in the square beyond.

The coffee shop is the centre of village life in both the Greek Cypriot and Turkish Cypriot zones—for the menfolk at least. It is a place of relaxation, of gossip and political debate, and of escape from the outside world.

'Come in, sit down. Welcome. How do you like your coffee?' Hospitality is the hallmark of the Cypriot coffee shop (*kafenion/kahvehane*) and this is easily extended to tourists hesitating in the doorway, uncertain whether to penetrate to the heart of the mystery within. In more worldly places by the coast, it will be accepted that tourists pay for their own, but in remoter villages rarely touched will the coffee may well be on the house.

Strong coffee it is too, the kind that puts hairs on your chest (perhaps another reason why women don't frequent these establishments). Given the sad division of Cyprus, it is as well not to call the drink by its usual name—Turkish coffee—in Greek Cypriot areas, but to speak instead of Greek or Cyprus coffee. Nowadays *ouzo*, *raki*, brandy, and even beer have all wormed their way into the coffee shop as well.

Fun time Politics, village gossip, the weather, and the prospects for harvest are all important staples of conversation, but only after the principal topic—soccer—has been exhausted. Card games and backgammon, played with vigorous gestures and bewildering speed, fill in the idle moments. Television, of course, has forced its way into the coffee shop, although it is generally only switched on for a football match or a racy film.

Starting the day at dawn with a strong cup or two, popping in at lunchtime for some more and settling down at the end of a day's work form an essential part of life's routine. And the younger men can look forward to their retirement, when they need never leave the coffee shop's warm, smoky embrace.

COFFEE TIME
Turkish coffee—or Greek coffee, if you prefer—is called *kafé* in Greek and *kahve* in Turkish. Made from fresh-ground coffee beans, it is prepared in a small pot, either with or without sugar according to taste. The steeped grounds are then poured into a cup. The result is a thick, strong-tasting coffee, which should be sipped slowly, but only as far as the 'muddy' residue in the bottom of the cup. Sugar is not added to the coffee afterwards, so the desired sweetness should be ordered: unsweetened (*sketo* in Greek, *sade* in Turkish), medium-sweet (*metrio/orta*) or sweet (*zahari/şekerli*)

215

TAKEN BY *TAVLI*
Coffee-shop denizens whizzing through a game of *tavli/tavla* (backgammon) are engaging in an activity that began some 5,000 years ago in Mesopotamia and was popular with the teenage Egyptian Pharaoh Tutankhamun, if the evidence from his tomb is anything to go by.

The coffee shop is a venerable and much-loved institution on both sides of the Cypriot divide

The North

VEGETABLE LEGACY
Kythrea (Değirmenlik) is said to have been the source of the cauliflower, which was introduced to a doubtless ecstatic Europe in 1604.

GROOVY FELINE
The distinctive pottery cats of Lapithos (Lapta) began their career when a British army officer ordered one for his house. More British residents followed suit, and soon a minor marketing phenomenon was under way. Other potteries joined in with their own styles, and cat-lovers from other countries placed orders. Since 1974, production has been transferred to south Cyprus, but the Lapithos cats' allure remains.

Statue of Kemal Atatürk at Lefka (Lefke)

▶ **Kythrea (Değirmenlik)**   199D1

Water from Kythrea's spring of Kephalovryso used to make the long journey by aqueduct across the parched Mesaoria (Mesarya) Plain to ancient Salamis, where it filled the pools and fountains of the city's elegant Roman-era baths.

The aqueducts have long since crumbled to the ground, and Kythrea has declined also to a sprawling township on the southern slopes of the Pentadaktylos (Beşparmak) Mountains. However, the Turkish Cypriot government has assigned funds for the restoration of Ottoman-period houses in the town, and some of these are very fine indeed.

North of Kythrea lie the remains of the ancient Greek city of Chytroi, founded around 1200 BC and cited by the second-century AD Greek geographer Ptolemy, in his *Geographica*, as one of the principal Roman cities of Cyprus. To the southeast of Kythrea, at the village of Voni (Gokhan), was found the magnificent lager-than-life-size bronze statue of the Roman emperor Septimius Severus, which is now one of the principal exhibits of the Cyprus Museum in Greek Cypriot Nicosia.

▶ **Lapithos (Lapta)**   198C2

Situated in the foothills of the Pentadaktylos (Beşparmak) Mountains overlooking the sea, this farming village has become popular with expatriates. Surrounded by lemon and lime groves, which owe their richness partly to the perpetual springs rising in the mountains that lie behind the town, Lapithos was one of Lawrence Durrell's favourite Cypriot villages; in *Bitter Lemons* he notes that it was famous for its 'woven stuff and silk'. To these can be added pottery. The village was settled by refugees from ancient Lampousa, who abandoned their coastal city in the face of constant Arab depredations in the seventh century and headed inland for greater security.

▶ **Lefka (Lefke)**   198A1

A spectacular equestrian statue of the Turkish statesman Kemal Atatürk greets visitors to this pleasant university town looking across a fertile plain towards the nearby UN buffer zone and the distant Troodos Mountains. Lefka has always had a strong Turkish Cypriot community, even in Cyprus's pre-partition days. All the bitterness of the events that led to the island's division is captured in a stark cemetery with a memorial to 'unarmed and defenceless civilians' massacred by Greek Cypriot and Greek 'thugs'. Yet Lefka is a peaceable place and well worth a casual wander through its streets.

▶▶ **Morfou (Güzelyurt)**   198B1

Deep in the heart of citrus territory, this handsome town, whose Turkish name means 'lovely country', is the fourthmost important in the Turkish zone of Cyprus. The town's **Agios Mamas Monastery**▶▶ (*Open* summer daily 9–7; winter daily 9–1, 2–4.45. *Admission: moderate*), although no longer in use, is maintained in excellent condition by its current guardians. Built over an early Christian church, which itself replaced a Roman temple, Agios Mamas was rebuilt in the 15th and 18th centuries. It contains the tomb of

the third-century hermit St. Mamas, the tax-dodgers' friend. Outraged at being taxed when he lived in a cave, so the story goes, St. Mamas of Morfou refused to pay. As he was being hauled before the Byzantine duke, he saw a passing lion attacking a lamb. Mamas subdued the lion (a species unknown to Cyprus) with a gesture and hopped up on to its back for the balance of the trip. The duke was sufficiently impressed to cancel the saint's taxes.

Güzelyurt Museum▶ (*Open* summer daily 9–7; winter daily 9–1 and 2–4.45. *Admission: moderate*), installed in the adjacent bishopric, houses on its ground floor a curious collection of stuffed birds and animals, most of them indigenous to Cyprus. The stuffing has been done with less than commendable skill, giving the creatures a ragged look, as if they have just been dragged through a hedge. Upstairs is a small but altogether more impressive archaeological section, displaying finds from the locality stretching from the Stone Age, through the Bronze Age to classical times. Particularly impressive are a terracotta figure of a bird-faced goddess and a statue of Artemis.

Some 3km (2 miles) north of Morfou is **Toumba tou Skourou▶**, a Bronze Age site famed for its copper industry. Excavations have uncovered faint traces of temples and other buildings.

Agios Mamas Monastery in Morfou (Güzelyurt), now a museum

TAX DODGERS
During Cyprus' centuries of occupation by the Ottoman Turks, many Christians engaged in a tax-dodging scheme that might have warmed the heart of St. Mamas of Morfou. They became *linobambakoi*, Christians who pretended to be Muslims to avoid paying tax. The word means 'flax-cottons', a strange mixture of substances, because they retained their Christian faith, practising it in secret and presumably skipping over the commandment 'Thou shalt not bear false witness…'

View over the Morfou (Güzelyurt) Plain, towards the distant Troodos Mountains

The five distinctive indentations of Mount Pentadaktylos (Mount Beşparmak)

▶ Mount Pentadaktylos (Mount Beşparmak)   *199D1*

The Byzantine hero Dighenis (not to be confused with the EOKA leader Grivas, whose *nom de guerre* was also Dighenis) once apparently leapt from Asia Minor to Cyprus while escaping from the Arabs, leaving the impression of his fingers in this 'five-fingered' mountain as he landed, thus giving its name. This is among the roughest terrain in the Pentadaktylos (Beşparmak) Range, and rewards properly equipped hikers with some tough but satisfying walks in the scented mountain air. There are trails to Mount Pentadaktylos from the vicinity of Klepini (Arapköy) and Trapeza (Beşparmak), and from the point where the Kythrea (Değirmenlik) road is crossed by the rough road from Voufaventon (Buffavento) Castle to the Halevga (Alevkaya) Forest Station.

▶ Myrtou (Çamlıbel)   *198B2*

The Turkish army is exceedingly active in this area, a fact that has led to the abandoned 16th-century **Agios Panteleimon Monastery** being out of bounds to visitors. About 1km (0.5 miles) south of Çamlıbel, following an unmarked track to the right, stand the remains of the Bronze Age sanctuary of **Myrtou-Pigadhes**, with a *temenos* (sacred precinct) and an altar.

▶ Pentageia (Yeşilyurt)   *198A1*

This was an important town in medieval times, and near by it preserves the remains of the 12th-century **Xeropotamos Monastery**, with fragments of colonnades and marble from ancient Soloi. Pentageia also boasts Turkish Cyprus' only golf course, an eccentric but lovingly maintained nine-hole affair, on which enthusiasts will search in vain for a green among the sun-scorched grass.

▶ Profitis Ilias   *198B1*

Near the village of Skylloura (Yılmazköy) and beyond, to Agia Marina (Gurpınar), the road seems to run through an almost unbroken series of restricted military zones, one of which has swallowed up this monastery.

►► Soloi (Soli) 198A1

Open: summer daily 9–7; winter daily 9–1 and 2–4.45.
Admission: moderate

Occupying a position among fields beside a beautiful stretch of shore marred only by the rusting remains of copper-ore loading terminals, the ancient city of Soloi was the subject of slow excavation before 1974. Soloi apparently got its name when King Philokypros was persuaded by the Athenian philosopher and statesman Solon to relocate an existing city, which the king did, renaming it in Solon's honour. Now the site has a slightly forlorn look, as if it has been abandoned once again as it was in the 7th century AD.

Little remains above ground of what were until the last century extensive ruins of the Hellenistic and Roman city, for the British found its ancient stones to be just the thing they needed for construction purposes in the Suez Canal. There is an early Christian basilica with some fine mosaic floors depicting birds and fish, but how long these will remain intact is uncertain, despite recent attempts to cover and protect them. This basilica, like most of Soloi, was razed to the ground by Arab raiders in the seventh century, and in the 12th century a smaller church was built within the ruins. Nearby is a Roman-style theatre, partially restored in the 1930s in an unattractively blocky style, like a Prussian interpretation of a Roman theatre's graceful lines. Among the sheep-fields are the paltry remains of temples and other buildings.

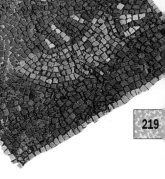

Mosaic floor in the basilica at Soloi (Soli)

219

Partially restored Roman theatre at Soloi (Soli)

The ruins of Buffavento

Drive

See map on pages 198–199

The Pentadaktylos (Beşparmak) Mountains

Driving along the Pentadaktylos (Beşparmak) Range involves several flanking operations and outright retreats in the face of Turkish army bases, but crusader castles show military power to be no newcomer to these slopes. The section suggested here ideally requires a day, although it could be done in about four hours as a non-stop drive. The sights are covered in more detail on pages 202–225.

Take the coast road eastwards out of Keryneia (Girne), turning inland and

Admiring the view from Mount Pentadaktylos

following the sign for **Belapais (Beylerbeyi)**▶▶. The road snakes up through lemon groves, just as Lawrence Durrell described it in *Bitter Lemons*, but with the addition of some unsightly ribbon development. You arrive in the village square at Durrell's 'Tree of Idleness', with the great Gothic **Abbey of Belapais**▶▶▶ laid out before you. Driving up the steep, narrow main street to the house where Durrell lived is possible but not recommended in view of the difficulties of the ascent and the disastrous modernization of the house.

About halfway down the hill, a road turns off towards **Agios Epiktitos (Çatalköy)**▶, where Durrell and his Cypriot friend Panos ran into an arms search by British troops. After the village, the main road turns south towards Kythrea (Değirmenlik), climbing again into the mountains as it does so. An interesting diversion at this point is to branch off towards **Klepini (Arapköy)**▶. Durrell and Panos came this way a few days before Panos was shot dead by EOKA.

For **Voufaventon (Buffavento) Castle**▶▶, a public right of way ends at the signs indicating a Turkish army base, so either park the car or turn right up a much rougher slope to park beside a monument to those killed in an air crash here. From this point, if you want to play crusader knight, you must first play mountaineer. Actually, the track leading up to the castle is not so bad and the climb takes about half an hour.

Mount Pentadaktylos (Mount Beşparmak)▶ has five impressions along its summit, said to have been made by the fingers of the Byzantine hero Dighenis. The trail winds along

through forest beneath the mountain. Somewhere out of sight to the right are the ruins of **Panagia Plataniotissa Monastery**, while near the end, to the left, are the slightly more visible ruins of the 10th-century Coptic and later Armenian monastery of **Sourp Magar**. A little farther is the **Halevga (Alevkaya) Forest Station**, at the confluence of several forest trails. Another 300m (985ft) downhill to the right is a herbarium and a small restaurant.

Where the main road turns sharply to the left just before Agios Amvrosios (Esentepe), a rough track leads off to the right, towards the 12th-century Byzantine monastery of **Antifonitis**▶▶, which is downhill to the left at a crossroads of forest trails. Its ruinously dilapidated church, filled with the vandalized remnants of once-superb frescoes, is worth seeing, if only to have a better idea of what neglect followed by communal conflict can do to a priceless cultural treasure. A furious debate rages over which community is responsible for Antifonitis's sad state; meanwhile the monastery disintegrates.

Belapais Abbey

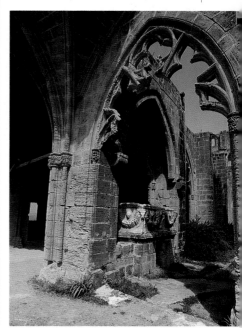

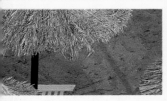

Holiday beaches are the stuff of dreams. The dream does not always match the reality, however. In the most popular parts of Cyprus, the picture is one of over-exploitation of the good beaches and a growing risk that the undeveloped ones will go the same way.

222

ON THE BEACH

Finding a deserted beach, even at peak holiday times, is not impossible. The main ones are in the Turkish Cypriot zone, particularly along the Karpasia (Karpaz) Peninsula, where there are great stretches of undeveloped, but also unsupervised beaches. Most are easily found, lying alongside the northern and southern coast roads. At the northern end of Famagusta Bay (Gazimağusa Körfezi), from Bogazi (Boğaz) onwards, some beaches can be found by taking one of many dirt trails running seawards from the inland stretch of road.

In the Greek Cypriot zone, the northern coast from Polis to Kato Pyrgos offers good possibilities, although the beaches are not wonderful. The Akamas Peninsula is better, but with beaches more difficult to reach. Parts of the coast between Larnaka and Limassol have beaches that, if not exactly deserted, are a lot quieter than those in the resorts.

Endangered turtles have their protectors

Cyprus has few outstanding beaches. A holiday paradise without paradisaical beaches is a difficult sell, so the brochures are filled with praise of places that, as described, do not appear to exist. Of course, it all depends on what is meant by 'good'. There is no Ipanema, no Bondi, no Malibu, but there are stretches of fine golden powdery stuff warmed by near-perpetual sunshine and washed by an azure sea. Yet it is hard, when trying to find a free spot at Fig Tree Bay, Agia Napa, or Coral Bay, to avoid the conclusion that most beaches are on the diminutive side of small.

In some parts of the Greek Cypriot south, the shortage of beaches has been tackled by shaving a few million years off nature's own beach-making process and delivering them by truck instead, creating the seaside equivalent of a moth-eaten fireside rug. Limassol and Larnaka beaches fall into this category, as do many of the pocket-handkerchief-sized beaches fronting resort hotels. The standard model, however, is a bay of modest dimensions whose beach is the major selling point of rather too many hotels, a familiar enough state of affairs throughout the Mediterranean.

Positive thinking None of this necessarily means that a beach holiday will be a disappointment. On the plus side, the facilities in terms of tavernas, beach cafés and watersports are good, the sea is warm, and sunshine is all but guaranteed. The atmosphere on the beaches is friendly, and there is little likelihood of theft of personal belongings. Besides, any parent knows their children only need a a small patch of sand to call their own and access to the sea to be as happy as sandboys and sandgirls right through from dawn until dusk.

Too many people in one place can even be good for other places. One of the best beaches, Lara Bay near the Akamas Peninsula in the Greek Cypriot sector, is reserved for turtles, which prefer quiet, sandy beaches when the time comes to do their duty by the next generation. This makes them unpopular with entrepreneurs, who take the view that if God had wanted turtles on the beaches, He would have provided them with money for hiring loungers. Yet Lara Bay is a vital environmental resource, and there are other fine beaches, in the so far unspoiled Akamas Peninsula particularly, that need protection. If Cyprus can withstand the pressures for more development it will be doing the natural world a service.

Beach invasion Northern Cyprus is better off when it comes to beaches. One of the Greek Cypriots' most bitter complaints about the island's division is that they lost the best holiday areas, around Keryneia (Girne) and Famagusta (Gazimağusa). Some beaches in the Turkish sector are open only to the Turkish army, either for military or recreational purposes. The Turkish troops may be duty-bound to blow their whistles at tourists who wander into unimportant places like tank depots and head-quarters map-rooms, but they get seriously irritated if you go anywhere near their beaches.

The long Golden Beach — typically all-but-deserted sands along the Karpasia (Karpaz) Peninsula

223

Deciding whether or not to bungee jump at Agia Napa... (she didn't)

SOLAR WARNING
Scientists at the National Council for Atmospheric Research in Boulder, Colorado, say that ozone cover over the northern hemisphere is down by 6–10 percent, implying a 15 percent increase in ultraviolet levels and a 20 percent increase in the incidence of skin cancer, although the explosion in such cases may have as much to do with excessive sunbathing as with increasing UV exposure. In any case, it makes sense to limit sunbathing and use high-protection-factor suncreams.

In compensation, the Turkish Cypriot zone has long stretches of wild and lonely golden sands with nary a hotel, nor a Coca-Cola stand, nor a lifeguard within 50km (30 miles). Their only visitor, apart from an occasional tourist trying to find a hotel, a cola drinks' stand or a lifeguard, appears to be a slovenly giant who spends half the year gathering up rubbish in black plastic bags and the other half spreading his collection out. Maybe it is fortunate that beach holidays are going out of style.

The Tekke Hazreti Ömer, dedicated to seven Islamic martyrs, clings to a rocky foreland

►► Tekke Hazreti Ömer (Hazreti Ömer Türbesi)   *199D2*

This important Ottoman-era Islamic shrine is dedicated to seven Arab soldiers killed in a 7th-century raid on Cyprus and considered martyrs for the faith. The whitewashed mosque stands on a rocky headland beside the sea, forming a simple but hauntingly beautiful scene. Its guardian can recite the outline of its history in several languages.

Beside the road to the shrine is a residence of the Turkish ambassador, incorporating the little church of Agios Georgios, cracked and crumbling, and the 'Fortuna' villa that belonged to Lawrence Durrell's friend Marie.

► Vavilas (Güzelyalı)   *198C2*

A farming village so close to the sea as to be in it as much as beside it, Vavilas has little to recommend it—other than its perfect situation, its tranquil character, and a little seaside restaurant.

►► Voufaventon (Buffavento) Castle   *199D1*

Open: permanently. Admission free

Lodged atop a 940m (3,084ft) high crag on the southern face of the Pentadaktylos (Beşparmak) Range north of Kythrea (Değirmenlik), Buffavento is reached via a rough track from the Keryneia (Girne)–Kythrea road. Getting there involves a climb, either from a parking area beside a military base, or from a little higher up, beside a memorial to all those who died in an airliner crash there in 1988. The exhilaration of the half-hour climb, with its widening vista of the Mesaoria (Mesarya) Plain, may be augmented by the desire not to step on one of the poisonous vipers that frequent the area.

GIVING UP GRACELESSLY
Poor old Isaac Komnenos. For a tough usurper who defied the Byzantine government in Constantinople, he put up a pathetic show after insulting Richard the Lionheart's betrothed. There is scarcely a medieval location in Cyprus that is not said to mark one of his defeats or surrenders. The picture gained is of him fleeing from one doomed strongpoint to another, before being hauled before his tormentor in chains. At Voufaventon (Buffavento), his daughter did the surrender honours.

Buffavento, 'buffeted by the winds', is a bit disappointing, especially given the exertion required to get there, but the view makes up for this. The castle was surrendered in 1191 by the daughter of Byzantine usurper Isaac Komnenos to England's King Richard the Lionheart. The Venetians later dismantled it when they concentrated their anti-Ottoman firepower at Nicosia (Lefkosia/Lefkoşa) and Famagusta (Gazimağusa).

Visible far down the valley, although no more than a few kilometres away as the swallow flies, is the 11th-century monastery of **Agios Ioannis Chrysostomos**, one of Cyprus's finest—or so it was reputed before the Turkish army established a base in and around it after 1974. Now it is a binocular-range attraction marked by an enormous cypress tree, and its icons have been evacuated to Keryneia. Equally inaccessible, out of sight to the west, is the church of Panagia Koutsovendis.

The climb to Buffavento Castle starts here

Left: Vouni Palace

►►► Vouni (Vuni) 198A1

Open: summer daily 10–5; winter 9–1 and 2–4.45. Admission: moderate

Say what you will about the ancient Persians, they knew a good place for a palace when they saw one. High above the Mediterranean, the great fortress-cum-palace at Vouni commanded more than a scenic outlook. It loomed large above the nearby Greek city of Soloi, which had rebelled against Persia in 498BC, encouraging the locals' loyalty by its presence. This wasn't enough, and by the middle of the century the Greeks held both city and palace.

Each set of owners gave something to Vouni: an oriental architecture subsequently altered by the addition of Greek forms. Today's visitor is liable to have difficulty distinguishing between them, thanks to the minimal vestiges left behind by two-and-half millennia of looting and decay. This does not seem important, however, as the main attraction of Vouni is still its superb location overlooking the sea and the fragmentary remains of Soloi.

► Vounon (Taşkent) 199D1

This village, formerly a Maronite community, now hosts the **Martyrs' Museum**, dedicated to Turkish Cypriots massacred by EOKA, whose mass grave was exhumed by the Red Cross. Outside the village the mountainside has been inscribed with a colossal Turkish Republic of Northern Cyprus flag and a declaration of Turkish pride by Kemal Atatürk, founder of modern Turkey: highly visible symbols understandably considered provocative by Greek Cypriots.

North of the village lies the Byzantine monastery of **Panagia Absinthiotissa**, rebuilt in the 15th and 20th centuries, whose treasures have been looted.

TURKISH DELIGHT
For anyone whose Turkish is a little rusty, the slogan of Kemal Atatürk beside the giant Turkish Republic of Northern Cyprus flag on the hillside near Vounon (Taşkent) is *Ne Mutlu Turküm Diyene*, meaning 'How fortunate is the person who can say "I am a Turk".'

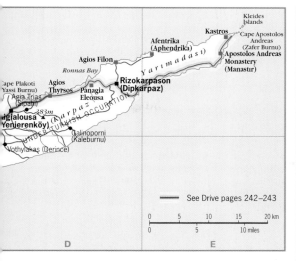

See Drive pages 242–243

THE EAST

One by-product of war and the Turkish Cypriots' former diplomatic and commercial isolation is that the coastline from Famagusta (Gazimağusa) all the way to the tip of the Karpasia (Karpaz) Peninsula at Cape Apostolos Andreas (Zafer Burnu) has been virtually a tourist-free zone. This is changing, however, and it is slowly waking from its long sleep.

Pre-1974, eastern Cyprus represented the single most important slice of the country's tourism pie. Specifically, this was concentrated in the hotel-and-beach playground south of Famagusta, in the days when a Mediterranean holiday meant quite simply sun, sea and sand. Now, solitude can be added if you want to get away from the sunworshippers for an activity-based or 'green' vacation.

Crowds, if they ever were a problem in this part of Cyprus, are one no longer. Famagusta's resort suburb Varosha (Maraş) is a ghost town, its once-proud holiday hotels ruined and collapsing after almost 30 years' abandonment, and its golden sands deserted under the summer sun. There have been proposals to reopen the town as part of a UN attempt to find a settlement but so far no agreement has been reached. Tourism is getting going again in eastern Cyprus and a resort area under construction between Agios Theodoros (Çay rova) and Koma tou Gialou (Kumyalı) is planned to give it a boost.

Left: Old shoreside church at Agios Thyrsos
Far left: A fisherman in the harbour at Bogazi (Boğaz)

A shoeshiner in Famagusta (Gazimağusa)

228

LUSIGNAN JEWEL Famagusta (called Ammochostos by the Greek Cypriots and Gazimağusa by the Turkish Cypriots) is the town on which the east is based. The walled city has lost much of its sparkle since the 14th century when it was the jewel of the Levant and Christendom's forward outpost. Europe's trade with the Orient passed through here, and profits from spices, silks, precious metals and stones filled the city's coffers.

'I dare not speak of their precious stones and golden tissues and other riches', wrote one awestruck visitor,'for it were a thing unheard of and incredible.' The poet James Elroy Flecker (1884–1915) captured the city's romantic image in his poem 'The Old Ships' (1915):

I have seen the old ships sail like swans asleep
Beyond the village which men still call Tyre,
With leaden age o'ercargoed, dipping deep
For Famagusta and the hidden sun
That rings black Cyprus with a lake of fire

INCOMERS
Many of the immigrants from Turkey who came to northern Cyprus after the 1974 invasion live in the sparsely populated and mainly agricultural Mesaoria Plain (Mesarya Ovasi) and Karpasia Peninsula (Karpaz Yarımadasi). The result is that these areas have a much more pronounced Turkish, as compared with Turkish Cypriot, character.

Shrunken and diminished as it is, Famagusta still wears its history like a glove. The Lusignans' Gothic legacy stands out in ruined churches, although only a fraction remains of the 300 or more churches to which travellers of that period refer. Nor has the city neglected publicity, especially that penned by William Shakespeare. Famagusta has taken on the mantle of *Othello*, based on Shakespeare's scene-setting note for the play: 'Cyprus. A sea-port'.

PERFECT PEACE The farther from Famagusta you travel, the emptier of people the landscape gets. The remains of ancient towns and cities are dotted along Famagusta Bay (Gazimağusa Körfezi) and out into the long, narrow Karpasia Peninsula, the 'panhandle' of Cyprus, but almost nothing in the way of tourist development. Instead, wild donkeys roam the Karpasia and are the subject of scientific research. By the time the windy tip of Cape Apostolos

Bastion and gateway in Famagusta's powerful defensive walls

Andreas is reached, with Syria and Turkey just across the water, the solitude is absolutely complete.

On the extensive spirit-level-flat plain called the Mesaoria (Mesarya Ovası), agriculture continues to be the mainstay for the inhabitants of a hundred little villages, and even then it can only be practised in winter and spring when the rains have brought life to what would otherwise be semi-desert.

Put all of this together and it can be seen that eastern Cyprus still commands one of the 21st century's most precious resources: nothing, and plenty of it.

The coastline near Cape Apostolos Andreas (Zafer Burnu)

229

CROWNING GLORY

During the coronation of Cyprus's Lusignan ruler, Peter II, the representatives of Genoa and Venice had an argument about who should take precedence in the procession. The Venetians won the argument, so in 1372 the Genoese invaded Cyprus and captured Famagusta (Gazimağusa).

BORN FREE

A unique feature of the Karpasia (Karpaz) Peninsula of eastern Cyprus is its wild donkeys, whose numbers are estimated at anywhere between a couple of hundred and a couple of thousand. The latter figure is often cited by irate farmers who accuse the scavenging donkeys of destroying their crops. Roaming donkeys were noted in the area as far back as the 19th century, but their number increased considerably after 1974 when many Greek Cypriot villagers fled the peninsula, abandoning their domestic animals. The donkeys are protected in a fenced-off national park area beyond Golden Beach.

▶ Afentrika (Aphendrika) 227E3

Archaeologists will, eventually, no doubt reveal much from the site of this important settlement of the Hellenistic period, one of Cyprus' main cities in the 3rd century BC, according to Strabo, who was writing in the first century AD. An extensive area along the shore northeast of Rizokarpaso (Dipkarpaz) throws up some slight evidence of its former glory in the remains of a citadel, traces of an ancient harbour and clusters of tombs. The best that can be said now is that its founders chose the setting wisely, the shoreline still presenting a memorable prospect today.

▶ Agia Trias (Sipahi) 227D3

This is one of the villages populated by post-1974 Turkish immigrants. It is most notable for the ruins of the sixth-century Christian basilica of Agia Trias. On the shore is **Agios Thyrsos**, a hamlet so small that the Turkish Cypriots haven't bothered to rename it. The salient points of Agios Thyrsos, apart from a fine prospect of the sea and coastline, are two neglected Orthodox churches, dating from the 10th century and the 15th century, the older of which stands under the cliff-face beside the sea.

Church on the coast road at Agios Thyrsos

▶▶ Aigialousa (Yenierenköy) 227D3

The Turkish Cypriots have named this village after the enclave of Erenköy on the northwest coast, whose handful of defenders in 1964 repelled (with help from the Turkish air force) an all-out onslaught of Greek Cypriot troops led by General Grivas. Aigialousa is a quiet enough farming village surrounded by fine countryside and is one of the few centres of shops, filling stations and cafés in the Karpasia (Karpaz) Peninsula. The beaches at Cape Plakoti (Yassi Burnu) north of the village are particularly fine, so much so that loggerhead turtles nest here. Soon after Aigialousa, the road to Cape Apostolos Andreas (Zafer Burnu) narrows as if in sympathy with the peninsula, which likewise narrows towards its tip, providing views of the sea on either side.

▶▶▶ Apostolos Andreas Monastery (Manastır) 227E3

Open: irregularly. Admission free, but donation welcome

Cyprus has no shortage of dramatically sited monasteries, but it could be that Apostolos Andreas (the Apostle Andrew)—which is targeted for a UN-sponsored renovation that is held up by Greek Cypriot objections to the plans—occupies the finest position of all. It stands on the shore at a rocky headland a short distance from the needle-tipped Cape Apostolos Andreas (Zafer Burnu), at the end of the Karpasia (Karpaz) Peninsula. The approach is through magnificent countryside, with views on either side of the sea washing deserted sand and jagged rock.

When the Mediterranean is in angry mood, waves crash over the rocks, drenching anyone at the spring said to

WATCHFUL PRESENCE
A Turkish Cypriot policeman notes the names and car licence-plates of all visitors to Apostolos Andreas Monastery. Access has improved greatly since the days when the Karpas was a restricted military zone, however, and the monastery is well enough cared for.

Inside the church of Apostolos Andreas, still used by the isolated Greek Cypriot community at nearby Rizokarpaso (Dipkarpaz)

have been brought forth by St. Andrew. The apostle was sailing for Palestine in a ship with a one-eyed captain. Perhaps not surprisingly they went off course and came ashore at this point. St. Andrew struck the rock with his staff, the spring gushed forth and the captain's full sight was restored. An alternative explanation is that the spring already existed and the apostle's ship merely put in for water. In any case, the spring became a major place of pilgrimage and miraculous cures. A small chapel dating from the 15th century stands by the shore, while a less noteworthy 18th-century church lies at the heart of the 19th-century monastery buildings.

In 1974 a small population of Greek Cypriots at nearby Rizokarpaso (Dipkarpaz) remained behind during the flight from the Turkish army. As its young people grow up and depart to the south for jobs, the population has been ageing. After decades during which visiting was impossible for Greek Cypriots from the south, Orthodox pilgrims are coming again to Apostolos Andreas, which has had a UN-sponsored renovation effort, matching that of the Hala Sultan Tekke near Larnaka (see page 82).

SLEEP-IN

In *Journey into Cyprus* Colin Thubron describes the miraculous healing of a paralysed girl at Apostolos Andreas shortly before his own visit to the monastery in 1972. She had dreamt that the apostle told her that if she slept the night in the chapel there she would be cured. The practice of 'incubation' (sleeping in the temple of a healing power) goes back to the rites of the pagan god of medicine, Asclepius, whose devotees overnighted in his sanctuaries.

231

Apostolos Andreas Monastery and its sacred spring are full of life once more

The East

BROTHER MONKS
The monastery of
Apostolos Varnavas used
to be noted as much for
three of its monks as for
its associations with St.
Barnabas. The three
monks were brothers in the
family as well as the religious sense. Chariton,
Stephanos and Barnabas
remained at the monastery
for three years after the
Turkish army occupied this
area in 1974, but were
finally evacuated to
Stavrovouni.

232

*The Icon Museum at
Apostolos Varnavas
Monastery*

▶▶▶ Apostolos Varnavas Monastery   226B1

Open: summer daily 9–7; winter daily 9–1 and 2–4.45
Admission: moderate

On the road from Salamis to Egkomi (Tuzla), the
monastery is dedicated to the Apostle Barnabas, a native
of Salamis, who, along with St. Paul and St. Mark, founded
the Christian church in Cyprus. It was here in AD488 that
Archbishop Anthemius of Salamis, facing a threat to the
Cypriot church's independence, opportunely discovered
the burial-place of Barnabas, containing a Gospel of St.
Matthew written in Barnabas' own hand and placed there
by St. Mark! Anthemius sent the gospel to the Emperor
Zeno at Constantinople, who was so impressed that he
confirmed Cyprus's religious autonomy and authorized
the archbishop to carry an imperial sceptre in place of a
pastoral staff, to wear robes of imperial purple and sign his
name in imperial red ink. The good archbishop was either
extraordinarily fortunate, or a shrewd hand at poker.

The foundation no longer functions as a monastery, but
houses instead an Icon Museum in the church and an
Archaeology Museum in the monks' former cells around
the cloister. Both are well presented, particularly the
archaeology section, in which the exhibits are arranged
chronologically through the cells, from the neolithic
period to the Byzantine. The cloister, a pleasant stroll, is a
blaze of well-watered flowers, with shade available under
trees. Items in the Archaeology Museum include Stone
Age tools, Greek pottery in both the black-on-red and red-
on-black styles, jewellery, Roman glassware and statuary.
Many of the finds come from the archaeological zone
surrounding Agios Varnavas, with Salamis and Enkomi-
Alasia being the main sources.

►► Bogazi (Boğaz)   226C2

The harbour of this delightful fishing village commands some sweeping views across Famagusta Bay (Gazimağusa Körfezi), although these are spoiled in one direction by a cement plant and oil-storage tank and the beginnings of considerable residential and touristic development to the north. Most of Bogazi has been devoted to the preparation and sale of fish, in a string of seafood restaurants along the main street and shoreline.

For travellers heading into the Karpasia (Karpaz), this is one of the last place with the main facilities.

►►► Cape Apostolos Andreas (Zafer Burnu)   227E3

It seems entirely appropriate that there should have been a temple of Aphrodite (the site of which has been covered with asphalt by the Turkish military) at this emblematic piece of coast, the farthest limit of the Karpasia (Karpaz) Peninsula, complementing her principal sanctuary in the far west at Palaia Pafos. The Christians razed the temple and named the point after the Apostle Andrew, who is said to have landed near here (see page 230).

Reached along a rocky track from Apostolos Andreas Monastery (Manastır), the cape is as wild and lonely a spot as any on Cyprus, pounded by the sea and ringing with the plangent cries of seabirds. It looks out across a flotilla of tiny islands towards the distant shores of Turkey and Syria. In the neolithic era, contemporary with Khirokitia (Choriokoitia) in southern Cyprus (see page 108), the settlement of Kastros was one of the first known human habitations in Cyprus.

►► Egkomi (Enkomi-Alasia)   226B1

Open summer daily 9–7; winter daily 9–1, 2–4.45
Admission: moderate
Near the village of Egkomi (Tuzla), ancient Enkomi is, on one level, an archaeological treasure trove containing priceless knowledge about Cyprus's most important city of the second millennium BC; on another it is a confusing jumble of old stones. Enkomi is thought to have been the 'Alasia' referred to in the Tel el-Amarna tablets, recording letters sent by foreign kings to the Egyptian pharaohs Amenophis III and Akhenaten. The city seems to have been a victim of the mysterious, violent 'peoples of the sea', and an earthquake in 1075BC finished the job they had begun.

► Eptakomi (Yedikonuk)   226C2

This village marks the last gasp of the Pentadaktylos (Beşparmak) Mountains, and it is notable for its 18th-century Orthodox church of Agios Loukas.

Fishing boats in the harbour at Bogazi (Boğaz)

BIRTH OF A NOTION
The little village of Trikomo (Iskele) near Bogazi was the birthplace of General George Grivas (also known as Dighenis), the leader of the pro-Greek armed Cypriot movement EOKA. You can be sure that there is no celebration of this fact in the Turkish Cypriot village.

233

View off Cape Apostolos Andreas (Zafer Burnu)

BIRD SANCTUARY
The tiny Kleides (Zafer) islands off the tip of Cape Apostolos Andreas (Zafer Burnu) are the haunt of the rare Audouin's gull. This whole area has, however, been declared a maritime exclusion zone by the Turkish armed forces, and sailing is not permitted.

The East

234

RAIL LINK

Famagusta used to be the terminal of the British-built Cyprus Government Railway, which ran from Morfou (Güzelyurt) through Nicosia, and was used principally for transporting copper from the mines around Morfou to the port at Famagusta. The railway was closed in 1951 after operating for 50 years.

►►► Famagusta (Gazimağusa)   226B1

Turkish Cypriots often still call it Famagusta, although the word is nowhere to be seen on road signs; Greek Cypriots call it Ammochostos. Whatever its name, the city's great days are firmly behind it, a history that dips and soars gracefully through Byzantium, the Lusignan period, and even the rule of venal Genoese and despotic Venetians. Under the Ottomans and the British, Famagusta went into hibernation and seems never to have woken up.

Refugees from the earthquake-stricken and Arab-ravaged city of Salamis (Constantia) moved in the 7th century to the small town of Arsinoë, which was to develop as Famagusta. During the crusades the town became a forward base, a safe haven after defeat in the Holy Land, and finally a retirement home for washed-up crusaders. By the 14th century Famagusta was renowned for its ostentatious wealth, not necessarily a prudent development in what was a rough neighbourhood. Muggers, in the shape of the Genoese and the Venetians, were not long in striking. The Venetians, with the Ottoman Turks breathing down their necks, ringed the city with the powerful walls that continue to enclose it today. In 1571, after an epic ten-month siege, Famagusta, under the command of Marcantonio Bragadino, surrendered to the far more numerous Ottoman forces of Lala Mustafa Paşa.

Nowadays, old Famagusta fits more than comfortably inside its walls. There is a curious mismatch between the import of those great walls and the dusty, down-at-heel city in their charge, dotted here and there with crumbling or ruined structures (mostly churches) from the good old days. Yet present-day Famagusta has an undeniable charm, a refined and leisurely Turkish Cypriotness that exists in parallel

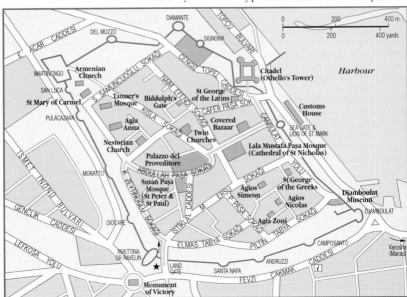

with the grandiose monuments and could easily get along fine without them. Beyond the walls lie the usual nondescript suburbs that you find in any city, but within them is a historic gem attractively dulled by time and circumstance.

THE DEFENCES AND HARBOUR

Famagusta's Citadel►►► (*Open* summer daily 9–7; winter daily 9–1 and 2–4.45. *Admission: moderate*) was originally a moated castle built on the seaward side of the city in the 14th century and later massively strengthened by the Venetians to withstand artillery fire. It is also known as Othello's Tower—actually, mainly known as Othello's Tower, which is judged to be a better tourist draw than plain old 'Citadel'. A few bits and pieces of ancient columns and statues 'adorn' its lower level, and a stroll around the battlements and through the galleries is an interesting diversion, but the Citadel's main attraction, to anyone other than medieval citadel buffs, must be its superb view over the harbour, which still has some of its medieval structures more or less intact.

The Citadel's connection with Shakespeare's *Othello* is purely speculative, although the play's stage directions speak of 'Cyprus. A sea-port' and 'Cyprus. The citadel'. It has also been suggested that the bard's 'valiant Moor' in the service of Venice may have been modelled on either Cristoforo Moro, a 16th-century lieutenant-governor of Cyprus, or Francesco de Sessa, a later Italian mercenary in Cyprus who was apparently nicknamed 'the Moor'. Shakespeare penned the play more than 30 years after the conquest of the island by the Ottomans, so he needed no great prescience when he composed the statement:

...When we consider
The importancy of Cyprus to the Turk...
We must not think the Turk is so unskilful
To leave that latest which concerns him first.

The Ottoman Turks laid siege to Famagusta in 1570, with an army reportedly 200,000 strong facing 8,000 Venetian defenders across the city's stone walls. Ten months later, the Turks were still on the wrong side of the 5km (3-mile) defensive circuit and had lost 50,000 men in the process of discovering just how stoutly built the walls were. Starvation and attrition of the small garrison achieved what direct assault could not, and finally forced Famagusta's surrender on 1 August, 1571.

The original walls were built by the Lusignans when arrows and an occasional catapulted rock were the primary threat. By Venetian times, powerful siege artillery required a redesign and vast increase in their strength. A tour of the walls leaves one in no doubt about that strength. The siege has left little visible trace.

Turkish Cypriot Freedom Monument recording the 1974 siege of Famagusta

235

HIDDEN MEANINGS

Gazimağusa, the Turkish name for Famagusta, means 'unconquered' and refers to the unsuccessful siege of the Turkish Cypriot quarter by Greek Cypriot forces in 1974. The city's original name (since restored by the Republic of Cyprus) was Ammochostos, meaning 'sunken in the sand', when it was founded in the third century BC by the Hellenistic ruler Ptolemy Philadelphus of Egypt.

SHOPPING LIST—1343

Joan Benet, a Catalan merchant, made a business trip to Famagusta in 1343 to buy luxury goods for resale in Barcelona. His account book lists: pepper, cinnamon, ginger (from Sri Lanka and Mecca), lac (a resin for varnishes and red dye), incense, borax (for medicinal use), cloves, cinnamon flowers, sugar, cotton and a conserve of black plums called myrobalans (also for medicinal use).

ROUGH INJUSTICE
The Venetian commander of Famagusta's garrison, the valiant Marcantonio Bragadino, having surrendered to Lala Mustafa with full military honours in 1571, was double-crossed by the Ottomans. Once in Lala Mustafa's power, his nose and ears were cut off and, after two weeks of further horrific tortures, he was flayed alive as a reward for the skill and heroism of his ten-month defence of the city.

Some of the fiercest fighting of the 1570–71 Ottoman siege of Famagusta took place around the Rivettina bastion at the southwest corner of the walls. The Turks eventually captured it, at which point both bastion and conquerors were blown sky high by the Venetians. Farther up the line, the arrow-shaped Martinengo bastion was clearly designed to skewer any outfit unwise enough to try storming it, and the besiegers left it well alone. Between the main bastions, the defences are dotted with smaller strongpoints equipped with side-mounted cannon ports from which flanking fire could sweep any force attacking the wall.

The best view of the **Harbour▶** can be had from the Citadel (Othello's Tower), from where a comparison between the various old prints of its galley-era operations and today's rust-bucket merchantmen may be made. Ferries connect Famagusta with Turkey, while cargo ships from all over the world tie up at the quays. The city is considered an illegal port by the Greek Cypriots, and any ship's captain who subsequently turns up at Limassol or Larnaka in the Republic of Cyprus is liable to arrest and imprisonment.

CHURCHES AND MOSQUES The church of **Agios Simeon▶** is the remnant of Famagusta's Byzantine cathedral, which was heavily damaged by the Turkish cannonade of 1570–71.

Once the foundation of the Christian Nestorian sect from Syria, the mid-14th-century **Nestorian Church▶** is now a cultural centre operated by the Eastern Mediterranean University.

St. George of the Greeks▶ was once Famagusta's Orthodox cathedral. The Byzantine basis of the 14th-century church was added to in Gothic style, making it a rare, but ruined, specimen of this hybrid form.

St. George of the Latins is the ruined stump of a 13th-century Gothic church, which still displays some signs of its former glory.

It would be interesting to know how much Christian forbearance was displayed by the congregations of the **Twin Churches▶**, two side-by-side 14th-century crusader churches. One was owned by the Knights Templar and the other by the Knights Hospitaller, whose sworn enmity towards the infidel hordes defiling the Holy Land was matched only by their hatred of each other. The Templars' church is now an art gallery and theatre; the Hospitallers' church is a music conservatory.

Famagusta's Ottoman conquerors so admired the imposing Gothic lines of the Lusignans' great 14th-century Cathedral of St. Nicholas, where the Kings of Cyprus had been crowned also as Kings of Jerusalem (Famagusta being a safer location for this ceremony than Saracen-occupied Jerusalem), that they added a

St. George of the Latins, one of the city's many Gothic remnants

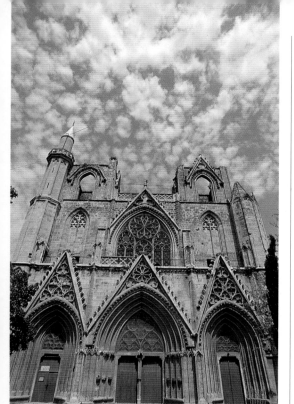

*Lala Mustafa Paşa
Mosque, formerly the
grand cathedral of the
Lusignan kings*

minaret and a *mihrab* and converted it to a mosque, the
Lala Mustafa Paşa Mosque▶▶▶ (Generally *open*
dawn–dusk. *Admission free*, but donation expected). The
muezzin's cry still wails forth from the minaret,
summoning the faithful to prayer—although if the
response to the summons is anything to go by, the faithful
of Famagusta have other things to occupy their time.
Inside, the cool silence and simplicity of the mosque compete harmoniously with the Gothic vaulting, columns and
rose windows of the underlying cathedral.

The **Sınan Paşa Mosque▶** (Generally *open* dawn–dusk.
Admission free, but donation welcome; closed for restoration at the time of writing), formerly the 14th-century
Church of St. Peter and St. Paul, is a more intimate place
than the more imposing Lala Mustafa Paşa Mosque.

ITALIAN PALACE Little remains of the **Palazzo del
Provveditore▶▶** (*Open* permanently. *Admission free*), the
proud structure built by the Venetians over the existing
Lusignan royal palace around 1550 to house their gover-
nors in style. In later years it was used as a police station
and prison, and today it is more like a small ornamental
park decorated with ancient columns and sculptures. The
building includes the tiny prison of the 19th-century
Turkish poet Namık Kemal, who criticized the sultan in
his works and lived to tell the tale—if only to his guards.

Walk

Above: Famagusta's small but colourful bazaar

See map on page 234

Within the walls of Famagusta

Famagusta is not very big and is lightly populated, so a stroll within its Venetian walls does not degenerate into a struggle against traffic fumes and crowds. This walk is a short one: allow an hour at the most. The sights on this walk are covered in more detail on pages 234–237.

Start at the seemingly impregnable **Rivettina bastion** (also known as the Ravelin). In 1570 Famagusta's Turkish besiegers apparently saw some weakness in its design or construction and concentrated their anti-Venetian firepower there. Walk north on Kemal Zeytinoğlu Sokağı. This short stretch allows for a view of the walls more or less as the Venetian defenders saw them as they hurried from one threatened sector to another. Two bastions, Diocare and Moratto, are on this section, and by climbing to the walls you can see how they are mutually supporting, taking any force assaulting the space between them under enveloping fire. Turn right along Abdullah Paşa Sokağı, which leads eventually to the monumental heart of Famagusta, but begins with a section of ordinary housing. You arrive at the Latin Church of St. Peter and St. Paul, now the **Sinan Paşa Mosque▶**. Its quiet interior may be visited. To the mosque's left are the ruins of the **Palazzo del Provveditore▶**, once the royal palace of the Lusignans, taken over and rebuilt by the Venetians.

Continue in this direction and next in view is the Latin Cathedral of St. Nicholas, now the **Lala Mustafa Paşa Mosque▶▶▶**, an imposing Gothic structure with a minaret attached. Finally, you arrive at the walls again, beside the sculpted Lion of St. Mark standing before what was formerly the city's Sea Gate.

Turn left on to Canbulat Yolu, and beyond a traffic oval is the **Citadel▶▶▶**, otherwise known as Othello's Tower.

At harbours all around Cyprus, fishermen still go through the age-old late afternoon ritual of putting to sea in high hopes of a good catch. By dawn, the fruits of their labours are heading for dining tables all over the island.

Stock take Fishing is not nearly so important an industry in Cyprus as you would expect of a Mediterranean island. The problem lies with marine conditions in the eastern Mediterranean basin rather than with any lack of piscatorial enterprise on the Cypriots' part. Yet at ports all round the island, fishermen can still be seen tending their nets and scrubbing their brightly coloured boats before heading out into the wide blue yonder to harvest the deep.

Therein lies the problem. The eastern Mediterranean is deep, and situated at the farthest possible remove from the nutrient-rich tides flowing through the Straits of Gibraltar from the Atlantic Ocean. The reduced freshwater flow from the River Nile since construction of the Aswan Dam is also said to have had a negative impact on fish stocks. The waters around Cyprus simply do not contain sufficient plankton, the basis of the marine food chain, to support vast numbers of edible species. In partial compensation, the plankton-poor, unpolluted waters make for excellent scuba-diving conditions.

Fleet operations The main fishing-fleet bases in the Greek Cypriot area are Pafos, Lakki, Potamos Creek, Limassol, Larnaka and Agia Napa, as well as some smaller locations dotted around the coast. In the Turkish Cypriot zone there are fishing harbours at Keryneia (Girne), Famagusta (Gazimağusa), Bogazi (Boğaz), Koma tou Gialou (Kumyalı) and some smaller places. The ordinary boats go after species such as sole, red mullet and whitebait, while specially equipped vessels sail in search of that well-armed knight of the pelagic depths, the swordfish. Octopus and squid are also picked up for the menu.

Some fish come from the dry land, in a manner of speaking: freshwater trout, for example, from reservoirs and fish farms using perpetual springs in the Troodos Mountains. The hard fact is that most of the fish consumed in Cyprus is imported.

FISHY STORY
Long, hot summers, dried-up riverbeds and chronic water shortages meant that until recently freshwater fish were strangers to Cyprus. The construction of dams to retain the rains of winter, combined with the opening of the Department of Fisheries Experimental Station at Kalopanagiotis in 1969, have been the basis of Cyprus's new-found appetite for freshwater fish. The station has been responsible for introducing such species as trout, eel and crayfish.

239

Still the boats go out

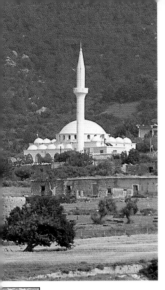

A newly built mosque dwarfs the houses of Galounia

The windy heights of Kantara Castle still dominate the surrounding plains

► Galounia 226C2

Little remains above ground of this ancient city on the north coast of the Karpasia (Karpaz) Peninsula which some scholars believe to have been the capital of Cyprus' Hittite kingdom from 1450 to 1200BC, when it was destroyed by the mysterious 'peoples of the sea'.

► Gastria (Kalecik) 226C2

Faint traces of a ruined 12th-century Templar castle stand on the shore near an oil terminal and factory complex south of here, as does a ruined Byzantine church, **Agios Ioannis**, dating from the 11th century.

►► Kantara Castle 226C2

Open: summer daily 10–5; winter 9–1 and 2–4.45
Admission: moderate

Isolated among the Pentadaktylos (Beşparmak) Mountains like its cousins Agios Ilarion (St. Hilarion) and Voufaventon (Buffavento), Kantara Castle retains all the romance associated with the crusaders, even though it too was partially dismantled by the Venetians. Begun in the ninth century under the Byzantines, Kantara was strengthened in succeeding centuries, particularly by the Lusignans in the 14th century. The climb to its battlements is not so steep or long as at Voufaventon.

Outside the castle gate is a large water-cistern, well covered by arrow-slits in the nearby towers—presumably as a deterrent to illicit dipping.

Within its elaborate battlements the castle contains living quarters, storage rooms and stables, as well as a high watchtower and a beacon platform from which signals could be transmitted westwards across the mountains to Voufaventon and Agios Ilarion. Kantara is surrounded by the picnic and barbecue sites of a forest station.

►►► Karpasia (Karpaz Yarımadasi) 227D3

The region of Karpasia, comprising the Karpasia (Karpaz) Peninsula, must have been one of the most heavily populated parts of the island at the high point of classical Greek and Roman civilization, with the ancient writers Strabo and Ptolemy both recording important cities in the area during this period. Unfortunately, such places as

Afentrika (Aphendrika), Afrodision (Aphrodision), Carpasia, Galounia and Knidos have left few visible traces. The contrast with today's virtually unpopulated, entirely agricultural peninsula could hardly be more pronounced. Yet the Karpasia is a ruggedly beautiful part of the island.

Travelling on the peninsula gives the visitor a real sense of 'getting away from it all', far from the increasing traffic and development of the rest of the island; a glimpse of unspoiled nature and how life has been lived in Cyprus for decades. Spring is a particularly rewarding time to visit, when the long stretches of open countryside are a carpet of colourful wild flowers.

▶ Kırklar Tekke   226A1

Near Tymvou (Kırklar), in an area of restricted access lying close to the buffer zone between Nicosia (Lefko a) and Famagusta (Gazimağusa), the Tekke is a tiny 19th-century mosque dedicated to 40 unknown martyrs.

▶ Knidos   226C2

The wreck of an old coastal vessel lies rusting on the rocky coast at scenic Cape Elaia (Zeytin Burnu), almost the only identifiable landmark in an area where the olive trees come down virtually to the sea. The ancient Phoenician harbour town of Knidos, inhabited from the fifth century BC to the secnd century AD, is buried here at the end of a track from Agios Theodoros (Çayırova), but only fragmentary remains can be seen.

▶▶ Mesaoria Plain (Mesarya Ovası)   226B1

This great agricultural plain extends from Nicosia (Lefko a) eastwards towards the sea and the Karpasia (Karpaz) Peninsula, and northwards towards the Pentadaktylos (Beşparmak) Mountains. Thoroughly dried up in summer except in areas where irrigation has been established, the Mesaoria comes into its own in winter, when wheat, potatoes and other crops are grown in abundance. Three things stand out about the Mesaoria: It is spirit-level flat, it is enormous, and the fields that cover it are also huge.

After these impressive characteristics have been absorbed, the most interesting thing about the Mesaoria is its people's total commitment to ordinary everyday life, usually involving a great deal of hard work in the fields, followed (for the menfolk at least) by concentrated rest and recuperation at the local coffee shop. The simple, and often ragged, villages are an indication of how many of the unfailingly hospitable Turkish Cypriot and immigrant Turkish people live. Both of northern Cyprus's two airports, Ercan and Geçitkale, are in the Mesaoria.

PARKS DEPARTMENT
Greek Cypriots have their ongoing debate about making a national park of the wild and unspoiled Akamas Peninsula, so it seems only fair that Turkish Cypriots should have come up with a similar solution for the Karpasia (Karpaz) Peninsula at the opposite end of the island. Although not so leg-numbingly rugged as the Akamas, and more affected by agriculture and village development, Karpasia is bigger and has its share of wild spaces, including unspoiled beaches and hilly areas where wild donkeys roam.

241

LOOTED TREASURE
The Church of Panagia Kanakaria at Lythragkomi (Boltaşlı) in the Karpasia (Karpaz) Peninsula was the source of a landmark legal ruling in America in 1989. The church's sixth-century apse mosaic of the Virgin and Child was ruled to have been looted since the Turkish intervention after it appeared on the international art market. It was ordered to be restored to the Republic of Cyprus.

Wild and isolated, the Karpasia (Karpaz) Peninsula gives a hint of what the Mediterranean was like before tourism was invented

Drive

See map on page 226–227

Famagusta to Cape Apostolos Andreas

The Karpasia (Karpaz) Peninsula, the 'panhandle' of Cyprus, is an extensive, sparsely populated area bordered by a coastline that is alternately wild and rugged or carpeted with long stretches of open, deserted beach. It is almost totally untouched by tourist development. This is an exhilarating but day-long return drive, so don't attempt to do more than a couple of the suggested diversions.

Window on two worlds —Greek and Turkish—in Rizokarpaso (Dipkarpaz)

The sights on the drive are covered in more detail on pages 230–249.

Roughly 10km (6 miles) out of Famagusta (Gazimağusa), on the main highway heading north, a cluster of historic sites can be visited. First, on the left of the coast road, is **Apostolos Varnavas Monastery▶▶▶**, now a superbly maintained and presented museum of icons and archaeology. A little farther along this side-road through the countryside, at Egkomi (Tuzla), are the ruins of ancient

Enkomi▶▶, also known as Alasia, a settlement that was founded around 2000BC and flourished under the Mycenaeans 500 years later.

Return to the coast road and continue north. Soon you arrive at the entrance to ancient **Salamis**▶▶▶, the ruins of a city with a rich history under the Greeks and the Romans, and whose finest monuments date from the late-Roman period following extensive destruction caused by earthquakes. Little of the city has been excavated, yet what there is gives a good idea of how wealthy Salamis was. From here the road curves around the broad sweep of Famagusta Bay (Gazimağusa Körfezi), through mostly agricultural country (with some sprawling development), passing some modest tourist developments.

Near the bay's northern end lies **Bogazi (Boğaz)**▶▶, a small fishing village with a fishermen's wharf and a cluster of seafood restaurants. (Bogazi is also the ideal place to divert north to **Kantara Castle**▶▶, high in the easternmost edge of the Pentadaktylos (Beşparmak) Mountains, but the diversion, although interesting, costs considerable time followed by a fair amount of twisting and turning to regain the main road.)

Head north from Bogazi towards **Aigialousa (Yenierenköy)**▶▶. You now enter the Karpasia Peninsula proper and the road, which has been quiet enough up to now, slides still deeper into tranquillity. The scenery opens up into a rolling green picture-postcard image of the ideal pastoral landscape, dotted with sleepy and rather ragged-looking villages whose inhabitants wave as you pass. Curving farther north towards Aigialousa, the landscape gets more rugged as the trailing edge of the Pentadaktylos range is reached, and the road shifts from hugging the southern coast to skimming the northern one.

At Aigialousa take the direction for **Rizokarpaso (Dipkarpaz)**▶. Here live the last remaining Greek Cypriots in the Turkish Cypriot zone, an elderly community watched over by a UN detachment and whose days, in the absence of a comprehensive settlement between the two communities, are inevitably numbered by the slow but sure process of ageing, although the opening of a Greek secondary school in the village may help to reverse that decline. The coast from Aigialousa to Rizokarpaso is dotted with Byzantine churches.

Beyond Rizokarpaso follow the road to the Apostolos Andreas Monastery (Manastır). As the peninsula narrows towards its tip, spectacularly rugged vistas open up on either side and the narrow road dips and soars on its own wild course. The empty beaches draw you, but ahead now can be seen the white gleam of **Apostolos Andreas Monastery**▶▶▶, clinging to the rocky, wave-battered coast. After this, the peninsula's needle-tipped point at **Cape Apostolos Andreas (Zafer Burnu)**▶▶▶, with its escort of rocky islets, is almost anticlimactic—but forms a definitive end of the road.

You can divert north at the fishing village of Bogazi for Kantara Castle

243

Although tourism is the main foreign-exchange earner, and manufacturing, shipping, banking and offshore business services are important economic sectors, agriculture remains a vital industry. Hard-working farmers also give the Cypriot countryside its distinctive flow of life and colour through the seasons, and keep the island's village roots alive.

DRUG DEALER
Cyprus was an early centre of the drugs trade, at least in the sense that it produced and exported opium. Ancient Egypt was one of the countries on the delivery list.

Olives ripening nicely for the press

Sowing the seeds of future wealth in the fields near Kiti

Water shortage Early morning and late-afternoon showers casting shimmering rainbows through the golden sunlight are as characteristic of summer in Cyprus as bathing suits and suntan lotion. Not that there is likely to be the tiniest amount of precipitation falling from the clear blue sky; it's just farmers spraying precious drops of water on their crops. Irrigation is an essential ingredient of almost all agriculture on this sun-parched island, the factor that makes the difference between life and death for the farmers' produce and businesses.

Stocks of vital water are monitored with the kind of care more usually associated with gold or oil production. Reservoirs, underground aquifers and the few perennial springs are drawn on heavily from spring to autumn, and when the first rains begin, usually in November, a Cypriot will observe the deluge with great satisfaction even if late-season tourists have a more jaundiced opinion. As well as guaranteeing the survival of agriculture in the following summer, the rains also make possible winter crops that form an important part of production.

Market strategies A visit to a market gives an idea of how successful the strategy can be. Cyprus is a cornucopia of fresh fruit and vegetables. Just to list the main ones is to range across the gamut of fragrance and taste and to show that Cyprus deserves its reputation as a vegetarian paradise: grapes, melons, tomatoes, aubergines, peppers, cucumbers, figs, peaches, cherries, strawberries, apricots, oranges, apples, lemons, limes, artichokes, avocados, celery, onions, carrots, potatoes. Then there are bread, cheese, pulses and nuts. Lamb

and chicken are the principal meat products (beef is available but is not nearly so common).

Around 70 per cent of agricultural production is exported, mainly to the European Union—which the Republic of Cyprus joined in 2004. The Turkish Cypriots were not party to an agreement despite a majority from their commuity being in favour of membership, and the EU is still working out how to aid and integrate the Turkish Cypriots in the absence of a political settlement on the island. Much of the added value in agricultural produce comes from additional processing rather than the basic commodity (for example, from making and packing fruit juice instead of just exporting the fruit).

On location Cyprus's geography is sufficiently varied for there to be different kinds of agriculture suited to different locales. The principal areas in this repect are the Mesaoria (Mesarya) and the Morfou (Güzelyurt) plains. The Mesaoria is a primary source of winter wheat. In summer it dries up to a state not far short of a desert. The Morfou Plain west of Nicosia is a more rolling landscape but also rich in winter crops. Both areas are in the Turkish Cypriot zone, a situation that creates one of the angriest Greek Cypriot complaints about partition.

Equally impressive is the great sweep of the southern and western Troodos given over to vineyards. Although many of the grapes are destined for wineries or dried for raisins, they are every bit as satisfactory just as grapes. In addition, the Marathasa Valley in the northwest Troodos is renowned for its cherries; the Kokkinochoria red-earth district around Agia Napa produces three crops of potatoes in a year; tobacco is still produced, on a small scale, in the Karpasia (Karpaz) Peninsula; bananas make their appearance along the coast north of Pafos; olives and carobs are all but ubiquitous; and market gardening is squeezed in wherever there is space—and irrigation, of course.

Crops near Agia Napa

245

DUSTY DEATH
Great tracts of the Cypriot countryside are as dry as a stick during the long, hot, rain-free summers. An inevitable side-effect of this is dust, which thoughtless drivers exacerbate by speeding along dusty tracks, kicking up great clouds of the stuff. Apart from the literal irritation this causes farmworkers busy in the fields near such tracks, the dust lands on crops, clogging the plants' pores and stunting their growth.

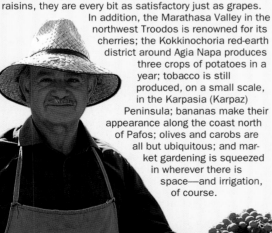

Grapes today, wine tomorrow—although it takes a little longer

Agios Filon, on the coast near Rizokarpaso (Dipkarpaz)

CLASS ACTION
The ageing of the remaining Greek Cypriot population at Rizokarpaso (Dipkarpaz), with youngsters for years having to go to school in the south once they were past primary age, may have been stemmed by the opening in 2004 of a Greek-language secondary school in the village. The move by the Turkish Cypriot authorities was hailed by the Council of Europe as a 'positive' contribution to building confidence between the two communities. Reciprocal agreement was reached to form a Turkish-language school in Limassol, but at the time of writing it had not opened.

▶ **Rizokarpaso (Dipkarpaz)**   *227D3*

Rizokarpaso is a fading ember of Greek Cypriot culture in North Cyprus, with an ageing population provided for by the UN. Although no obvious physical pressure is placed on the community, and their church of **Agios Synesios** is still operating, the steady loss of young people to the Greek Cypriot south has up to now told its own story.

In the immediate vicinity are the fine beach at **Ronnas Bay▶▶**; the small 16th-century church of **Panagia Eleousa▶**; and the 10th-century **Agios Filon▶▶** on the shore, the fittings of which have been removed, apparently by tourists. Finally, there are some ruins and traces of the Roman-era harbour of ancient **Carpasia▶**, whose zenith was in the 4th and 3rd centuries BC. The city flourished into Roman times before declining under the Byzantines and finally succumbing to the Arabs in the 9th century.

▶▶▶ **Salamis**   *226B1*

Open: summer daily 9–7; winter daily 9–1 and 2–4.45. Admission: moderate

Legend tells that Salamis was founded by Teucer, a Greek hero of the Trojan War, and named after his native Salamis, an island near Athens. The city joined the revolt against Persian rule in 498BC, but by changing sides at a critical moment ensured the Greeks' defeat. Salamis made amends under King Evagoras, a pro-Greek usurper who united most of the island under the Greek banner.

During the Roman period, Salamis remained wealthy and important. In AD342, however, an earthquake levelled it. Rebuilt under Emperor Constantius, the city was renamed Constantia and became the seat of the Byzantine governor and Orthodox archbishop. In the seventh century, Arabs attacked, and the city never recovered.

The site of the ancient city is spread over a considerable area along the coast north of Famagusta (Gazimağusa). Most of the remains lie buried beneath a forest of acacias and tangled undergrowth, although new summer excavations led by Turkish academics have begun to uncover further elements of the ancient city.

THE RUINS The colossal fourth-century marble basilica of

Intricate mosaic at the Kampanopetra Basilica, Salamis

Agios Epifanios►►, even in ruins, gives some idea of the power and glory of the Christian church in Cyprus at a time when it was taking over the reins as state religion from paganism. The tomb of St. Epifanios, archbishop of Salamis, can be seen but his remains were removed to Constantinople in the 10th century by the Emperor Leo.

The **agora**►► of Salamis is said to have been the largest monumental public market-place of the Roman Empire, marked by long colonnades of which only fragments remain. An inscription found here records that the agora was restored by the Emperor Augustus. At its end is the ruined Temple of Zeus, in which an inscription honouring Livia, the wife of Augustus, was found.

The **harbour**► of Salamis was one of the most important in the ancient eastern Mediterranean. Now its secrets lie under the sands of 13 centuries, awaiting the hand of the archaeologist. Some sections of its sea wall and of installations along the shore can still be discerned, and the sand is jumbled with sherds of sea-smoothed potsherds, as well as bricks and stone.

As impressive as the ancient city's main basilica, the **Kampanopetra Basilica**►► commands a wonderful location beside the ancient harbour. Its ruins contain a vivid mosaic of concentric circles rendered in a complex pattern of coloured marble tiles, a beautiful work which, sadly, is suffering from exposure to the wearing effects of the elements.

The **gymnasium and baths**►►► are a photogenic image of classical civilization, also providing unmistakable evidence of Salamis's straitened circumstances following the 4th-century earthquake. The exercise yard is surrounded by a peristyle whose columns have been salvaged from other demolished buildings rather than built anew. In the southwest corner is a fascinating piece of history: A semicircular latrine with places for 44 people who presumably shared the latest news while sitting side by side engaged in their business. The public baths are an institution of such marble-lined grandeur, with pools, fountains and hot and cold rooms, that visitors to the 16-centuries-old ruins can only lament that there is nothing like them in Cyprus today. Also called the Byzantine Cistern, Salamis's **Roman cistern**► is an underground water reservoir used for refuge by early Christians, who left wall-paintings as a record of their stay.

247

The Roman theatre at Salamis is still used occasionally for musical, dance and artistic performances

NOT JUST THE TICKET
The regular curator of the tombs of Salamis is a man of considerable enthusiasm for his work and for the history of the site in his charge. He is happy to pass on his knowledge of its history as opposed to just taking visitors' money and handing them tickets.

A restored chariot, recovered from one of the Mycenaean-era Royal Tombs at Salamis

The Roman-style **theatre▶▶▶**, built on the site of an Augustan-age (late first century BC) amphitheatre, has been partially restored, with rows of seating ascending in steps from the proscenium, and 'backstage' installations also visible.

Tombs for heroes and paupers Outside the main Salamis site, near the village of Egkomi (Tuzla), the **Tombs of Salamis▶▶▶** are in two sections: the Royal Tombs, destined for prominent soldiers and citizens, and the ordinary folks' tombs, called the Cellarka, both dating from the 8th and 7th century BC. The former are an astonishingly vivid confirmation of the burial ceremonies of Mycenaean heroes described by Homer in the *Iliad* for the funeral games of Patroclus. There are several large *tumuli* (mounds) inside which the monumental tombs of noblemen were discovered. Each has a trapezoidal *dromos* (entranceway), where the skeletons of sacrificed horses and other funerary tributes were excavated. The burial chambers are made from limestone blocks and are entered via an ornamental *propylaeum* (porch). One tomb was built up with limestone blocks during the Roman period, and tradition is that the building became the prison of St. Catherine of Alexandria, an early Christian martyr.

Some distance away from the Royal Tombs is the poor people's necropolis, a partially excavated mass of burial chambers carved into the rock.

► Trimithos   226A1

This was recorded by the Roman-era geographer Ptolemy as being among the principal cities of Cyprus. Now the Turkish Cypriot village of Tremetousia (Erdemli) covers whatever traces of the ancient city remain, and a Turkish army military zone in this area beside the demarcation zone makes movement difficult. Also out of bounds is the 7th-century Byzantine monastery of **Agios Spyridon,** named after a local shepherd-boy who became a bishop and who is now patron saint of Corfu. The monastery was formerly a centre for icon restoration and many important works remain there, apparently in good condition according to independent experts.

►► Varosha (Maraş)   226C1

Varosha is awesome. A tour of the outer fringe of this town on the southern edge of Famagusta (Gazimağusa) leaves one open-mouthed at a scene reminiscent of a science-fiction film in which the earth's population has been wiped out by some deadly disease. Before 1974 it was a mainly Greek Cypriot resort town with a permanent population of 40,000, and in those days it was the focus of Famagusta's—indeed, of Cyprus's—tourism industry.

Varosha's population fled from the Turkish army, and although the town lies inside the Turkish ceasefire line it has never been occupied since. For more than 30 years, Varosha has been disintegrating. Its hotels and houses are derelict and collapsing; a jungle of weeds, flowers and plants has sprouted; and rusting irrigation windmills creak eerily as their blades turn idly in the sea breeze. The beach, once the most popular in Cyprus, is deserted. Varosha is isolated by a barbed-wire fence marked with stern warnings that it is a first-degree military zone, with photography and entrance strictly forbidden.

Varosha cannot be visited, but it can be seen. At night, its dark mass looms against the surrounding street lights like a black hole in space. By day, it is a ghostly but gruesomely fascinating sight, a festering sore incongruously superimposed on a background of blue sea and sky, bordered by ordinary houses where people carry on with everyday life. One of North Cyprus's most stylish hotels, the Palm Beach, stands beside the barbed-wire fence, and tourists sunbathe a short distance away.

Reopening Varosha is one of the 'confidence-building measures' regularly proposed by the United Nations as part of the search for agreement between Cyprus's divided communities, but in the absence of an overall settlement this has never happened. In any case the entire town would now need to be demolished and rebuilt from scratch.

249

Baskets are the stock-in-trade at this shop in Tremetousia (Erdemli)

LOST CITY
In his book *Cyprus: Images of a Lifetime* (1992), Reno Wideson looks back in anguish on his memories and photographs of Famagusta and its resort suburb Varosha (Maraş): 'It is difficult to believe and accept that this happy, busy, blossom-scented small town I have known, where visitors came in their thousands and where the sound of Orange Festival songs filled the air, is now an uninhabited ghost town. I hope and pray that sanity will prevail in the not-too-distant future and that Famagusta will be restored to its previous happiness and glory.'

Despite the rapid growth of the island's cities and resorts, Cypriot society is still very much grounded in the village. Experiencing the warmth of an unaffected village far from the tourist track is a quiet privilege, whose memory will remain long after the suntan fades.

SATURDAY NIGHT FEVER
Saturday night is usually the best night to be in the hill and mountain villages. Families are reunited as the younger people return from their jobs in the cities or at the coast, and the local tavernas are at their liveliest.

250

In a way, all villages in Cyprus are remote: if not physically distant from the cities and tourist centres, they are sufficiently far removed in spirit to merit the description. Self-contained, close to the land and unhurriedly engaged in the simple life, if not necessarily the good one, villages are the great undiscovered country of Cyprus.

Or at any rate they used to be. Inroads are being made by tourist and expatriate developments, in both the Greek and Turkish Cypriot zones, into the most scenic villages and those most conveniently located for the holiday areas, while sparing their incomer occupants the distress of mingling with the common-or-garden package-holiday tourist. Omodos and Arsos fall into this category in the Greek Cypriot zone, and Bellapais (Beylerbeyi) and Lapithos (Lapta) in the Turkish zone.

Shared experience In areas far from the main roads and farther still from casinos and discos, Greek and Turkish Cypriot villagers have much more in common than perhaps even they have been aware of during the decades of separation that followed the 1974 Turkish invasion. Everywhere the coffee shop is the centre of the village universe, with the church or mosque somewhere near by.

Young people in both areas leave for the bright lights and fatter pay-packets of the resorts and cities. Yet the fields, orchards and vineyards remain the keys to prosperity and continued life for the village.

Threatened by progress and depopulation, Cypriot villages retain their graces even as they struggle to survive

Remote villages can be found everywhere: in the Karpasia (Karpaz) Peninsula and Tilliria, among the peaks of the Troodos and Pentadaktylos (Beşparmak) Mountains, in the Solea Valley and on the Mesaoria (Mesarya) Plain. They are best approached on foot or by bicycle, rather than by jeep or roaring dirt-bike. This is a Cyprus that works to another agenda and moves at its own pace and rhythm. The residents may sometimes be surprised to see you, but they will always be hospitable.

Travel Facts

Arriving and departing

The Republic of Cyprus is the recognized government of Cyprus. Since 1974, however, almost 38 per cent of the island has been under the military occupation of Turkey. In 1983 this territory declared itself to be the 'Turkish Republic of Northern Cyprus (TRNC)', a declaration that the UN states is legally invalid.

The TRNC is not recognized by any country except Turkey; this situation can affect visitors. For the official UN position see page 288.

Citizens of the European Union may travel freely in both directions; citizens of other countries should be able to travel without hindrance but may be subject to restrictions. At the time of writing there are five crossing points open along the intra-island border, and a sixth is being prepared. The principal crossing points in Nicosia are at the Ledra Palace Hotel on Leoforos Markou Drakou and, for cars, in the western Agios Dometios suburb. Be sure to check the current position before going across.

Republic of Cyprus

Passports must be valid for three months beyond the date of arrival. Tourists from European Union member states, from most other European countries, North America, and from some other countries may stay for up to three months without a visa. Other visitors must apply for a visa. When arriving you may enter only through Larnaka and Pafos International Airports and the ports of Larnaka, Limassol and Pafos. Entry stamps from the Turkish Cypriot zone are considered illegal, and visitors bearing such stamps on their passports may be refused admission into the Republic of Cyprus and Greece.

By air

Larnaka International Airport is the main airport for both scheduled and charter flights, while **Pafos International Airport** is mainly a charter airport. Airport tax is included in the ticket price. (Nicosia International Airport is currently closed and occupied by the United Nations Force in Cyprus.)

Car rental, catering, currency exchange, and other passenger facilities are available at the airports (not always on a 24-hour basis). Duty-free shops are in the departure lounges.

By sea
Vehicle-only ferries (with space for a mere handful of passengers) connect Piraeus/Keratsini near Athens, the island of Rhodes (occasionally), and Haifa in Israel, and with Limassol. The regular car ferry service from Piraeus remains suspended.

Northern Cyprus
Passports are valid for a stay of three months. Prior visas are not required; entry visas are issued on arrival. Immigration officers will not stamp passports, if requested, to avoid difficulties for those planning visits to the Republic of Cyprus and Greece.

By air
The main airport is **Ercan**, with a second one at **Geçitkale**. Flights to either are only possible via Turkey (usually Istanbul or Izmir).

By sea
Ferry services operate to the ports of Keryneia (Girne) and Famagusta (Gazimağusa) from Mersin and Ta ucu in Turkey.

Transfers
Bus services are available to and from the airports. One bus connects Pafos Airport with Kato Pafos; Larnaka Airport has no direct bus to Larnaka, but a bus passes within 1km (0.5 miles) of the airport. Metered taxis, plentiful and reasonably priced, operate from the airports to all locations.

Unmetered taxis, but with fixed official tariffs, operate from both airports in the Turkish Cypriot zone.

Customs
The import of wildlife souvenirs sourced from rare or endangered species may be illegal or require a special permit. Check your home country's customs regulations.

Republic of Cyprus The Republic of Cyprus is a member of the European Union; travellers within the EU no longer have access to duty-free goods. Visitors to Cyprus from EU countries have essentially no restrictions on the import of legal goods for personal use (there are guidelines).

Visitors may import without payment of duty: 250g tobacco (or the equivalent in tobacco products, for example 200 cigarettes); 1 litre spirits; 2 litres wine (no tobacco or alcohol allowance for under-17s); one bottle of perfume up to 600cl, and 250cl eau de toilette; articles of any other description (excluding jewellery) up to the value of CY£100.

There is no limit to the amount of currency that can be imported or exported, but amounts above the equivalent of €12,500 must be declared. Agricultural product and propogating-stock importation without permission is prohibited.

Northern Cyprus Duty-free quantities are 500g tobacco (or 400 cigarettes); 1 litre wine; 1 litre spirits; 100cl perfume. There is no limit on importing foreign currency, which can be exported freely up to US$10,000, if it has been declared on arrival.

253

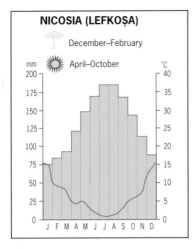

NICOSIA (LEFKOŞA)

☂ December–February

mm ☀ April–October ˚C

summer; otherwise you will require little beyond a swimsuit and shorts and T-shirts. The best time to visit for temperate weather is from March to May and from about mid-September to November. At the earlier time, there is fine weather and carpets of spring flowers and greenery. July and August together comprise the hottest, busiest and most expensive holiday period, but in compensation this time is also the liveliest and best for getting that holiday tan. Winter has its bonus points too, when skiing in the morning and swimming in the afternoon are possible; for residents of the cold, northern latitudes, this is an ideal time for a warm-weather break.

254

Essential facts

Climate

The island has a long, very hot and dry summer, a short spring and autumn, and a usually mild, relatively wet winter, which can see snow in the Troodos Mountains. The average daytime temperature in July and August is 35°C (95°F) and in January 15°C (59°F), although maximum summer temperatures inland can reach above 40°C (105°F), and minimum winter temperatures drop below 0°C (32°F) in the mountains.

There is little or no rainfall, as a rule, between June and September, and by the end of the summer dust can be a problem. A sweater or other warm clothing is desirable for evenings in the mountains, even in

National holidays
Republic of Cyprus
- **New Year's Day** 1 January
- **Epiphany** 6 January
- **Green Monday** variable (7 weeks before Greek Orthodox Easter)
- **Greek Independence Day** 25 March
- **Anniversary of Cyprus Liberation Struggle** 1 April
- **Good Friday** (Greek Orthodox Church) variable
- **Easter Saturday** (Greek Orthodox Church) variable
- **Easter Sunday** (Greek Orthodox Church) variable
- **Easter Monday** (Greek Orthodox Church) variable
- **Labour Day** 1 May
- **Pentecost–Kataklysmos** (Festival of the Flood) variable

Thanks to 3,000 hours of sunshine, suntans are all but guaranteed

- **Assumption of Our Lady**
  15 August
- **Cyprus Independence Day**
  1 October
- **'Ochi' Day (Greek National Day)** 28 October
- **Christmas Day** 25 December
- **Boxing Day** 26 December

Turkish-occupied Cyprus
- **New Year's Day** 1 January
- **Şeker Bayram** (Sugar Festival) variable (end of Ramadan); lasts three days
- **National Sovereignty and Children's Day** 23 April
- **Labour Day** 1 May
- **Youth and Sports Day** 19 May
- **Kurban Bayram (Festival of the Sacrifice)** variable; lasts four days
- **Peace and Freedom Day** 20 July
- **Communal Resistance Day**
  1 August
- **Victory Day** 30 August
- **Turkish National Day** 29 October
- **Prophet Muhammad's Birthday** variable
- **Independence Day (Turkish Republic of Northern Cyprus)**
  15 November

Time
Cyprus is on central European Time: Greenwich Mean Time (GMT) plus two hours in winter and plus three hours in summer. For most of the year Cyprus is one hour ahead of western Europe, two hours ahead of the UK and Ireland, six hours ahead of US Eastern Standard Time and eight hours behind Australia (Sydney).

Money matters
Republic of Cyprus The unit of currency is the Cyprus pound (CY£). Notes are available in denominations of CY£20, CY£10, CY£5 and CY£1; coins in 50¢, 20¢, 10¢, 5¢, 2¢ and 1¢. the euro (€) will eventually replace the CY£, but it seems not before 2008 at the earliest.

Northern Cyprus The unit of currency is the new Turkish lira (YTL).

International credit and charge cards are widely accepted in the Republic of Cyprus, but less so in Turkish Cyprus, and at some filling stations in both zones. Traveller's cheques can be exchanged for Cyprus pounds or Turkish lire, as appropriate, at banks, exchange bureaux and hotels, and can be used to settle bills in some hotels, restaurants and shops.

Automatic cashpoint machines are widely available in both zones and accept foreign Eurocheque cards, credit cards and charge cards.

All 'hard' currencies are accepted at banks, hotel exchanges and so on in the Republic of Cyprus. In Turkish Cyprus only US dollars, British pounds and euros have general acceptance. Many businesses will exchange these currencies at favourable rates.

Banking hours in the Republic of Cyprus are Monday to Friday 8.15–12.30. Banks in the main resort areas and all towns provide an afternoon tourist service of 3.30–5, occasionally later than this. In Northern Cyprus, banks open 8–12 in summer; 2–4 in winter.

Credit and charge cards are widely accepted in towns and resorts

Getting around

Finding your way

It is essential to obtain up-to-date maps (see page 268) as place-name spellings have been changed to a new transliteration system. Be warned, however, for although your map may use Larnaka and Pafos, the signs you come across in the towns

Car-rental companies will supply you with a telephone number to dial in the event of a breakdown. Other situations in the Republic of Cyprus may be handled by the Cyprus Automobile Association, tel: 22313131—24 hours, or by telephoning a vehicle recovery service (see the Yellow Pages business telephone directory).

There are good roads in most areas

themselves may still use the old spellings of Larnaca and Paphos.

Car rental

Republic of Cyprus Rental cars are called 'Z cars', for their distinctive red licence-plates with a 'Z' prefix. There are three categories of operator: the major international rental companies, with a reputation for reliability but usually at a higher price; national groups which offer the advantages of the majors but usually at a lower price; and local firms with very good rates but whose cars may be older or less well maintained. Jeeps are popular, but those with open tops put passengers at risk of severe sunburn, as well as being dusty in dry conditions. If collision-damage waiver insurance is not taken, you may be liable for a large initial sum in the event of an accident, although this may be covered by your own travel insurance.

Northern Cyprus Similar points to those raised above apply in Turkish-occupied Cyprus, except that the major international groups do not operate and car rental is cheaper. Most companies offer both left-hand- and right-hand-drive vehicles, but as driving is on the left it is safer to opt for right-hand drive.

Car-rental companies should provide a telephone number to call in the event of a breakdown.

Driving tips

National and international driving licences are valid in both north and south. Cyprus is a member of the international Green Card insurance system. Third-party cover is the legal minimum, but comprehensive cover may make more sense.

Traffic moves on the left, and road-traffic signs are on the left. Distances and speed limits are posted in kilometres and kilometres per hour (kph). Speed limits are 50kph (30mph) in built-up areas, 80kph (50mph) on main roads and 100kph

(60mph) on motorways. Dipped headlights are mandatory from 30 minutes after sunset to 30 minutes before sunrise. The intense glare of the sun can require the use of sunglasses.

Front seat-belt use is compulsory. Children under five cannot sit in the front passenger seat, and children aged from five to ten can only do so if a child's seat-belt is fitted.

Filling stations are plentiful in towns and major resorts, but not outside them, particularly in the mountains and other remote areas, and in all cases are rarer in Turkish-occupied Cyprus. Leaded petrol and diesel are both widely available, unleaded petrol less so. Most fuel stations are open Monday to Friday 6am–6pm and to 4pm on Saturdays; most close on Sunday; automatic vending is available in all the towns and resort areas on a 24-hour basis, with payment by bank notes and, less widely, by credit card.

Most aspects of driving are an improvement on the norm in Mediterranean countries. The major exception is local drivers overtaking recklessly on busy roads, even where corners and gradients hide oncoming vehicles. Farmers in pick-ups may force tourists' Z-registration cars into the verge on roads not wide enough

for two vehicles, though this is less evident in Northern Cyprus.

The Republic of Cyprus has excellent two-lane motorways (Nicosia– Pafos, Nicosia–Larnaka, Larnaka– Agia Napa and Limassol–Larnaka), as well as many well-maintained roads. There are also some good mountain roads. On the roughest stretches, however, drivers need to exercise caution and be determined to reach their objective.

On many roads in Northern Cyprus, Turkish military transport may have priority.

Public transportation

Buses Three kinds of bus service exist in both zones: urban, interurban and rural. Urban services in Nicosia, Limassol, Larnaka, Pafos, Keryneia (Girne) and Famagusta (Gazimağusa) are adequate, if hardly luxurious. Interurban services are regular, fares are cheap and most buses run direct from town to town.

Rural buses connect villages with the nearest town, generally with only one return service per day, leaving in the morning and returning in the evening. Many smaller villages have no bus service.

Public transport is adequate in the towns, less so in the countryside

Getting around

Taxis

Republic of Cyprus There are three
types of taxi service: urban, rural and
interurban.

Urban taxis are available 24 hours a
day in towns, major resorts and from
airports, and can be booked by telephone or rented from their rank or
base. These taxis have meters, minimum rates and waiting charges, and
charges for luggage weighing more
than 12kg (26.5lbs), which may be
waived.

Rural taxis operate in country areas,
are unmetered and can be rented
from their base or by telephone; a
charges chart is carried by the driver,
although it may be wise to ask for an
estimate of the fare.

Shared service taxis, which can be
booked by telephone, are a direct and
convenient alternative to the slow
and roundabout bus service. They
directly between towns, from the
main bus stops, and whose journey
begins when they are full.

Cycling

Bicycles can be a good way of getting
around in the resorts and even, with a
little caution, in the towns. Bicycles are
easy to rent in most resorts, and offer a
more tranquil way of getting close to
Cyprus's nature than the mopeds or
motorcycles which are also available.

Mountain-bikes can be rented for
the kind of rugged trails which are
common all over Cyprus, as well as in
the actual mountains: the Troodos
and Pentadaktylos (Beşparmak)
ranges. Mopeds are the most popular,
but high-powered dirt-bikes are also
available for off-road expeditions.

On foot

Hitch-hiking is permitted in both
north and south, except on motorways
and motorway accesses. Some

*Reasonably priced, taxis are a popular
means of getting around*

carry between four and seven
passengers on regular journeys
between the four main towns,
picking up and dropping off at the
passenger's requested location, for a
low fixed charge.

Northern Cyprus Similar conditions
apply to those in the Republic of
Cyprus, except that taxis are not
metered. Instead, they have a list of
official charges from which the fare
can be established for long journeys.
Dolmuş are minibuses which operate

walking and hiking routes have been
established in the Troodos and
Pentadaktylos (Beşparmak)
Mountains and in the Akamas
Peninsula. For these and more individual expeditions, water and food
should be taken along. Serious climbing and hill-walking requires proper
equipment. Local tourist offices can
often provide or suggest guided or
independent walking itineraries in
their localities. See also the various
walking itineraries in this book.

Student and youth travel

Cyprus has not really developed the
kind of low-cost infrastructure that

258

Walking and hiking are popular activities in the Akamas Peninsula

makes 'bumming around Europe' part of the rites of passage of many students, preferring to concentrate instead on package tourism. The shortage of accommodation at the low end of the price scale is being made up only slowly and without official encouragement. Nevertheless, there are some youth hostels, while the 'hotels without star' classification offers other possibilities.

There are a number of youth hostels catering for members of the IYHA (International Youth Hostels Association). Non-members are also accepted. There are youth hostels at:

● **Nicosia** 5 Odos Tefkrou,
    tel: 22674808.
● **Larnaka** 27 Odos Nicolaou Rossou,
    tel: 24621188.
● **Pafos** 37 Loeforos Eleftheriou
    Venizelou,
    tel: 26932588.
● **Troodos** Troodos–Kakopetria road,
    Troodos village, tel: 25420200. The
    hostel is open from April to
    October.

Further information is available from the **Cyprus Youth Hostel Association**, PO Box 24040, 1700 Nicosia, tel: 22670027; fax: 22672896; email: montis@logos.cy.net. In addition,

there is the **Stavros tis Psokas Rest House**, Pafos Forest, tel: 26999144. Advance reservations are essential at this small guest-house near the moufflon reserve in the Pafos Forest.

Arranging excursions
Most tour operators arrange day-trips to archaeological, historical, religious and scenic sites. These include monasteries and Byzantine churches in the Troodos Mountains, the Sanctuary of Aphrodite, the ruins of Salamis and Kourion, the wild and scenic Akamas and Karpasia (Karpaz) peninsulas, crusader castles in the Pentadaktylos (Bešparmak) Mountains and Nicosia within the Venetian walls. Tourist guides can be contacted via tourist information offices or, in the Republic of Cyprus, through the **Cyprus Tourist Guides Association**, PO Box 24942, 1355 Nicosia, tel: 22765755; fax: 22766872; www.cytourguides.com.

259

Facilities for young and independent travellers are slowly improving

In the Republic of Cyprus you need never go without your daily paper

Communications

Media
Republic of Cyprus There is a daily English newspaper, the *Cyprus Mail* and a weekly, the *Cyprus Weekly*. In addition, the *International Herald Tribune* is obtainable on the day of publication and many British and Irish newspapers are widely available one day after publication, as are newspapers of most western European countries.

Many hotels have satellite television, with stations including CNN International, BBC World and BSkyB. The Cyprus Broadcasting Corporation (CyBC), Logos, Antena, Pafos TV and Sigma stations broadcast movies and programmes from Britain, the USA and other English-language countries with their original soundtrack and Greek subtitles. CyBC2 has a 5-minute news summary in English every day at about 9PM. In addition, CyBC Radio's Channel 1 has a daily English news broadcast, and Channel 2 features occasional programmes in English and, from Monday to Saturday, June to September, the information programme *Welcome to Cyprus*.

BBC World Service Radio and Voice of America can also be picked up. The British Forces Broadcasting Service (BFBS) is on the air 24 hours a day, with a diet of music, magazine programmes and news aimed at the British Sovereign Bases' personnel and their families.

Northern Cyprus There is a weekly English newspaper, *Cyprus Today*. *Kibris Monthly*, a soft-propaganda organ of the Public Information Office, includes much general information. International newspapers are rarely found. The Bayrak Radio and Television Service (BRTK) broadcasts occasional programmes in English.

Post offices
Republic of Cyprus Most post offices are open: September to June Monday to Wednesday and Friday 7.30–1.30, Thursday 7.30–1.30 and 3–6; July and August Monday to Friday 7.30–1.30. In addition, the District Post Office and Palteia Eleftheria Post Office in Nicosia, District Post Office and City Centre Post Office in Limassol, District Post Office in Larnaka and District Post Office in Pafos are open: September to June Monday, Tuesday, Thursday and Friday 7.30–1.30 and 3–6, Wednesday 7.30–1.30, Saturday 8.30–10.30; July and August Monday, Tuesday, Thursday and Friday 7.30–1.30 and 4–7, Wednesday 7.30–1.30, Saturday 8.30–10.30.

As well as selling stamps and delivering letters, post offices also provide airmail, express, registered, courier, package, poste restante and other services.

Northern Cyprus Offices open May to October Monday 7.30–2 and 3.30–6, Tuesday to Friday 7.30–2; November to April Monday to Friday 8–1 and 2–5. Post intended for this zone has to be addressed c/o Mersin 10, Turkey, not direct to Cyprus.

Telephone and fax
To telephone abroad from both north and south, dial 00 + country code + area code (minus the initial 0) + subscriber number.

Some country codes:
Australia 61
Canada 1
Eire 353
New Zealand 64
South Africa 27
UK 44
USA 1

Republic of Cyprus Public telephones accept 5¢, 10¢ and 20¢ coins, or CY£3, CY£5 and CY£10 telecards (available from post offices, souvenir shops and newsagents). The country code for the Republic of Cyprus is 357. Area codes have been abolished and telephone numbers have eight digits. But you can identify the location of a number by its first two digits: 22 is Nicosia, 23 is the Agia Napa/Protaras area, 24 is Larnaka, 25 is Limassol and 26 is Pafos and Polis; a 9 indicates a mobile phone. Fax machines are generally available.

Northern Cyprus The same kind of direct-dialling system as in the Republic of Cyprus operates from both coin-operated and telecard phones. Public telefax units are not widely available, but most hotels will allow guests the use of their fax.

The country code for Northern Cyprus is 90392. There are no area codes, only seven-digit subscriber numbers, though you can identify the location of a number from the first two digits—eg Nicosia 22, Keryneia (Girne) 81, Famagusta (Gazimağusa) 36 and Morfou (Güzelyurt) 71.

Language guide
The island's two languages are Greek and Turkish. English is widely spoken, and German is quite common in Northern Cyprus, and increasingly so in the Republic of Cyprus.

261

SOME USEFUL WORDS AND PHRASES

ENGLISH	GREEK	TURKISH
good morning	kaliméra	günaydın
good afternoon	kalispéra	iyi günler
good night	kaliníkta	iyi geçeler
goodbye	chérete	allaha ısmarladık
please	parakaló	lütfen
thank you	efcharistó	mersi/teşekkür ederim
yes	ne	evet
no	óchi	hayır
how much?	póso káni?	fiyati nedır?
where is...?	pou íne...?	nerede...?
how are you?	ti kánete/te kánis?	nasılsınız?
sorry/excuse me	signómi	ozür dilerım
one	éna	bir
two	dío	iki
three	tría	üç
four	téssera	dört
five	pénde	beş
six	éksi	altı
seven	eptá	yedi
eight	októ	sekiz
nine	enéa	dokuz
ten	déka	on
Monday	Deftéra	Pazartesi
Tuesday	Tríti	Salı
Wednesday	Tetárti	Çarşamba
Thursday	Pémpti	Perşembe
Friday	Paraskeví	Cuma
Saturday	Sávato	Cumartesi
Sunday	Kiriakí	Pazar

Emergencies

Crime and police

Crime is hardly a worry, as most Cypriots are much too civilized to take part in it. Some of one's fellow tourists can be less engaging, however. The usual precautions ought to be taken with regard to items left in open cars, handbags and valuables left lying around, particularly in busy tourist areas. Violent offences such as muggings are rare, although Cyprus is not completely immune to the imported hooligan syndrome. Offences and thefts should be reported to the police, if only for insurance purposes.

Most policemen in both south and north speak at least some English and are disposed to be tolerant of tourists on minor matters, although not to the extent of allowing them to take advantage of this. In Turkish-occupied Cyprus, the military police (ASIZ) are more in evidence than the civilian police, but in practice this makes little difference.

Visitors should note that it is a criminal offence to export antiquities, and possession of illegal narcotics will be treated seriously.

Embassies and consulates
Republic of Cyprus
Australian High Commission
2nd Floor, 4 Odos Annis Komninis, Nicosia, tel: 22753001
British High Commission
1 Odos Alexandrou Palli Nicosia, tel: 22861100
Canadian Consulate
1 Odos Lampousas, Nicosia, tel: 22775508
US Embassy
Leoforos Metochion and Odos Street, Nicosia, tel: 22393439.

Northern Cyprus With the exception of Turkey, Turkish-occupied Cyprus has no diplomatic representation, as the Turkish Republic of Northern Cyprus is not an internationally recognized state. However, the **British Council,** 23 Mehmet Akif Caddesi (tel: 2283861), **American Centre,** 6 Saran Sokak (tel: 2273930), and **Australian Representation Division,** 20 Güner Türkmen Sokak (tel: 227

7332) in the Turkish Cypriot sector of Nicosia fulfill some consular duties.

Emergency telephone numbers
Republic of Cyprus
Ambulance 112
Police 112
Fire service 112
Night pharmacies 192
Doctors on call Larnaka: 90901424; Limassol: 90901425; Nicosia: 90901422; Pafos: 90901426; Paralimni (Agia Napa–Protaras): 90901423.
General hospitals Larnaka: 24800500; Limassol: 25801100; Nicosia: 22801400; Pafos: 26803260; Paralimni (Agia Napa–Protaras): 23821211; Polis 26321431.

Northern Cyprus
Ambulance 112
Police 155
Fire service 199
Night pharmacies Information is posted on pharmacy doors and published on Saturday in *Cyprus Today.*
General hospitals Nicosia 228 5441; Keryneia (Girne) 815 2266; Famagusta (Gazimağusa) 366 2876; Morfou (Güzelyurt) 714 2125.

Lost property
Items left at restaurants and cafés, and on buses and taxis have a high chance of being recovered. When credit cards and cheques are lost, the issuerss should be informed immediately. If the property has been stolen you should report it to the police, if only for insurance reasons.

Health
There are no mandatory vaccination requirements for either the south or the north. Health services and standards of hygiene range from adequate to excellent, although in remote areas health services are minimal and other standards may be rough and ready.

Blood which is intended for transfusions is AIDS-screened. Mosquitoes are common but are not malarial. Food and tap water are safe, but outside the mountains the taste of water is often poor; bottled mineral water is widely available.

Poisonous vipers can be encountered in spring and summer

in rough country and in the mountains, and while the chance of this is very small and ought not to be exaggerated, a bite from one is potentially fatal. Caution, a hiking-stick and stout footwear are the best safeguards, and anti-venom serum from pharmacies can be self-administered. Anyone who has been bitten and has no serum should remain calm and reach medical assistance speedily with minimum exertion—advice which is designed to slow the spread of venom through the bloodstream.

Less arcane emergencies are more common. Sunburn is liable to be the commonest complaint of all. Free emergency medical care is available at the casualty departments of state hospitals and clinics in both the south and north. Your own country's insurance may cover other medical expenses; but you should have travel insurance to cover medical emergencies. Many medicines are available at chemists without a prescription, and pharmacists can offer advice on treatment of simple ailments. See Emergency Telephone Numbers, opposite, for telephone information numbers of out-of-hours chemists.

The local hospital at Pedoulas in the Troodos Mountains

263

Other information

Bed-and-breakfast accommodation
This is not one of Cyprus' strong selling points, particularly in the main resort areas. That said, there is a growing trend for local houses in villages in and around the Troodos Mountains and around Polis to offer accommodation as part of an effort to spread the monetary benefits of tourism around, without swamping villages with apartment blocks.

Camping
Republic of Cyprus Campsites are licensed by the Cyprus Tourism Organisation and there are only six. Farmers and private landowners might grant permission to pitch a tent if asked, and there are isolated places along the coast and in the mountains where a modest campsite might be set up (but note that fires are forbidden in the forests and it is officially prohibited to camp outside registered sites).

Official campsites, with showers, toilets, shopping, restaurant, and washing facilities, are at:
- **Forest Beach** On the beach 8km (5 miles) east of Larnaka centre, tel: 24644514.
- **Feggari Camping** Coral Bay, Pegeia, 11km (7mi) north of Pafos, tel: 26621534.
- **Governor's Beach** Located 20km (12 miles) east of Limassol, tel: 25632878.
- **Geroskipou Zenon Gardens** Some 3km (2 miles) south of Pafos Harbour, near Geroskipou Beach, tel: 26942277.
- **Polis** Set amid eucalyptus on the beach 500m (550yds) from the village centre, tel: 26815080. Open April to October.
- **Troodos Mountains** Among pine forests 2km (1 mile) north of Troodos, off the road to Kakopetria, tel: 25420205. Open May to end October.

Northern Cyprus As in the Republic of Cyprus, farmers and landowners may give camping permission if asked, and there are many out-of-the-way beaches and forest groves where it can't do much harm if campers are

tidy and respectful of the environment (and light no fires in tinder-dry forests). A properly equipped site is:
- **Riviera Bungalows** On the sea, 5km (3 miles) west of Keryneia (Girne), tel: 822 2026.

There are a number of other small sites, without much in the way of facilities, at **Onur Camping** near Trikomo (Iskele), north of Famagusta (Gazimağusa) at **Nese Beach** south of Bogazi (Boğaz), and at **Aigialousa (Yenierenköy) Public Beach** and **Teresa Beach** near Aigialousa in the Karpasia (Karpaz) Peninsula.

Self-catering accommodation
Apartments, studios, apartotels and villas are burgeoning, usually in the same locations as package-holiday hotels, but in some cases (villa developments, for example) in off-resort areas where isolation is part of the attraction. Again it is possible to book such accommodation after arrival, but the more usual method is to arrange it in advance as part of a package.

Children
International and locally produced brands of baby foods, disposable nappies and other items are available from pharmacies and supermarkets in both the north and south. There are few specifically child-orientated attractions, and some poorly protected historic and archaeological sites may be positively dangerous for children. Offsetting this, children are greatly valued

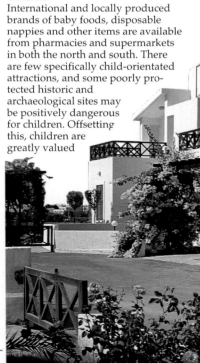

by the Cypriots, and are made welcome in cafés and restaurants. Beaches and swimming pools offer endless diversions, so long as children are properly supervised and protected against sunburn. Most resort hotels can arrange baby-sitting services.

Visitors with disabilities

Services and access for people with disabilities are limited, but the situation is improving, especially with the implementation of new hotel regulations in the Republic of Cyprus. Some hotels, museums, and public buildings have ramps for wheelchairs. Public transport is also a difficult proposition. A few parking spaces are reserved for drivers with disabilities at public places and at most parking areas. The Cyprus Tourism Organisation publishes a guide for travellers with disabilities. Some addresses for further details:
UK: Royal Association for Disability and Rehabilitation (RADAR), Unit 12, City Forum, 250 City Road, London EC1V 8AF, tel: 020-7250 3222; fax: 020-7250 0212; minicom/

textphone: 020-7250 4119; www.radar.org.uk.
US: Society for Accessible Travel and Hospitality, 347 Fifth Avenue, Suite 610, New York, NY10016, tel: 212/447-7284; fax: 212/725-8253; www.sath.org.

Opening times

Republic of Cyprus Shops are generally open as follows:
Summer Monday, Tuesday, Thursday, and Friday 8–1 and 4–7; Wednesday and Saturday 8–2.
Winter Monday, Tuesday, Thursday, and Friday 8–1 and 2.30–6; Wednesday and Saturday 8–1.

Northern Cyprus zone Shop opening times can vary greatly, but bigger stores are generally open as follows:
Summer Monday to Saturday 8–1 and 4–7; Saturday 7.30–1.
Winter Monday to Saturday 9–1 and 2–6.

265

Apartments at Agia Napa

CONVERSION CHARTS

FROM	TO	MULTIPLY BY
Inches	Centimetres	2.54
Centimetres	Inches	0.3937
Feet	Metres	0.3048
Metres	Feet	3.2810
Yards	Metres	0.9144
Metres	Yards	1.0940
Miles	Kilometres	1.6090
Kilometres	Miles	0.6214
Acres	Hectares	0.4047
Hectares	Acres	2.4710
Gallons	Litres	4.5460
Litres	Gallons	0.2200
Ounces	Grams	28.35
Grams	Ounces	0.0353
Pounds	Grams	453.6
Grams	Pounds	0.0022
Pounds	Kilograms	0.4536
Kilograms	Pounds	2.205
Tons	Tonnes	1.0160
Tonnes	Tons	0.9842

MEN'S SUITS

UK	36	38	40	42	44	46	48
Rest of Europe	46	48	50	52	54	56	58
US	36	38	40	42	44	46	48

DRESS SIZES

UK	8	10	12	14	16	18
France	36	38	40	42	44	46
Italy	38	40	42	44	46	48
Rest of Europe	34	36	38	40	42	44
US	6	8	10	12	14	16

MEN'S SHIRTS

UK	14	14.5	15	15.5	16	16.5	17
Rest of Europe	36	37	38	39/40	41	42	43
US	14	14.5	15	15.5	16	16.5	17

MEN'S SHOES

UK	7	7.5	8.5	9.5	10.5	11
Rest of Europe	41	42	43	44	45	46
US	8	8.5	9.5	10.5	11.5	12

WOMEN'S SHOES

UK	4.5	5	5.5	6	6.5	7
Rest of Europe	38	38	39	39	40	41
US	6	6.5	7	7.5	8	8.5

266

Places of worship

Greek Orthodox churches can be found all over the Republic of Cyprus; even small villages will have one. They hold services on Saturday and Sunday, as well as on saints' days, and at other times are invariably locked. There are similarly large numbers of mosques in Northern Cyprus, as well as a few in the Republic of Cyprus. Maronite and Armenian churches exist in various locations, as well as those dedicated to Roman Catholics, Anglicans, Baptists and other denominations in the main towns and resorts.

Sports and other activities

Cyprus is well endowed with outdoor sports possibilities: angling, both at sea and in reservoir lakes; cycling and mountain-biking; hiking and hill-walking; swimming; skiing; water-skiing; scuba-diving and snorkelling; shooting; tennis; golf; horse-riding; and aerial sports, such as sky-diving and hang-gliding. In addition, there are activity holidays based on archaeology, architecture, arts and crafts, athletics, bird-watching, bridge, Byzantine art, motorsport (the Cyprus Rally is held in September), cooking, the environment, fruit-picking, geology, philately, photography and wines. These are mostly practised in the Republic of Cyprus.

Further information is available from the Cyprus Tourist

Flat out in the Troodos Mountains during the Cyprus Rally

Organisation and specialist tour operators.

Electricity
The electricity supply throughout Cyprus is 240 volts AC, 50 cycles, with 5-amp and 13-amp three-pin plugs. Adaptors for connecting more than one low-current appliance are available from many hotels and are on sale in shops. Hotel rooms often have a 110-volt outlet for shavers.

Etiquette and local customs
Casual dress is acceptable in most non-business situations, whether for the theatre, dinner or visiting. Not all Cypriots, however, are delighted to see sweaty, all-but-naked bodies, straight off the beach, wandering into their shops and tavernas.

The sensitivities of Christian and Islamic religious institutions such as churches, mosques, monasteries and convents should be respected, with both men and women covering up properly and, in the case of mosques, removing their shoes. Worshippers should not be pestered with cameras.

Topless bathing at beaches and pools is usually acceptable, but is much less common in Northern Cyprus. Nude bathing is not acceptable in Cyprus, although at remote, unfrequented beaches such as those of the Akamas Peninsula, and private beaches in Northern Cyprus you may be able to get away with it.

Girls, both Greek Cypriot and Turkish Cypriot, are far less sheltered than they used to be, particularly in the towns and bigger resorts, but family and religious safeguards—and sanctions—still exist and unwanted attentions can lead to trouble.

Photography
In what is surely one of the most photogenic islands in the Mediterranean, photography has become a security risk in many places. Military personnel and installations, including those of the UN and the British Sovereign Bases, are strictly off limits for photography, and this can also apply to innocent locations and family snapshots taken close to military personnel and installations.

Museums may require a permit for photography. Flash photography is generally forbidden in historic churches, especially those with fragile icons and frescoes; visitors tempted to sneak a few are reminded that the flash causes damage to the works of art. Cameras, film, memory cards, batteries and rapid processing are all widely available, although less so in Northern Cyprus.

Tipping
Restaurants and hotels include a ten per cent service charge in the bill, and VAT at 5 per cent is levied on all customers' bills (15 per cent for alcohol), but a small extra amount for good service is still appreciated.

Taxi-drivers, hairdressers and chambermaids are as fond of tips as anyone, but they don't hustle for them.

Tipping is rather less common in Northern Cyprus, especially for taxi-drivers, but here, too, customs are changing.

Toilets
Public toilets are few and far between in Cyprus. There are, however, lots of bars, cafés and tavernas with toilets, but being polite and buying a drink before using the facilities, as one should, tends to diminish the effect of the exercise. Toilet paper is normally not flushed away but placed in the receptacle provided, a practice intended to keep the plumbing unblocked.

Women travellers
A low crime level means there is little likelihood of women travelling alone being subject to assault in Cyprus. Nevertheless, the risk cannot be ruled out completely and it makes sense to adopt commonsense measures, such as not hitch-hiking alone.

There is no need to be over-concerned about dress in most circumstances, but women must respect Christian and Muslim religious sensitivities. Few women in Northern Cyprus are veiled. In remote areas, social attitudes tend to be conservative.

267

Tourist offices

Republic of Cyprus

The **Cyprus Tourism Organisation (CTO)** offices, mail enquiries only, are at PO Box 24535, 19 Leoforos Lemesou, 1390 Nicosia, tel: 226911000; www.visitcyprus.org.cy. Branches can be found at:

Agia Napa 12 Leoforos Kryou Nerou, tel: 23721796.

Larnaka Plateia Vasileos Pavlou, tel: 24654322.

Larnaka Airport Passenger terminal, tel: 24643576.

Limassol (Lemesos) 115a Odos Spyrou Araouzou, tel 25362756; 22 Odos Georgiou A', Potamos tis Germasogeias, tel: 25323211.

Limassol Harbour Passenger terminal, tel: 25571868.

Nicosia (Lefkosia) 11 Odos Aristokyprou, Laïki Geitonia, tel: 22674264.

Pafos 3 Odos Gladstonos, tel: 26232841.

Pafos Airport Passenger terminal, tel: 26423161.

Pano Platres Plateia Seferis, tel: 25421316.

Paralimni-Protaras 356 Leoforos Protara-Kavo Gkreko, tel: 23832865.

Polis 2 Odos Vasileos Stasioikou A', tel: 26322468.

Overseas offices

UK Cyprus Tourist Office, 17 Hanover Street, London W1S 1YP, tel: 020-7569 8800; fax: 020-7499 4935; www.visitcyprus.org.cy.

US Cyprus Tourism Organisation, 13 East 40th Street, New York, NY 10016, tel: 212/683-5280; fax: 212/683-5282; www.visitcyprus.org.cy.

Northern Cyprus

The address of the **Ministry of Tourism** is Lefkoşa, c/o Mersin 10, Turkey; www.tourism.trnc.net. Tourist information offices are at:

Ercan Airport Passenger terminal, tel: 231 4003.

Famagusta (Gazimağusa) Fevzi Cakmak Caddesi, tel: 366 2864.

Keryneia (Girne) Kordon Boyu (yacht harbour), tel: 815 2145.

Nicosia (Lefkoşa) Selcuklu Caddesi, tel: 228 9629.

Overseas offices

UK TRNC Tourist Office, 29 Bedford Square, London WC1B 3EG, tel: 020-7631 1930; www.tourism.trnc.net.

US TRNC Tourist Office, 1667 K Street, Suite 690, Washington DC 20006, tel: 202/887-6198; www.tourism.trnc.net.

European Union TRNC Office, Tourism Section, 207 Avenue Louise, 1050 Brussels, Belgium, tel: 02 648 4870; fax: 02 648 7088.

Maps and information

Republic of Cyprus The CTO and its local offices provide free maps and information. Bookshops, news-vendors, and souvenir shops also sell maps, guidebooks, and other information books. A good road map (such as the AA/Macmillan *Cyprus Traveller's Map*) is essential when travelling off the main highways.

Northern Cyprus Offices at Nicosia, Keryneia (Girne), Famagusta (Gazimağusa) and Ercan Airport dispense free maps and brochures, as well as more detailed, paid-for information.

Hotels & Restaurants

HOTELS

The Cyprus Tourism Organisation (CTO) publishes a list of officially registered and classified hotels. Local CTO offices have lists for their areas. Hotels are rated from one to five stars, with a 'hotels without star' category. Room and other rates are approved by the CTO for a fixed period, and must be displayed in rooms. Overcharging is an offence. Off-season prices show considerable reductions.

Cyprus is mainly a tourist destination, although the towns and resorts have business- and conference-orientated establishments. The mainly package-tourism market means that most hotel rooms are block-booked. Independent travellers will find a lack of family hotels and pensions that make staying a day or two then moving on an integral part of their vacation experience. Package-orientated hotels will not, however, turn such customers away if they have room.

In attempting to change the face of its tourist industry, the CTO has limited growth in new hotel construction and favoured four- and five-star hotels. With no corresponding improvement in the tourism 'product', many hotels operate below capacity, offering the chance of negotiating favourable rates. The two major exceptions are in the Troodos Mountains and around the Akamas Peninsula, where hotels are subject to limits on size, and development is discouraged.

The situation in the Turkish Cypriot zone is marked by a lack of accommodation compared with the Republic of Cyprus, and fewer resort areas. Lower demand does not offset this. Most visitors are from Turkey, but arrivals from Europe show a steady increase. Growth has been given a significant boost by the opening of the intra-island border and the liberalization of travel between the two zones, but is still impeded because the international community does not recognize the Turkish Republic of Northern Cyprus.

The following hotels have been divided into three price categories:
£££ = expensive
££ = moderate
£ = inexpensive

NICOSIA

Greek Cypriot sector

Averof (£)
19 Odos Averof tel: 22773447;
www.averof.com.vy
This modern, family-run hotel with its own restaurant and bar, in a quiet residential area near the Green Line, has rustic warmth and character. Some of the 25 rooms have a balcony, some have television and all have a private bathroom and air-conditioning.

Castelli (£)
38 Odos Ouzounian tel: 22712812;
www.castelli-hotel.com

A small bed-and-breakfast hotel with reasonable facilities for the price, it occupies a good position next to the walls, near the Pafos Gate.

Classic (££)
94 Odos Rigainis tel: 22664006;
www.classic.com.cy
Business and holiday visitors should both appreciate this hotel in a fully renovated old building near the Pafos Gate. Rooms are modern, air-conditioned and comfortable; double-glazed windows cut out noise from the busy street. There are fitness and business centres and an international restaurant.

Cleopatra (££)
8 Odos Florinis tel: 22440000;
www.cleopatra.com.cy
Somewhat more expensive than higher-star-rated hotels, the Cleopatra has excellent facilities, including a swimming pool, fine restaurant, health centre and conference suite.

Denis (£)
19 Odos Diagorou tel: 22330315;
fax: 22335046
Good-value hotel that lies close to the city's lung at the Athalassa Forest Park.

Hilton Cyprus (£££)
116 Leoforos Archiepiskopou Makariou III
tel: 22377777; www.hilton.com
Nicosia's premier hotel is a modern and efficient five-star establishment, with superbly appointed rooms and excellent service. The hotel's swimming pool is a big plus in Nicosia's scorching summer; there's also a well-equipped business centre.

Holiday Inn Nicosia City Centre (££)
70 Odos Rigainis tel: 22712712;
www.holiday-inn-cyprus.com
This high-quality hotel lies just inside the city walls near the Pafos Gate, and provides the standard of room and comfort you'd expect from a flagship member of this chain. It has a fine Japanese restaurant, the Bonzai, and the French Café Opera, next door.

Hilton Park Nicosia (££)
Leoforos Georgiou Griva Digeni tel: 22695111;
www.hilton.com
A business-orientated hotel set amid landscaped gardens.

Rimi (£)
Odos 5 Solonos tel: 22680101;
email: rimi@cytanet.com.cy
For a budget hotel, this recently modernized establishment in a restored town house in the middle of the Laïki Geitonia district has good facilities. These include air-conditioning, bathroom and television in each of the 26 rooms. The surroundings can be noisy until late.

Turkish Cypriot sector

Ender Hotel (£)
12 Şehit İsmail Dümenci Sokak tel: 227 8612
Simple, friendly and clean hotel, midway out of town from the city walls.

Gönyeli Kent Hotel (£)
Gönyeli tel: 223 7610
A small and pleasant hotel in a suburb on the northwestern fringe of the city.

Royal (££)
19 Kemal Asik Caddesi tel: 228 7621
This modern hotel includes a casino, indoor
swimming pool, sauna, Turkish bath and
massage facilities.

Saray (££)
Atatürk Meydani tel: 228 3115
Turkish Cypriot Nicosia's premier hotel, the
Saray is a fairly uninspired-looking place, but it
is a good hotel. Traditional Cypriot and standard European cuisine are available in the
restaurant overlooking the square.

THE SOUTHEAST

Agia Napa area

Adams Beach (££)
Leoforos Nissi tel: 23725000;
www.adams.com.cy
An international holiday hotel rated a shade
below five stars, this hotel has its own pocket-
handkerchief-sized beach and an enormous
range of sports and leisure facilities, including
(if you require it) bungee-jumping.

Alion Beach (£££)
Leoforos Kryou Nerou tel: 23722900;
www.alion-beach.com
As with all top-class hotels in Agia Napa, the
Alion Beach is devoted to beach holidays with
an added touch of style.

Anesis (£)
7 Odos Oktovriou 1 tel: 23721104;
www.aquasolhotels.com
Regular tourist hotel, midway between the
resort centre and the harbour, with facilities to
suit a higher-grade establishment.

Asterias Beach (££)
Makronisos tel: 23721901; email:
asterias.beach.hotel@cytanet.com.cy
A well-regarded hotel on the beach west of Agia
Napa, the Asterias is embedded in an area of
sand dunes and greenery. The hotel's happy
hours, barbecues and entertainment evenings
sum up its fun-orientated approach.

Bella Napa Bay (££)
47 Leoforos Kryou Nerou tel: 23819900;
www.bellanapa.com.cy
A straightforward and unpretentious hotel,
renovated and upgraded, occupies a hillside
not far from the shore.

Christofinia (££)
112 Leoforos Nissi tel: 23721610;
www.christofinia.com
Part of a line of hotels commanding the
approaches to Nissi Bay, the Christofinia lacks
an ideal waterfront position but gets close
enough.

Chrysland (£)
82 Odos Tefkros Anthias tel: 23721311;
www.chryslandhotel.com.cy
In a quieter district than is the norm in Agia
Napa, the Chrysland is good value for money.

Dome (££)
Makronisos tel: 23721006;
www.domehotel.com.cy
A remarkably big hotel even by Agia Napa's
usual standards, with two extensive stretches

of beach, the Dome is a beach-holiday hotel
par excellence. Its fair-sized swimming pool is
surrounded by lush gardens.

Luca-Cypria Florida (££)
Leoforos Kryou Nerou tel: 23721781;
www.dhcyprotels.com
The Florida is a reasonably priced resort hotel,
considering the range of facilities on offer,
although there is a road to cross on the way
to the beach and it is a fair walk to the
resort centre.

Grecian Bay (£££)
32 Leoforos Kryou Nerou tel: 23842000;
www.grecian.com.cy
A top-flight hotel on its own sandy beach, the
Grecian Bay boasts an unrivalled range of facilities, including those for conferences. This is
the kind of place that some of its guests never
find the need to leave.

Grecian Sands (££)
44 Leoforos Kryou Nerou tel: 23721616;
www.greciansands.com
Not far from its starrier sister hotel, the
Grecian Bay (see entry above), the Grecian
Sands offers a slightly slimmer diet of holiday
facilities, but an equal proximity to the beach.

Kermia Beach (££)
74 Leoforos Kavo Gkreko, Korakistres
tel: 23721401; www.kermaibeach.com
This modern but quite charming bungalow
complex on a marvellous strip of coast midway
between Agia Napa and Cape Gkreko has an
isolated feeling, which is far from typical of the
Agia Napa area.

Leros (£)
41 Leoforos Archiepiskopou Makariou III
tel: 23721126; fax: 23721127
Small and inexpensive, this hotel aimed at the
budget traveller of a kind that Agia Napa
could do with more of.

Pavlonapa Beach (££)
71 Leoforos Nissi tel: 23722400;
www.pavlonapa.com.cy
A smaller establishment than is the norm in
this area, the Pavlonapa Beach lacks a few of
the facilities that are available at the bigger
establishments nearby, but its superb
location on the first fine bay out of Agia Napa
to the west more than makes up for this.

Sancta Napa (££)
9 Odos Oktovriou 1 tel: 2321011;
www.sanctanapa.com.cy
This has an ideal, moderately priced position
for those who like to have the sea, the pool
and the nightlife high-spots all within easy
reach. If the bustle gets too intense, the harbour is equally close by for a fast getaway by
cruise boat.

Larnaka area

Beau Rivage Beach (££)
Larnaka–Dhekelia road, Pyla tel: 24646600;
www.beaurivagecyprus.com
The Beau Rivage is an excellent mid-range
hotel, with scented gardens, its own wide
stretch of beach on Larnaka Bay and good facilities for children.

271

Cactus (£)
*6–8 Odos Saixpir tel: 24627400;
www.cactus.com.cy*
A popular family-run in-town hotel, thanks to a simple but elegant style and a staff who are far from prickly. It also has a small swimming pool.

Eva (£)
*Larnaka–Dhekelia road, Oroklini
tel: 24645100; fax: 24644203*
One of the cheaper hotels on the coast road, near the village of Oroklini, the Eva is a friendly, family-run hotel.

Faros Holiday Village (££)
Perivolia tel: 24422111; www.farosvillage.com
Found 14km (9 miles) south of Larnaka, near the lighthouse at rugged Cape Kiti. The Faros Holiday Village is one of this area's better properties and has fine sea views.

Flamingo Beach (££)
*152 Odos Piyale Paşa tel: 24828224;
www.flamingobeachhotel.com*
A good seafront property in southern Larnaka, well placed for the Salt Lake though perhaps a little too close to the airport.

Golden Bay (£££)
*Larnaka–Dhekelia road, Pyla tel: 24645444;
www.lordos.com.cy*
Larnaka's top hotel provides high-quality service and comfort in its 193 rooms. It stands on the beach midway along Larnaka Bay and has a range of watersports and beach sports facilities, including a pitch-and-putt course. Most rooms have a sea view and, among other facilities, there's an outdoor pool and a heated Roman-style colonnaded indoor pool.

Harry's Inn (£)
*2 Odos Thermopylon tel: 24654453;
email: harrysinn@cytanet.com.cy*
A small, friendly, typically Cypriot hotel. It has just nine rooms and 15 beds and does only bed and breakfast. It is just a few minutes walk from the seafront, near the tourist information office in the heart of town. Hard to find better value for money.

Ireon (£)
*74 Leoforos Archiepiskopou Makariou III
tel: 24637444; www.crownresortsgroup.com*
Not far from the harbour and on a busy main thoroughfare, the light and airy Ireon has a swimming pool at the back.

Karpasiana Beach Sunotel (££)
*Larnaka–Dhekelia road, Oroklini
tel: 24645001; www.crownresortsgroup.com*
The Karpasiana is fairly typical of the hotels along the shore north of Larnaka, but it does have a sheltered stretch of beach and good value to recommend it.

Larco (£)
*Odos Pontou tel: 24657006;
www.larco-hotel.com.cy*
Embedded in Larnaka's old Turkish quarter, this is a quite large and busy hotel, serving breakfast-only to guests.

Lenios Beach (££)
*Larnaka–Dhekelia road, Oroklini tel:
24646100; email: lenios@cytanet.com.cy*
An attractive, smaller hotel on a fairly deserted stretch of sand just outside Larnaka, offering a quieter scene for swimming and sunbathing than some of its neighbours.

Les Palmiers (£)
*12 Leoforos Athinon tel: 24627200;
fax: 24627204*
An excellent bet for travellers who want to be in town, this well-managed hotel has a first-class seafront location on Foinikoudes Promenade. Its sense of style offers a welcome contrast to the big resort hotels.

Lordos Beach (££)
*Larnaka–Dhekelia road tel: 24647444;
www.lordos.com.cy*
The Lordos Beach lies no more than a ten-minute drive north of Larnaka centre. Its balconies gaze sideways at the sea, but there is a patch of sand for getting a closer look, and there are ample amenities for families.

Onisillos (£)
*17 Odos Onisilou tel: 24651100;
fax: 24627204*
In the Turkish quarter, not far from Larnaka Fort, this small and presentable but otherwise unremarkable hotel is good value and well-positioned.

Palm Beach Hotel & Bungalows (££)
*Larnaka–Dhekelia road, Oroklini
tel: 24644500; www.palmbeachhotel.com*
On the coast road just to the north of Larnaka, the Palm Beach offers a high level of facilities for a slightly lower price than could be expected. On-site bungalows are available.

Sun Hall (££)
*6 Leoforos Athinon tel: 24653341;
www.aquasolhotels.com*
This big, blocky hotel lies across the road from a palm tree-lined stretch of sand near Larnaka's marina overlooking the Foinikoudes Promenade. The town's main shopping and taverna centre is right next door.

Sveltos Beach (£)
*Piyale Paşa Street tel: 24657240;
fax: 24658334*
A block of apartments beside Mackenzie Beach at the southern end of Larnaka, offering in-town access to another kind of ambience from that of the coast road to the north.

Three Seas (£)
*Perivolia tel: 24422901;
www.3seashotel.com*
The Three Seas occupies a fine position beside the lighthouse at scenic Cape Kition, 14km (9 miles) south of Larnaka, and its modest prices add to the attraction.

Vergi (£)
*Larnaka–Dhekelia road, Pyla tel: 24645900;
fax: 24645790*
A relatively quiet position off the highway recommends the Vergi to visitors who want to be near the beach but without the bustle of the seafront resort hotels.

Protaras–Pernera area

Adelais (££)
Green Bay tel: 23832600; fax: 23832601
Set a little way back from the beach in a quieter area south of Protaras, Adelais offers a slight

272

variation on the standard beach hotel, with some good nature walks nearby.

Anaïs Bay (££)
Pernera Harbour tel: 23831351; www.anaisbay.com
A quite charming, smallish hotel by Protaras standards. It is family-run and has a Cypriot, as opposed to international, feel.

Golden Coast (££)
64 Odos Pinias, Pernera tel: 23831366; www.lordos.com.cy
Stylish hotel overlooking the fishing shelter on a stunning stretch of coast. The hotel's greenery-bedecked swimming pool adds to the exotic feel.

Grecian Park (£££)
81 Odos Konnou, Konnos Bay tel: 23832000; www.grecianpark.com
A superbly equipped resort hotel, the Grecian Park's vast blue swimming pools compete with the translucent waters of the nearby sea.

Konnos Bay (££)
Kavo Gkreko–Protaras road tel: 23832870; fax: 23831632
What sets this complex of mid-brow, modern apartments grouped around a swimming pool apart is its setting overlooking Konnos beach. The white-sand beach is not big, but it shelves gently into the clear blue water, creating an extensive safe-bathing zone for children.

Odessa (££)
Odos Amfititis, Protaras tel: 23831645; www.tsokkos.com
Set slightly back from the main road in Protaras, near Flamingo Beach, with the resort's bustling nightlife happening all around it.

San Antonio (£)
123 Odos Grigori Afxentiou, Paralimni tel: 23821561; fax: 23826097
Set well back from the coast, at Paralimni village, the San Antonio has local ambience and gives a focus away from the beach.

Silver Sands Beach (££)
3 Odos Demokritos, Protaras tel: 23831590; www.tsokkos.com
The Silver Sands Beach stands on Flamingo Beach, the next stretch of sand along from the renowned Fig Tree Bay, and provides a little more in the way of peace and tranquillity.

Sunrise Beach (££)
Protaras tel: 23831501; www.sunrise.com.cy
Around the northern corner from Fig Tree Bay, the top-class Sunrise Beach Hotel has an unsurpassed position on the beach.

THE SOUTHWEST

Limassol area

Acropole (£)
21 Odos Georgios tel: 25362706
A dinky little place in a good central location near Limassol's seafront promenade. The room rates will suit the thinnest wallet.

Alasia (££)
6 Odos Haydari tel: 25332000; email: alasiahotel.com.cy
For those who prefer an in-town hotel to a seafront one, the Alasia is just off the inner ring road in Limassol. A heated outdoor swimming pool may compensate for the lack of beach.

Amathus Beach (£££)
Leoforos Amathous tel: 25832000; www.mathushotel.com
Tombs from ancient Amathous lend a historical touch to an unwaveringly modern establishment 5km (3 miles) east of Limassol. One of the Leading Hotels of the World, it is an oasis of calm, with its own beach, health and recreational amenities, and Cypriot and international restaurants (including a highly regarded seafood eatery).

Arsinoe (££)
620 Amathus Avenue tel: 25321444; www.cyprus2000.com/arsinoe
Midway between the Potamos Germasogeias seafront and ancient Amathous, 6km (4 miles) east of Limassol, this is a medium-sized hotel at the mid-point of its price bracket.

Avenida Beach (££)
Leoforos Amathous tel: 25321122; email: avenida@cytanet.com.cy
Smaller and more personable than the average beachfront hotel, thanks to its family ownership, the Avenida is beside the sea, 11km (7 miles) east of Limassol.

Azur (££)
Odos Georgiou 'A', Potamos Germasogeias tel: 25322667; fax: 25321897
Quite a stylish place lying just a few minutes away from the beach, the Azur has its own swimminhg pool and easy access to the nightlife whirl.

Best Western Pavemar (££)
147 Leoforos Oktovriou 28 tel: 25587000; www.allwinhotels.com
The rooftop swimming pool here gives a superb view over Akrotiri Bay—or more accurately over the hotels that line Akrotiri Bay.

Chez Nous (£)
2 Odos Aktinou, Potamos Germasogeias tel: 25323033; email: cheznous@cytanet.com.cy
This fairly small hotel has the family touch, in a busy area surrounded by hotels that may look more impressive but do not necessarily deliver better service.

Continental (£)
115 Odos Spyrou Araouzou tel: 25362530; fax: 25373030
Budget travellers often do best in terms of location and don't mind having fewer facilities considering the price differential. These factors, together with its popularity among Cypriot families, make the Continental a good bet.

Curium Palace (££)
11 Odos Lordou Vyronou tel: 25891100; www.curiumpalace.com
A family-owned hotel, which proudly displays an interesting collection of *objets d'art* and antique furnishings, Curium Palace is back from the beach, overlooking Limassol's Municipal Gardens with its tiny zoo and open-air theatre.

Elias Beach (££)
Leoforos Amathous tel: 25636000; www.eliasbeach.com

Hotels & Restaurants

A big plus-point here is that the hotel has its own horse-riding centre. It also has a reasonable position on the beach 11km (7 miles) east of Limassol.

Episkopiana (££)
Odos Kremastis, Episkopi tel: 25935093; www.episkopiana.com
A full refurbishment of this hotel has brought its facilities up close to the highest level in Cyprus and offers good value for money. Its location at Episkopi puts it in the heart of a scenic area.

Four Seasons (£££)
Leoforos Amathous tel: 25858000; www.fourseasons.com.cy
As well as its first-class beach hotel and sporting facilities, the Four Seasons is a spa resort of a kind unique in Cyprus. Thalassotherapy is the name of this particular game, with sea-water hydromassage and sea-weed therapy treatments adding up to a 'body holiday'.

Hawaii Grand and Resort (£££)
Leoforos Amathous tel: 25634333; www.hawaiihotel.com
Situated 11km (7 miles) east of Limassol, next to a boat marina, this resort-hotel has the full range of facilities, as is fairly standard on this stretch of coast.

Holiday Inn Limassol (££)
Odos Oktovriou 28, Agios Athanasios tel: 25851515; www.holiday-inn.com/limassolcyprus
This standard-bearer of the chain is towards the edge of Limassol, at a point where the town begins to give way to the ribbon development that stretches along the eastern shore.

Kanika Pantheon (££)
Kanika Centre, Odos Oktovriou 28 tel: 25591111; www.kanika-group.com/pantheon
Set in a complex of shops, restaurants and hotels near the centre of Limassol and across the main road from the beach, not far from the Municpal Gardens. The Pantheon's ambience makes for a change from the standard beach hotel.

King Richard (££)
63 Leoforos Amathous tel: 25321330; email: kingrichard.htl@cytanet.com.cy
Somewhat simpler than many hotels in this area, 8km (5 miles) east of Limassol, it nevertheless offers a good standard of service and comfort.

Le Meridien Limassol Spa & Resort (£££)
Leoforos Amathous tel: 25862000; www.lemeridien-cyprus.com
Part of the string of hotels running east along Akrotiri Bay outside Limassol, this is 13km (8 miles) from the city. It has two fine restaurants serving French and international cuisine, and an enormous swimming pool. A little bridge reaches across the hotel's private bay.

Le Village (£)
242 Odos Leontiou 'A' tel: 25368126; fax: 25348044
Only bed and breakfast are offered at this friendly little place, well sited for exploring Limassol.

L'Onda Beach (£££)
Odos Georgios 'A', Potamos Germasogeias tel: 25321821; www.londabeach.com
One of Cyprus's top-rated hotels, and a good deal smaller than the colossal hotels that dominate this area, L'Onda focuses on de luxe suites and offers a more personal service than is the norm hereabouts.

Louis Apollonia Beach (£££)
Odos Georgiou 'A', Potamos Germasogeias tel: 25323351; www.louishotels.com /apollonia
Right in the heart of Limassol's tourist district, the Apollonia fits the description 'bustling'. A good place for children, as it has a small but sheltered stretch of sand.

Luca-Cypria Poseidonia Beach (£££)
Leforos Amathous tel: 25321000; www.dhcyprotels.com
Only 6km (4 miles) from Limassol, between Potamos Germasogeias and ancient Amathous, this is one of the closer out-of-town hotels. It has a heated swimming pool.

Metropole (£)
6 Odos Ifigenia tel: 25362330; www.metropole.com.cy
Forget the stylish cosmopolitan name: it would be hard to find a place closer to the street scene than this modest little hotel.

Miramare (££)
Odos Amerikanas, Potamos Germasogeias tel: 25888100; www.miramare.com.cy
Surrounded by gardens in a slightly secluded spot, this is otherwise a standardly equipped mid-market hotel.

Sylva (£)
124 Odos Griva Digeni tel: 25591999; email: evisrots@spidernet.com.cy
Surrounded by more touristy establishments, this is a good standard town hotel in an area where the street doglegs towards the sea.

THE TROODOS MOUNTAINS

Agros

Rodon (££)
1 Odos Rodou tel: 25521201; www.rodonhotel.com
Off the beaten track in the eastern Troodos, the Rodon is a big, modern, low-rise hotel that doesn't do much to enhance the village's character but makes a good base for exploring the rugged and sparsely populated Pitsilia district. There's a swimming pool and sauna, and you have great mountain views from your window.

Kakopetria

Hellas (££)
4 Odos Mammantos tel: 22922450; email: hellas.hotel@cytanet.com.cy
Mid-range and mid-sized, with 30 rooms, the Hellas provides a comfortable introduction to the mountain lifestyle.

Kifissia (£)
20 Odos Aidonion tel: 22922421

With a scenic outlook over a plunging stream (more usually a dried-up stream-bed), the Kifissia has 37 rooms that are often full.

Linos Inn (££)
34 Odos Palaias tel: 22923161; www.linos-inn.com.cy
A group of restored traditional houses in the heart of the village form this character-filled, seven-room lodging. Wooden beams, frames and ceilings, antiques, craft items and four-poster beds create a friendly feel that's enhanced by old-fashioned hospitality. The facilities in the rooms include whirlpool-bath, sauna, satellite TV and underfloor heating.

Pano Platres

Edelweiss (£)
53 Odos Spyrou Kyprianou tel: 25421335; www.edelweisshotel.com.cy
This small hotel brings a touch of alpine charm to the Troodos.

Forest Park (£££)
62 Odos Kalidonias tel: 25421751; www.forestparkhotel.com.cy
Situated in its own extensive grounds amid the forest and with a heated swimming pool and tennis courts, this is the top-class resort hotel of the Troodos Mountains.

Lanterns (£)
tel: 25421434
This is one of several fine, unpretentious hotels that make the Troodos Mountains a pleasant change from resort-based coast culture

New Helvetia (£)
6 Odos Helvetia tel: 25421348; www.minotel.com
A fine restaurant and a shaded location distinguish this renovated hotel near the edge of Pano Platres village.

Pendeli (££)
12 Leoforos Archiepiskopou Makariou III tel: 25421736; www.pendelihotel.com
Modern facilities include a swimming pool in what is one of the most comfortable hotels in the village.

Pedoulas

Christy's Palace (£)
Main street tel: 22952655; email: anchristys@cytanet.com.cy
This modern, bright, family-run hotel combines straightforward home comforts with a friendly approach. It has a fair taverna and great views across the village to the surrounding hills.

Churchill Pinewood Valley (££)
Prodromos–Pedoulas road tel: 22952211; email: pinewood@churchill.com.cy
Set among pine and cedar forests, this is one of the most attractive hotels in the mountains.

Mountain Rose (£)
Main street tel: 22952727; fax: 22952555
The Mountain Rose, on the steep main street into the village, scores through its character and friendly welcome. Though minimally equipped, the rooms are reasonably comfortable and the in-house taverna is adequate.

Troodos resort

Jubilee (£)
Tel: 25420107; www.jubileehotel.com
Ideally placed for anyone looking to exploit the good hiking country in these parts.

Troodos (££)
Tel: 25420135; fax: 25420160
A small but pleasantly sited hotel, which is suitable for summer or winter breaks.

THE WEST

Coral Bay

Leptos Coral Beach (£££)
Coral Bay tel: 26881000; www.coral.com.cy
This big resort hotel, above the beach at Coral Bay, merits its five stars for facilities that include both an outdoor and a heated indoor swimming pool and a fitness centre, and its plush rooms and public areas. Service, though professional, tends towards the impersonal.

Thalassa (££)
Adjacent to Coral Bay tel: 26813777; www.thalassa.com.cy
Occupying a headland overlooking Coral Bay, this boutique hotel with spa offers guests luxury, thoughtful touches and personal care. You can even have your own butler. Its residences and suites are tastefully furnished and decorated. The main restaurant espouses a distinctive *nouvelle* Cypriot cuisine and there's a fine seafood restaurant.

Pafos area

Agapinor (££)
24–28 Odos Nikodimos Mylonas tel: 26933926; www.agapinorhotel.com.cy
The Agapinor is an efficiently run, modern hotel, with a mixed business and holiday clientele. It has a fine position in Ktima, near the market, main shopping centre and bus terminal.

Alexander the Great (££)
Leoforos Poseidonos tel: 26965000; www.kanikahotels.com
Just off the southern end of the harbour, the 'Alex' doesn't have a perfect beach location but is well up to standard in all other respects.

Almyra (££)
Leoforos Poseidonos tel: 26933091; www.thanoshotels.com
Well positioned at the eastern end of Pafos harbour, this is a first-class resort-hotel for those who like to be in the thick of the action.

Annabelle (£££)
Leoforos Poseidonos tel: 26238333; www.thanoshotels.com
Rocky groves around the swimming pool are the Annabelle's effort to fit in with its environment—not easy for such a big, though generally attractive resort hotel.

Atlantic Golden Beach (££)
Kisonerga tel: 26947777; www.atlanticahotels.com
With coastal development rapidly extending

north of Pafos, this resort hotel has claimed a rocky spot beside a tiny beach.

Cynthiana Beach (££)
Kisonerga tel: 26933900;
www.cynthianahotel.com
Near banana plantations on a headland with a small private beach near Kisonerga, 7km (4 miles) north of Pafos, this hotel combines relative isolation with resort-hotel facilities.

Louis Imperial Beach (£££)
Leoforos Poseidonos tel: 26965415;
www.louishotels.com
One of the many—perhaps too many—top-rated hotels in the Pafos area, offering much the same resort-hotel diet.

Kings (£)
38 Leforos Tafon ton Vasileon tel: 26933497;
www.tsiolis.com.cy
Good-value accommodation at this medium-sized hotel near the Tombs of the Kings.

Luca-Cypria Laura Beach (£££)
Chlorakas tel: 26944900;
www.dhcyprotels.com
Extensive garden, indoor and outdoor pools, and sports facilities all distinguish this fine resort hotel, 5km (3 miles) north of Pafos.

New Olympus (£)
12 Odos Lordou Vyronou tel: 26932020;
www.new.olympus.com
One of the small, friendly gems of Pafos, set in town. The New Olympus has a pool.

Paphiana (££)
Konia tel: 26960252; fax: 26962476
An inland hotel, just outside Konia, 4km (2.5 miles) east of Pafos, which is ideal for those who want to be a little closer to the country.

Park Mansion (££)
16 Odos Pavlou Melas tel: 26245645;
fax: 26246415
Bordering the Municipal Gardens this restored 18th-century mansion is a graceful departure from Pafos's usual resort-hotel style. The high-ceilinged rooms have wooden shutters, tiled floors and a mix of antique and modern furnishings; some have balconies. There is a swimming pool and a fine restaurant.

Pyramos (£)
4 Odos Agias Anastasias tel: 26935161;
email: pyramos@cytanet.com.cy
A small, family-run hotel with balustraded balconies above an arcaded bar.

Riu Cypria Maris Beach (££)
Leoforos Poseidonos tel: 26964111;
www.riuhotels.com
Sheltered swimming off its own beach at Geroskipou and a swimming pool surrounded by greenery are distinguishing features of this well-established beach hotel.

Roman (££)
Odos Agios Lambrianos tel: 26945411;
www.romanhotel.com.cy
Its Byzantine castle look sets this downtown hotel apart from the many nearby resort-hotels. It has a small rooftop tennis court.

Theofano (££)
Odos Danaïs tel: 26965700;
www.theofano-hotel.com
The Theofano is on a more human scale, for those visitors who cannot easily live with the colossal size that is more usual in Pafos.

Trianon (£)
99 Leoforos Archiepiskopou Makariou III
tel: 26232193
A small and, for the low-budget independent traveller, good-value guest-house.

Vasilias Nikoklis Inn (££)
Nikokleia village tel: 26432211;
www.vasilias-nikoklis-inn.com
This restored medieval inn occupies a tranquil spot overlooking scenic countryside. Its eight rooms have modern furnishings, and the restaurant serves traditional village food and wine.

Venus Beach (£££)
Leoforos Tafon ton Vasileon tel: 26949200;
www.venusbeachhotel.com
This hotel has an unrivalled seafront setting near the superb Tombs of the Kings.

Pissouri

Bunch of Grapes Inn (£)
9 Odos Ioannou Erotokritou Pissouri
tel: 25221275; fax: 25222510
Popularity seems perennial at this traditional taverna/hotel, in a restored 100-year-old inn, with basic accommodation in just 11 rooms.

Columbia Beach (££)
Pissouri Bay tel: 25221201;
www.columbia-hotels.com
The only hotel on a long expanse of beach, the Columbia is a taste of luxury. It nestles at the foot of the cliffs and is just about insulated from what is a busy place in summer. All rooms have a sea view and every comfort. There are tennis courts, a pool and a health and beauty centre.

Polis–Lakki area

Akamas (£)
14 Odos Griva Digenis, Polis tel: 26321521;
fax: 26321561
With a good position in Polis village, this fine little hotel is close to whatever action there is in this peaceful part of Cyprus.

Aphrodite Beach (££)
Lakki–Baths of Aphrodite road tel: 26321001;
email: aphroditebeachhotel@hotmail.com
When its blocky, modern lines are fully discounted, this is still a small and friendly, family-run hotel, beside the beach and within easy reach of the Akamas Peninsula.

Cyprotel Droushia Heights (££)
Drouseia tel: 26332351;
www.dhcyprotels.com
This modern hotel in the hill village of Droushia is popular with the hiking fraternity, as it's well-situated for exploring the western Troodos and the Akamas Peninsula. It's a bit lacking in character, but the local staff ensure friendly service. Outdoor pool and tennis courts.

Elia Latchi Holiday Village (££)
Lakki tel: 26321011;
email: elialaki@logos.cy.net
Close to the sea and Latsi fishing harbour, this small complex of studios and apartments is at the heart of a largely undeveloped coastal area.

276

Marion (£)
6 Odos Marion, Polis tel: 26321216;
www.marionhotel.com
This is a small, friendly hotel in a village where
Cypriot style has not yet been overwhelmed.
Souli (££)
Neo Chorio road tel: 26321088
This plain but comfortable hotel occupies a
beautifully isolated location overlooking the sea
and is an ideal place for getting away from it all.

Stavros tis Psokas

Stavros tis Psokas Rest House (£)
Pafos Forest tel: 26999144
With just seven rooms and a few suites with
shower and fireplace, this isolated wilderness
rest-house/hostel requires advance reservation.

THE NORTH
Belapais (Beylerbeyi) area

Altinkaya and Armonia (£)
Kazafani (Ozanköy) tel: 815 5001
This pretty, family-run establishment on the
Keryneia–Bellapais (Girne–Beylerbeyi) road,
consists of 42 bungalows grouped around a
swimming pool and across the road, and incor-
porates a restaurant that is popular with locals.
Ambelia Village (££)
Bellapais–Kato Dhikomo (Beylerbeyi–Dikmen)
road tel: 815 3655
Gardens screen this apartment complex, 300m
(980ft) above sea level and above the village
of Bellapais.
Belapais Gardens (££)
Keryneia–Belapais (Girne–Beylerbeyi) road
tel: 815 6066
Its pool fed by a spring once used by the ancient
Romans, this small, de luxe villa complex
nestles in an idyllic setting among lemon groves,
below the ruined Gothic abbey of Belapais.

Keryneia (Girne) area

Bristol (£)
Hürriyet Avenue tel: 815 6570
An excellent-value hotel on Keryneia's main
shopping street, with clean rooms and a good
Turkish restaurant.
British Hotel (£)
10 Eftal Akça Street tel: 815 2240
It would be hard to beat the location of this
friendly, family-run hotel with just 18 rooms on
the harbourside at Keryneia, overlooking the
open-air terraces and moored yachts.
Courtyard Inn (£)
Karakum tel: 815 3343
This small, inexpensive pension has a nice
restaurant and swimming pool and is just to
the east of Keryneia.
Dome (£££)
Kordonboyu tel: 815 2453
Modernization may not be popular with genuine
ex-colonials (it now has a casino) but this elegant hotel is still the place of choice for
holidaymakers in the know and in the money.

Dorana (££)
Hürriyet Avenue tel: 815 3521
A relaxing, friendly family hotel not far from the
harbour, the Dorana is on the main shopping
street—which ought to be noisy but isn't.
Grand Rock (£££)
Kordonboyu tel: 815 2238
The name here is appropriate, as its beach is
mostly rocks. A central location and efficiently
modern approach compensate for this.
Kyrenia Oscar Resort (££)
Karakum tel: 815 4801
Fairly standard holiday hotel, with pool and
other facilities, including beach. A courtesy bus
runs from the hotel to the nearby town centre.
Liman (££)
Kordonboyu tel: 815 2001
The Liman is in a bustling part of town around
the corner from the old harbour. The hotel's café
terrace across the road is shaded by the
entwined branches of Keryneia's 'Loving Trees'.
Socrates (£)
Hürriyet Avenue tel: 815 1291
A family hotel with a leafy courtyard café, on
the main shopping street, near the old harbour.

Lapithos (Lapta) area

Almond Holiday Village (£)
Karavas (Alsancak) tel: 821 2885
This 'village' of 20 bungalows nestles in the
foothills of the mountain range, a few minutes
from the sea. It has its own pool, restaurant and
bar, and is just 8km (5 miles) from Keryneia.
Celebrity Hotel and Bungalows (£££)
Keryneia–Vavilas (Girne–Güzelyalı) road
tel: 821 8751
This hotel has a private beach and a casino
among its full range of resort-hotel facilities.
Château Lambousa (£££)
Off Keryneia–Vavilas (Girne–Güzelyalı) road
tel: 821 8751
With superb Turkish architecture, the
Château Lambousa has shaded balconies
looking over palm-fringed gardens to the sea.
Deniz Kızı (££) **and Deniz Kızı Royal** (£££)
Karavas (Alsancak)
tel: 821 8710 and (Royal) 821 2676
These two hotels share a sandy bay near this
village, at a spot where the sea makes the out-
door pool almost superfluous.
Mare Monte (££)
Karavas (Alsancak) tel: 821 8310
A vine-shaded open-air restaurant beside the
Mediterranean is one of the attractions of this
hotel, along with beautifully scented gardens.

THE EAST
Bogazi (Boğaz) area

Bogaz (££)
Famagusta–Bogazi (Gazimağusa–Boğaz) road
tel: 371 2559
On the coast road across from the fishing
harbour, the Bogaz is a quiet, modern hotel.
Guests can use the swimming pool and tennis
courts at the nearby Hotel Seaview (see below).

Exotic (£)
Famagusta–Bogazi (Gazimağusa–Boğaz) road
tel: 371 2885
On the coast road on the fringe of Bogazi, this 22-room hotel is friendly and comfortable, and overlooks open countryside and the sweeping bay towards Famugusta (Gazimağusa).

Merit Cyprus Gardens (££)
Famagusta–Bogazi (Gazimağusa–Boğaz) road
tel: 371 3450
The Cyprus Gardens consists of a complex of bungalows and small villas beside the sea, in a fine, scented garden. Pool and tennis courts are complemented by horse-riding facilities.

Seaview Hotel (££)
Off Famagusta–Bogazi (Gazimağusa–Boğaz) road tel: 371 2651
The Seaview occupies a superb spot on a hill behind Bogazi, overlooking the sea. Beautiful gardens complement the hotel's stylish looks, and it also has good sports facilities and a pool.

Famagusta (Gazimağusa) area

Altun Tabya (£)
7 Kızılkule Yolu tel: 366 5363
A simple but clean and friendly small hotel inside the city walls. Evening meals are available on request in the Turkish restaurant.

Palm Beach (£££)
Havva Sentürk Avenue tel: 366 2000
This stylish, flamingo-pink hotel with a pool and casino is in a fine seafront spot, south of the walled city. Its outlook in another direction, however, is towards the adjacent barbed-wire barricades and dereliction of Famagusta's abandoned resort suburb of Varosha (Maraş).

Portofino (£)
Fevzi Çakmak Bulvarı tel: 366 4392
This is a family-run hotel close to the old town and the sea. Opened in 2000, it has 52 rooms and a wide range of facilities.

Karpasia (Karpaz) Peninsula

Blue Sea (£)
Rizokarpaso–Cape Apostolos Andreas (Dipkarpaz–Zafer Burnu) road tel: 372 2393
A tiny hotel with a superb seaside setting southeast of Rizokarpaso, in the beautiful but hotel-poor Karpasia.

Salamis area

Park (££)
Famagusta–Bogazi (Gazimağusa–Boğaz) road
tel: 378 8217
On its own beach right by the sea, this Bavarian-style country hotel has all the facilities you'd expect in a modern resort-hotel, yet in a fairly small and attractive package.

Salamis Bay Conti (£££)
Famagusta–Bogazi (Gazimağusa–Boğaz) road
tel: 378 8201
This principal resort-hotel on the sandy stretch of Famagusta Bay some 10km (6 miles) north of Famagusta is a large, well-equipped complex, with swimming pool, sauna and sports facilities.

278

Vazaro (££)
Famagusta–Bogazi (Gazimağusa–Boğaz) road
tel: 378 8212
Next to the Salamis Bay Hotel, the Vazaro is a more individual kind of place, and although it lacks some facilities, guests can use the pools and sports facilities at the Salamis Bay.

RESTAURANTS

Cyprus has a strong tradition of local cuisine combining Greek and Turkish elements with influences from Europe and the Levant, but this is not evident in the hotels that serve bland international fare. The resorts offer a vast choice of outlets where the ingredients of Cypriot cuisine may be present yet where quality has been sacrificed in the interests of speed. There are, however, restaurants and tavernas, in all areas and price categories, where the authentic taste of Cyprus is preserved and served with commitment and style. The trick is to go where the Cypriots go.

The following restaurants are divided into three categories:
£££ = expensive
££ = moderate
£ = inexpensive

NICOSIA

Greek Cypriot sector

Abu Faysal (££)
31 Odos Klimentou tel: 22760353 or 367785
An excellent Lebanese restaurant with an old mansion-style interior and atmospheric garden terrace. The Lebanese *mezza* (*meze*) is every bit as feature-packed as its Cypriot counterpart, but is more colourful and better considered.

Aegeon (£)
40 Odos Ektoros tel: 22433297
This is a fine traditional taverna near the Famagusta Gate, where several such venues rub shoulders with modern style.

Archontiko (££)
27 Odos Aristokyprou tel: 22450080
Dine on *meze*, either indoors or in good weather outdoors at a taverna that is more or less typical of the popular, tourist-orientated places in the Laïki Geitonia district.

Armenaki (£)
15 Odos Sans Souci, Akropolis tel: 22378383
This family-owned Armenian restaurant has plain tables and chairs in a bright, unadorned setting. Good taste and modest prices take the place of style. Look for small, spicy Armenian pizzas, kebabs and vegetarian dishes.

Axiothea (££)
8 Odos Axiotheas tel: 22430787
It seems incongruous to eat so well in such a relaxed setting, with Green Line barricades as a backdrop, but this unpretentious restaurant is traditional Nicosia at its best.

Bonzai (£££)
Holiday Inn, 70 Odos Rigainis tel: 22712712

Stylish and authentic, this is the place to go for original Japanese food—sushi, *sashimi* and *teppan yaki*. There's a daily buffet lunch.

Chang's China (££)
1 Odos Akropolis tel: 22351350
Considering that foreign cuisine is thin on the ground in Nicosia, this is an adequate if not overly memorable taste of China.

Erenia (£)
64a Leoforos Archiepiskopou Kyprianou tel: 22422860
A specialist in *meze* and Cypriot charm, this diminutive taverna is well worth the trip into suburban Strovolos.

Konatzin (£)
10 Odos Delfi tel: 22776990
Vegetarian *meze* and meat-based dishes at a romantic converted house with garden.

Mattheos Georgiou (£)
6 Palteia Oktovriou 28 tel: 22755846
This superior example of the working-class cafés near the Green Line offers simple traditional dishes at extremely low cost and with friendly service.

Plaka Taverna (££)
8 Odos Stlianou Lena, Egkomi tel: 22352898
One of Nicosia's essential eating experiences, and noted for its excellent *meze*. The service can be casual.

Ten Lanterns (£)
5 Odos Kefallinia, Akropolis tel: 22421410
This unpretentious local restaurant makes up in fine-tasting food for what it lacks in style.

To Stekki tis Chrysaliniotissas (££)
18–19 Odos Athins tel:22430772
Near the trendy Famagusta Gate, this taverna maintains a traditional Cypriot character. Cool and shady,the converted house has an arched interior, with a mix of wood and stone floors and a wicker ceiling. Grilled lamb's liver stands out as an individual dish, but *meze* is the best way to go.

Trattoria Romantica (££)
13 Odos Evagora Pallikaridi, Lykavitos tel: 22377276
Alfresco and indoor dining in a fine restaurant are on the menu here, along with home-made pasta and pure Italian ambience.

Xefoto (££)
6 Odos Aeschylou, Laïki Geitonia tel: 22666567
Smarter and a shade more adventurous than is the norm for Laïki Geitonia, Xefoto has a stylish café on the ground floor, a darkly romantic dining room on the first floor, and a terrace on the narrow, pedestrians-only street out front.

Zebras (££)
43 Odos Klimentos tel: 22458600
Cosmopolitan Nicosia finds a fresh outlet at the African eatery owned by a returned expatriate from South Africa. Restrained tribal interior sets the scene for a menu that features dishes from around the continent, including North Africa. There are no zebra steaks, but there is ostrich meat.

Turkish Cypriot sector

Moyra (££)
Osman Paşa Sokagi tel: 228 6800
For kebabs, *meze* and steaks in a stylish setting, you can't do better than at this authentic Turkish Cypriot restaurant.

Saray Roof (££)
Meydanı Atatürk tel: 228 3115
Turkish and European cuisine is served in the restaurant of Turkish Cypriot Nicosia's top-rated Saray Hotel, which overlooks the square.

THE SOUTHEAST

Agia Napa area

Georgis Flambé Restaurant (£)
9 Odos Ippocratou tel: 23721504
A hale and hearty kind of place that's not untypical of Agia Napa, serving brandy-flamed dishes outdoors in summer.

Potamos (£)
Potamos Creek tel: 24785065
This authentic, excellent if rather plain fish restaurant occupies a scenic spot beside the fishing boats at the harbour near Xylofagou.

Taverna Napa (££)
15 Odos Dimokratias tel: 23721280
The resort's oldest taverna, shaded by a vine arbour, has a friendlier feel than is common on these busy streets. Inside it is warm and romantic, and there's an outside terrace. You dine on typical Cypriot fare that includes a fine *meze*, cooked and presented with flair.

To Ploumin (££)
3 Odos Oktovriou 28, Sotira tel: 23730444
Local people prepare country cuisine in this restored farmhouse, decorated with photographs of generations of family members and villagers, and old household utensils and farming implements. In summer you can dine in the courtyard, in which stands an old windmill; in winter there's a blazing fire in each room.

Vassos (££)
51 Leoforos Makariou tel: 23721884
This harbourside taverna is the place for fish, much of it straight off the fishing boats nearby. It is popular with fishermen and Cypriots, as well as visitors. In summer you can dine either in the bustling interior or outside on the terrace.

Larnaka area

1900 Art Café (£–££)
6 Odos Stasinou tel: 24653027
The arched interior of a turn-of-the-19th-century house, ornamented with paintings and film posters, serves as restaurant, bar, tea house and coffee house. The inventive menu has vegetarian options, such as stuffed cabbage rolls, and delicately prepared meat dishes.

Archontiko (££)
24 Leoforos Athinon tel: 24655905
The Archontiko serves Cypriot dishes in a picturesque old building beside the seafront Foinikoudes Promenade; there's an associated Archontissa steak-house.

279

Hotels & Restaurants

I Mavri Chelona (££)
11 Odos Mehmet Ali tel: 24650661
The cluttered dining room here in the old Turkish Quarter is filled with plain wooden tables and chairs, and the walls are decorated with traditional household utensils. There is meat, fish and vegetarian *meze*, and more exotic dishes like rabbit in lemon sauce.

Monte Carlo (££)
28 Odos Piyale Paşa tel: 24653815
Stylishly named and stylishly done seafront restaurant with a balcony overlooking the Mediterranean and a nice line in traditional Cypriot cuisine.

Pyla Tavern (££)
Frenaritis Complex, Larnaka–Dhekelia road tel: 24645990
Specializing in fish, this simple seaside taverna is popular with Cypriot families and with tourists who appreciate hearty Cypriot cooking.

The Tudor Inn (££)
28a Odos Lala Mustafa tel: 24625608
Steaks are the house special, and their supporting dishes are well produced.

Protaras-Pernera area

Anemos Beach Restaurant (£)
Fig Tree Bay tel: 23831900
Almost the ideal of a seaside taverna in a busy resort, where low cost combines with good food, and local people are among the patrons.

Blue Bay (£)
Protaras Harbour tel: 23831048
In a place where few tourist tavernas have much to recommend them, other than low price, the Blue Bay has an enthusiastic proprietor and a reasonable setting.

Spartiatis (££)
Konnos Beach tel: 23821386
With a view of olive groves and across to the headland near Cape Gkreko on which stands whitewashed Agioi Anargyroi chapel, Spartiatis specializes in seafood fresh from the nearby harbour, and traditional Greek dishes. It serves them in a decent modern setting that runs to naïve Cypriot art.

THE SOUTHWEST

Lefkara

Lefkara Tourist Pavilion (£)
Pano Lefkara village square tel: 24342211
In an area of little other than tourist-orientated tavernas, this one is as good as any, and reasonably priced.

Symposium (££)
Agora Hotel, off Odos Timiou Stavrou tel: 24342901
You have a choice of eating in the bright, moderately chic main dining room, or outside in a shaded, flower-brightened courtyard below the pillared arcades of the hotel's upper floor. The menu ranges through typical Cypriot fare, to French and Italian dishes, and more adventurous local offerings such as game.

Limassol area

Glaros (££)
36a Odos Agiou Antoniou tel: 25357046
West of the Old Harbour, in a little enclave of tavernas popular with local people, plainly decorated Glaros has a waterside terrace that looks out over Akrotiri Bay. It gets especially busy with Cypriot family groups at the weekend. The house special is moderately priced fish.

Karatello (££–£££)
Odos Vasilissis tel: 25820430
A renovated carob mill and warehouse dating from the early 1900s now houses this chic modern restaurant. Beneath the high ceiling's exposed air ducts are a brick mosaic floor, and wooden tables and chairs laid out in neat rows. Interesting dishes include charcoal-grilled village rabbit and *saganaki* with king prawns.

Lefteris (££)
Germasogeia tel: 25325211
Germasogeia, in the hills above Potamos Germasogeias resort area, has become the out-of-town place of choice for residents of Limassol seeking a cool place to dine. Lefteris is the village's oldest and best performer and often fills up quickly. It's a romantic place to dine on *meze*, either outside on a rambling terrace or in the sentimentally embellished interior decked out with antiques, curios and old farming and household items.

Porta (££)
17 Odos Genethliou Mitela tel: 25360339
Good traditional Cypriot food is served here in the unlikely setting of a converted donkey stable in the old Turkish quarter, near the mosque.

Richard and Berengaria (£)
23 Odos Eirinis tel: 25363863
An ultra-cheap and modest little family-run bar suited to a snack-orientated break from sightseeing, across the road from Limassol Castle.

Scottis Steakhouse (££)
38 Odos Souli tel: 25575173
As its name implies, Scottis specializes in steaks, the quality of which makes this place popular with Cypriots and visitors alike.

Xydas (£££)
22 Odos Anthemidos, Amathous tel: 25728336
This first-class seafood restaurant serves fresh fish with a touch of class.

Zygi

Markos (££)
Village seafront tel: 24333404
In this fishing village and seafood centre, where taverna quality is variable, Markos is a steady performer. Choose your own freshly caught fish and eat it right beside the sea.

THE TROODOS MOUNTAINS

Agros

Iy Kiladha (£)
Village main street tel: 25521303
A good, if at first sight unprepossessing

taverna, hidden in a tree-sheltered corner off the main road. It's not much more than a village snack-bar, but it does a fine, primarily meat-based *meze* with a few vegetable choices.

Foini

Phini Taverna (££)
Odos Demos Herodotus tel: 25421828
Cypriot dishes, plus trout, steaks and the like are favourites at this taverna in a lovely village.

Kakopetria

Linos Inn (££)
34 Odos Palaias tel: 22923161
Set in Kakopetria's renovated conservation zone, the restaurant of the eponymous hotel has walls partly made from straw-brick and mud, and a wood-beamed ceiling. The interior—scattered with traditional household objects, utensils and knick-knacks—is not overdone. Neither is the food, with specials that include *meze* and vegetarian options.

The Mill (££)
Odos Mylou tel: 22922536
The spectacular outlook is reason enough for a visit to this restaurant in the Troodos foothills. The food, particularly the trout (from fish farms), is excellent, but the restaurant is rather touristy.

Omodos

Makrinari (££)
Adjacent to Troodos-Limassol crossroads tel: 25422151
Although a welcoming and worthwhile place, Makrinari, like Omodos in general, isn't quite as good as it looks. You can dine on Cypriot fare outdoors on the wicker-shaded courtyard terrace decorated with plants and giant *pitharia* storage pots, or indoors in the convivial old (or at least old-looking) stone-built house.

Pano Platres

Kalidonia (££)
31 Odos Olympou tel: 25421404
A no-frills but lip-smackingly good mountain taverna, Kalidonia specializes in *meze*.

Psilodhendro (££)
Troodos road, 0.5 km (0.3 miles) outside Pano Platres tel: 25421350
Set in the forest beside the Kryos stream, a short walk uphill from Platres, this is ideal for a lunch of trout from the fish farm that the restaurant belongs to. This and meat dishes are barbecued. In summer you can dine outdoors.

Skylight (££)
Kato Platres road, Pano Platres tel: 25422244
A restaurant with its own swimming pool is something of a special treat already, so it's doubly gratifying that this relaxed, family-run taverna serves a fine traditional *meze*, along with trout fresh from the waters of the village's fish farm, and grills and salads. There's an outdoor terrace and garden.

Pedoulas

To Vrysi (££)
Village centre tel: 22952240
Also known as 'Harry's Spring Water Restaurant', this place was founded in 1929. It still sells traditional food, a cut above the usual, in a friendly, cluttered setting.

THE WEST

Coral Bay–Pegeia area

Araouzos (£)
Kathikas tel: 26632076
For authentic village food, try this family taverna. In a rustic setting, with ingredients from local farms, accompanied by Kathikas's own excellent Vasilikon white wine.

Imogen's Inn (££)
Kathikas village tel: 26633269
Charactered, atmospheric restaurant run by a couple with origins among the Greek Cypriot community in Egypt. The food has an Egyptian and Lebanese tinge, with falafel, slow-baked vegetables and dishes with cumin and spices.

Peyia Tavern (£–££)
Leoforos Kyprianou, Pegeia village centre tel: 26621077
The same things are cooked here night after night—grilled meats, accompanied by side dishes and village wine—and night after night the place fills up to consume them. Ambitious the food isn't; tasty it certainly is. You can eat in the spare, rustic interior or outside on a sliver of veranda that's a little too close to the road.

Saint George (££)
Agios Georgios tel: 26621306
Few spots have a better view of the sunset than this otherwise uninspired-looking taverna over-looking Agios Georgios beach and fishing harbour. The house special is fresh fish, nicely cooked though unimaginatively accompanied.

Vineyards (££)
Coral Bay–Pegeia road tel: 26621994
Large and modern, with lots of glass through which you can see the surrounding vineyards. The menu consists of traditional grilled meat and vegetable dishes, home-cooked to a high standard. You can sit on an outdoor terrace, breathing scented air while watching the sunset.

Pafos area

Cavallini (£££)
65 Leoforos Poseidonos, Kato Pafos tel: 26964164
This modern, stylish restaurant focuses on north Italian cuisine, which it prepares with some sophistication. Service is both professional and attentive, and an outdoor terrace sheltered by a low wall and plants cuts most of the traffic noise from the busy road out front.

Demokritos (££)
1 Odos Dionysou tel: 26933371
Greek dance and other floorshows complement the menu in this very Cypriot taverna, which makes good use of its *kleftiko* clay oven.

Hotels & Restaurants

Koh-i-Noor (£)

7 Odos Kleios, Kato Pafos tel: 26265544
Tucked down a side street, this serves refined Indian cuisine in a cool (literally, due to fearsome air-conditioning), pastel-toned room that maybe squeezes a few too many tables for the space. The tandoori dishes are nicely done.

Nicos Tyrimos (££)

*71 Odos Agapinoros, Kato Pafos
tel: 26941731*
This bustling, family-owned seafood taverna isn't much for looks—blue-and-white checked tablecloths on café-style tables is as far style goes. Regulars come for the large choice of fresh fish, plainly cooked so that its taste shines through.

Paphos Grill House (££)

33 Odos Ioannis Agrotis, Ktima tel: 26937822
In a location that's virtually out of sight on a dimly lit sidestreet, Paphos Grill House has a plainly decorated dining room and an unforced welcome. It presents a range of thoughtfully prepared *meze* items that are suffused with flavour.

Pelican Inn (££)

102 Leoforos Apostolou Pavlou tel: 26946886
This specializes in fish and seafood dishes, including lobster. Congenial harbour setting.

Phuket (£££)

*Leoforos Tafon ton Vasileon, Kato Pafos
tel: 26936738*
Original Chinese cooking, which has made a big impact on Pafos since the restaurant opened.

Seven Saint George's (££)

*Odos Pavlou Krineou (off Leoforos Danaïs)
tel: 26263176*
An old Cypriot dwelling now a sophisticated *meze* house. Good vegetarian dishes, as well as meat, and excellent home-produced wine.

Pissouri

Bunch of Grapes Inn (£)

Pissouri village tel: 25221275
This fully restored, century-old inn in the centre of the village, with a romantic courtyard restaurant, is noted for its Sunday lunches.

Hani (£)

Limassol–Pafos road tel: 25221211
A transport café with good taste and friendly service, which make it popular.

Melanda (££)

Avdimou Bay, near Pissouri tel: 25991700
The drawn-out approach to this slightly ramshackle taverna is worth it, for fresh, good-tasting grilled and fried fish served on an open-air terrace right beside the beach.

Palio Limanaki (£)

Pissouri Bay tel: 25221288
In an area where choice is limited, the Palio Limanaki at least benefits from a fine beachside position and simple, tasty Cypriot food.

Simposio (££)

Pissouri Bay tel: 25221158
A modern stonebuilt taverna artfully designed to look like an old stonebuilt taverna, Simposio has a good position beside the beach and produces fine traditional Cypriot food, though its menu stretches beyond this to cover beach-type snacks and other international fare.

Polis–Lakki area

Archontariki (££)

*14 leoforos Archiepiskopou Makariou III, Polis
tel: 26323187*
This engaging restaurant is set in a stone-built house. The quaint dining room has a stone floor and chandeliers and is decorated with old photographs. On the terrace the air is filled with floral scents and birdsong. The Cyprus platter, a cold mini-*meze*, is a good starter.

Baths of Aphrodite (££)

*Opposite Baths of Aphrodite trail entrance
tel: 26321457*
This simple clifftop taverna does a good lunchtime salad and excellent fish, and is ideally placed for anyone emerging from a long, hot walk in the Akamas Peninsula.

Old Town (££)

Kyproleontos Street, Polis tel: 26322758
This stone-walled taverna with a large, tree-shaded outside terrace, a short way from the busy main square, is a local favourite. The menu is strong on vegetarian choices, though in typically eclectic Cypriot style, there is no intention of disappointing meat and fish eaters.

Paradise Place (££)

*Coast road between Pomos and Pachyammos
tel: 26342537*
This agreeably laid-back taverna attracts locals as well as visitors with delicately prepared, highly individual Cypriot and world cuisine, including vegetarian dishes, with added improvisational touches. You can watch the sunset to the strains of classical music and jazz.

Porto Latchi (££)

Seafront, Lakki tel: 26321529
Housed in a 17th-century Cypriot dwelling, this taverna takes a stellar part in the Lakki specialism of high-quality seafood.

Ttakkas Bay (££)

Lakki–Baths of Aphrodite road tel: 26321087
You eat right beside the pebble beach at this fine seafood taverna, off the main road, where the focus is on individually prepared fish dishes.

Yiangos and Peter (££)

Fishing harbour, Lakki tel: 26321411
The harbour at Lakki has no shortage of good seafood tavernas that also serve meat-based dishes. This was the first, and is still the best, with a fine waterfront setting and good cooking.

THE NORTH

Agios Epiktitos (Çatalköy)

Lemon Tree (££)

*Keryneia–Agios Epiktitos (Girne–Çatalköy) road
tel: 824 4045*
On the coast road near the turn-off for the Hazreti Ömer Mosque, this country house serves first-class fresh seafood.

Mardin (££)

Tel: 824 4027
A seafood restaurant on the southern fringe of the village, Mardin has a good reputation among local people.

Belapais (Beylerbeyi)

Kybele (£££)
Grounds of Belapais Abbey tel: 815 7531
Atmospheric bar, restaurant and wine house
with the ruined abbey as a back-drop.

Keryneia (Girne) area

Canlı Balik (££)
Kordonboyu tel: 815 2182
Good-quality seafood restaurant beside the
fishing boats in Keryneia harbour.
Courtyard Inn (££)
Karakum tel: 815 3343
The Courtyard caters mainly to expatriate
residents, chiefly British and German, as well
as to visitors from those countries. It is a
pretty place and its cuisine is good.
Efendi's House (£)
6 Kamil Paşa Road tel: 815 1149
Efendi's has a fine pedigree and a reputation
for the quality and style of its food, and the
Turkish atmosphere is guaranteed.
Harbour Club (£££)
Kordonboyu tel: 815 2211
In the shadow of Keryneia Castle, this is
expensive by Turkish Cypriot standards but its
quality seafood and French dishes are superb.
Its setting and decor add to the experience.
Harbour Taverna (££)
Kordonboyu tel: 815 5344
The traditional weekend taverna nights here,
with *meze*, kebabs and live entertainment, add
a different touch from Keryneia harbour's other
seafood restaurants.
The Hideaway Club (££)
*Trimithi–Karmi (Edremit–Karaman) road
tel: 822 2620*
Tasty international dishes are served here in a
relaxing poolside restaurant with superb moun-
tain views. The Hideaway puts on special and
party nights.
Niyazi's (£)
Kordonboyu tel: 815 2160
Around the corner from Keryneia harbour,
Niyazi's is a traditional Turkish Cypriot restaurant, which guarantees that kebabs are a
good buy.
Set (£)
Kordonboyu tel: 815 2336
Good seafood place beside the yacht harbour.
Yenihan (£)
*Keryneia–Lapithos (Girne–Lapta) road
tel: 815 1276*
Unpretentious and friendly, this restaurant on
the western fringe of Keryneia is popular with
locals and visitors, and serves a wide range of
good *meze* and simple but tasty Turkish
dishes. The restaurant also hosts Cypriot
nights with live music and a bellydancer.

Lapithos (Lapta) area

Ali Paşa's (£)
*Keryneia–Lapithos (Girne–Lapta) road
tel: 821 8942*
Although this is a large, quite ugly-looking

seafront taverna, the cooking and an enthus-
iastic proprietor more than make up for this.
Altinkaya (££)
*Keryneia–Lapithos (Girne–Lapta) road
tel: 821 8341*
A popular, high-quality restaurant on the coast
near the Turkish Cypriot Peace and Freedom
Monument, and specializing in seafood.
Shirley Valentine's (££)
Karavas (Alsancak) tel: 821 8922
On the seafront, this small restaurant beside a
pool and bar serves international cuisine.

THE EAST

Famagusta (Gazimağusa) area

Agora (££)
17 Elmas Tabya Street tel: 366 5364
Kebabs and other well-prepared Turkish fare.
Cyprus House (££)
Polat Paşa Bulvari tel: 366 4845
You dine Turkish-style here amid relics of
antiquity and *objets d'art* in the garden of
Famagusta's former British police station.
Koca Reis (££)
*On the beach beside the Salamis Bay Hotel
tel: 378 8229*
Specializing in fish, this restaurant boasts a
laid-back owner and an equally laid-back hen,
who wanders among the tables, secure in the
knowledge that the fish dishes are so good
nobody will ask for chicken.
Palm Beach Hotel Restaurant (£££)
Havva Sentürk Avenue tel: 366 2000
The in-house restaurant of one of Cyprus's
best hotels serves exceptional international
cuisine and Turkish dishes.

Karpas (Karpaz) Peninsula

Blue Sea (£)
*Rizokarpaso–Cape Apostolos Andreas
(Dipkarpaz–Zafer Burnu) road tel: 372 2393*
A small seafood restaurant attached to a
simple hotel, the Blue Sea has a superb
seaside setting southeast of the village of
Rizokarpason (Dipkarpaz).

Salamis–Bogazi (Boğaz) area

Akdeniz (££)
*Famagusta–Bogazi (Gazimağusa–Boğaz) road
tel: 378 8227*
A little north of the access road to the
Salamis Bay Hotel, this is a fairly typical
Turkish Cypriot restaurant, serving tasty food.
Eyva (££)
*Famagusta–Bogazi (Gazimağusa–Boğaz) road
tel: 378 8235*
Good-quality Turkish cuisine and atmosphere
are served up at this restaurant on the coast
road to Salamis. It has live entertainment.
Kocatepe (££)
Fishing harbour, Bogazi tel: 371 2620
Slightly more classy than is the norm in Bogazi,
Kocatepe, overlooking the harbour,
concentrates on seafood and does it very well.

283

285

Index

287

Index/Acknowledgements

Picture credits

The Automobile Association would like to thank the following photographers and libraries for their assistance in the preparation of this book.
Abbreviations for the picture credits are as follows – (t) top; (b) bottom; (c) centre; (l) left; (r) right; (AA) AA World Travel Library.

BRAND X PICS 72; **HEADQUARTERS BRITISH FORCES CYPRUS** (B. Gamble) 106t; **GETTY IMAGES** 29, 51, 197 **(TIME AND LIFE PICTURES)** 39, 40r 40b, 60, 61, **J LAMBROU** 18/9t, 18b, 138/9t, 138b, 139; **MARY EVANS PICTURE LIBRARY** 23b, 34t, 34b, 35b, 38t, 38b; **NATURE PHOTOGRA-PHERS LTD** 183 (P R Sterry) **PHOTODISC** 13, 67t; **REX FEATURES LTD** 41; **ROYAL GEOGRAPHIC SOCIETY LIBRARY** 36b.

The remaining photographs are held in the Automobile Associations own photo library (AA PHOTO LIBRARY) and were taken by Alex Kouprianoff, with the exception of: 3, 4, 5b, 6/7t, 7b, 12t, 20c, 26t, 31b, 32/3, 32, 43, 54, 56, 57t, 58b, 64, 69b, 71t, 73, 88, 91b, 94, 107, 112, 115t, 115b, 127t, 133t, 136t, 141, 146, 147, 154, 157b, 158, 161, 168/9t, 168, 169, 171t, 179t, 191, 196b, 201, 254, 260, 264/5, 266 which were taken by M. Birkitt; 12b, 19b, 162/3, 259t taken by Steve Day; 58t, 217t, 218, 225bl, 238, 240b, taken by R,Bulmar, 85b, taken by K. Paterson; 8, 22b, 27, 71b, 84b, 96/7b, 105, 113t, 119t, 119b, 125t, 132t, 148t, 181, 187b, 192t, 239b, 244b, 245c, 263, taken by R. Rainford and pages 21b, 30t, 35t, 198, 199, 203, 209b, 219b, 220b, 223t, 228/9b 229t, 242, 243, 249, taken by H. Ulucam.

Every effort has been made to trace the copyright holders, and we apologise in advance for any accidental errors. We would be happy to apply the corrections in the following edition of this publication.

Contributors
Revision verifier: George McDonald
Original copy editor: Jennifer Speake   Revision edit/design: Bookwork Creative Associates Ltd.

Statement on the position of the United Nations

There have been a great many debates on Cyprus at the United Nations and a veritable blizzard of Security Council and General Assembly resolutions. In a nutshell, the UN aims to restore the legal, constitutional basis of the Republic of Cyprus, reaffirm the rights of both communities in the constitution, and end military occupation. Inevitably, one or other community objects to some aspect of this approach, and the Secretary General's mission of 'good offices' has always run into the sand due to this kind of opposition. Security Council resolution 541 of 18 November 1983, following the unilateral Turkish Cypriot foundation of the 'Turkish Republic of Northern Cyprus', is a key element of the UN position.

The Security Council,
Having heard the statement of the Foreign Minister of the Government of the Republic of Cyprus,
Concerned at the declaration by the Turkish Cypriot authorities issued on 15 November 1983 which purports to create an independent State in northern Cyprus,
Considering that this declaration is incompatible with the 1960 Treaty concerning the establishment of the Republic of Cyprus and the 1960 Treaty of Guarantee,
Considering, therefore, that the attempt to create a 'Turkish Republic of Northern Cyprus' is invalid, and will contribute to a worsening of the situation in Cyprus,
Reaffirming its resolutions 365 (1974) and 367 (1975),
Aware of the need for a solution of the Cyprus problem based on the mission of good offices undertaken by the Secretary General,
Affirming its continuing support for the United Nations Peacekeeping Force in Cyprus,
Taking note of the Secretary General's statement of 17 November 1983,
1 Deplores the declaration of the Turkish Cypriot authorities of the purported secession of part of the Republic of Cyprus;
2 Considers the declaration referred to above as legally invalid and calls for its withdrawal;
3 Calls for the urgent and effective implementation of its resolutions 365 (1974) and 367 (1975);
4 Requests the Secretary General to pursue his mission of good offices, in order to achieve the earliest possible progress towards a just and lasting settlement in Cyprus;
5 Calls upon the parties to cooperate fully with the Secretary General in his mission of good offices;
6 Calls upon all States to respect the sovereignty, independence, territorial integrity and non-alignment of the Republic of Cyprus;
7 Calls upon all States not to recognize any Cypriot State other than the Republic of Cyprus;
8 Calls upon all States and the two communities in Cyprus to refrain from any action which might exacerbate the situation;
9 Requests the Secretary General to keep the Security Council fully informed.